D0323427

# The Supreme Court

# THE SUPREME COURT

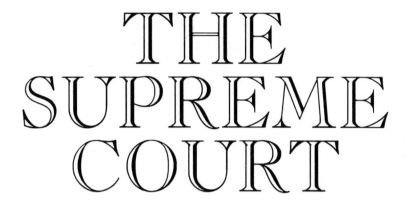

## A Citizen's Guide

Robert J. Wagman

**PHAROS BOOKS**
A SCRIPPS HOWARD COMPANY

NEW YORK

Copyright © 1993 by Robert J. Wagman

All rights reserved. No part of this book may be reproduced in any form
or by any means without permission in writing from the publisher.

Library of Congress Cataloging-in-Publication Data
Wagman, Robert J.
     The Supreme Court : a citizen's guide / by Robert J. Wagman.
         p.   cm.
     Includes bibliographical references and index.
     ISBN 0-88687-692-3 : $21.95
     1. United States.   Supreme Court—History.   2. Judges—United
States—Biography.   3. United States—Constitutional law—
Interpretation and construction—History.   I. Title.
KF8742.W34   1992
347.73'26—dc20                                                        92-24658
[347.30735]                                                              CIP

*Printed in the United States of America*

Jacket design by Janet Tingey
Interior design by Laura Hough

Pharos Books
A Scripps Howard Company
200 Park Avenue
New York, NY 10166

10 9 8 7 6 5 4 3 2 1

Pharos Books are available at special discounts on bulk purchases for sales promotions,
premiums, fundraising or educational use. For details, contact the Special Sales
Department, Pharos Books, 200 Park Avenue, New York, NY 10166

*For Patricia*

NOR

# Contents

# Contents

# Acknowledgments

This volume represents the hard work and generous assistance of a number of people. It would not have been possible without them.

First, thanks must go to my editor, Kevin McDonough of Pharos Books. The book was his idea originally and he steered it through to completion. Deep thanks, too, go to Carol Berglie for her perception and her unfailing copy editing skills.

Much research went into this volume. I am indebted to the staffs of the Library of Congress Law Library and the Library of the Supreme Court for their cooperation and assistance. I am most thankful to Catherine Fitts and Carrie Hendon of the Supreme Court's Curator's Office for their help and assistance. Donna Beardsley and DeBorah Smith are both young lawyers. The quality of their research shows that they have great careers in front of them. Holly Hagan provided invaluable help, as did Jennifer Wagman.

I am especially grateful to Dick Carelli, half the Associated Press's veteran reporting team covering the Court. He is mainly responsible for Chapter 6: The Court and Its People.

As always, Carol Wagman provided skilled proofreading and her unfailing instincts were never wrong. Patricia, Bob, and Molly Wagman provided help at critical times. To all, I am grateful.

# 1.
# How the Supreme Court Works

What follows is the story of an appeal, from the moment an alleged crime was committed in St. Paul, Minnesota, until it resulted in a potential landmark decision by the U.S. Supreme Court. The story illustrates not only how the Supreme Court works but how the dual judicial system—state and federal—operates in the United States, and how and when they mesh.

One aspect of this case is somewhat unusual: the speed with which it moved through the court system. The alleged crime was committed in June 1990; the case was heard at the state trial court and state appeals court and then was appealed on the federal level and ruled on by the Supreme Court only two years later. While the pace of the case is far from unprecedented, the fact that it did move expeditiously is testimony to the basic and wide-ranging constitutional issues involved—and the recognition by all parties at every level of the process how important the resolution of these issues were.

## R. A. V., Petitioner v.
## City of St. Paul, Minnesota
## (In the Matter of the Welfare of R. A. V.)

Shortly after 1:00 A.M. on the morning of June 21, 1990, Laura Jones was awakened from a light sleep by strange noises outside her home on Earl Street, in the Dayton's Bluff section of St. Paul, Minnesota. At first, she

1

says, she was not all that concerned, because the house sits on a busy street and some noise at night is not uncommon. But then she realized the noise was coming from almost directly beneath her bedroom window, so she got up to investigate.

When Laura Jones looked down from her bedroom window, she was shocked to see a small wooden cross burning on the lawn below. The cross had been fashioned from a pair of two-foot-long pieces from a wooden lawn chair, taped together, then doused with paint thinner and set ablaze. A group of young men were standing nearby shouting something that Mrs. Jones could not make out. Terribly frightened, she woke her husband and called the police.

Just a few weeks earlier, Russell and Laura Jones and their five children had moved into the comfortable home in the middle-class residential neighborhood. They were the first black family on their block, and one of the first to move into the area. Their arrival had raised tensions in the neighborhood. A few days before this incident, the tires on one of their cars had been slashed and a window had been shattered. On another occasion, one of their children had been taunted with racial slurs by a classmate.

The police arrived and extinguished the cross. Within a matter of days they arrested six young men who they said burned the cross on the Jones's lawn, then hid in a home across the street. Later the same night they burned a second cross on the grass median in the street, and then a third in the parking lot of a nearby apartment complex that had some black tenants.

Two of the young men, eighteen-year-old Arthur Miller III and seventeen-year-old Robert A. Viktora, Jr., who would be identified only by his initials—R. A. V.—because he was a juvenile, were charged with committing an assault under both a Minnesota state statute (Count 1), and a St. Paul city ordinance (Count 2). Miller, the eighteen-year-old, pleaded guilty. The minor, who claimed he could not afford to hire a lawyer, was assigned the services of Ramsey County Public Defender Ed Cleary. Cleary decided to contest the arrest. Because the laws R. A. V. was alleged to have violated were state and local, the Minnesota state court system had jurisdiction. This put the case into the Ramsey County District Court, and because R. A. V. was under age, it specifically put the case in the Juvenile Division courtroom of Judge Charles A. Flinn, Jr.

On June 25, 1990, R. A. V., represented by Cleary, appeared at a preliminary hearing in front of Judge Flinn to answer what was technically a delinquency petition. A not-guilty plea was entered, and R. A. V. was ordered bound over and held in custody pending the formal hearing (juvenile trial).

In part because of the public outcry over the event, Ramsey County Attorney Tom Foley decided to amend the charges against R. A. V. He dismissed the original Count 2, dropping the simple city ordinance assault misdemeanor in favor of a seldom used, much more serious hate-crime statute that had been on the books since 1982. The statute, also a St. Paul city ordinance, provides:

> Whoever places on public or private property a symbol, object, application, characterization or graffiti, including but not limited to a burning cross, or Nazi swastika, which he knows or has reasonable grounds to know arouses anger, alarm or resentment in others on the basis of race, color, creed or religion or gender, commits disorderly conduct and shall be guilty of a misdemeanor.

If convicted under the previous Count 2, R. A. V. would have faced a maximum of ninety days in custody. Under the hate-crime ordinance, the maximum penalty is five years incarceration. So R. A. V. immediately objected. Through Cleary he challenged the constitutionality of the law he was now being charged under.[1] He asked for an immediate hearing, and the motion was granted by Judge Flinn.

On July 13, 1990, a hearing was held at which defense attorney Cleary and assistant county attorney Steven C. DeCoster met to argue the constitutionality of the St. Paul hate law.

Cleary argued that what the 1982 law sought to ban was constitutionally protected expressive action guaranteed under the First Amendment. Moreover, he argued that the law was constitutionally flawed for two technical reasons: it was "vague," meaning that a reasonable person reading it would not know on its face what specific acts are prohibited; and that it was "overbroad," meaning that while seeking to prohibit some acts that might not be constitutionally protected, it also banned actions that are afforded constitutional protection.

---

1. It should be noted that R. A. V. challenged only the second of the two counts under which he was charged. He did not challenge the count brought under the state assault statute. As this is being written, he will either have to stand trial on that count or work out some plea bargain with the prosecution.

DeCoster, in turn, conceded that the city ordinance did proscribe expressive conduct, but only conduct of a type that the state clearly has an overriding interest in regulating. He argued that some kinds of expression can be regulated by the state if an ample reason is present, and that the kinds of actions covered under the statute are exactly the kind the state has a duty to ban.

Judge Flinn did not agree. On July 16, he agreed with Cleary and ruled the statute unconstitutional. The prosecution announced that it would immediately appeal the ruling.

Since the action was in the Minnesota state court system, the initial appeal of Judge Flinn's ruling had to be made within the state court system. So on July 23, 1990, DeCoster, on behalf of Ramsey County, filed a Petition For Accelerated Review with the Minnesota Supreme Court. On August 3, that court agreed to hear the matter, and in due course both Cleary and DeCoster appeared before the state's high court to argue the case and to submit written briefs. Their arguments changed little from what they had been before Judge Flinn. In fact, when they made their oral arguments before the nine justices of the U.S. Supreme Court, the parameters of the dispute were about the same as for the first hearing before Flinn.

On January 18, 1991, the Minnesota high court handed down its opinion. It ruled that the hate-crime ordinance was not vague, and while it might be construed as partly overbroad as originally drafted, the specific acts that the defendant was accused of clearly fell outside of constitutionally protected expressive action and thus were not constitutionally protected. To this extent, the court ruled, the statute was constitutional.

The U.S. Supreme Court has always held that certain aspects of speech and communication are outside of any protection by the First Amendment. One of those exceptions is so-called fighting words. In a 1942 decision (*Chaplinsky* v. *New Hampshire*) the Court ruled that "there are certain well-defined and narrowly limited classes of speech, the prevention and punishment of which have never been thought to raise any constitutional problems. These include the lewd and obscene, the profane, the libelous, and the insulting or 'fighting words,' those which by their very utterance inflict injury or tend to incite an immediate breach of the peace."

Now the Minnesota Supreme Court ruled that the actions R. A. V. was accused of all fell within the definition of fighting words. Thus, to this extent, the ordinance fell within the guidelines of Chaplinsky, and was constitutional. In upholding the ordinance, Justice Tomljanovich said "burning a cross in the yard of an African American family's home is deplorable conduct that the city of St. Paul may without question prohibit. . . . It is the responsibility, even the obligation, of diverse communities to confront such notions in whatever form they appear."

The ruling specifically overturned Judge Flinn's dismissal of the second count of the indictment, and ordered the case sent back to him for trial on both counts.

With the Minnesota Supreme Court having ruled, R. A. V. and Cleary now had two options. They could return to the courtroom of Judge Flinn and try the case on its merits, or they could lodge one last appeal. The court that had ruled was the highest court in the state system. So the only place they could go to appeal that ruling was the U.S. Supreme Court, if it would agree to hear the case.

Article III of the Constitution grants the Supreme Court "original jurisdiction" over only a very limited range of issues, mainly lawsuits brought by one state against another (usually over boundary or water rights[2]), the very rare occasion of a suit brought by a state against the federal government, or vice versa, or any action arising out of matters concerning ambassadors and foreign counsels. In these unusual situations, occurring only once every few sessions, if that often—the Supreme Court acts as the trial court, with no right of appeal from its final judgment.

The same article gives the entire federal court system jurisdiction over all "cases and controversies"[3] arising under the Constitution and laws of the United States, arising under treaties to which the United States is a party, and between citizens of different states or between a citizen of the United States and a foreign country. The Supreme Court, in turn, is given "appellate jurisdiction" to review decisions of lower federal courts as to

---

2. A famous example is a 1952 suit by Arizona against California over diversion of water from the Colorado River. Sitting as a trial court, the justices amassed a trial record of more than 26,000 pages and heard more than thirty hours of oral argument over a two-year period. Arizona won the suit and California was ordered to end the diversion.

3. The use of the term "cases and controversies" is important because it means that there must be a real dispute involving real parties before the federal court system will get involved. As it pertains to the Supreme Court, the cases and controversies threshold has meant that the Court will not involve itself in hypothetical situations or in the abstract. Nor will the Court be placed in the position of giving advisory opinions. That issue was settled quickly in 1793, when President George Washington sought the legal advice of John Jay and the other justices of his first Court on various legal matters. They refused to render such counsel and that has remained the fact ever since.

both law and fact, and a right to review the decisions of the highest court of a state where U.S. constitutional questions are presented.

Article III specifies that this appellate jurisdiction shall be exercised "under such regulations as Congress shall make." The Court from its very beginning has always held that in exercising its appellate jurisdiction, it may pick and choose from among the cases presented to it, looking for those that present the most vital issues. With the passage of the Judiciary Act of 1925, Congress codified the right of the Supreme Court to be the final arbiter of what cases it will hear. The 1925 law divided cases coming to the Court on appeal into two classes: appeals, which the Court is obliged to hear; and petitions for writs of certiorari[4] in which review is totally discretionary.

Under the 1925 act, the Court was virtually obliged to grant review of any federal court ruling that a state law is unconstitutional or any decision of a state high court that a federal law is unconstitutional. For decades, successive chief justices tried to get Congress to further narrow the Court's mandatory review. In 1988, Chief Justice William Rehnquist finally succeeded, and now almost all appeals must come through the certiorari process. Thus, if Cleary was to get the Supreme Court to overturn the ruling of the Minnesota Supreme Court sending R. A. V.'s case back to Judge Flinn for trial on the hate-crime count, he would first have to get at least four justices to formally vote to accept the case.

In most instances, that is very far from assured. In a normal annual Supreme Court term, lasting from the traditional first Monday in October until sometime in mid-June, the justices will hear and decide between 150 and 180 cases. In a recent year, the 1991–92 term, it received in excess of 7,000 petitions for certiorari. This means that fewer than one in fifty cases is granted. These are daunting odds for any litigant.

Under Rule 20 of the Court, all appeals of a criminal nature must be made no more than ninety days after the lower court has given its final ruling. In this case, the Minnesota Supreme Court ruled on January 18, 1991. That meant that Cleary had until April 18 to lodge his appeal with the Supreme Court. He pushed the window. On April 11, his seventeen-

---

4. From the Latin *certiorari volumnus*, meaning "we wish to be informed." A writ of certiorari is an order by the Supreme Court to a lower court, asking for a formal record of a proceeding that has taken place there in order to review it.

page Petition For A Writ of Certiorari arrived in the clerk's office at the Court in Washington.

The petition conformed with the Court's Rule 21: It was less than thirty pages long, it presented the question(s) for review (in this case whether the St. Paul ordinance was unconstitutional because it was vague, over-broad, and in conflict with the First Amendment protection of free speech), and it contained a concise statement of the facts and a listing of the authorities and prior Court precedents that were being relied upon. The petition was also accompanied by a motion that asked that R. A. V. be allowed to proceed *in forma pauperis* (in the manner of a poor person). If granted, this meant that he would not have to pay filing fees, that he would need to supply the Court with only a single typed copy of briefs rather than expensively printed documents,[5] and that the Court would pay travel expenses for his lawyer to argue the case. Finally, in accordance with the Court's regulations, Cleary included a certificate attesting that a copy of the petition had been sent to Assistant County Attorney DeCoster.

The name of the case also changed now. Since it was a juvenile case within the Minnesota court system, the case's name was like that of most juvenile cases: In The Matter Of . . . Now that it was going to the Supreme Court, it had become a contest between R. A. V. and the city of St. Paul. From now on, the case would be known as R. A. V., Petitioner v. City of St. Paul, Minnesota (or simply *R. A. V. v. St. Paul*).

The clock was now running for Ramsey County. It had thirty days in which to file with the U.S. Supreme Court, if it so desired, a brief in opposition to Cleary's petition for certiorari. It definitely wanted to. On May 10, the clerk of the Court received the requisite forty copies of County Attorney Foley's twelve-page Brief In Opposition, which argued that the Court should not accept the case because no important Constitutional questions were being presented, since the "fighting words" exception to the First Amendment was long established and generally accepted. Further,

---

5. The Court's requirements (Rule 33) as to form and style of documents filed with it are very exacting. The rule not only sets forth the maximum length of various documents, and the precise wording and information to be placed on the cover, but prescribes the exact typeface that must be used in printing and the exact color of the cover of different documents: light orange for writs of certiorari, light blue for appellants' briefs, light red for respondents' briefs. The different cover colors is a practical necessity because it allows the justices and their clerks to quickly find a given document in a crowded case file.

the county's brief argued, the Minnesota Supreme Court's opinion had narrowed the interpretation of the statute to the point it was not overbroad.

Now began what is probably the most important and least understood of the Court's processes. In a very real sense, the justices can decide a case by deciding not to hear it. If this is their decision, then the final judgment of the lower court stands. Quite often, a justice will vote not to hear a case because he believes that the lower court has rendered a correct verdict for the correct reason. Likewise, most of the time, a justice will vote to hear a case because he either believes the lower court's ruling to be wrong or that it is a correct holding, but for the wrong reason. Since it takes four justices voting yes to accept a case, and only one more to actually form a majority for a decision, getting the original four votes is often more difficult than actually winning the case once it is heard.

With both a petition and reply in hand, the staff of the clerk's office of the Court examines both to ensure that they are correct as to form. Assuming that they are, the clerk places the case "on the docket," assigns a docket number to it (*R. A. V. v. St. Paul* became docket number 90-7675, a high number because it was filed near the end of the Court's 1990–91 term), and sends a copy of both the petition and the reply to each of the justices' chambers.

Each justice handles the review of cert petitions differently. Some personally browse through the piles of petitions they receive weekly, looking for cases that contain interesting legal issues. Others assign one of their clerks to prepare a short memo on each petition, which the justice then reviews. Still other justices have formed what around the Court is called the "cert pool," where the incoming petitions are divided up among the clerks of several justices working together, with the resultant case memos distributed to all the justices participating in the pool.

On June 7, 1991, shortly before 9:30 A.M., a bell rang in each of the chambers of the nine justices, summoning them to one of the most secret regular meetings held in a city known for its secret meetings. Each Wednesday afternoon and Friday morning,[6] the justices gather in the small white-oak–paneled conference room adjacent to the Chief Justice's chambers. It is an ornate room, with a marble fireplace and walls covered with bookcases

---

6. Prior to 1955 the Court heard oral arguments Monday through Friday and then held an all-day conference on Saturday. In 1955 it was decided to change the conference day to Friday, which meant that oral arguments would be held Monday through Thursday.

filled with the reports of previous Court decisions. From its high ceiling a large crystal chandelier overhangs the conference table. Looking down on the setting from a spot over the fireplace is the stern portrait of former Chief Justice John Marshall.

As the nine justices file into the room, they exchange ritual handshakes at the door before settling in to decide cases that have been orally argued so far that week, and on Friday mornings to review the cert petitions that are pending. Only the justices are present at conferences. Since 1907, when a decision was leaked out of a conference session, all clerks, legal assistants, and other staff have been strictly forbidden. Most of the justices bring notes with them to the conferences or make notes about the cases being discussed during the conference. By tradition, as soon as they finish their personal use of such notes, they are destroyed.

The seating at conference is carefully prescribed. The Chief Justice sits at the east end of the table. Directly opposite him at the west end sits the senior associate justice. The other justices align themselves beginning on the Chief Justice's left, and in clockwise order according to their relative seniority. Since there are no staff or clerks present, the most junior justice, currently Justice Clarence Thomas, acts as a sort of doorkeeper, accepting messages for the various justices or sending out messages for legal research materials.

About 100 cert petitions are up for review each week the Court is in session. Because of this large number, it is simply not possible to discuss every one at the conference. So the Chief Justice prepares a Discuss List containing the names of the cert petitions to be discussed each Friday. Any justice can have a case added to the Discuss List simply by asking that it be placed there. By one estimate, most Discuss Lists contain about thirty cases, of which perhaps five or six are accepted for review. Three out of four cert petitions do not even make it to the Discuss List. They are summarily rejected without further consideration.

In the Rehnquist Court, the disposition of cert petitions moves quickly. Each justice is supposed to be familiar with the facts of each case on the Discuss List, and to generally have already made up his or her mind as to whether the Court should accept it or not, before the Friday morning session. The day-long Friday conference is primarily for deciding argued cases and assigning justices to write opinions. By tradition, the justices work from 9:30 or 10:00 A.M. until 11:00 A.M., when they take a short coffee break. The Chief Justice reportedly likes to have all the cert petitions dealt with by the coffee break.

On the morning of June 7, *R. A. V. v. St. Paul* was on the Discuss List. The Chief Justice started off the discussion about the case by summarizing the facts and the legal points being challenged. Then each justice, in turn by seniority rank, had an opportunity to state a position on whether the case should be accepted for review. Then a vote was taken. Although no regulation demands it, by tradition it takes four affirmative votes for the Court to accept a case for review, although at times Chief Justices will reschedule a case for a second look at conference if it gets only the bare four votes. Any justice who feels strongly enough that a case should be accepted, even though it initially lacks the required four votes, may ask the Chief Justice to schedule a second discussion of it at a later conference. In the interim, he may send a memo to the other justices setting out his arguments as to why the case should be accepted. In the end, if it is not accepted, he may have it noted in the final printed Orders that he dissented from the decision not to accept the case for review and why. It is also possible, although very rare, that in agreeing to review a case the Court will at the same time issue an order vacating, staying, or even striking down the ruling of the lower court that is being appealed. These rare summary reversals take place when it is clear from the conference discussion that a majority of the justices already know how they are going to eventually rule on the case, and that the majority believes that some damage will be done by allowing the lower court ruling to stand in the interim.

Although the exact vote count will never be known, reportedly on this morning there was little doubt among the justices that the St. Paul hate-crime ordinance raised significant First Amendment questions that the Court should address, and thus there was agreement to place it on the Oral Argument List. In turn, all the cases that were also accepted for review, and those that were rejected, were placed on the Orders List to be announced the following Monday morning by the Chief Justice before that day's oral arguments began.[7]

On the morning of June 10, 1991, Chief Justice Rehnquist announced that in the case of *R. A. V.*, *Petitioner* v. *City of St. Paul, Minnesota*, the Court was issuing a writ of certiorari, and was granting R. A. V.'s companion motion that he be allowed to proceed *in forma pauperis*.

---

7. From the earliest days, the Court fell into the tradition of only announcing decisions on "Decision Monday." But since 1965 decisions may be announced any day the Court is in session.

\* \* \*

Now that the justices had agreed to hear the case, several things happened immediately. The clerk received it back in his office. His first act was to send an official notice to the Minnesota Supreme Court that the U.S. Supreme Court was going to review its decision, and ask that an official, certified copy of the case record be forwarded immediately.[8] He also officially notified both counsels of record, Cleary and DeCoster, that the case had been accepted for argument. He then, in consultation with them and looking at the Court's own calendar, scheduled the time for oral argument—10:00 A.M., Wednesday, December 4, 1991.[9]

Under Court rules, oral arguments cannot be scheduled for at least ninety days after a case has been accepted for review, except under extraordinary circumstances. In practice, depending upon when during a term a case is accepted, oral arguments are usually scheduled six to eight months in the future.

As soon as the clerk notified Cleary that his writ had been granted, another clock began running. Under Court Rules 30, 34, and 35, Cleary now had forty-five days in which to file his brief arguing his case, and to reach an agreement with DeCoster on a "joint appendix," and to file it with the Court.

The brief, which is the main written presentation that is made to the Court, is usually only a more detailed statement of the arguments that were contained in the petition for the writ of certiorari. As with the rules for the filing and the content of a petition for a writ of certiorari, Rules 33 and 34 spell out the form and general content of the appellant's brief.[10] Because the Court had agreed to allow R. A. V. to proceed *in*

---

8. Technically, this is exactly what a writ of certiorari is—a request to a lower court for the official record of a case.

9. Previously, oral arguments were scheduled every week the Court was in session. Today, the justices hear cases in two-week cycles, hearing oral arguments Monday through Thursday for two weeks, and then recessing for two weeks while the justices work on writing opinions on previously decided cases and preparing for upcoming oral arguments. On arguments days, it used to be that the justices would sit from eleven in the morning until perhaps five in the afternoon. These days, oral argument is scheduled from 10:00 A.M. to noon and from 1:00 P.M. until 3:00 P.M. This means that at most four cases will be heard in a day, although three is usually the maximum.

10. A brief may not be longer than fifty typeset pages in length (110 pages typewritten), with typefaces, size, and margins the same as required in writ petitions. Each brief must contain a statement of the questions presented for review; a list of all parties to the proceeding; a table of

*forma pauperis*, the brief did not have to be expensively printed—only a single typewritten copy had to be sent. The required forty printed copies were made by the Court itself.

On July 25, 1991, Cleary submitted his brief. What the Supreme Court had agreed to review technically was the decision of the Minnesota Supreme Court upholding the constitutionality of the St. Paul ordinance. So while making the underlying argument that the ordinance was unconstitutional, Cleary also had to specifically argue how and why the Minnesota high court justices had erred in their ruling, and how they had misapplied previous U.S. Supreme Court rulings, especially *Chaplinsky*. Basically, he argued as he had since the first hearing before Judge Flinn, that the ordinance was overbroad, vague, and a content-based restriction of free expression prohibited by the First Amendment.

As with most briefs filed before the High Court, Cleary's was generally technical and academic in tone.[11] This was not a case of "first impression," when the Court is asked to rule on a point of law or a subject it has never considered before. Rather, it was a case in which the appellant was asking the Court to invalidate a state law by applying previously annunciated precedents applying both to freedom of speech and the defects found in statutes both overbroad and vague. So Cleary couched his argument in terms of past Court decisions that he thought supported his positions.

---

contents; a listing of authorities (previous precedents being relied upon); a table of citations of all opinions delivered in the lower courts; a concise statement of the facts of the case; a summary of the argument; the argument set forth in such a way as to clearly establish the points of fact and law being relied upon and citing completely the authorities and precedents being cited; and a conclusion summing up the argument and specifically setting out the relief the party thinks he is entitled to. Rule 34.6 states "Briefs must be compact, logically arranged with proper headings, concise and free from burdensome, irrelevant, immaterial and scandalous matter. Briefs not complying with this paragraph may be disregarded and stricken by the Court."

11. Actually, Cleary inserted an interesting literary reference in his brief to try to drive home his point that the First Amendment guarantee of freedom of speech must apply in the case of a cross burning, if it is to apply elsewhere. His excerpt was an exchange from the play *A Man for All Seasons*:

WILLIAM ROPER: So now you'd give the devil benefit of the law?
THOMAS MORE: Yes. What would you do? Cut a great road through the law to get
    after the devil?
ROPER: I'd cut down every law in England to do that.
MORE: Oh? And when the last law was down, and the devil turned round on you,
    where would you hide, the laws all being flat? . . . I'd give the devil benefit
    of the law, for my own safety's sake.

At the same time he submitted his brief to the Court, Cleary also submitted the required "joint appendix"—a compilation of documents from the lower courts, including docket sheets, rulings, and parts of the transcripts of previous Court proceedings that might be of interest or use to the justices in their review of the case. In R. A. V., since there was no real trial court record or complex appeals court proceedings, the appendix was short, easy to assemble, and easily agreed upon by both sides. Often the assembly of a joint appendix can become a major struggle between opposing counsel, as each seeks to include what will bolster its case and exclude what it believes might help the opponent. In those circumstances, Court rules provide that each side may submit its own appendix. But the justices are clearly unhappy when this happens, and both sides in disputes are better served if they can jointly agree on an appendix.

When Cleary submitted his brief in support of R. A. V.'s argument that the ordinance should be overturned, he delivered a copy to Ramsey County Attorney Foley. Now another clock began running. Under Rule 35, a respondent has thirty days in which to file forty copies of his brief stating his arguments.

On August 23, Ramsey County filed its respondent's brief. Foley's arguments now differed slightly from what had been argued by his assistant DeCoster in both the district and state supreme court. They had sought to protect the ordinance in the abstract; now their respondent's brief had to be geared to arguing that the Minnesota high court justices had correctly applied past U.S. Supreme Court rulings, as well as to directly respond to arguments that Cleary had raised about the underlying constitutionality of the ordinance. Since Ramsey County was not considered a pauper, its forty copies had to comply with Rule 33 and be professionally printed in a 6 ⅛ by 9 ¼-inch format with at least ¾-inch margins, using greater than 11-point type, with 2 points of leading (space) between the lines, footnotes in 9-point type or larger (footnotes may be single spaced), and bound with a light red cover.

Rule 33 gave both sides one more written shot. R. A. V.'s attorney, Cleary, had a new thirty days during which he could file a reply brief, limited to a direct response to any arguments raised by Ramsey County in its respondent's brief. He chose to do so, and on September 24, 1991, he filed a short brief arguing that Foley was improperly seeking to apply certain past Court precedents. Under the rule, Ramsey County now had yet another thirty days to file its own reply brief, countering specifically anything that Cleary had argued in his reply brief. Foley chose not to file one, believing his side of the case was adequately spelled out in his previous brief.

As far as the Supreme Court was concerned, both sides had now completed their written arguments. It was still three months before the oral argument was scheduled, and the justices used the time to prepare.

As with the review of cert petitions, each justice prepares for oral argument differently. Some carefully read each set of briefs, check outside references that both sides have cited, and do independent research in order to frame both sides' arguments in their minds before listening to the advocates. In this process most justices make extensive use of their law clerks, having them review the briefs and citations and prepare memos and suggested questions that might be asked during oral argument.

While the written arguments from the two sides is closed at this point, there are times when the issues being argued in a particular case are of wider interest than of simply the two litigants who are directly involved. Often the Court's potential ruling could substantially impact on another individual or group, and thus that individual or group wants to make the Court aware of that impact and to lobby the Court to decide the issue in a certain way. Under the rules of the Court, this is possible by filing of what is known as an *amicus curiae* (friend of the court) brief.

Technically, a person or organization wishing to file an *amicus* brief must petition the Court to be allowed to do so. In practice, the petition is made part of the brief, and the justices are free to consider or not consider what is contained in the brief. An *amicus* brief must conform to the same rules as to content and style as the briefs of the litigants, and except in the most extraordinary of circumstances, no *amicus* is allowed to appear *in forma pauperis*.

Quite a few organizations and individuals believed they had a substantial interest in whether or not hate-crime statutes are held to be constitutional under the First Amendment. Numerous cities and states themselves have similar laws on their books. So the attorneys general of seventeen states[12] filed a joint *amicus* brief arguing that the ordinance should be upheld, as did counsel for the National League of Cities, the League of Minnesota Cities, and the National Governors Association in separate briefs. Most hate-crime statutes are specifically written to protect blacks

---

12. Minnesota, Alabama, Arizona, Connecticut, Idaho, Illinois, Kansas, Maryland, Massachusetts, Michigan, New Jersey, Ohio, Oklahoma, South Carolina, Tennessee, Virginia, and Utah.

from things like cross burnings and Jews from harassment through the defacing of their properties with Nazi symbols. So groups representing both minorities felt they had a vested interest in seeing that the constitutionality of such laws is upheld. Thus counsel representing the National Association for the Advancement of Colored People (NAACP), the National Black Women's Health Project, the Anti-Defamation League of B'nai B'rith, and the American Jewish Congress all filed *amicus* briefs arguing that the ordinance should be upheld. So too did other organizations ranging from the Asian-American Legal Defense Fund, and the People for the American Way Foundation, to the Center for Constitutional Rights in a brief subscribed to by a dozen organizations including the National Council of Black Lawyers, the United Church of Christ, the National YWCA, and the National Council of LaRaza. Each filed an *amicus* brief in support of Ramsey County, arguing that the decision of the Minnesota Supreme Court should be upheld.

On the other side, organizations dedicated to upholding rights under the First Amendment are particularly troubled by any law that seeks to regulate certain kinds of expression based on the content of that expression. While they do not support the kinds of actions that the St. Paul ordinance covers, they believe those actions can be regulated through other types of criminal statutes. They fear that every time the Court upholds a content-based regulation of expression for any reason, it opens the door for other content-based restrictions to be adopted and upheld. So in this case, the American Civil Liberties Union and the Association of American Publishers filed *amicus* briefs against the St. Paul ordinance. Also filing briefs in support of the ordinance were several conservative legal organizations as well as groups representing what they claim are the interests of white people.

Before 1849, the Court was not all that busy, and oral arguments lasted until the lawyers ran out of things to say—usually many hours, sometimes even days. Lawyers on both sides wore formal clothing, and soaring oratory was the norm. But on December 4, 1991, as Ed Cleary and Tom Foley fidgeted in their seats behind the counsel tables shortly before 10:00 A.M., oral argument before the Court had become a much different thing from how it was a century and a half earlier.

Long gone was the tradition of open-ended argument. In the days when the Court might deliver thirty decisions a year, it could spend days listening to arguments in a single case. But as the docket became more crowded, a time limit had to be adopted. The first change came in 1849, when argument was limited to two hours for each side, with as many advocates appearing as each side wanted. This new time limit was rather elastic, depending on the importance of the case. When the famous Dred Scott slavery case was argued in 1857, oral arguments lasted four full days and nights and into the fifth morning. In the 1880s, the time limit was dropped to ninety minutes for each side, with the number of permitted advocates reduced to two for each side. In the 1920s, the time for oral argument was further reduced to one hour on each side. Since 1970, except in very rare cases of unusual complexity or importance, each side is given a firm thirty minutes; and since 1980, unless special leave is granted by the Chief Justice, each side is limited to a single advocate.

Lawyers address the Court from behind a podium that sits in the center of the courtroom. On it are two clocks, one for the petitioner and one for the respondent. On top of the clocks are two lights: one green, one red. The clocks tell the lawyers how much of their allotted thirty minutes has expired. As long as the green light is on, the advocate may continue. The moment the red light goes, a similar light goes on in front of the Chief Justice who will say, often interrupting a lawyer in mid-sentence (unless he or she is in an answer to a question from a justice and then the attorney may finish the answer), "Thank you, counsel. The case is submitted." The timing system is operated by an assistant marshal sitting to the left of the bench. He also has a signal system from the Chief Justice, who may during the course of an oral argument allow extra time if something has occurred in the courtroom that has allowed events to stray away from the argument at hand, or more commonly when there have been so many questions asked a lawyer he or she has not had a chance to make the argument.

One regular exception to these rules is when the U.S. government has intervened in a case as an *amicus curiae*. In those situations, the government, in the person of the solicitor general,[13] is allotted thirty min-

---

13. The solicitor general is the third highest ranking official in the Justice Department after the attorney general and deputy attorney general. His only duty is to represent the United States before the Supreme Court. He and his staff prepare all the government's briefs that are filed with the Court and they argue the cases. Although he is the official advocate of the United States before the Court, he actually plays an important role within the Supreme Court system. Potentially the federal government could file hundreds, if not thousands, of cert petitions annually. But the solicitor general is expected to pick and choose carefully, bringing before the Court only those issues that

utes to argue the government's position. Often when this occurs, the Chief Justice will automatically allot the other side additional time during which *amicus* favoring them can appear. The Chief Justice occasionally will allow *amicus* parties to argue if he thinks their views are important to the case. Or one of the other justices can request a particular *amicus* be allowed to appear, or even be required to appear, in order to expand upon something argued in an *amicus* brief. Usually, if an *amicus* appears, the time he or she uses is subtracted from that side's thirty minutes. But the Chief Justice can grant additional time at his discretion.

On this December morning it was only going to be Ed Cleary for R. A. V. and Tom Foley for Ramsey County. Both were dressed in dark business suits. The Court had long since abandoned the tradition that all lawyers appearing before it had to wear formal dress. These days usually only the solicitor general and his assistants regularly wear tails and striped trousers when appearing before the Court, although every session a few lawyers will appear formally attired to make their arguments.

Since their case was to be the first of three to be argued that morning, the two lawyers and several assistants were at the four counsel tables well before the session began. As they arrived, they found a pair of white goose-quill pens crossed on each of the four counsel tables (they are big souvenir items and few counsel ever leave without them). As they sat in the huge vaulted courtroom, they stared at the raised, slightly rounded bench, with the nine odd-sized black chairs arrayed behind it, four forty-foot-high Italian marble columns behind the bench, and the huge, 40 by 40-foot deep red curtain that fills the front of the courtroom.[14] At each justice's

---

are of importance. In recognition of this, the justices are ten times more likely to accept a case for review if the cert petition has been filed by the solicitor general.

The staff of the Office of Solicitor General has grown as its work load has increased. These days it may be required to file briefs and make appearances in 150 to 175 orally argued cases a year, and file hundreds of petitions urging the denial of certiorari in response to petitions that have been filed in cases where the United States is a party.

Four solicitors general have gone on to become justices: William Howard Taft, Stanley Reed, Robert H. Jackson, and Thurgood Marshall.

14. The bench was redesigned in 1972 in the shape of a half hexagon with the ends set at a 10-degree angle. Before that, it went straight across. This meant that a justice sitting at one end could not see, or often hear, a justice at the far end. It was not unusual for a lawyer to be asked an identical question by two justices seated at opposite ends of the bench. Now with the slightly curved bench all justices can see one another, and a sound system has been installed to ensure that all justices can hear one another and the lawyers making their arguments. As for the chairs, each

place were the pens and pencils they preferred, legal pads, copies of all the briefs that had been filed in each of the cases to be argued, and a pewter mug of ice water. Out of sight at each justice's feet was an ornate brass spittoon. In the days of chewing tobacco, these were a necessity. Today they have been converted to wastebaskets whose contents are shredded and burned after each Court session.

Although no one in the courtroom had heard it, about five minutes earlier a bell had sounded in each of the justices' chambers. It is the same bell that calls them to conferences. Now it commanded them to assemble in the robing room directly behind the courtroom. As each justice arrived to robe, they again went through the ritual handshake with all the other justices, even though they may have been sharing coffee in the adjoining lounge only moments before.

A minute or two before 10:00 A.M., the marshal of the Court, or one of his deputies, and the clerk of the Court, or one of his deputies, both dressed in cutaways, entered the courtroom and took their places to the left of the bench. At precisely 10:00 A.M., the marshal, acting as crier, pounded his gavel, and requested quiet and that all present come to their feet. He intoned in a loud voice: "The Honorable, the Chief Justice and the Associate Justices of the Supreme Court of the United States. Oyez! Oyez! Oyez! All persons having business before the Honorable, the Supreme Court of the United States, are admonished to draw near and give their attention, for the Court is now sitting. God save the United States and this Honorable Court."

With this the justices arrived through the red curtain and the four tall marble pillars that stand behind the bench. They took their seats according to a rigid order based on seniority. The Chief Justice took his seat directly in the middle of the bench. The eight associate justices are placed alternating between the Chief Justice's right and left. On this day, Justice Byron White, as the senior associate justice, sat to Chief Justice William Rehnquist's right. To Rehnquist's left sat Justice Harry Blackmun. To White's right was Justice John Paul Stevens. To Blackmun's left, Justice Sandra Day O'Connor. To Stevens's right sat Justice Antonin Scalia. To O'Connor's left, Justice Anthony Kennedy took his seat. To Scalia's right sat the second most recent addition to the Court, David Souter. And to Kennedy's left,

justice is allowed to choose the size and style preferred. Therefore, some of the chairs have high backs, some do not, and they look quite different, which they are.

and the far left-hand side of the bench, sat the Court's newest member, Clarence Thomas.

As the justices took their seats, court attendants took seats behind them. Their jobs are to pass messages to and from justices, refill water glasses, fetch research materials from a justice's chambers or the third-floor law library, or in other ways serve any justice's needs.

On any day the Court is in session, pending business is conducted before the first of the day's cases is called for argument. At the start of a Monday session, the Chief Justice will read off the Orders List indicating which cases were accepted for argument at the previous Friday's conference, and which certiorari petitions are being denied. On other days, opinions of the Court may be announced, with the Chief Justice or the associate justice who wrote the majority opinion reading aloud a summary of the opinion. When opinions are announced, a justice who is in dissent has the option of announcing and even reading his dissent.

This day, there was no pending business, so immediately Chief Justice Rehnquist intoned, "First, we will hear the case of *R. A. V.*, *Petitioner* versus *St. Paul.*" As counsel for the appellant (petitioner), Ed Cleary went first. A lawyer has the option to use as much of his allotted half-hour at this time as he wishes. Most use only a portion initially, so there will be time remaining from their half-hour to reply to arguments raised by opposing counsel. But under the rules, in most cases, the appellant has the right both to open and close the argument.[15]

Cleary approached the lawyers' podium and used its hand crank to adjust it to a comfortable height. As he began he had to keep in mind the explicit provisions of Rule 38 governing oral argument: "Oral argument should undertake to emphasize and clarify the written argument appearing in the briefs theretofore filed. Counsel should assume that all Members of the Court have read the briefs in advance of argument. *The Court looks with disfavor on any oral argument that is read from a prepared text* [emphasis the Court's]."

This often places a lawyer in a damned if he does, damned if he doesn't position. The rule says that he should assume that the justices have

---

15. There are times when neither side is happy with the decision of a lower court, and both file petition for writs of certiorari. In these unusual circumstances, if the Court accepts the petition and cross-petition, it will designate who is the appellant for purposes of who has to file the first brief and who shall lead off the oral argument and who shall have the right to close.

read the briefs and have a working understanding of the case. But he can't be sure that in his particular case all the justices have really done their homework and really remember and understand both the facts and the law of the case. So most lawyers try to begin their presentations with a summary of the facts and the legal principles involved and then are prepared either to move on or go into greater detail about the facts and the law if they can tell by the justices' reactions that they have not read or have mostly forgotten about the case.

Court scholars differ sharply on how important oral argument is. In a 1967 Harvard Law School publication, recently retired Justice William Brennan said, "Oral argument is the absolute indispensable. . . . Often my whole notion of what a case is about crystallizes at oral argument. This happens even though I read the briefs before oral argument." Some of the justices seem to have their minds made up well before they come to the oral arguments. They seem to pay little attention. But most lawyers who appear before the Court believe that oral argument is important because it can allow them the opportunity to put some flesh on the otherwise academic and legalistic arguments they have made in their written briefs, and that they can use the opportunity to try to make the justices see the wider and more personal ramifications of what a particular ruling might bring.

Oral arguments are not sessions in which advocates lecture to a panel of nine justices for thirty minutes. They are very much interactive exercises, with a great deal of give-and-take between the justices and the lawyers arguing in front of them. Perhaps the most important aspect of oral argument are the questions asked by the justices. Often a lawyer will barely finish with his traditional opening of "Mr. Chief Justice, and may it please the Court," when some of the justices begin firing questions. Many of the justices have worked with their clerks outlining and digesting the briefs into bench memorandums with lists of questions to be asked each counsel. Other times a lawyer will argue something that prompts a question from a justice who doesn't understand. Still other justices are famous for using sharp questioning to try to throw off balance, and even to harass, a lawyer arguing a side with which they do not agree; or to effectively coach a lawyer into making a point the justice wants made. Leading questions are often the rule, not the exception. By the time they sit down, most lawyers feel they have been thrust back into law school with nine professors all firing questions at the same time.

How questioning dominates oral arguments was seen in R. A. V. v. St. Paul. Cleary began by arguing, "Each generation must reaffirm the guarantee of the First Amendment with the hard cases. We are once again faced with a case that will demonstrate whether or not there is room for freedom for the thought that we hate, whether there is room for the eternal vigilance necessary for the opinion that we loathe."

He then continued: "The conduct in this case is reprehensible, is abhorrent and is well known by now. I'm not here to defend the alleged conduct, but just as Justice Felix Frankfurter showed forty years ago, history has shown that the safeguards of liberty are generally forged in cases involving generally not very nice people."

This is as far as he got when the questions began. One justice wanted to know if he wasn't arguing the wrong case because the Minnesota Supreme Court had narrowed the focus of the ordinance in its decision, and now Cleary seemed to be arguing against the statute as originally written. Another wanted to know if Cleary believed a state could proscribe words that caused alarm twenty-four or even forty-eight hours later as opposed to immediately and face-to-face. Another wanted to know about a statute that proscribed some "fighting words" but not others. In answer to one of a dozen and a half additional questions, Cleary argued if the Court were to validate the St. Paul ordinance, "there is nothing to stop another state from adopting a law like this to outlaw another symbol—the Star of David, for example."

County Attorney Foley did not even get a chance to start before he was answering questions. Justice Harry Blackmun, a St. Paul native, wanted to know exactly where the house was at which this happened, down to the nearest cross street. Then he wondered why, if it were a St. Paul city ordinance that was being challenged, the Ramsey County attorney was appearing. (Ramsey County handles all juvenile matters in the county including those occurring in the city limits.) Finally Foley was allowed to begin, and he argued "the First Amendment was never intended to protect a person who burns a cross in the middle of the night in the fenced yard of an African-American family. The city of St. Paul has the right to proscribe such conduct."

That is as far as he got before more questions began. Many were the same as had been fired at Cleary. In answering, Foley did concede that the ordinance, as originally written, was probably overbroad because it would have, for instance, outlawed the burning of a cross at a public rally on the county courthouse steps. He agreed that such a cross burning would be protected in the same way the Court had protected flag burning. But then he argued that the Minnesota Supreme Court, in its ruling on the case, had narrowed the law's focus when it said the law could be used in the "fighting words" context.

"This is more than just outrageous conduct," Foley argued. "It causes direct harm to people. It is a precursor to violence and hatred in this country." After a short rebuttal by Cleary, Chief Justice Rehnquist intoned, "Thank you, counsel. The case is submitted."

Supreme Court decisions serve two purposes. They are the final resolve of specific disputes between specific parties. But they are much more than that. The Court uses the specific cases it hears to interpret and explain the law to lower courts and to the legal community. Take R. A. V. v. *St. Paul* as the obvious example. While the Court's decision ultimately told both R. A. V. and St. Paul whether the youth would have to stand trial under the potentially harsher hate-crime ordinance, the justices' decision also told the wider legal community whether laws like St. Paul's are constitutional. In doing so, the Court continued its now two-centuries-old defining of the First Amendment and the Constitution as a whole.

Given this function, what becomes centrally important to the orderly operation of the system is some degree of consensus. If the Court intends its decisions to give direction to lower courts on interpreting the law, its opinions must contain some level of consensus. If the justices cannot agree, then their opinions lose authority as guideposts for the legal community. The worst situation is a case in which a majority of justices might agree on an outcome—who wins and who loses—but not agree as to why. When this happens you can end up with four justices agreeing in a plurality opinion that A prevails over B for a certain set of reasons, while several other justices also agree that A should prevail over B, but not for the same reasons. So they write one or more concurring opinions. The remaining justices disagree completely—they believe that B should prevail over A—and they write one or more dissenting opinions. In the end, you are left with a situation where as far as the litigants are concerned, they now know that A wins. But the case is largely useless in explaining and defining the law and legal concepts involved.

This is not to say that dissent should in any way be stifled. The tradition of dissent is one of the strongest virtues of the Supreme Court and of our legal system. Looking back in history, we see that many of the most famous cases ever decided by the Court are so because of a well-reasoned and impassioned dissent. The Court is well able to instruct and interpret in 5–4 and 6–3 decisions, even with sharp divisions. It is not instructive when the justices cannot agree among themselves why one side should prevail. So the entire opinion process is geared to developing some level of consensus.

Because of the absolute secrecy of the process we cannot be sure, but we can assume at conference on Friday, December 6, 1991, the justices decided the case of *R. A. V. v. St. Paul*. The justices like to decide a case soon after it is argued, while it remains fresh in their minds. The Wednesday afternoon conference is usually reserved for deciding cases argued on Monday and Tuesday, the Friday conference for cases argued on Wednesday and Thursday. Thus we can assume that sometime after the Discuss List of cert petitions was finished, and the morning coffee break completed, the justices got around to deciding whether the St. Paul ordinance was constitutional.

The Chief Justice starts the discussion of the cases. Then, in turn by seniority, each justice who wants to can discuss the case. By tradition, once a justice speaks no other justice is supposed to interrupt. We are told that decorum always rules in conference, with all justices respecting the views of all others and each giving deference to the other. But we know from interviews, memoirs, and other sources that conferences can get argumentative, raucous, and at times downright nasty and personal. But these situations are usually the exception. In most cases, as the justices speak in turn, it becomes clear what the outcome will be. At the end of the discussion, a vote is taken and the case is decided.

Even though the vote has been taken, and the case has been decided, a critical part of the process remains: the writing of the opinions. If the Chief Justice is part of the majority, he can reserve the writing of the opinion for himself or he can assign it to any of the other justices in the majority. In doing so, he usually takes into consideration the current work load of each justice, the degree of interest each justice might have in the case, and what special expertise a justice might have in a certain subject. If the Chief Justice is not part of the majority, the assignment of the opinion is made by the senior justice in the majority. Those justices in opposition choose among themselves which of their number will write the dissent. In the case of *R. A. V. v. St. Paul*, Chief Justice Rehnquist probably[16] assigned Justice Scalia to write the majority opinion, while the minority chose Justice White to write a dissent.

16. One has to say "probably" because the final sets of opinions are so convoluted that it is possible

What now ensues is this quest for consensus. The justice writing the majority opinion will begin work with his clerks marshaling his arguments and citations and will begin a first draft of the opinion. Others of the justices might prepare memorandums of their own, outlining their thinking on a case and what previous cases they would cite, and send these to the justice writing the opinion. When the first draft is completed, it is circulated among the justices. Their input will result in further drafts, until an opinion is completed that all can agree on. In the meantime, the same kind of process goes on among those who are dissenting.

This is a fluid process. It is not altogether rare, in a case that resulted in a very close 5–4 vote at conference, that during the months-long opinion-writing process one of the justices will come to the conclusion that he or she is not being persuaded by the arguments in the majority draft opinion, and upon further reflection will decide to change his or her vote. In this circumstance, the draft dissent might suddenly become the draft majority opinion.

This is unusual, however. Much more common is that at some point in the opinion-writing process some justices making up the majority will realize that they do not agree completely with the line of reasoning that is developing in the majority opinion. They decide to strike out on their own and write a concurring opinion. Typically, a justice in a concurring opinion will say that he or she agrees with the majority on the outcome (A prevailing over B, or vice versa) and on certain points as to why, but that he or she disagrees on others. Or that the justice agrees in part and believes that the decision should also rest on some other legal theory that the majority-opinion writer has not included. As with the majority opinion, drafts of concurring opinions are circulated, and other justices from the majority might decide to join in the concurrence rather than in the majority opinion. Occasionally, enough justices decide to abandon the draft majority opinion so that, by the time the opinion is released, what started as the concurrence has become the majority opinion.

Finally, the majority opinion and any concurrences or dissents are completed, and all the justices have signed off on the final drafts. The completed opinions are then forwarded to the clerk's office, where the staff reviews each carefully, rechecking every citation and writing the so-called

that Scalia started out writing a dissent only to have it become the majority opinion and Justice White started out writing the majority opinion only to have it end up a dissent.

head notes that will appear in the final printed version summarizing the points of law covered. Once the head notes have been added and all citations reverified, the clerk sends the opinion to the printer's office, where it is prepared and printed. When this is completed, copies are sent to all justices, and the Chief Justice schedules it to be announced. As he begins his reading, copies are delivered to the public information and press rooms for distribution to the public.

At precisely 10:00 A.M. on Monday, June 23, 1992, the justices entered the Court chamber through the massive red curtain behind the bench. It was the beginning of the last week of the term, and numerous decisions still had to be announced. Veteran Court observers knew that some major decision was going to be announced because of the unusually large number of justices' law clerks who had slipped into the chamber to watch. The justices had stopped hearing new cases more than a month earlier, and for the last four weeks had come to the bench once or twice a week to announce decisions. Now, the two most eagerly awaited still to be announced were an abortion rights case which might result in the modifying, or even the overturning, of the landmark *Roe* v. *Wade*, and the St. Paul hate-crime case: *R. A. V.* v. *St. Paul.*

The rumor around the Court for the last several months had been that the justices were having unusual difficulty with R. A. V. That seemed obvious. The case had been argued in early December, yet weeks and then months had passed without the opinion being announced. Decisions on cases argued in February and March were announced, but still nothing on the hate-crime ordinance. But exactly how much difficulty the justices had had only become clear once the multiple decisions on the case were released.

After the packed chamber had settled down, Chief Justice Rehnquist began the session by announcing that the justices had agreed to hear an important alien asylum case at the start of the new term in October. Then he announced the Court's decision, which he authored, in a habeas corpus case. Then Justice Anthony Kennedy announced his majority decision on the question of the burden of proof in determining the mental competency of a criminal defendant. Finally, Justice Antonin Scalia began to read the majority decision he had authored in *R. A. V.* v. *St. Paul.*

The importance of the case was underscored by the fact that Scalia read from his decision for almost eight minutes, an unusually long time. Normally a justice will only indicate what the result is, and perhaps will underscore the main legal reasoning. But Scalia read at length from his opinion, including why he and the other five justices in the majority were correct in their reasoning on the case while the remaining four justices were not. In doing so, Scalia made it absolutely clear exactly how difficult reaching this decision had become.

Given the secrecy of the justices' conferences, it is impossible to know exactly what happened. But an educated guess is that when the justices met in conference on the Friday after the case was argued in early December, they quickly agreed, unanimously, that the St. Paul ordinance was unconstitutional. Chief Justice Rehnquist then assigned the writing of the opinion to Justice Scalia. But as drafts of the opinion began to circulate among the justices it must have become clear that while all nine were in agreement that the ordinance must be struck down, there was a fundamental and absolute disagreement among them as to why it was unconstitutional. In the end four other justices—Chief Justice Rehnquist and Justices Kennedy, Souter and Thomas, signed the Scalia opinion making it the majority ruling. Justices White, Blackmun, Stevens, and O'Connor agreed only with the outcome of the majority opinion. Justice White wrote a concurring opinion in which the other three generally agreed. And to underscore the level of disagreement, both Blackmun and Stevens wrote separate concurring opinions. So in the end, in a unanimous case, you had four separate and very different opinions.

Scalia, and the four justices joining him, ruled that the St. Paul ordinance is constitutionally flawed because the First Amendment prohibits government from "silencing speech on the basis of its content." The law, noted Scalia, makes it a crime to engage in speech or behavior likely to arouse "anger or alarm" on the basis of "race, color, creed, religion or gender." Yet people who might commit many of the same acts of insult or harassment on the basis of "political affiliation, union membership or homosexuality" would not be breaking the law.

Scalia used an example of an imaginary confrontation between Catholics and anti-Catholics. If the anti-Catholics waved virulent signs denouncing Catholicism, they would be violating the St. Paul law. But their opponents, saying and doing exactly the same thing, in exactly the same way, denouncing them, would not violate the law. Wrote Scalia: "St. Paul has no such authority to license one side of a debate to fight freestyle, while requiring the other to follow Marquis of Queensbury Rules." The law must fall, he ruled, because of this selectiveness.

Wrote Scalia:

The dispositive question in this case, therefore, is whether content discrimination is reasonably necessary to achieve St. Paul's compelling interests; it plainly is not. An ordinance not limited to the favored topics, for example, would have precisely the same beneficial effect . . .

St. Paul has not singled out an especially offensive mode of expression. It has not, for example, selected for prohibition only those fighting words that communicate ideas in a threatening (as opposed to merely obnoxious) manner. Rather, it has proscribed fighting words of whatever manner that communicate messages of racial, gender, or religious intolerance. Selectivity of this sort creates the possibility that the city is seeking to handicap the expression of particular ideas . . .

Let there be no mistake about our belief that burning a cross in someone's front yard is reprehensible. But St. Paul has sufficient means at its disposal to prevent such behavior without adding the First Amendment to the fire.

One interpretation of the majority opinion is that it might well be constitutional for the state to ban cross burning, but that the problem with the St. Paul law was that it was specific about some acts being banned, while not including others. Inherent in that reasoning is the idea that the law might have stood if only St. Paul had included enough acts—if the law had been even more overbroad. If this interpretation is correct, then the majority, while overturning the St. Paul law, actually narrowed the scope of the First Amendment.

This, at least, is what the four dissenting justices believed the majority was saying. The depth of the philosophical disagreement among the justices was apparent in the opening sentence of Justice White's concurring opinion: "I agree with the majority that the judgment of the Minnesota Supreme Court should be reversed. However, our agreement ends there . . . the Court's reasoning in reaching its result is transparently wrong."

White, and the other three minority justices, believe the St. Paul ordinance can be struck down "within the contours of established First Amendment law" by holding it "fatally overbroad"—that in proscribing certain speech and conduct that does fall outside the protection of the First Amendment, it also proscribes speech and conduct that clearly is protected.

In the majority opinion, Scalia ruled that since the statute was "flawed on its face," the Court did not even have to consider whether it might be overbroad. With this characterization, White had serious problems.

As White saw it, in an unclear and indirect way, the majority was overturning past Supreme Court decisions that had held that "fighting words" were outside the scope of constitutional protection by now placing them on "at least equal constitutional footing with political discourse and other forms of speech that we have deemed to have the greatest social value, the majority devalues the latter category."

Wrote White:

> . . . the majority holds that the First Amendment protects those narrow categories of expression long held to be undeserving of First Amendment protection, at least to the extent that lawmakers may not regulate some fighting words more strictly than others because of their content . . . *such a simplistic, all-or-nothing approach to First Amendment protection is at odds with common sense and with our jurisprudence as well.* [17] It is inconsistent to hold that the government may proscribe an entire category of speech because the content of that speech is evil, but that the government may not treat a subset of that category differently without violating the First Amendment; the content of the subset is by definition worthless and undeserving of constitutional protection.
>
> Today, the Court has disregarded two established principles of First Amendment law without providing a coherent replacement theory. Its decision is an arid, doctrinaire interpretation, driven by the frequently irresistible impulse of judges to tinker with the First Amendment. The decision is mischievous at best and will surely confuse the lower courts. I join in the judgment, but not the folly of the opinion.

Had the Court adopted the reasoning of the four minority justices that the St. Paul ordinance should be struck down on the established constitutional grounds of being overbroad, then the city, and the dozens of other states, cities and communities that have adopted similar hate-crime ordinances could redraft them in such a way that hate crimes would still be specifically outlawed, but the laws would not also ban constitutionally protected speech and acts. But under the majority ruling, redrafting the statutes to make them acceptable would seem impossible. It would also appear from the majority ruling that the "politically correct" speech codes

17. This is an exact phrase that Scalia used in his majority opinion to dismiss White's objections. The use of it by White underscores the bitterness of the split.

that have been adopted by hundreds of colleges and schools, cannot stand up to constitutional scrutiny.

That fact was at the heart of Justice Blackmun's concurring opinion. Writing: "I regret what the Court has done in this case . . . I fear the Court has been distracted from its proper mission by the temptation to decide the issue over "politically correct speech" and "cultural diversity," neither of which was presented here." On the specific issue being presented, Blackmun said: "I see no First Amendment values that are compromised by a law that prohibits hoodlums from driving minorities out of their homes by burning crosses on their lawns, but I see great harm in preventing the people of St. Paul from specifically punishing the race-based fighting words that so prejudice their community."

Justice Stevens in his concurring opinion, which was joined by the other three in the minority, also centered on the idea that creating subsets of prohibited acts to punish differently, should cause no constitutional problem. "Conduct that creates special risks or causes special harms may be prohibited by special rules."

Stevens noted that past First Amendment rulings had established three levels of protection for speech: "core speech" deserving of the most protection, commercial speech and non-obscene expression of a sexual nature that deserves less protection, and obscenity and fighting words that deserve little or no protection. Stevens worries that the majority opinion has inadvertently raised this last category now to an equal level with the first and made fighting words more deserving of protection than corporate speech.

Finally, Stevens says he thinks the majority is simply illogical in its conclusion: ". . . the Court recognizes exceptions to its new principle, those exceptions undermine its very conclusion that the St. Paul ordinance is unconstitutional. Stated directly, the majority's position cannot withstand scrutiny."

But while the Supreme Court struck down St. Paul's hate-crime ordinance, and in so doing the second count against R. A. V., the justices' ruling is not an end to Robert A. Viktora's legal problems. He did not challenge the first count of his indictment, and he will still face trial.

# 2.

# The History of the Court

## The Origin of the Judiciary

X By the summer of 1783, men like George Washington, John Jay, Alexander Hamilton, and Gouverneur Morris realized that the new government that had been set up in the United States after the Revolution wasn't working. Jay wrote from England that Europe was looking with great jealousy at the situation and noted "jealousy is seldom idle." He predicted that unless the central government was strengthened and assumed more control, the new nation was ripe for invasion by France, Spain, or England.

The new government had been established under the Articles of Confederation and Perpetual Union, which had been drafted even as the Revolution was being waged. There was naturally a great fear that the hated British government, which was being rebelled against, would simply be replicated here. So the drafters of the Articles went far out of their way to ensure that would not happen by establishing a very weak central government consisting only of a legislature in which each of the thirteen states would have a single and equal vote. No separate national executive was established, and the powers of national legislature were limited to issues of foreign policy and war, operating a postal service, issuing a common currency, and some other minor matters. Most of the real power was left with the individual states. Article II of the Articles said it all: "Each state retains its sovereignty, freedom and independence, and every power, jurisdiction and right, which is not by this confederation expressly delegated to the United States, in Congress assembled." This meant that the new national legislature had wide responsibilities, but little actual authority.

As far as a central federal judiciary was concerned, that was not even considered. The Articles assumed that state courts would retain jurisdiction over all civil suits, including suits between residents of one state and another, and over all criminal matters including cases of high treason. It was further assumed that each state would recognize the legal proceedings of all the others, and they would take judicial notice and would respect the laws of all other states.

Congress itself was granted some quasijudicial functions, in that it was made the final arbiter of boundary, jurisdictional, and other disputes between or among the states, as well as given the power to settle any land disputes that might arise from conflicting land grants declared by more than one state. Congress was given the power—so long as no member served as a judge—to establish a court with jurisdiction limited to certain admiralty issues, including cases of piracy and other high crimes committed at sea.

The Articles did not take effect until 1781, and within eighteen months it was clear to most that the new system simply was not working. The finances of the new government were a shambles. Congress had no power to raise funds through the direct levy of taxes; instead, it had to ask the states for what amounted to donations. It could sell bonds, but it could not guarantee repayment. With no constitutionally designated head of state—a president or a prime minister—the new Congress found it had the power to negotiate international treaties, but it could not enforce them. It had no power to regulate commerce between the states, or between individual states and foreign nations. Serious interstate disputes broke out, and no court existed to adjudicate them. Some states were developing what amounted to their own foreign policies and international relations.

By 1785 there was talk in every state about ways of strengthening the central government. These informal talks led to a convention in Annapolis in September of 1786. That gathering, in turn, issued a call for a convention of all thirteen states to find ways to strengthen the government under the Articles. Congress reluctantly agreed, and called for a national convention to convene in Philadelphia in May 1787, "for the sole and express purpose of revising the Articles of Confederation." Every state, save Rhode Island, sent delegates.

By and large the delegates who gathered at State House (now Independence Hall) in Philadelphia represented the very best from each state. George Washington was there from Virginia, as were James Madison, George Mason, John Marshall, and Edmund Randolph. Ben Franklin, at age eighty-two, was the gathering's elder statesman, while Jonathan Dayton of New Jersey, at age twenty-seven, was the youngest. Alexander Hamilton and Gouverneur Morris, probably the most outspoken proponents of a strong central government, represented New York, as did George Clinton, who was probably the strongest proponent of what today we would call states' rights. About the only men of real note who were not in Philadelphia that hot summer of 1787 were Thomas Jefferson and John Adams, who were serving as ambassadors to France and Great Britain, respectively; Virginia's Patrick Henry, who so opposed a strong central government that he boycotted the convention; and Charles Carroll of Maryland and George Wythe of Virginia, who did not attend for health reasons.

The Philadelphia convention was called for what Congress had seen as the limited purpose of "amending" the Articles. But except for George Clinton, almost all the strongest willed delegates had come for the express purpose of establishing a strong central government. The convention actually began with Virginia's governor Randolph's broad-based attack on the Articles and offer instead of a Virginia Plan that called for scrapping the whole system under the Articles and adopting a strong central government with wide powers. Quickly a consensus began to build among the delegates that Morris was right. Simply amending the existing Articles would not be sufficient. Rather, they would have to be junked and a whole new document drafted. The Virginia Plan became the draft document around which the debate swirled.

As the delegates debated, they struggled with three major problems: how to give the national government the broad powers it needed without endangering the continued existence of the states; how this broad national power could be restrained so as not to infringe upon individual liberties; and how to assure that the new Constitution would remain preeminent, while striking some balance between the executive branch and Congress. Their answer, and to many the genius of the Constitution, was the transfer of powers from the state to the federal government in international, interstate, and specific national areas like finance, taxation, and regulation of commerce, while leaving the states with broad but generally unspecified powers in other more local matters. To restrain the executive and legislative branches, the two were made equal through the processes of checks and balances.

As for limiting the power of the central government over individual rights, the Convention bogged down in a major philosophical argument over whether the new Constitution should contain specific guaranteed rights of citizens. George Mason had drafted a "declaration of rights" that had been included in the Virginia state constitution. It stipulated that all governmental authority comes from the people, and it enumerated a list of specific rights guaranteed all citizens, including the right of an accused to face his accuser and to a trial by jury, protection from being forced to give testimony against himself, prohibition of cruel and unusual punishment, subordination of the military to civilian control, and guaranteed right of freedom of the press and of speech.

George Mason and Charles Pinckney wanted to include the same kind of specific guarantees in the new constitution. According to Madison's journal, Mason asked the convention "to attend to the rights of every class of the people." He was joined in this call by Pinckney and Madison, and James Wilson and Elbridge Gerry of Massachusetts.

A majority of the delegates, however, opposed the idea of including any explicit listing of individual rights. It was not that they were opposed to a guarantee of individual liberties. Rather, as they saw it, what they were in Philadelphia to do was to establish a strong new central government based on specific enumerated powers. They did not want to start the process by making a list of what the new government could not do. But more basically, they simply assumed that any powers not specifically given to this new central government were reserved to the states. Since every state but New Jersey at the time had a delineation of individual rights as part of its state constitution, most in Philadelphia felt individual liberties were adequately protected.

Not including a specific statement of individual rights almost proved a serious enough error to have kept the new Constitution from ratification. In the end, six of the eleven states initially ratifying the new Constitution did so on the understanding that the new national legislature would modify the document with a Bill of Rights. That proved one of the first orders of business for the new Congress, and the mistake was rectified with the passage and adoption of the Bill of Rights in 1791.

That left the question of constitutional superiority. In his opening speech, Randolph had listed the Articles' major defects: the supremacy of state constitutions to it; its lack of authority to decide conflicts between and among states; and its inability to prevent the states from encroaching on the power of the central government. The obvious answer to Randolph, and to others like Madison and eventually to Hamilton, was an independent federal judiciary. Once this concept found agreement, the convention's lawyers spent months in hot debate over the form and powers of a federal court system.

The idea of a separate judicial branch was not really foreign to the delegates. Six of the original thirteen states had separate judiciaries. As with the other aspects of the proposed new government, Randolph's Virginia Plan acted as the basis for the debate over the judiciary. It called for a separate judicial branch, equal to the executive and legislative and consisting of a Supreme Court as well as a system of inferior courts. Many of the delegates had major problems with the idea of inferior federal courts, especially sitting within the states. They viewed this as a direct challenge to the jurisdiction of state courts.

Charles Pinckney of South Carolina was one who distrusted the idea of a strong federal judiciary. He brought forward his own plan for a new central government that included only a limited federal court system composed of a "supreme court of error" empowered to try government officials charged with official misconduct and to take appeals from the highest courts of each state on matters arising out of treaties, international law, trade (both foreign and interstate), and cases in which the government itself was a party. Pinckney's plan did not call for any inferior court system, but it did grant Congress the ability to establish an admiralty court, with a branch in each state, to hear only maritime cases.

William Paterson of New Jersey then introduced a series of amendments to the existing Articles that stopped far short of the complete overhaul contained in the Virginia Plan. While it recognized that the central government needed more power, Paterson's amendments—which became known as the New Jersey Plan—reflected the fear of the small states that they would lose their power and even their identity in a strong union dominated by the larger states.

Paterson's New Jersey Plan adopted the underlying philosophy of a weak national judiciary contained in Pinckney's plan. It called for establishment of a single supreme federal court whose sole function would be to protect national rights and to assure uniformity in constitutional interpretations by state courts. This court would hear cases of impeachment of national government officials and would have appellate rights to review state court decisions involving ambassadors, all foreigners, crimes on the high seas, interpretation of treaties, and the interpretation of national commerce, trade, and revenue laws. The New Jersey Plan did not provide for any inferior courts, but it did give the highest courts of each state quasijoint jurisdiction in federal matters with the federal high court, with the latter to act as an arbiter when state courts could not agree.

In the end there were at least five competing proposals for a federal judiciary on the table: the Virginia Plan, the New Jersey Plan, Pinckney's, one drafted by Roger Sherman of Connecticut that also called for a single federal court with most of the power continuing to reside in the state judiciaries, and a plan drafted by Alexander Hamilton.

Hamilton appears to be something of a late convert to the idea of a strong central judiciary. He came to Philadelphia perhaps the strongest advocate of a powerful, highly centralized, almost aristocratic government, but not one based on democracy because he distrusted the people's ability to choose their own leaders. He was suspicious of a strong judiciary. However, as the debate evolved, Hamilton realized that there would be no strong central government without a strong federal judicial system. So when he finally came forward with his own blueprint for a new central government, it contained a federal judiciary headed by a supreme court with jurisdiction over all cases to which the United States is a party, all cases of disputes between the states, and all cases involving diplomats. Hamilton's supreme court also would have had appellate jurisdiction over all questions of law arising in cases involving citizens of a foreign country, citizens of different states, and all others involving "fundamental rights of this Constitution." In addition, Hamilton's plan called for establishment of those inferior federal courts that Congress would, from time to time, deem necessary.

Much of the work of the delegates to the Constitutional Convention that summer involved reaching compromises between the advocates of a strong central system, as outlined in the Virginia Plan and advocates of leaving vast powers with the states, as outlined in the New Jersey Plan. The most important compromise was the so-called Great Compromise, establishing a dual-chambered legislature with the upper chamber containing two senators from each state regardless of size and the equal lower chamber, the House of Representatives, with proportional representation based on population. This same kind of compromise was struck in establishing a new federal judiciary—a compromise between the competing Virginia Plan as modified by Hamilton and the New Jersey Plan as modified by both Pinckney and Sherman.

Debate on the judiciary began on June 4. Randolph introduced his plan in the form of a motion. After almost a day of debate, John Rutledge of South Carolina introduced a motion eliminating the inferior courts contemplated by the Virginia Plan. A short but bitter debate ensued, with Madison leading the effort to retain the inferior court system. In the end those supporting lower courts lost, and Rutledge's motion deleting inferior courts was adopted.

Now came the critical compromise. Madison put forward a motion seeking to adopt Hamilton's idea of giving Congress the power to establish those lower courts it would think necessary. The debate continued, with some delegates arguing that any inferior courts would limit states' rights. But Madison argued that by resting the power of the establishment in the hands of Congress, states would be protected. In the end the motion was adopted.

More than six weeks passed before the convention returned to the subject of the judiciary, this time to consider its scope of jurisdiction. After several days of debate, the delegates agreed that "the jurisdiction of the national Judiciary shall extend to cases arising under the laws passed by the general Legislature, and to such other questions as involve National peace and harmony."

That was not specific enough for Randolph. He formulated a new draft on judicial jurisdiction, and this was ordered and referred to the Committee on Detail, along with several resolutions by Paterson aimed at limiting even further federal jurisdiction. Then the convention adjourned for three weeks.

There was no accurate record kept of the proceedings of the convention. Much of what we know about what happened comes from notes and diaries kept by individual delegates, and by comparing various drafts of the same documents. So some of what happened, and why it happened, remains a mystery. One such mystery concerns the judiciary. When Randolph's draft was sent to the Committee on Detail, it talked about the jurisdiction of the judiciary as a whole. But when it emerged, seemingly almost intact, it now spoke only about the jurisdiction of the proposed new high court. How and why this change occurred is not clear, but it was very significant—the Constitution would not establish a set jurisdiction for the lower courts. Off and on over the next three weeks, the debate over lower court jurisdiction continued, until in the end it was agreed that any lower courts would be both established, and their jurisdiction set, from time to time by Congress.

Other lesser matters still remained, including a measure about judges' tenure, compensation, and conduct (including Congress's ability to impeach); a safeguarding of the right to trial by jury; and clarification of the difference between the specific jurisdiction of the Supreme Court and the jurisdiction of the federal judiciary in general. A compromise ended still another dispute—whether the president or Congress should appoint Supreme Court justices. Here, too, the answer was a compromise—the president would appoint, with confirmation by the Senate. Finally, the judicial measure was adopted in principle, and was forwarded for formal drafting to the Committee on Style, chaired by Gouverneur Morris.

Now another compromise in forming the new federal judiciary took place. Morris insisted that the new Constitution be written with clarity, precision, and detail. If you read Article I, setting up the scope of congressional power, and Article II, detailing the powers of the executive, you see in them Morris's passion for clarity and detail. But with the judiciary article, Morris decided that since deep differences still existed among the delegates, and since states might object should the wording be too definitive, he would resort to simplicity and deliberate ambiguity. It is a bit of a shock to reach Article III, and see both its brevity and generality relative to the first two articles. But Morris knew that this was the only way to win agreement for the compromise between the sharply differing competing plans.

As finally adopted, Article III contained only three short sections, with the third pertaining only to the crime of treason.

### ARTICLE III

Sec. 1. The judicial power of the United States, shall be vested in one Supreme Court, and in such inferior courts as the Congress may from time to time ordain and establish. The judges, both of the Supreme and inferior courts, shall hold their offices during good behavior, and shall at stated times, receive for their services, a compensation, which shall not be diminished during their continuance in office.

Sec. 2. The judicial power shall extend to all cases, in law and equity, arising under this Constitution, the laws of the United States, and treaties made, or which shall be made, under their authority; to all cases affecting ambassadors, other public ministers and consuls; to all cases of admiralty and maritime jurisdiction; to controversies to which the United States shall be a party; to controversies between two or more States, between a State and citizens of another State; between citizens of different States; between citizens of the same State claiming lands under grants of different States, and between a State or the citizens thereof, and foreign states, citizens or subjects.

In all cases affecting ambassadors, other public ministers and counsels, and those in which a State shall be party, the Supreme Court shall have original jurisdiction. In all other cases before mentioned, the Supreme Court shall have appellate jurisdiction, both as to law and fact, with such exceptions, and under such regulations as the Congress shall make.

The trial of all crimes, except in cases of impeachment, shall be by jury; and such trial shall be held in the State where the said crimes shall have been committed; but when not committed within any State, the trial shall be at such place or places as the Congress may by law have directed.

Sec. 3. Treason against the United States, shall consist only in levying war against them, or in adhering to their enemies, giving them aid and comfort. No person shall be convicted of treason unless on the testimony of two witnesses to the same overt act, or on confession in open court.

The Congress shall have power to declare the punishment of treason, but no attainder of treason shall work corruption of blood, or forfeiture, except during the life of the person attained.

Actually, a provision of the Constitution that became central to the development of a strong judiciary was not even contained in Article III. Luther Martin, a Maryland delegate, was a lawyer of significant repute. He was not a strong advocate of centralized government; in fact, he is said to have abhorred the proposed limitation of states' rights. But he was too good a lawyer to let pass what he considered a major drafting flaw. He believed that something was needed to help connect all the parts of the document. So near the end of the convention, Martin moved a sentence be added to Article VI:

This Constitution, and the laws of the United States which shall be made in pursuance thereof; and all treaties made, or which shall be made, under the authority of the United States, shall be the supreme law of the land; and the judges in every state shall be bound thereby, any thing in the Constitution or laws of any State to the contrary notwithstanding.

Known as the supremacy clause, these words became the fuel for the engine of the federal judiciary ever since.

# The Early Years

With the new Constitution ratified after eleven months of bitter debate, the First Congress met in 1789, in the nation's temporary capital of New York City. The Senate's first order of business was to fill in the details of the judiciary. A committee was formed under two of the framers who were now senators (both of whom would go on to serve on the Court)—William Paterson of New Jersey and Oliver Ellsworth of Connecticut. In a way the Constitutional Convention's debate was played out all over again, with senators worried about the diminished prerogatives of the states fighting to prevent the establishment of an inferior court system, while senators favoring a strong central government, with a strong federal judiciary, fighting to establish a broad-based system of lower courts with an extensive jurisdiction.

Again the debate ended in a compromise. The lower federal courts were established—in fact, a dual system of lower federal courts was created—but they were still to share much of their jurisdiction with state courts. On September 24, 1789, Congress adopted its first new law, the First Judiciary Act (or the Judiciary Act of 1789, as it is now known).

The new law began by filling in the details of the new Supreme Court. It would have a Chief Justice and five associate justices, and could conduct business only with a quorum of four. A majority of only three, then, would be necessary to render a decision. The Court would hold two sessions annually, beginning on the first Mondays of February and August. In addition, Congress thought it important that the justices keep closely attuned to local law and opinion, so each of the justices was put in charge of a judicial "circuit" and required twice a year to "ride circuit" and oversee the district courts.

The Constitution had given the Supreme Court original jurisdiction over disputes between states and those involving ambassadors, ministers, and counsels. But it had been left up to Congress to set the scope of the new High Court's appellate jurisdiction. The new Judiciary Act was strict in this regard: it allowed the Court to review civil cases only, and then only when the amount "in controversy" was in excess of $2,000; and to review only those state court decisions arising out of provisions of the Constitution.

But whereas the new act provided for only a very limited Supreme Court appellate jurisdiction, it established a much more elaborate lower court system than might have been envisioned. The new law established a dual system of lower courts. At the bottom, the country was divided into thirteen judicial districts, one for each state, with a district court presided over by a district judge set in each. Then in addition, the country was also divided into three larger judicial circuits—East, Middle, and South. These circuits had no judges of their own; rather, one district judge and two Supreme Court justices were assigned to ride circuit in each.

On the matter of jurisdiction, the new lower courts were given a broader base of jurisdiction than the Supreme Court's. The district courts received exclusive jurisdiction in maritime and seizure cases, and a limited number of crimes arising under the laws of the United States. The new circuit courts had an even wider original jurisdiction, including suits between citizens of different states, most criminal cases, and disputes involving the United States as a party. In addition, the circuit courts could hear appeals from district courts in all cases involving more than $50.

The new law also contained other clauses that were to prove significant in the growth of the federal judiciary. Section 12 allowed for the removal from state courts, to the federal district courts, of any dispute in excess of $500. Section 13 allowed the Supreme Court to issue "writs of mandamus" to government officials—effectively, orders compelling them to undertake specified actions. But the most far-reaching section of the new law, and one that would be debated and litigated for more than fifty years, was Section 25, which sought to implement the supremacy clause. It gave the Supreme Court the right to reexamine and reverse or affirm, or remand for retrial, any final judgment or decree of the highest court of any state that involves the validity of a treaty or statute of the United States; any authority exercised by the United States concerning any right or privilege claimed under the Constitution; any question of the construction of the Constitution; or of the construction or interpretation of any statute or treaty of the United States. Eventually, this section would be deemed to have given federal law supremacy over state law and the federal courts supremacy over state courts.

President Washington signed the legislation into law on September 24, 1789. He immediately submitted to the Senate, for its ratification, his first nominees for Chief Justice and the five associate justices. To give the initial Court instant prestige, he chose as Chief Justice John Jay of New York, a diplomat and statesman. For the five associate justices he carefully picked to assuage sectional rivalries, choosing William Cushing of Massachusetts, James Wilson of Pennsylvania, Robert Hanson Harrison of Maryland, John Blair of Virginia, and John Rutledge of South Carolina. All had been very involved in drafting or ratifying the new Constitution, and all were lawyers. Nothing in the Constitution or the Judiciary Act required that justices be lawyers. But with this first set of picks, Washington established a precedent that has never been broken.

The new Court did not get off to an auspicious start. Its first session began on February 1, 1790, in the Royal Exchange Building at Broad and Water streets in what is now the heart of New York City's financial district. Only three of the six new justices managed to reach New York in time for the first session, and without a quorum they were forced to adjourn quickly. The next morning John Blair arrived from Virginia, and the Court could officially conduct business. But that didn't matter much, because there were no cases on the docket and virtually nothing for the new justices to do. A few days later the Court reached its fullest initial strength when James Iredell arrived from North Carolina. Iredell, thirty-eight, had quickly been nominated by President Washington to replace Harrison of Maryland, who had died. The only member of the Court not to arrive in New York was John Rutledge, but then he never did attend a Court session. He was so angered at not being named Chief Justice that he boycotted Court sessions, although he did ride his circuit.

When it became apparent that the five justices would have absolutely nothing to do, the session was adjourned after ten days. Actually this was the Court's longer session its first year. On August 2, the Court convened for its second session as required by law. Again its docket was empty. So the justices spent a few hours over two days taking care of some administrative matters and admitting new lawyers to the bar, and then adjourned for the year.

This is not to say the justices themselves were not busy. As required by the Judiciary Act, they rode circuit twice a year. This was an arduous task involving months of travel. As an example, between crisscrossing the Carolinas and Georgia, and then traveling twice to New York for Court sessions, Justice Iredell spent eleven months away from his home the first year. Things did not get much better. As early as 1792 the justices began to complain bitterly. First they wrote to President Washington asking to be relieved of their circuit duties. When he responded that because of the Judiciary Act he could do nothing, several of the justices, including Chief Justice Jay, took their complaint to Congress—threatening to quit if the circuit riding was not eliminated. But Congress would not relent completely. It said the justices must continue to oversee circuits, but said they need only make the circuit once annually.

In 1791, the nation's temporary capital was moved from New York to Philadelphia, until the permanent capital in the District of Columbia was ready. So the Court's third session, in February 1791, met at the State House. Again, nothing was on its docket. So the justices enjoyed a good dinner together, told stories about what was going on in their circuits, and adjourned. The same thing happened again in August—the justices came to order, found their docket empty, and adjourned. The Court had not yet considered its first case after two years. About the only thing of note to have occurred was Justice Rutledge's resignation in 1791, still having never attended a session, to become a state judge. He was replaced by Thomas Johnson of Maryland. It was also probably a good thing the Court was not too busy, because Chief Justice Jay was able to use his free time to run unsuccessfully for governor of New York. (He later was elected and served two terms.)

The Court held only one session in 1792, deciding some minor matters during a few days in February. There was only a single session that year. A yellow fever outbreak in Philadelphia, in the summer, caused the August session to be canceled. This same thing would happen twice more before the Court moved at the end of the decade to the new capital in what would be called Washington, D.C.

One thing of note did occur in 1792. Congress passed a new law expanding the jurisdiction of the Court, or more correctly the duties of the justices, to include hearing the claims of pensioners while riding circuit. But the justices refused to accept the new duties, saying that Congress had overstepped its authority in requiring the justices to perform what amounted to nonjudicial administrative functions. This holding, coupled with Chief Justice Jay's refusal to allow the Court to issue advisory opinions and to act as a sort of legal counsel to President Washington, established that the Court would play a strictly judicial role.

Business finally began to pick up for the Court in February of 1793. When the Court reassembled it was now housed in the east wing of the new Philadelphia City Hall, under crowded conditions. Part of the building housed the Congress. The Pennsylvania legislature and Philadelphia city offices were in another. In the same wing as the Supreme Court were also the state and municipal courts, and the Supreme Court had to share a courtroom with the local mayor's court.

That February the Court heard its first important case, †*Chisholm* v. *Georgia*. In deciding that a citizen of one state could sue another state in federal court, the Court exercised its Article III authority for the first time. That its authority was accepted was shown by the fact that the states became so alarmed by the decision that they persuaded Congress to pass the Eleventh Amendment forbidding states to be sued in federal court without their permission.

In *Chisholm*, the justices delivered their opinions *in seriatim*—an individual opinion for each justice. This was a practice that would continue for a decade. It meant that the Court was speaking in many voices, and without consensus underpinning many of its rulings, they were of little value as precedents or as guidance for the lower courts.

In 1794, President Washington sent Chief Justice Jay to England as a special envoy to lessen growing tensions between Britain and the United States. He would never return to the Court. While still in England, he was elected governor of New York, and upon learning of this he resigned as Chief Justice. Washington immediately named John Rutledge to the post. Because the Senate was not in session, Rutledge was able to preside over the August 1795 term. But when the Senate came back into session, it was so angered over his previous boycott as an associate justice that it refused to confirm him. Washington then elevated Justice William Cushing, who the Senate quickly confirmed. But despite the fact he would serve another eleven years as an associate justice, Cushing turned down the job claiming that at age sixty-four he was too old. Finally, Washington named Senator Oliver Ellsworth of Connecticut who, with John Patterson, had been an author of the Judiciary Act.

Actually what were probably the two most important decisions of the Court's first decade, and certainly the two most important of the Ellsworth Era, if such a thing ever really existed, were both made without Ellsworth because he was sworn in too late to take part. Both were decided in February 1796. In †*Hylton* v. *United States*, the justices for the first time declared an act of Congress unconstitutional—a new tax on carriages that Congress had ruled was a direct tax that had to be apportioned back to the states. The Court ruled that Congress had no authority to declare it a direct tax and, thus, if collected, the revenue could be retained by the federal

*For more information on cases marked †, see Chapter 3, *The Decisions of the Court*.

government. Then in †*Ware* v. *Hylton,* the Court for the first time struck down a state law—a Virginia statute that allowed its residents to pay off old pre-Revolutionary debts to British creditors with devalued money in contradiction to the terms of the treaty with Britain that had ended the war. The Court ruled that the terms of federal treaties take precedent over any conflicting state laws.

The remainder of the decade passed very quietly for the Court. Two of its next four summer sessions were called off because of yellow fever outbreaks, and the August 1880 session could not find a quorum. As with John Jay before him, Chief Justice Ellsworth was borrowed by President Adams and sent on an ambassadorial mission to France to soothe feelings between France and the United States. Justice Cushing did not attend because of illness. Justice Chase was out campaigning for President Adams. Only three justices showed up: Paterson and the two newest justices: Bushrod Washington and Alfred Moore. This nonsession in August 1800 was the Court's last in Philadelphia. When it would next meet in 1801, the session would be the first to be held in the nation's permanent new capital in Washington, D.C. In its first decade, the Court heard and decided fewer than fifty cases.

Actually, 1800 is important in the history of the Court because the Court became a major issue in President Adams's reelection campaign. Republicans accused the Court of being a Federalist instrument for two presidents, Washington and Adams. As proof they offered the strong nationalist views of every justice—mostly exhibited in rulings while riding circuit—and the fact that both Chief Justices had been used by successive presidents as personal emissaries to foreign nations. In 1799, the Federalist Congress had passed the Sedition Act, making it a crime to criticize high government officials. The law was designed to end criticism of Adams and his cabinet, and a number of justices, riding circuit, were among its most enthusiastic enforcers.

As the Court reassembled for its February 1801 term, it had two big problems. The lesser was where it would hold sessions. Enough of the White House and the Capitol had been completed for the government to move from Philadelphia to its new permanent home. But no one had made any provision for quarters for the judiciary in the planning. Congress suddenly realized the Court was arriving for its first Monday of February session with no place to meet. So a resolution passed on January 23, 1801, allowing the Court to meet in the Capitol. It was one of those better said than done kind of resolutions. With most of the Capitol still unfinished, the only space that could be found was a small twenty-five-by-thirty-foot room in the basement of the north wing. For almost the next 135 years, the Court would call the Capitol home.[1]

A more significant problem was who would lead the Court. The rigors of the trip to France had proved too much for Chief Justice Ellsworth. He remained in France, but in failing health, and was forced to resign from the Court. Adams first turned back to John Jay, nominating him to a second term as Chief Justice. Jay was confirmed by the Senate, even before his letter arrived from New York declining the job. He said he had left the post believing the system of judicial service was badly flawed, and that nothing had changed. He said he simply was too old to continue riding circuit.

The election of 1800 had been a disaster for President Adams. He had actually run third to his two Republican opponents, Thomas Jefferson and Aaron Burr, who had tied in electoral votes. The House still had not decided how to break the tie when the lame duck Adams was faced with the question of whether to replace Ellsworth or allow his successor to do so. The election had left Adams bitter, and he wasn't about to give any political favor to either Jefferson or Burr. So on January 20, 1801, Adams nominated his secretary of state, John Marshall, to be the new Chief Justice. On January 27, 1801, Marshall, then only forty-five, was confirmed to the post he would hold for the next thirty-four years. He was sworn in on February 4, 1801, the second day of the Court's new term.

About two-thirds of the way through Marshall's tenure, Adams would write: "My gift of John Marshall to the people of the United States was the proudest act of my life. There is no act of my life on which I reflect with greater pleasure."

The Supreme Court, as the institution we know today, was about to be born.

## The Marshall Era

John Marshall's tenure got off to a very slow start. On the day he was sworn into office, he was only the second justice present in Washington. It was not for several days that enough justices had arrived to achieve a quorum;

---

1. The Court would end up having more than a dozen homes before its own building was finally finished in 1935. For more detail, see Section V, The Court and Its People.

when the Court had enough members present to conduct business, it found, once again, that it faced an almost empty docket. No decisions were published from this first session presided over by Chief Justice Marshall.

But outside the cramped new Supreme Court chambers, momentous events were happening that would help set the course of Court history. The embittered Federalists, led by Adams, decided to leave a present for the incoming Republican administration. The deadlock between Jefferson and Burr had been broken in Jefferson's favor, and he was due to be sworn into office on March 4. But even as Congress was deciding that the winner of the election was Jefferson, it passed Adams's gift to his successor: a new judiciary law, the Circuit Court Act of 1801.

The new law created six new federal circuits, and appointed sixteen new circuit judges. It also established many jobs for federal prosecutors, civil lawyers, marshals, clerks, and other court employees. Naturally, Adams appointed Federalists to all the new judgeships and other positions created by the law. At the same time, the new law decreased the membership of the Supreme Court from six to five (to be achieved by attrition) in the belief that having to wait for two justices to die or retire would mean that Jefferson would probably never get a chance to make a nomination. Finally, the law eliminated the requirement that the justices ride circuit.

Then on the day before Jefferson was to take his oath, Congress passed yet another job creation law, establishing forty-five new justices of the peace, each to serve a five-year term. Adams sat at his desk until the stroke of midnight signing commissions for party loyalists who were being given the jobs. Technically, to be valid, these commissions had to be physically delivered to their intended recipients; that was the job of the acting secretary of state (now Chief Justice), John Marshall. He and his brother delivered some, but not all. At midnight they quit, with Marshall saying that physical delivery was not important. As far as he was concerned, the undelivered commissions were valid.

The next day when Jefferson took over, he immediately ordered his new secretary of state, James Madison, not to deliver the remaining commissions. They sat undelivered in Madison's office (or were destroyed— that was never clear) when in December one William Marbury, a Georgetown landowner, and three other appointees arrived to demand that Madison deliver their commissions. He refused, so Marbury went immediately to the Supreme Court and filed suit, seeking a writ of mandamus under Section 13 of the Judiciary Act of 1789. Chief Justice Marshall accepted the case and issued a show-cause order requiring Madison to appear before the Court in its next session to show why the Court should not issue a mandamus order compelling him to release the commissions.

Madison simply ignored the show-cause order. In the meantime, the new Republican Congress had passed a new law repealing the Circuit Court Act of 1801. The new law abolished all the new circuit courts that had been established, eliminated all the jobs that had been created, fired all the people hired to fill them, and put the justices back to riding circuit. With the repeal law, Congress also changed the two sessions a year now mandated for the Supreme Court to a single session beginning in February. By doing this, the Republican Congress knowingly pushed back the showdown between Madison and Marshall until February of 1803.

Starting on February 10, 1803, the Court began the direct examination of witnesses in †*Marbury* v. *Madison*. Representing Marbury was Adams's former attorney general, Leonard Levi, who argued that the commissions were proper and valid, and that the Court had the power under Section 13 of the Judiciary Act to order Madison to deliver them. He then produced a string of witnesses to testify to the fact that the commissions had been signed, that some had been delivered, and that others were left in the secretary of state's office for delivery. The Jefferson administration took no part in the hearing. It had no lawyer present, and it called no witnesses.

It took the Court two weeks to render its verdict. Marshall faced a seemingly impossible dilemma. If he found for Marbury, and granted the writ, then almost certainly Madison—acting on Jefferson's orders—would still refuse to deliver the commissions. The Court would be shown to be powerless to enforce its orders, and the result would be an all but fatal diminishing of the Court's stature. But if Marshall found against Marbury and refused to issue the order, then Jackson would have won by default, and the Court would be seen as backing down in the face of a presidential challenge. It was a classic no-win situation, and that is why the utter genius of Marshall's decision shines through. On February 24, 1803, Marshall delivered the Court's long and complicated ruling. There was only one opinion: Marshall's.

Marshall began by noting that the commissions themselves were clearly valid. Then he upheld the right of Marbury and the other plaintiffs to receive them, while rebuking Madison for withholding them "in plain violation of national law." Finally, he said that when a public official fails to exercise his authority, a writ of mandamus is the proper remedy; and that in deciding to issue such a writ the courts do not involve themselves in political questions because they are protecting individual rights, and not invading the authority of the executive.

But having said all this, then Marshall took a sudden turn. He ruled that Congress had exceeded its authority in passing Section 13 of the Judiciary Act. That section, ruled Marshall, gave the Supreme Court original jurisdiction to hear such cases and to issue writs. But, said Marshall, Article III of the Constitution allows the Court to issue writs in such cases only on appeal from lower courts. Thus, he ruled, Section 13 of the Judiciary Act is unconstitutional. In effect, Marshall ruled that Marbury was right, but that he lost because he had brought his action in the wrong court. In so ruling, Marshall managed to escaped from the sure trap.

What was historic about the opinion, and what makes it one of the handful of most important Court rulings ever, is that it was the first time the Court held invalid an act of Congress. That is something that the Court would not do again for almost fifty years. But that it was asserting it had the power to rule on the constitutionality of acts of Congress was shown again only a week later, when in another decision, the Court surprisingly upheld the constitutionality of the Repeal Act of 1802.

During the Constitutional Convention there had been considerable debate about whether to include in Article III the express authority to allow the new federal judiciary to enforce constitutional supremacy over acts of Congress and state laws. The principle of judicial review was well known to lawyers in the time of the convention, both in terms of legal precedents from British law and from the powers invested in many state high courts by their state constitutions. According to Madison's notes, at least twenty-six delegates had spoken at one time or another during the convention's debates about the need for such judicial review. George Mason, in fact, had offered a motion that would have established within the federal judiciary a kind of quasicourt, the Council of Revision, whose sole purpose would have been to review congressional acts to pass on their constitutionality.

But in the final drafting, for reasons that have been lost, the power of judicial review was not expressly stated. Some argued this meant that the Court had no such power. But in *Marbury*, Marshall simply went out and assumed the power; from that point on, although it would not be exercised again until 1857, it was accepted that the Court did have the power to strike down an act of Congress.

Early in his tenure, Marshall instituted a change in the way the Court issued its opinions that would revolutionize the operation of the Court. First, Marshall reached an agreement with William Cranch, then the judge of the district court in the District of Columbia, that Cranch would, on a regular and continuing basis, collect and publish the decisions of the Court. Previously in Philadelphia, a local lawyer, Alexander Dallas, had done so on an ad hoc basis. Now it would be done semi-officially. Because of this, ruled Marshall, all opinions of the Court would have to be written. Moreover, no longer would the Court issue its rulings *in seriatim* opinions, with each justice writing separately. From now on, said Marshall, the Court would attempt to speak in a single voice, with only one justice writing the opinion. He did not exactly say so, but it was assumed that it would be he who would write the opinions.

This was fine as long as all the justices were Federalists who shared Marshall's nationalist views. But it did not sit well with William Johnson, the first Republican named to the Court in 1804. He is called the "Father of Dissents" because it was he who insisted on publishing his own opinions in opposition to Marshall's when they disagreed—which was most of the time.

President Jefferson was outraged by the *Marbury* decision. He interpreted it as a political warning shot across his bow, Marshall saying the Federalist Court stood ready to veto legislation passed by the newly elected Republican Congress. So he and his supporters hatched a plan: impeach the Federalist members of the Court.

Their first target was the most political of the justices, Samuel Chase. After Chase gave a particularly firebrand political speech to a grand jury in Baltimore, the Republican House voted impeachment, charging him with high crimes and misdemeanors for the speech, and for the enthusiastic way he conducted Sedition Act trials aimed at opponents of Adams.

A major constitutional crisis was narrowly averted when the Senate failed to muster the votes for impeachment. Jefferson had pushed very hard for impeachment. But Vice-President Burr, still smarting from his loss to Jefferson in the election, presided over the Senate in a very neutral way. Moreover, some of the Republican fury against the Court dissipated when Marshall had upheld the Repeal Act of 1802. Although a majority did vote to impeach, the total fell a few votes short of the necessary two-thirds. To Jefferson and his supporters in the Senate, it was obvious that if they could not win the impeachment for the most political of justices, there was little hope of winning the impeachment of any. The plan was abandoned. It was the last time the Court would ever have to face this kind of political challenge.

The next major political involvement of the Court came through another impeachment effort of Jefferson's. This time the target was Burr. Their relationship had worsened to the point that, in 1807, Jefferson had Burr arrested and charged with treason, accused of plotting to set up his own country in the west.

Marshall first became involved when two of Burr's associates, arrested with him, filed for writs of habeas corpus, claiming there was no evidence on which to hold them. Jefferson tried to head off the maneuver by getting the Congress to pass a bill suspending habeas corpus. But the House refused to go along, and Marshall and the Court found for the two, and ordered their release. Then Jefferson became even more incensed when Marshall, sitting as circuit judge in Richmond, held a preliminary hearing for Burr and ruled that there was only enough evidence to try him on a single misdemeanor—violating the neutrality law by planning an expedition against Mexico.

Jefferson managed to get a grand jury to issue more serious indictments against Burr, and this led him to yet another showdown with Marshall when the Chief Justice issued—on Burr's behalf—a subpoena ordering the president to appear at the trial, and to bring with him certain documents. Jefferson took the position that as president he did not have to honor the subpoena, but he sent lawyers to appear before Marshall to argue the point. In the end, Marshall ruled that Jefferson did not have to personally appear, and that he had only to give Burr's defense abridged copies of the documents. It did set a precedent, however, that would a century and a half later become a basis for the demand that Richard Nixon turn over the Watergate tapes to the special prosecutor.

Jefferson pulled out all the stops to win Burr's conviction, including bribing many of the witnesses. Marshall, again in his capacity as circuit judge, sat as the presiding trial judge. The government argued that, under English common law, to contemplate treason is the same as to actually commit it. But Burr's attorneys argued that Article III sets out a clear definition of treason; whatever Burr might be guilty of, it fell far short of waging war against the United States. Marshall thought the whole episode held the potential for setting a precedent that unhappy politicians could use the courts to get rid of political opponents. So he charged the jury with such a narrow definition of treason that it would have been all but impossible for them to have convicted Burr. It took the jury less than a half-hour to acquit him.

Jefferson was enraged. He tried to get the Senate to pass a law ending life tenure for judges, and allowing a president to remove a judge with a two-thirds concurrence by both House and Senate. The bill went nowhere. Then he tried to get a law passed greatly expanding the definition of treason. It failed also.

The Court returned to its business. In 1807, with the population increasing in what were then the western territories, a new circuit was added that included all of Ohio, Kentucky, and Tennessee, and an additional seat was added to the Supreme Court. President Jefferson named the area's top jurist, Kentucky state chief justice Thomas Todd, to fill the new seat.

The Marshall Court's next important milestone came in 1810, when it agreed to review a case from Georgia. A group of land speculators had paid off every member but one of the state legislature to pass a land grant act that resulted in the speculators being sold most of what is today Alabama and Mississippi for a cost averaging about two cents an acre. Even in those days that was literally pennies. The speculators were quickly able to resell the land at huge profit, with much of it sold in smaller parcels to farmers and other speculators. A new legislature was elected the next year, and it passed a new law rescinding the land-grant act and canceling all the grants. The new law effectively repossessed all the land that had been resold. A group of land owners who had never been involved in the bribery, and who had bought the land in arms' length transactions, filed suit seeking to force the state to grant them title.

The case, †*Fletcher* v. *Peck*, was argued for two days before the Court. Marshall ruled for a unanimous Court, and for the first time struck down a state law as violating the Constitution—the new Georgia law overturning the land-grant act. He ruled that under the contract clause (Article I, Section 10) of the Constitution, a state may not pass a law invalidating what otherwise is a valid contract. He ruled that a state legislature could invalidate laws passed by its predecessors, but it could not extinguish obligations that might have been entered into as a result of the previous law. In so ruling, Marshall not only exercised the power to overturn a state law for the first time but expanded the scope of the contract clause in a way that would be repeated many times in the years to come.

After 1810, the Court seemed poised to greatly expand its role. But that expansion would have to wait for intervening events. In September, William Cushing, the last of the original justices, died. His death left the Court evenly divided between Republicans (Livingston, Johnson, and Todd) and Federalists (Marshall, Bushrod Washington, and Chase). Madison was now president, and he was under great pressure from his predecessor, Jefferson, to name a Republican to the Court and thus create a

Republican majority. Little did he dream what lay ahead. His first choice was Jefferson's attorney general, Levi Lincoln. The Senate quickly confirmed the choice, but Lincoln refused the job. His second choice was Alexander Wolcott of Connecticut, the state's Republican leader. Wolcott complained that he was unqualified, but would accept. But the Senate agreed that he was totally unqualified, and rejected the nomination. Next Madison turned to John Quincy Adams, but he too said no.

Much of the 1811 term passed without a nomination to fill the vacant seat. The vacancy, coupled with various reasons, resulted in the Court's inability to muster a quorum through much of the term. No cases were decided. Then Justice Chase died, and Madison now had two vacancies to fill. He finally did so, nominating Gabriel Duvall of Maryland and Joseph Story of Massachusetts. Both were quickly confirmed.

But now the War of 1812 intervened. For the next four years, when the Court was in session, it was mainly presented with cases and issues arising out of the war. Over and over it refused to hear many of the issues referred to it, ruling that they were political questions and properly the business of Congress.

Finally, in 1816, the Court was able to return to a normal docket. Over the next seventeen years, under Marshall's firm guidance the Court vastly expanded its influence into every facet of American life, and vastly expanded the abstract powers contained in various clauses of the Constitution.

This expansion began with the 1816 case, †*Martin* v. *Hunter's Lessee.* The Court was asked to rule on a disputed title to some 300,000 acres of Virginia land. One set of owners claimed title based on an old Crown grant, while the competing claim was based on a state grant. The Virginia courts had ruled in favor of the state grant, so the heirs to the British grant brought a writ of error to the Supreme Court under Section 25 of the Judiciary Act of 1789. Marshall himself apparently owned a piece of the disputed land, so he disqualified himself. Another justice did also. In the end only four justices voted; by a vote of 3–1—with Justice Story writing the opinion—the majority upheld the original Crown grant because provisions of several treaties with Britain guaranteed British subjects the right to continue to own land in America.

But when the case was sent back to the Virginia courts with instructions to settle the title, the presiding judge of Virginia's highest court, Spencer Roane, a states' rights zealot, refused to accept the verdict. Instead, he declared Section 25 unconstitutional in Virginia. The case went back to the Supreme Court, and three weeks later the unanimous Court issued a stinging decision upholding Section 25. Justice Story again wrote the opinion, a wide-ranging defense of the principle that the Court is the final arbiter of the Constitution and of federal law, whether the case originates in a federal or a state court. Story said flatly that a state court may not declare any part of federal law to be in violation of a state constitution, and thus rule it null and void in that state.

Later the same year, the Court all but took itself and the lower federal courts out of the criminal law business. In *United States* v. *Hudson,* Marshall ruled that federal courts have jurisdiction over criminal matters only in those limited areas that Congress has specifically designated by statute to be federal crimes.

The 1819 term became one of the most important in the history of the Court. In the final days of the previous term, the Court had heard oral arguments in what seemed like a minor squabble between a small college and the state of New Hampshire. But when Marshall announced the Court's decision on the opening day of the 1819 term, the case suddenly became very important to the development of American law.

Dartmouth College in those days was a small New Hampshire private college. Its trustees had become unhappy with its president, and they fired him. But he refused to go quietly. He had friends in the state legislature, and they concocted a plan whereby the college's private charter would be revoked, the college would be turned into a public institution, and its new board would be packed with friends of the ousted president, who would reappoint him.

Daniel Webster, a graduate, argued tearfully that the college's charter was inviolate and could not be rescinded. Chief Justice Marshall writing for a unanimous Court agreed, and in doing so used the opinion to establish the supremacy of the contract clause. Marshall expanded the definition of a contract to include state-granted charters. Although this case involved a nonprofit educational institution, the Supreme Court continued to apply the principles established here to other organizations. Eventually, corporate, business, industrial, and financial entities also were protected from potential state government regulation abuses. This decision was primarily responsible for the growth of the corporate form of ownership in American business.

Shortly after announcing its opinion in the *Dartmouth* case, the Court heard one of the most extraordinary oral arguments in its history. The case, †*McCulloch* v. *Maryland,* centered on a challenge to Congress's power to charter a new national bank. Then treasury secretary Alexander Hamilton had chartered the United States' first national bank in 1798, but the Republican Congress had let its charter expire in 1811. In 1816, President Madison realized that had been a mistake, and convinced Congress to charter a second bank. It was not a very beloved institution. It saw as its principal function the reining in of state banks who were issuing huge amounts of almost worthless currency. That did not make it very popular, nor did its reputation for quick foreclosures on borrowers who ran even slightly behind on their repayments.

James W. McCulloch was the manager of the bank's branch office in Baltimore, one of eighteen around the country. Apparently he was as corrupt as most of the bank's employees, and would eventually be convicted of lending himself and three associates almost a million and a half dollars of the bank's deposits. But he came to the Court's attention because in 1818 the state of Maryland, in an attempt to drive the bank out of Baltimore, imposed on it an annual tax of $15,000, as if it were a state-chartered institution. Five other antibank states also were trying to tax the national bank out of existence. In Maryland, McCulloch refused to pay. A flurry of lawsuits ensued, with the bank calling the tax unconstitutional and the state calling the bank illegal.

The issue went far beyond the bank to exactly what Congress's powers are. There is nothing in the Constitution that specifically grants Congress the power to establish and charter a bank. So the basic question came down to whether Congress is limited to exercising only those powers that have been expressly granted to it by the Constitution's Framers.

The bank was represented by Daniel Webster and a brilliant young Baltimore lawyer, William Pinckney. Oral argument continued for nine days. When Marshall eventually gave the Court's decision, it was obvious that he had long ago made up his mind. He used the case to set forth his basic philosophy of nationalism, and the supremacy of the federal government.

Marshall based his decision on two underlying principles: (1) that the federal government's power does not come from the states, but rather comes directly from the people; and (2) a constitution, of necessity, can only be an outline and must be adaptable to changing circumstances and cannot itself be expected to cover all contingencies.

The people, said Marshall, had made the Constitution supreme over the states "within its sphere of action." The Constitution, he said, had clearly given the government the power to tax, to regulate commerce, to form a central economy. Inherent in these powers were the powers to use the means necessary "for their execution." He found this power within the "necessary and proper" clause (Article I, Section 8), which gives Congress the prerogative to make "all laws which shall be necessary and proper for carrying into execution" its responsibilities. In the case of chartering a bank, this is national fiscal management.

Turning to the subject of the Maryland tax, Marshall quickly struck it down, saying that the power to tax is the "power to destroy." In so doing he restated the principle that state constitutions, and state laws, do not control federal law or the Constitution. But he tempered this slightly by noting that, while federal law is supreme, there must be a balance between federal supremacy and sovereignty, and between state autonomy and federal intrusion.

In 1821, in †*Cohens* v. *Virginia*, Marshall again came in conflict with Virginia's Judge Roane. The case involved a seemingly minor criminal violation, but in Roane's actions, Marshall immediately saw potentially devastating ramifications for the Court.

The Cohen brothers were accused of selling District of Columbia lottery tickets in Virginia, in violation of state law. They claimed that the federal government, which had sanctioned the lottery, had given them an effective license to sell the tickets anywhere. They were found guilty, and they appealed to Roane's state high court. But he refused to entertain their appeal. When he would not hear it, the brothers appealed under a writ of error to the Supreme Court. The issue came down to whether the Court could hear a case under Section 25 before there had been a final ruling by the highest court of the state involved.

The issue was critical. If the Constitution was adhered to strictly, then a state could duck Supreme Court review of its actions simply by avoiding a final ruling from its highest court. That would all but render moot the supremacy clause. Marshall was quick to rule. Using Story's basic premise in *Martin* v. *Hunter's Lessee*—that it is the case and not the court that determines the Supreme Court's jurisdiction—he ruled that the Court has the power to issue writs of error to any state court, at any level. In his opinion, Marshall again launched an eloquent defense of federal supremacy, and of his vision of a nation that was one and unified. "The American people are one," he wrote.

Marshall had greatly expanded Congress's power through the contract clause. Now, in 1824, he would do the same with the commerce clause, and in so doing, he would give Congress the principal means of regulation it would exercise for a century. The case was †*Gibbons* v. *Ogden*, and it represented the Court's first attempt to define exactly what the extent of Congress's power is to regulate interstate commerce.

Gibbons and Ogden were partners who operated ferry boats that ran between New York and New Jersey. They split and became bitter competitors. They got into a dispute about who was licensed to carry passengers between New York and New Jersey, and between certain ports in New Jersey. Ogden had bought his license from the monopoly that had been created by the New York legislature to carry passengers to and from the shores of New York. Thus he claimed the sole right to use the waterway between New York and New Jersey, including between ports solely in New Jersey. Gibbons held a federal license granted under the Coastal Licensing Act of 1793, and he argued that it allowed him to pick up passengers anywhere, even if he did not have a state license.

The issue for the Court was whether the commerce clause gives Congress the right to regulate navigation, and, if so, what powers are left to the state to regulate both navigation and commerce generally. Daniel Webster argued for Gibbons that the commerce clause should be read broadly, and that New York's ferry monopoly was illegal and served to limit "commercial intercourse." Thomas Emmett, Odgen's lawyer, argued that the commerce clause must be read narrowly, and that states must be given great leeway to control commerce arriving at and within their borders.

Marshall ruled for Gibbons's federal license. Congress's powers under the commerce clause (Article 1, Section 8), he said, are very broad. The constitutional phrase "among the several states" means that federal control extends to all commerce that concerns more than one state, including commerce that passes through one state on its way to another. Moreover, commerce is not simply buying and selling. It includes "all commercial intercourse" and this includes navigation. In so ruling, Marshall wisely ducked one of Webster's central arguments—that the commerce clause precludes any regulation by the state of interstate or foreign commerce. Marshall said only that states control "their own purely internal affairs, whether trading or police." This, in turn, was the Court's first reference to a police power of a state, and was the basis for an 1829 ruling (*Wilson* v. *Blackbird Creek*), in which Marshall ruled that a state could exercise this police power over aspects of interstate trade that Congress had not yet regulated.

In his thirty-four years on the Court, Marshall found himself in the minority only once. He believed in the absolute right to contract and that the contract clause absolutely barred any state's interference with the right to contract, or with an existing contract. In 1819 (*Sturges* v. *Crowninshield*), he had used the contract clause as the basis for invalidating a new New York State bankruptcy law because it freed debtors of their obligations under contracts entered into before the law was passed. Eight years later, in 1827, the Court was presented (*Odgen* v. *Saunders*) with the logical next question: what about a bankruptcy law that potentially extinguishes debts from contracts entered into after the law is passed? Again Marshall thundered that no state act can invalidate the terms of a contract freely entered into. But for the first time he could not get a majority of the Court to support his view. By a 4–3 vote, the majority found bankruptcy laws constitutional and not in conflict with the contract clause because both parties should be aware of their existence and possible effect before their contract is entered into.

Marshall's final years on the Court were not happy ones. Andrew Jackson was elected president in 1828, and he and Marshall would prove to be thorns in each other's sides for almost Jackson's entire two terms.

A week after he was elected, Jackson nominated John McLean—who had been Adams's postmaster general—for an opening on the Court. Certainly there has never been a more political justice than McLean. He ended up serving more than three decades on the Court, and every four years for that entire time, when there was a presidential election, he was a potential candidate. In between, he was constantly maneuvering for whatever political advantage he might gain, and was not above using his decisions for his own political ends.

If McLean was a questionable nominee, then Jackson's choice for the Court's next opening in 1829 was a disaster. Henry Baldwin was a prominent lawyer and the political leader of Allegheny County (Pittsburgh), Pennsylvania. He had worked in Jackson's campaign, so when the Court opening occurred, Jackson nominated him. He ended up serving fourteen years. Perhaps the most charitable thing that can be said about Baldwin was that he was extraordinarily eccentric. Actually, it is more likely that he suffered from some sort of mental illness, and for his entire career he was given to bouts of extreme temper, fights with the other justices, and strange—even bizarre—decisions and written opinions.

Both of these appointments reportedly greatly distressed Marshall, who saw in them an attempt, by states' rights advocate Jackson, to diminish the stature of the Court. But his real differences with the new president were philosophical and political.

Jackson's election had marked a rebirth of the frontier spirit in America. One way it manifested itself was in the treatment of Native American people. Jackson did not much care for Native Americans, but he did at least believe they should be paid fairly for their lands and then resettled someplace far in the west where the white man had not yet settled. In those areas where Native Americans resisted this resettlement plan, he did not hesitate to send in the cavalry. But in Georgia, the Cherokees tried a more novel approach to resisting resettlement. They assimilated into the white culture, built settlements, began to farm, and established the "Cherokee Nation" in northern Georgia. The state didn't care very much for this, and passed several laws dissolving this so-called nation. One law required any white man attempting to live in this area to obtain a license from the state. To show how assimilated they had become, the Cherokees tried to file a writ of error directly with the Supreme Court to invalidate these new laws. As they were doing this, they also filed an appeal to stay the execution of a Cherokee convicted of murder, on the grounds that he should have been tried under Cherokee law.

Georgia simply refused to appear to defend its anti-Cherokee laws. As far as the murder appeal was concerned, the state immediately executed the man before the Court could consider his case. Marshall was incensed, but he went ahead and issued an opinion in the writ action, ruling the Court lacked the jurisdiction to consider the matter. "This is not a tribunal which can redress the past or prevent the future," he wrote.

But Marshall got another chance to rule on Georgia's anti-Cherokee laws. Two white missionaries were arrested for attempting to live in Georgia's Cherokee territory without first obtaining a state license. They were convicted and sentenced to four years at hard labor. They appealed to the Supreme Court, and again the state of Georgia refused to appear to defend itself. This time (*Worchester* v. *Georgia*), Marshall struck down the Georgia Cherokee laws, ruling that the federal government had sole jurisdiction over Native American affairs, and that a state could not make laws that affect Native Americans. Because its licensing law was null, said Marshall, Georgia "should" release the missionaries.

Marshall said *should*, as opposed to *must*, because he suspected—quite correctly—that Georgia was not going to comply, and he did not wish to provoke a major constitutional confrontation. This was especially true since he knew that the Court was not going to be supported by President Jackson. It wasn't. Jackson did nothing to support the verdict, or the Court, and all but publicly sided with Georgia. The missionaries remained in jail, and Marshall worried publicly that respect for the Court and its decisions, which he had carefully built up over thirty years, was being destroyed; he felt that Jackson's attitude toward states' rights might even lead to a dissolving of the union.

As this was going on, Jackson was staging a major fight over the recharter of the national bank. Jackson, and those who believed in states' rights, hated the bank as a symbol of federal dominance. So when Congress passed a rechartering bill in 1832, Jackson vetoed it. His veto message was very upsetting for Marshall. In it, he declared the bank to be unconstitutional, and in so doing simply dismissed the Court's opinion in *McCulloch*. And he went even further, setting up the president, and not the Supreme Court, as the ultimate arbiter of what is and what is not constitutional. Marshall believed this signaled the end of the Court.

But then Jackson surprised Marshall, and almost everyone else, in a new showdown with South Carolina. Emboldened by Georgia's defiance of the Court's decision, South Carolina passed a new law—the Nullification Ordinance—which held "unconstitutional" within South Carolina a new federal tariff law. It also proclaimed the right of any state to declare unconstitutional any federal statute, and for good measure made it a crime for any citizen of the state to appeal the new law to the U.S. Supreme Court. Had Jackson stood by and allowed South Carolina to put this law into effect, clearly it would have spelled the end of the Supreme Court and probably of the union. But his reaction was instant. He branded the South Carolina legislature a traitor, and threatened to send in federal troops to enforce the tariff. South Carolina quickly backed down.

Overnight, the incident turned Jackson into a nationalist. He ordered the governor of Georgia to release the two missionaries who were still being held, and the governor complied. Then, in a total about-face, he asked Congress in 1833 for a new judiciary act, one that would both expand and strengthen the federal judiciary. Congress complied.

The crisis for the Court had passed, but the Marshall era clearly was in descent. Marshall was almost eighty and had visibly slowed. Justices Johnson and Duval were ill and missed most of the sessions. In the Court's last three terms, only a single major decision was rendered. In *Barron* v. *Baltimore* (1833), Marshall ruled that the Bill of Rights is applicable only to federal laws and actions, and not to state laws or actions. This decision had a profound effect on the growth of the American legal system because it ended for almost a century any attempt to shield individual rights from state action, and eventually made it necessary to pass the Fourteenth Amendment.

In August 1834, Justice Jackson, the "Great Dissenter," died. President Jackson named James Wayne of Georgia to succeed him. Then in January of 1835, Duval, now in rapidly failing health, resigned. Jackson named Roger B. Taney, his former attorney general and treasury secretary, to the seat. But Taney had problems with the Whigs in the Senate. He had been Jackson's point man in the war on the national bank, and that had made him very unpopular in nationalist circles. On the last day of the session, the Senate voted to table the nomination. So they adjourned without a confirmation vote, and the Duval seat remained empty.

On July 6, 1835, Chief Justice Marshall died. The Liberty Bell in Philadelphia was tolled to mark his passing. It cracked, and was never rung again. Perhaps the most important era in the development of the Supreme Court had ended. Under Marshall, the Court had established its right to review laws passed by Congress and by the states. It had struck down one federal statute and more than a dozen state laws. It had established the ability of the federal government to control state actions through the contract and commerce clauses. It had established federal supremacy, and the supremacy of the Court, over state judiciaries. For these three decades, John Marshall had been more than just the Chief Justice. In a very real sense, he had been the Court. Over his tenure he personally had written more than half the Court's decisions. Of the major decisions of his era, he had written every one except *Martin* v. *Hunter's Lessee*, when he had disqualified himself. Through dint of intellect and personality, he had shaped and molded the Court, and deserves to be called its father. In doing so, he reserved for himself a place as a leading figure in the history of the United States.

# The Taney Court

Probably no Chief Justice has been as vilified as Roger B. Taney (he pronounced it "Tawney"). He came very close to not being confirmed. At the time his tenure was widely regarded as a giant step backward from that of his predecessor, and today his name often heads lists of worst justices. Taney is certainly the most misunderstood man ever to serve prominently on the Supreme Court. He was, in fact, a brilliant lawyer and a more than able Chief Justice, a man of generally moderate legal philosophy who guided the Court in a direction that actually built on the foundation left him by Marshall. But in the end, it is probably fair to say that Taney is one of the most tragic figures in American history, a man whose reputation was forever and irrevocably sullied by his decision in the *Dred Scott* case.

Taney was born and grew up in western Maryland. He became a leading lawyer in the county seat of Frederick, and then went into Federalist politics and was elected to the state senate in Annapolis. There he was one of that body's experts on banking law, and thus was thrust into the controversy over the second national bank, its branch in Baltimore, its manager James McCulloch, and the events that became *McCulloch* v. *Maryland*.

Interestingly, Taney was against the tax that the state tried to impose on the bank. On the issue of the bank itself and its activities, he began as a neutral. He realized that there had to be some check on the practices of many state banks, and that the national economy needed some overall guidance. But this neutrality ended abruptly when Taney learned of McCulloch's gross dishonesty and embezzlement. Overnight Taney turned completely against the bank.

When he finished his State Senate term, Taney moved to Baltimore and resumed his law practice. His opposition to the bank had grown so great that he began to support Andrew Jackson solely because Jackson was opposed to the bank. He became Jackson's Maryland campaign manager in 1824, and was rewarded in local politics by being named state attorney general in 1826. In 1831, he was brought to Washington by Jackson as U.S. attorney general, and in 1833 Jackson named him treasury secretary for the express purpose of destroying the bank.

Its hard to exaggerate how strongly feelings ran over the issue of the bank. It was the first defining test of states' rights versus nationalism—the central issue of its day that would eventually be replaced by the issue of slavery. Things became so heated that Vice-President Martin Van Buren took to wearing his pistols to preside over the Senate. Into this highly charged atmosphere came Taney to do the job that Jackson had delegated to him—destroy the bank. He virtually succeeded by withdrawing all federal government funds from it and redepositing them into state banks. Then he authored Jackson's veto message on the bank's rechartering.

Is it any wonder, then, that his nomination first as an associate justice, and then as Chief Justice after Marshall died, was the source of great controversy? Whig newspapers labeled him a "political hack" and worse. The Whigs were able to block a vote on his nomination as associate justice. Then at the start of the next Senate term, when the debate began on his appointment as Chief Justice, the Senate was far from ready to confirm him. Off and on, the debate lasted more than three months, but finally, the Senate did vote narrowly to confirm.

Philosophically, Taney did not agree with Marshall's view of nationalism. Marshall based his "national supremacy" philosophy on the belief that the Constitution represents a contract directly between the people and the national government, an "ordinance of the people." Taney believed in a philosophy of "dual federalism," which centered on the Constitution as a "compact among sovereign states." Taney was especially concerned that the states have the power to deal with particular problems occurring within their borders and had the power to act in the very many areas where Congress had not spoken, even if it apparently had the authority.

The Court that Taney began to preside over was dominated by justices who shared this view of the Constitution. Of the seven justices on the Court, five were Jackson appointees. And shortly Congress added two new judicial circuits and two new justices, and Jackson would appoint them also. So Taney presided over a Court made up almost totally of men who shared his basic views.

Given this overwhelming shift away from the nationalist views of a majority of the justices of the Marshall era, the stage seemed set for wholesale revision of Marshall's positions. As Taney began his tenure there was a general belief, especially among those who opposed his nomination, that he would place the Court in a period of decline and would swing power back to the states and to the state courts. The Court's docket was certainly ripe for this to occur, because for the twenty years prior to the start of the Civil War, a majority of the cases the Court heard were situations in which federal interests were pitted against state interests. But Taney surprised everyone, including many of his fellow justices, by charting a very moderate course, and over the next two decades—until the clouds of war settled over the Court, as they did over the country—the justices expanded, not contracted, the Court's influence over the legal system.

Conservatives were in great fear that this new Jacksonian Court under Taney would all but wipe out those private property rights that had been so jealously guarded by the Marshall Court for more than three decades. But the new Chief Justice's first major decision in *Charles River Bridge* v. *Warren Bridge* (1837) showed that while his legal philosophy was very different from Marshall's, and that he viewed the contract clause in a very different light, the conservatives and Federalists had no worry about the future of personal property rights.

The issue was the kind that Marshall would have loved: does the right of the public ever take precedence over private property rights? The Massachusetts legislature had granted a charter to the Charles River Bridge Company in 1785 to construct a bridge over the Charles River between Boston and Cambridge, and to collect tolls for passage across the new bridge. Company stock was gradually bought up by Harvard University, and by the 1820s the people of Boston were growing tired of paying daily commuting tolls to what had become the richest private institution in the city, if not America.

The people demanded the city build a new bridge across the Charles and make passage free. In 1828, the state legislature chartered a new company to build a free bridge to be named after a physician-hero of the Revolution, Dr. Joseph Warren, who died at Bunker Hill. Predictably, Harvard was outraged at the chartering of the new bridge company. So it and the Charles River Bridge Company sued, claiming that issuance of the new charter violated their rights under their charter, and this in turn violated the contract clause of the Constitution. After Massachusetts's highest court deadlocked over the case and was unable to render a verdict, the issue was appealed to the U.S. Supreme Court.

The case was first argued before the Marshall Court in 1831. It seemed clear that Marshall was very sympathetic to the arguments advanced by the Charles Bridge Company's lawyer, Daniel Webster. But because of illnesses, deaths of justices, and absences of quorums, the case was never ruled on. It was argued and reargued three times, and by the time the Taney Court heard it argued again for another five days, the new Warren Bridge had been built, and it had put the Charles River toll bridge out of business. Some said this made the case moot, but Taney and the rest of the justices realized that the issues were so basic, and so important to the development of the country, that the case had to be resolved.

The new Warren Bridge Company was called a public service corporation in those days. Today, we would call it a public utility, and thus central to the case being argued was a determination of the legality of public utilities. America was seeking to expand west by developing a great rail network, and the new railroad companies were seeking investors, and these investors were seeking monopolistic charters that would protect their investments. Both interests—public service corporations, and private corporations granted monopolistic charters—would be vital to the future growth of America. The Court was being asked to choose between them and the wrong decision could have done great damage. But in the end, Taney, writing for a 4–3 majority, found a tightrope that he could use to walk right down the middle, as Marshall had often done before him.

Taney and the Court ruled against the Charles Bridge Company, but did so in such a way that the sanctity of contracts and private property were upheld while the way was opened for public-service corporations to play a leading role in future development. The state of Massachusetts must, Taney said, adhere to the exact terms of the original grant. But the fact that the Charles Bridge Company thought it had been granted a monopoly did not make it so. The original charter, noted Taney, did not explicitly rule out the chartering of competing bridges, nor of establishing them as free bridges. He ruled that the state had a vital interest in promoting transportation within its borders, so it could foster transportation through building new bridges. The states must have power "over their internal improvement." Property rights, wrote Taney, must be "sacredly guarded." But at the same time, "we must not forget that the community also have rights, and that the happiness and the well being of every citizen depends on their faithful presentation."

What Taney was saying with this decision is that he intended to construe contracts more narrowly and states' power more elastically than had Marshall, but the change was going to be a gradual change of inference, rather than a judicial revolution.

While his *Charles River Bridge* decision is the more famous, another decision in his first term probably is more important to the development of American law. In *New York* v. *Miln*, the Court was asked to rule whether a New York law that required all ships entering its harbor to immediately report the names, dates of birth, place of previous residence, and occupation of everyone on board—passengers and crew—before the ship could unload, was an unconstitutional invasion by the state of the federal government's power to regulate interstate commerce. The case presented a dilemma for the Taney Court. It wanted to back away from Marshall's all-encompassing definition of federalism, but clearly this particular state law did impinge upon commerce. So Taney had to find a way to uphold the law, and thereby give states more power, while not specifically limiting the power of the federal government. He did so by ruling that states have "police power" under the Tenth Amendment—a power that Marshall himself had first found in *Gibbons* v. *Ogden*. Part of that police power, ruled Taney, is the power to regulate and control immigration.

Taken together—*Charles River Bridge, Miln,* and a third decision from Taney's first term, *Briscoe* v. *Bank of Kentucky*—these decisions stood for the proposition that states should be granted more powers. It is likely that Marshall would have voted the opposite way in all three of these decisions. But Taney wrote all of them in such a way that the changes were evolutionary, not revolutionary. While he attempted to grant the states broader powers, he tried to do so in a way that did not directly diminish federal power.

But in *Miln,* the Taney Court did not answer a central question: can states exercise some level of direct control over commerce? In fact, the Taney Court spent a decade and a half, in case after case, trying to avoid having to answer that question. So *Miln* became the first of many cases in which the Taney Court would hold valid—as an exercise of police power— state laws that were attempting to deal with social and economic problems, but were in areas of seeming federal jurisdiction. In 1847 in the licensing cases, the Court was asked whether state laws regulating the manufacture and sale of liquor, including liquor shipped in from out of state, constitute an unconstitutional restraint of interstate commerce. The Court said no, that this falls within a state's police powers. But among the nine justices, they wrote six opinions. There was nothing approaching real consensus on the Court on this vital subject.

Finally in 1852 the Court faced squarely the question of whether states could have some role in regulating commerce. In *Cooley* v. *Pennsylvania,* the question was whether a state law requiring pilots aboard ships traversing certain waters violated Congress's power to regulate navigation. Congress had never considered the matter, and the Court decided it was not a matter of police power. So it was up to the Court's newest member, a brilliant young Boston lawyer named Benjamin Curtis, to fashion a compromise between Marshall's federal view and Taney's state view. The compromise allowed Pennsylvania to keep its pilot law through a theory that Curtis called "selective exclusiveness." This he defined as the situation where Congress has a right, but chooses not to exercise it and thus it is left to the states. Curtis found that two kinds of commerce exist: a national kind that needs national rules and regulations to provide order, and a local kind that Congress has the right to regulate, but if it doesn't, then the state can exercise the authority.

But while this battle saw the states emerging with expanded power to regulate at least some aspects of commerce, the Taney Court refused other expansions of states' rights. In *Holmes* v. *Jennison* (1840) it refused to allow states to engage in foreign affairs. In *Swift* v. *Tyson* (1842) it ruled that federal courts are not bound by state-court interpretation of state laws. And in still another case, *Dobbins* v. *Erie County*, it ruled that states could not tax the salaries of federal judges.

This was also a time of significant internal difficulties in the Court. When President William Henry Harrison died after only a month in office in 1841, his vice-president, Whig leader John Tyler, succeeded him. Tyler and Congress just didn't get along. In 1843, Justice Smith Thompson died. Tyler nominated Treasury Secretary John Spencer; the Senate rejected the choice. Next he nominated New York judge Reuben Walworth; the Senate refused to vote before adjourning. Then Justice Henry Baldwin died, leaving the Court with a second vacancy. Tyler nominated Philadelphia lawyer James King; again the Senate refused to vote, so Tyler withdrew both Walworth's and King's nominations. Now Tyler was getting desperate, so he nominated New York's respected jurist Samuel Nelson to fill the Thompson seat. He was confirmed. But Tyler was all but told by the Senate that it would not consider any more of his nominees. So Baldwin's seat remained vacant for almost two years. Then Justice Story died, and this meant that when President James Polk took office in 1845, he had two seats to fill. He chose George Woodward of Pennsylvania to fill the still-vacant Baldwin seat and Senator Levi Woodbury of New Hampshire to fill Story's. Woodbury was quickly confirmed, but the Baldwin seat remained vacant when the Senate rejected Woodward. Finally, after twenty-eight months, the Baldwin seat was filled when the Senate confirmed Pennsylvania judge Robert Grier.

This was also an era that saw the Court's work load mushroom. In 1844, Congress recognized this and lengthened the Court's term by two months, moving the starting date back to the first Monday of December. The Court itself, for the first time, instituted a time limit on oral argument. Each side was to limit its argument to two hours, unless given special leave. Finally, for the first time the Court required all motions and arguments to be made in writing.

But most of all, this was the era when slavery was becoming the predominate social and political issue. The Court had tried to steer as neutral a course as it could on the issue. In 1842 it was presented with one of its first slave cases: *Prigg* v. *Pennsylvania*. The question was whether

Pennsylvania could pass a law requiring a court hearing for a person accused of being a fugitive slave before the person was removed from the state. The Court ruled it could not because fugitive slaves were exclusively the concern of the federal government, and states could not adopt their own fugitive slave laws or procedures.

More and more the slavery issue evolved into two central questions: did Congress have the power to forbid or to regulate slavery in the newly developing territories? Were blacks, either free or slave, citizens of the United States and entitled to the protection of the Constitution and the Bill of Rights?

The Court had a chance to face these issues head-on in an 1850 case, *Strader* v. *Graham*, when it was presented with the question of whether runaway slaves became free by reaching free states, and whether slaves became free by the fact that they worked for some period in a free state or territory. The Court ducked these central issues by ruling that the laws of the state where the slave currently resides should rule, and that it was not a matter for the federal courts.

The Court did not know it at the time, but ducking the ruling in *Strauder* was going to play a pivotal role in the case that would come to define the Taney Court—and do so much to tarnish the reputation of its Chief Justice.

By now the *Dred Scott* case was working its way through the Missouri Courts.[2] When the Missouri Supreme Court ruled on whether Scott's living in the Wisconsin Territory had made him a free man, it answered by citing *Strauder* and saying that since Scott was back in Missouri, Missouri law prevailed, and that made him still a slave. The case reached the Supreme Court, and in it the justices found the two key questions of slavery clearly presented: could Congress establish slavery territories and were blacks citizens? The case was argued in February of 1856. By August, the justices were nowhere near resolving the issues. It was decided to order it reargued in December, in order to put off a decision until after the November election. It was reargued and, after another two months of groping, by February of 1857 the justices finally thought they had found a way out. Seven of the justices were now in agreement that the Court would issue a very limited opinion, again restating what it had stated in *Strauder*—that state law should prevail—and thus they would dismiss the suit ruling that

2. For a complete examination of the *Dred Scott* case, see pages 169–70.

Scott had no standing in federal court to have brought the appeal. In this way they could continue to duck the central issues at least a while longer.

But that would not do for either Justice John McLean or Benjamin Curtis. Both were morally opposed to slavery, and both decided to write dissents in which they would argue that not only had residence in the Wisconsin Territory made Scott a free man, but he and all other Negros were citizens of the United States and, as such, were free to sue in federal court under the same guidelines as other citizens.

That was too much for the other justices, especially the Southern conservatives who strongly backed slavery. Each of the seven, including Taney, decided to issue their own separate opinions, with each addressing those issues they thought important.

This became a turning point in American history. When Taney was made Chief Justice, many saw him undoing Marshall's work and leading the Court into decline. But just the opposite had occurred. Under Taney the Court's authority and stature had grown to the point that by 1850 a majority of the nation—North and South—believed that somehow the Court would find for the country a way out of the growing slavery dilemma. The belief was so universal that President Buchanan, in his Inaugural Address, told the nation that he considered slavery to be a "judicial problem," and one that the Court was preparing to answer. But only two days after Buchanan made this promise, the Court released its opinions in *Dred Scott*—all nine of them—and they were in such conflict that the nation knew immediately slavery was not an issue that was going to be solved judicially or politically.

Although his was only one of the nine decisions, Taney's became the most famous because he was the Chief Justice, and his was the most decisive and inflammatory. He began by absolutely ruling out citizenship, not only for blacks living then, but for their descendants as well. Then he ruled that slaves were property, and that it was the duty of government to protect property. Next, through a convoluted flight of reasoning, he held that the Missouri Compromise, which had banned slavery in the Wisconsin Territory, was unconstitutional. Finally, he ruled that Scott's fate was to be determined under Missouri law, and that the federal courts were bound by Missouri's judgments.

In his decision, Taney went further than any of the other six justices who had found against Scott. His decision was particularly galling to the antislavery movement because Taney used the Bill of Rights—the Fifth Amendment—to rule against Scott by declaring the Missouri Compromise unconstitutional. Some historians have said that the decision was a root cause of the Civil War. That is perhaps overstating its effect. But what can't be argued are that the decision ended any hope that some easy solution could be found to the slavery question, that it tore apart the fabric of the Court that was never repaired, that it brought such waves of indignation and disrespect to the Court that it took future justices decades to rebuild its reputation, and that Taney's opinion undid two and a half decades of hard work by him and consigned him to the scrap heap of history.

To show the extent of damage to the Court, when Lincoln ran for president in 1860, he did not run against his Democratic opponent Stephen Douglas so much as he ran against the Court and Chief Justice Taney. He was cheered in his Inaugural Address when he said that he believed a president has equal power to interpret the Constitution, and that he would henceforth exercise that power.

As the Civil War broke out, Taney and Lincoln were destined to clash frequently. Lincoln believed that the Union must be preserved at all cost. Taney believed that a Union without the rule of law was not worth preserving. When Lincoln ordered habeas corpus suspended under Article I, Section 9 of the Constitution ("in cases of Rebellion or Invasion"), Taney issued a blistering opinion, ruling that only Congress had the power to suspend it. Lincoln ignored the opinion. By 1863, Lincoln had named a majority of the justices on the Court, including a new tenth justice who had been authorized by Congress. They voted for Lincoln in †The Prize Cases (1863), in which they upheld his ability to order a blockade of Southern ports and to press on with the war. Taney was in the minority. But the justices also found reason to unanimously deny military courts the jurisdiction to try cases so long as the civilian court system remained operational.

But other then these few decisions, the Court had little work to do while the war raged. Even as the war continued, Chief Justice Taney died in October 1864, at age eighty-seven and after twenty-eight years on the Court.

So in the end, what do we make of Chief Justice Roger Taney? Perhaps one of the most interesting perspectives came from the liberal justice and constitutional scholar, Felix Frankfurter. Of Taney, Frankfurter wrote:

> The intellectual power of his opinions and their enduring contribu-
> tions to a workable adjustment of the theoretical distribution of author-

ity between two governments for a single people, place Taney second only to Marshall in the constitutional history of our country.

# The Chase & Waite Courts

With the Civil War at an end, it was time for the Court to return to some semblance of normalcy. Five of the ten justices had been appointed by Lincoln, with each chosen because Lincoln believed he could be trusted to approve the president's war policies and to provide a pro-Union majority that would deal strongly with the South once hostilities ended. But as the war drew to an end, there was no consensus among the justices as how to proceed into the postwar environment.

The Court's newest member was Justice Stephen J. Field, a transplanted New Yorker who had moved to California to set up a gold-rush law practice, and was now sitting on the Court representing the new 10th Circuit, which Congress had added in 1863. Field had been recommended to Lincoln as a conservative who could be trusted to back the president's policies and help provide that solid pro-Union majority. What he turned out to be was an iconoclast and rugged individualist who had little time for government and who would end up, after a thirty-four-year tenure, with the reputation as the Court's all-time foe of government regulation. He was an activist, and almost immediately he became the intellectual center for the justices who favored finding judicial solutions to the nation's problems. These justices wanted the Court to quickly find cases to make broad rulings that would win public favor. In this way, they believed, the Court could win back some of the support and favor it had lost with the *Dred Scott* decision.

This group was balanced by other justices who believed that the political realities of the day required the Court to take a go-slow approach while keeping a low profile, in order to give the country time to heal. They believed that if the Court attempted to address some of the more controversial problems of the day, the only possible result would be for it to lose even more stature.

Falling somewhere between these two groups was the new Chief Justice, Salmon P. Chase. When Lincoln had appointed Chase—his former treasury secretary—to succeed Chief Justice Taney, many people thought he was trying to eliminate a potential political rival. Chase had served as governor of Ohio, a leader of the antislavery wing of the Senate, and then as Lincoln's wartime treasury secretary. He had been the architect of both the financing of the war and the newly installed national banking system. Chase had resigned in an argument with Lincoln early in 1864. There was talk he might challenge the president for reelection, but it was only talk. When Chase learned of Taney's death, he went immediately to Lincoln to beg for the job. He said he wanted to overrule all the pro-slavery decisions of the Taney Court. Lincoln was only too happy to oblige him, and the Senate confirmed him within a half-hour of receiving his nomination from the White House.

If Congress was counting on the justices to support its vision of radical reconstruction, it was brought up short by the Court's first major postwar decisions. To the justices it must have seemed as if they were doomed to revisit issues that had caused so much grief in the final years of the Taney Court.

In 1863, the army had arrested Indiana lawyer Lambdin P. Milligan and charged him with treason for plotting to raid Union arsenals to steal guns for Confederate troops. He was tried by a military commission, under Lincoln's order giving military tribunals the right to try "disloyal citizens," and he was found guilty. Milligan brought a writ of error to the Supreme Court, arguing that he should have been tried in a civilian court, in front of a jury. In *Ex parte Milligan*, the Court unanimously agreed with him. The justices ruled that no matter how shocking the charges against a person, so long as civilian courts were "open and ready to try them," the Constitution demanded civilian courts try "all classes of men, at all times, and under all circumstances."

The Court heard the case in April 1866, and ruled on it almost immediately, but it did not release its opinion until December. It knew that the radical Republicans who now dominated Congress were going to be unhappy with the decision, and they wanted to avoid any kind of showdown. Congress was waging war with President Andrew Johnson, and the Court was already finding itself thrust in the middle.

Justice John Catron had died in May 1865. President Johnson, having just succeeded the assassinated Lincoln, wanted to wait a while before sending a name to the Senate. But then the Senate let Johnson know it was not in a mood to confirm any nominee he sent up for confirmation. So Johnson let the seat remain vacant for a year before finally nominating his attorney general, Henry Stanbery. But instead of confirming Stanbery, the Senate simply abolished the seat; in so doing, it reduced the Court's membership from ten to nine. Moreover, it announced it would do the same as the next two openings occurred, until the Court's membership stood at seven. What the Senate was really saying was that it was not going to approve any nominee sent up by Johnson. That proved true in July 1867, when Justice Wayne died. He was not replaced, and the Court's membership was allowed to drop from nine to eight.

In April 1866, Congress passed a wide-ranging civil rights law, making blacks citizens and wiping out many of the Southern laws aimed at limiting the rights of former slaves. President Johnson vetoed it, and for the first time in the history of the Republic, Congress overrode a presidential veto. But Congress felt that it had not gone far enough in trying to protect the rights of former slaves. A law passed today, it realized, can be undone tomorrow by another law or a Supreme Court opinion. The Congress especially did not trust the Court, so the obvious answer was a constitutional amendment. Despite Johnson's attempts to stop it, in June 1868 Congress approved the Fourteenth Amendment, in which it tried to accomplish three things: overturn the *Dred Scott* decision by redefining American citizenship so broadly it included blacks and former slaves; outlaw all clearly discriminatory state legislation, especially the Southern "black codes"; and protect the right to vote for all citizens and do it in such a way as to force Southern states to allow blacks to vote.

Not a single Southern state would ratify the new amendment. Although it was quickly approved by all Northern states, it would take almost three years to receive enough Southern and border-state support to be ratified. In the interim, conflicts within the Congress and between the Republicans in Congress and President Johnson deepened, as the Court tried desperately to stay out of the line of fire.

That attempt did not get off to a good start in 1867. Congress had passed a Reconstruction law, whereby lawyers could not practice law in the federal court system without first taking a retroactive loyalty oath, swearing that they had been, and would always be, loyal to the Union. Augustus Garland, a distinguished Arkansas lawyer who had argued many cases before the Supreme Court and who was well known to the justices, would not take the oath. Instead he filed suit. At the same time, Missouri had passed a law forbidding ex-Confederate officials from practicing any profession. Cummings, a lawyer, also filed suit. The Court decided the two cases—*Ex parte Garland* and *Cummings* v. *Missouri*—at the same time as the "test oath" cases. The justices unanimously struck down both laws, ruling that they constituted bills of attainder—laws which exert a punishment without any judicial proceeding.

Now Congress decided to try to force the hand of the Southern states and back them into a corner, where they had to ratify the Fourteenth Amendment. Again, over President Johnson's veto, Congress passed the Reconstruction Act, which divided the Confederacy into a half-dozen military districts and placed them under marshal law and military control. The state of Mississippi filed suit, seeking a writ from the Court preventing President Johnson from enforcing the new law. This one was just too explosive for the Court—it ducked. In *Mississippi* v. *Johnson*, the justices ruled unanimously that the case involved a political question, and therefore the Court had no jurisdiction.

But try as hard as it could, the Court simply could not avoid involving itself in the deepening political morass. In 1867, as part of a judicial act, Congress broadened the Court's appellate power to include review of denials of writs of habeas corpus by lower federal courts. The Court received an appeal by a Mississippi newspaper publisher, William McCardle, who had been denied a writ on his claim that he was being illegally held after having been arrested to stop his publication of inflammatory editorials aimed at Mississippi's military governor. In his petition to the Court, McCardle asked the justices to strike down the Reconstruction Act, a prospect that Congress greatly feared.

The case could not have come at a worse time. President Johnson's Republican foes in the Congress had finally mustered enough support in the House to vote articles of impeachment against him. His two-month-long trial began in the Senate, with Chief Justice Chase presiding (Chase had insisted he be allowed to preside) on the same day that arguments began in †*McCardle* v. *United States*. Those arguments continued for three days, while Senate Republicans watched with growing anger Chase's very even-handed handling of the impeachment trial. Finally they could stand it no longer. They quickly passed a bill removing, retroactively, the Court's jurisdiction to hear habeas corpus appeals. Johnson vetoed it, but within hours Congress repassed it.

Now, what to do? Congress had said it no longer had jurisdiction. McCardle's lawyers asked to be allowed to argue against Congress's action. The government's lawyers asked for time to consider what they would do. The Court agreed to adjourn the argument.

No further argument was ever held, and it was a full year before the Court ruled. In the meantime, President Johnson slipped through, avoiding impeachment by a single vote. Finally in April of 1869, the Court unanimously dismissed McCardle's suit, ruling that Congress had an absolute right—no matter what its motives—to set the Court's appellate jurisdiction. Instead of a case defining the limits of Reconstruction, *McCardle* became the Court's definitive restatement of Congress's constitutional prerogatives.

In the year that the Court had been trying to decide *McCardle*, it also wrestled with another of the great postwar issues: the validity of the paper money that then Treasury Secretary Chase had issued in 1862–63 to finance the war. Prior to Chase's action, paper money was not common, and when it was issued by the federal government or the states, it was directly backed by gold, silver, or some other form of specie. But to pay the Union soldiers and debts, Chase had issued some $450 million in "greenbacks"—paper money not backed by any specie, just the promise of the U.S. government that it could be redeemed. At the same time, Congress has passed the Legal Tender Act, which declared the greenbacks to be valid for payment or repayment of all private or public debts, contracted before or after the law was passed.

The result was a flurry of lawsuits in almost every state. Most involved creditors suing to prevent debts incurred before the law was passed from being repaid in greenbacks. Fifteen of sixteen lower federal courts and state courts declared the law constitutional. Most of these cases were appealed to the Supreme Court.

The Court first heard arguments in the †Legal Tender Cases, as they were called, in December of 1867. The specific case, *Hepburn* v. *Griswold*, was held over and ordered reargued in December 1868. Still there was no decision. Part of the problem was that Justice Grier kept changing his mind. Finally the justices held a vote and by a margin of 5–3 informally agreed that the Legal Tender Act was unconstitutional. Grier, having changed his vote at least three times, voted with the majority. His vacillating so annoyed his fellow justices that they convinced Congress to pass a law allowing justices to retire and continue receiving half their salaries. That served as sufficient inducement, and Grier retired. The Court was now reduced to seven members. Without Grier to change his mind again, the two sides solidified over the legal tender issue and finally released a formal decision. A week after Grier resigned, the Court struck down the law 4–3, ruling that creditors could refuse payment in greenbacks for debts incurred prior to the passage of the law. Although he had caused the law to be passed, and the greenback plan was his, Chief Justice Chase wrote the majority opinion.

The president was now Ulysses S. Grant, elected in 1868. He convinced Congress to reverse itself, and return the Court's size to nine seats.

He clearly had an ulterior motive. Grant had been shocked when the Court had struck down the Legal Tender Act, and he could count. If he could get two new justices appointed who would support the law, he could change the majority from 4–3 against to 5–4 in favor. This is exactly what he did, although Congress, and fate, did not make it very easy.

The Senate wanted Grant to name Secretary of War Edwin Stanton to the Court. But the man Grant wanted first was Attorney General Ebenezer Hoar, a man definitely not very popular with the Senate. Grant sent up Hoar's nomination, and it was greeted with silence from the Senate. Hoping to help Hoar's nomination, Grant acquiesced and nominated Stanton for the other seat. Stanton was quickly confirmed, but he died four days later. Then the Senate rejected Hoar, and Grant found himself back to square one.

So he changed his strategy. Instead of nominating politicians or government figures, Grant went out of town to find noncontroversial nominees (but still men he could count on to vote in favor of the Legal Tender Act). He found the two he needed in Joseph Bradley, a New Jersey lawyer, and William Strong, a Pennsylvania judge. They were both quickly confirmed. Within a month of their joining the Court, the justices agreed to hear another challenge to the Legal Tender Act, †*Knox* v. *Lee,* and to rethink their previous opinion. They decided by a 5–4 vote—with the two new justices providing the difference—to reverse the decision in *Hepburn* and to uphold the constitutionality of the Legal Tender Act. President Grant was reportedly very pleased.

The pressure that Congress had put on the South with the Reconstruction Act finally worked. Enough Southern states fell into line so the Fourteenth Amendment was ratified in 1868. But the Court had not yet been called upon to begin interpreting it. Given the fact that the amendment was passed to protect the rights of blacks and former slaves, it is an historical oddity that the amendment's first test in the Supreme Court came on the appeal of a large number of white Southern butchers.

In 1869, Louisiana had granted a twenty-five-year monopoly to a slaughterhouse company to operate in New Orleans. A number of butchers brought suit, claiming that the monopoly deprived them of the opportunity to earn a living, and thus was a violation of the Fourteenth Amendment's privileges and immunities clause, which says in part, "[n]o state shall make or enforce any law which shall abridge the privileges or immunities of citizens of the United States." They lost in the Louisiana Supreme Court and they appealed to the U.S. Supreme Court.

Writing for a five-member majority, Justice Samuel Miller ruled in †*The Slaughterhouse Cases* that the right to earn a living as a butcher was neither a right nor a privilege guaranteed by the amendment. The Fourteenth Amendment, said Miller, protects U.S. citizens against the unconstitutional exercise of state power to infringe on fundamental rights. But the right to exercise a specific trade is not such a right. What makes the case so important is that Miller went on to list what are fundamental rights, and in doing so to give meaning to the new amendment. What is striking is that the list was so short: freedom to travel, freedom to petition for redress of grievances, the privileges of habeas corpus, and the right of a citizen of the United States to become a citizen of any state (but not to protect any rights of state citizenship as opposed to the rights of federal citizenship).

Then Smith and the majority went on. The amendment had not, they ruled, "intended to bring within the power of Congress the entire domain of civil rights heretofore belonging exclusively to the states." The subject of the case might have been white butchers, but the decision severely limited the reach of the Fourteenth Amendment. The four dissenters, led by Justice Field, joined in a stinging dissent in which Field lamented that the majority had not seen fit to include the right of labor as among the fundamental rights. This sharp split on this issue was to come up again and again in years to come.

Chief Justice Chase suddenly died of a stroke in May 1873, at the age of only sixty-four. America seemed genuinely shocked and saddened at his untimely death. Grant then began an almost year-long exercise to find a successor who would accept the job, and who the Senate would approve. Six times he tried; with four of his choices turning him down, and the Senate rejected the two others—Oregon Attorney General George Williams and Massachusetts Attorney General Caleb Cushing. Finally, almost in desperation, Grant turned to an almost totally unknown Ohio lawyer, Morrison Waite, a man with no judicial experience, but also with no known enemies in the Senate. Almost at the point of exhaustion over Supreme Court nominees, the Senate voted to confirm him in March 1874.

Waite was a bit of a contradiction as Chief Justice. The Court was entering an unprecedented period of growth. The press of business was forcing it to change many of its traditional ways of doing business, as it struggled to become more efficient. For this task, Waite was perfect. He proved to be better than a capable manager; in fact, he turned out to have a flair for administration. He was clearly a man of integrity and honesty, and was without political ambition. That worked greatly in the Court's favor. But philosophically, Waite was a conservative who agreed completely with a very narrow interpretation of the Fourteenth Amendment's privileges and immunities clause. That was shown in his first decision on the Court, *Minor v. Happersett*,[3] in which he ruled that voting is not a guaranteed right of citizenship, and therefore women could be denied the right to vote.

He quickly followed up this ruling with another based on the same theory of voting not qualifying as an automatic right of citizenship. Since voting is not a right, Waite ruled in *Reese v. United States*, white poll officials can stop blacks from voting through the use of poll taxes, or simply by refusing to register them. He said that Congress, in outlawing such practices, had overstepped its authority.

On the same day in 1876 that the Court announced its opinion in *Reese*, Waite announced what many believe is the single worst decision in the Court's history, including *Dred Scott*. In *United States v. Cruikshank*,[4] the majority found that the federal government could not try a group of whites in Louisiana who killed numerous blacks who were protesting their lack of a right to vote, because voting is not a guaranteed federal right and therefore the federal courts have no jurisdiction.

Throughout the final quarter of the nineteenth century, the Court found itself dominated by two issues: the state regulation of business, and the civil rights of individuals.

In this era, the National Grange of Patrons of Husbandry—known simply as the "Grange"—had developed into an effective national organization representing the interests of farmers. Among the farmers' biggest problems were the high cost they were being charged by the railroads to ship their crops and the high rates charged by grain elevators to store those crops. So the Grange took the farmers' cause to the state legislatures, and the legislatures responded by passing laws regulating rail freight rates and storage charges. When lower federal courts upheld these new laws, the railroads and their lawyers quickly beat a path to the door of the Supreme Court. They alleged, the Slaughterhouse Cases notwithstanding, that state regulation was unconstitutional under the commerce clause, that it repre-

---

3. For a full discussion, see pages 171–72.
4. For a full account, see pages 170–71.

sented a violation of the due process clause of the Fourteenth Amendment, and that it represented a taking of private property. Nine Granger cases reached the Court together, including that of Ira Munn and George Scott, who owned a grain elevator in Chicago. Illinois had adopted a new law regulating the rates grain elevators could charge and opening them up to safety inspections. Munn wanted the law struck down.

In what he later said was the most important decision he ever wrote, Chief Justice Waite sided with the state in Munn's case and the other eight rail cases. In †Munn v. Illinois, Waite said that grain elevators serve a public function, and thus the public has a direct interest in how they are operated and what they can charge. Private property, through its public use, can come under government regulation. Public use does place such property within the reach of the due process clause. Such a law, Waite said, was properly a function of the state's police power. This theory became known as the "Munn public interest rule."

As for intrastate railroad rates, Waite said that Congress clearly had the right to set freight rates. But until Congress did so, the states had a right to regulate rates for transportation within their borders.

But he went further than simply declaring the laws constitutional. He admitted that a state could go too far in setting rates, or regulating business. Then realizing that the courts would be burdened with many such allegations, Waite sought to get the courts out of the business of deciding rate cases. He ruled that under such circumstances, courts can play only a minor role. A court, he said, would have to assume that the legislature possessed the facts when it set rates, and had some basis to arrive at the rate schedule that it did. Thus it was not for the courts to get involved in the rate-setting business. If someone had a problem with a rate schedule, he should take that problem to the legislature for redress, and not to the courts.

States saw in Munn a green light to regulate, and almost every state responded by adopting numerous regulatory measures. What the states overlooked in Munn was Waite's admonition that in areas where the federal government has the power to regulate, states can regulate only in those intrastate areas where Congress has not yet spoken. Once Congress speaks, then federal preemption exists, and the issue is closed to the states. Between Munn in 1877, and Wabash Railroad v. Illinois in 1886, on twenty-three separate occasions the Court had to issue decisions striking down state regulatory schemes on the basis of federal preemption.

Wabash Railroad was its most definitive ruling. In it, the Court actually overruled part of Chief Justice Waite's opinion in *Munn*. Central to Waite's *Munn* decision was the idea that railroads were essentially no more than joined local entities. If that had been true in 1877, it certainly wasn't true a decade later, by which time a truly national interstate rail system had been established. So in *Wabash*, the majority, with Waite dissenting, ruled that it was entirely up to the federal government to regulate rail rates for any railroad linked to the interstate system.

This growth of a truly national commerce resulted in the passage of the Interstate Commerce Act in 1887 and the Sherman Antitrust Act in 1890.

This was also a period of significant internal changes in the Court. In 1877, in an unusual move, Justice David Davis resigned to take a Senate seat. President Hayes chose as his successor John Marshall Harlan, a lawyer who had been named after the Chief Justice and who would go on to serve thirty-four years with great distinction. By 1880, the Court numbered among its nine justices three who were in such failing health that they could barely function. Justice Ward Hunt suffered a stroke in 1879 and went into semiretirement, but had not made it official. Justice Noah Swayne had become mentally impaired, and could not really take part in decisions. Justice Nathan Clifford had also likely suffered a stroke, but would not resign until a Democrat was in the White House. Even as these three held on, Justice William Strong resigned. William Woods of Georgia was named to replace him, the first Southerner named to the Court since the Civil War. Then Swayne resigned, and he was replaced by Senator Stanley Matthews of Ohio, who won confirmation by a single vote. Then Clifford died and was replaced by the chief judge of the Massachusetts Supreme Court, Horace Gray. Finally, Justice Hunt did retire, and after some difficulty, President Arthur named federal judge Samuel Blatchford to succeed him. This meant that only three of the justices from the Slaughterhouse Cases decision were still on the Court and two, Field and Bradley, had been in the dissent. Only Miller remained on the Court from among the justices who had voted a narrow interpretation of the Fourteenth Amendment.

But the change in justices did not signal a change in attitude. Although six of the nine justices now sitting on the Court had not heard the Slaughterhouse Cases, the decision would have been little different if they had. As events would soon show, the new justices shared this narrow view of what the Fourteenth Amendment meant. And this view would be critical to the development of American law because, over the last thirty years of the nineteenth century, and the first twenty of the twentieth century, there was an explosion of Fourteenth Amendment cases. Between 1870 and 1890, more than seventy decisions involved the amendment. Then over the next thirty, more than seven hundred cases would revolve around interpretations of the amendment's clauses.

The first real test of personal civil rights came in a test over the constitutionality of the Civil Rights Act of 1875, which Congress had passed relying on the Fourteenth Amendment as its constitutional basis. The law made it a federal crime to deny any persons the "full and equal enjoyment" of public facilities, which included hotels, modes of transportation, and other public venues.

There was massive resistance to the law all across the South, and even in the North. Hundreds of lawsuits were filed by persons denied access to public accommodations. Despite the Civil Rights Act, many lower courts upheld the right to privately discriminate, while others found the law to be constitutional because of the Fourteenth Amendment. Eventually, six cases were ready for Supreme Court review. They involved denying black ticket holders access to theaters, refusals to rent hotel rooms to blacks, and denying access to a first-class train car to a black woman who had bought a ticket for a first-class car. The cases were combined and decided as the Civil Rights Cases.[5]

By a vote of 8–1, the Court struck down the Civil Rights Act as an excessive exercise of Congress's authority. As the majority saw it, what the law attempted to do was regulate social relationships, which was beyond the ability of Congress to do and outside the scope of the Fourteenth Amendment. The Court held that acts of "private" discrimination were beyond the reach of Congress, because to hold otherwise would diminish the value of private property.

Moreover, on the same day as they released their opinion in the Civil Rights Cases, the justices also announced a key decision that further limited the Fourteenth Amendment. In *Hurtado* v. *California*, the Court ruled that a state could utilize criminal procedures that differed from federal criminal procedures. In so ruling, the Court restated Chief Justice Taney's central holding in *Barron* v. *Baltimore* that the Bill of Rights does not pertain to state laws or actions. Specifically, the Court rejected the idea that the Fourteenth Amendment had extended the protection of the Bill

---

5. For a fuller description of these cases, see pages 173–74.

of Rights to state action—this, despite the ample legislative history that it was exactly the intention of the drafters of the Amendment.

All this is not to say that the Court was uniformly against civil rights in this era. While the justices continued to shield state laws and actions regarding personal liberties from constitutional interference, they gave both the Bill of Rights and the Fourteenth Amendment an expansive interpretation as regards federal laws and actions. In a few isolated instances they issued rulings protecting rights. In 1884, in *Ex parte Yarbrough*, Jasper Yarbrough and six other Ku Klux Klan members were charged with beating a black man to keep him from voting. You might have expected they would have got off from a Court that allowed the deaths of dozens of blacks in *Cruikshank*. But this time the Court unanimously upheld the conviction of Yarbrough, on the basis that the man who was beaten was on his way to vote in a national, and not a state, election. Therefore, federal law predominates and the federal courts have jurisdiction. Left unstated was the inference that, had the man been on the way to vote in a state election, the state law would have ruled; if the state had a law allowing whites to beat blacks on their way to the polls, then the men would have been free to have administered the beating.

In March 1888, Chief Justice Waite died. As his successor, President Cleveland chose a successful Chicago railroad lawyer, Melville Fuller. Illinois was going to be an important state for Cleveland in the upcoming election of 1888, and Fuller was an important Democrat there, thus the appointment was viewed as political. Fuller had no judicial experience, and had never even held public office or any governmental position, so the Senate was very wary. It debated the nomination for more than three months, but finally confirmed the new Chief Justice by a vote of 41–20.

# The Fuller Court

The Supreme Court that Melville Fuller inherited was a very different institution from the one that Morrison Waite had joined fourteen years earlier. In 1875, Congress had passed the Removal Act, which contained a major change in federal jurisdiction, allowing the moving of cases from state courts to federal courts whenever federal questions were involved. As a result, the work load of the entire federal court system skyrocketed, and this included the work load of the Supreme Court. Between 1875 and 1880, the Court's docket more than doubled to 1,200 pending cases. During most of the 1880s, the Waite Court labored under what the Chief

Justice called "a treadmill of uninterrupted work." During the period a four-year backlog developed, even though the justices were deciding almost 200 cases a year.

On the day that Fuller arrived at the Court to take his oath of office, the docket had 1,561 pending cases. By the end of his first term, the Court had managed to rule on 400 of them. But that still meant a carry-over of more than six hundred cases into the next term, where they would be joined by a record number of new cases. Fuller knew that something had to be done. So he went to the Senate Judiciary Committee to lobby for changes. After months of effort, the senators told Fuller to draft what changes he wanted, and in 1891 the Senate, and then the House, passed Fuller's Circuit Court of Appeals Act. The new law created nine circuit courts of appeals with jurisdiction to hear appeals from the rulings of the lower federal courts. The law gave the Supreme Court selective jurisdiction: the power to accept or reject on appeal—through the device of writs of certiorari—those cases that had already been decided by the new intermediate appeals court. And significantly, the new law freed the justices from their duties to ride circuit at least once annually, in order to allow them to concentrate fully on their Supreme Court duties. Finally, the starting date of the Court was moved back another two months to the first Monday of October. This meant the Court was now in session nine months a year.

The new law worked. Within eight years, the backlog had dropped by more than a third, and the number of full opinions that the Court was issuing had dropped from an average of 260 a year to about 200.

Fuller's twenty-two years marked another passage in the Court's history. He was Chief Justice as the Court moved into the twentieth century, and as the United States forever lost its frontier youth and became the urban-centered culture it is today. More and more, the Court was called upon to rule on issues that justices fifty years earlier would scarcely have imagined. Fuller's tenure also marked another significant shift in the Court's membership, as the leading justices from the past—Field, Bradley, and Miller—all left the bench to be replaced by some of the sharpest conservative minds ever to serve on the Court.

It would be Fuller's Court from the perspective that he was the able administrative leader who efficiently organized the Court to face its growing work load. But he was not the intellectual center of his Court. That role fell to three of the Court's new justices: David Brewer, who replaced Miller, who died in 1890; Edward White, who arrived in 1894; and Rufus

Peckham, who arrived in 1896. Fuller's first decade on the Court would be a time of rapid turnover of justices. Besides Brewer, White, and Peckham, other new justices included Henry Brown (1890), George Shiras (1892), Howell Jackson (1893), and Joseph McKenna (1898). What all these men shared in common was their conservatism. By the turn of the century, the Fuller Court was one of the most conservative in history.

That conservatism showed clearly in three major decisions in the 1894–95 term. For the first time, the Court was asked to rule on the constitutionality of the Sherman Act, which had been passed to curb monopolies and monopolistic trade practices. The case was brought by the E.C. Knight Company, a sugar monopoly that refined and sold 90 percent of the sugar available for sale in the United States. It wanted the law declared unconstitutional, but the Court refused and in †*U.S.* v. *E.C. Knight Co.* found that the Sherman Act was a legitimate exercise of Congress's power over commerce. But at the same time as it found the law constitutional, the majority gutted its enforcement ability. In a radical departure from the theory that had stood since 1824 (*Gibbons* v. *Ogden*), the majority now established a distinction between what directly affects interstate commerce and what only "indirectly" affects it. It ruled that Congress had no power—and therefore neither did the Sherman Act—to regulate manufacture, even though the manufactured product is sold in interstate commerce, and even though it might represent a virtual monopoly. The act of manufacturing a product, said the Court, only "indirectly" affects interstate commerce.

Then a few months later, the Court struck down the nation's first attempt at imposing a tax on income. The case, *Pollock* v. *Farmers' Trust*, was complex and difficult. Congress had passed a tax on income derived from real estate, and ruled that it was not a direct tax that had to be apportioned back to the states. Clearly, under the Constitution, a tax directly on real estate would have to have been apportioned. Thus the case presented multiple issues, the first of which was whether a tax on income from the land was really any different from a tax on the land.

The case was argued, and with eight justices ruling, the Court held, 6–2, that the proposed tax was unconstitutional because it was a direct tax that had to be apportioned. But it left a broader issue that the justices could not decide: were all income taxes unconstitutional? They ordered that issue reargued, and within six weeks they were ready with an answer. Yes, they ruled, all income taxes are unconstitutional because they are unapportioned. Justice Henry Brown, in dissent, said the majority was doing nothing short of "surrendering the taxing power to the moneyed classes." As a direct result of this decision, Congress passed the Sixteenth Amendment in 1913.

Then a week later, the Court refused (†*In re Debs*) to reverse the contempt conviction of labor leader Eugene Debs and other union officers who led a strike in defiance of a court injunction. The justices held that it was proper for a court to issue injunctions to stop even peaceful strikes, because the strikes interfere with the orderly flow of interstate commerce. Until Congress passed a series of laws almost forty years later to prevent judges from interfering with peaceful strikes, this decision was used countless times by judges to end strikes.

As the *Debs* decision showed, the Fuller Court was not a friend to organized labor. In a 1908 decision, *Adair* v. *United States*, the justices ruled broadly that labor relations per se do not directly affect interstate commerce. Thus, any number of federal labor laws could be invalidated, including the one under review in *Adair*, which had made it a crime for employers to force workers to sign contracts agreeing not to join a union as a condition of employment.

A year later, the justices came down with another antilabor decision in *Loewe* v. *Lawlor*, usually called the Danbury Hatters' case. A union was trying to organize a Danbury, Connecticut, hat manufacturing firm, by organizing a boycott of its products in retail stores. The nine justices unanimously found that labor unions fell within the "any combination" definition of the Sherman Act, and thus were subject to federal antitrust legislation. Moreover, the justices ruled that the "secondary boycott" this union was engaged in was a restraint of trade. This decision forced Congress to later amend (1914) the Clayton Antitrust Act to specifically exempt labor unions.

If the justices of the Fuller Court had conservative economic views, their social views were even more conservative. The Court's first landmark civil rights case of the Fuller era ended up having a profound effect on the nation for generations to come. Justice Harlan called it potentially as damaging as *Dred Scott*.

Louisiana had passed a law requiring railroads carrying passengers in the state or through the state to provide separate cars for whites and blacks. The railroads opposed the law because it was expensive for them to comply. So they rigged a test case in which a black man, Homer Plessy, tried to ride in a whites-only car. He was arrested and convicted. The railroads financed his appeal to the Supreme Court.[6] In May 1896, the Court ruled, 7–1, that the Louisiana law did not violate the constitution because it provided for "separate but equal" facilities. Separate but equal remained the law of the land for fifty-eight years, until 1954 when the Court held in *Brown* v. *Board of Education* that separate is "inherently unequal."

Two areas in which at least a few of the Fuller Court justices began to have some second thoughts were the Sherman Act and their decision in *Knight*. While the Court had not declared the law unconstitutional, the majority had rendered it virtually unenforceable. Now, two years later, it took a short step back. The case was *United States* v. *Trans-Missouri Freight*. A group of sixteen railroads argued that the Sherman Act did not prevent all combinations or "reasonable" restraints of trade, which is what they argued they were. All the law banned was "unreasonable" restraints— which they did not try to define—and bad combinations—which they also did not seek to define. By a 5–4 vote, which means that only one justice changed his mind, the majority found that the Sherman Act bans all combinations, good or bad, and that by definition no restraint of trade is reasonable. This began a whole series of identical 5–4 verdicts in which the majority upheld the Sherman Act against other combinations.

A more wholesale modification of *Knight* came in 1904, in the case of †*Northern Securities* v. *United States*. The company was an interlocking holding company that controlled other holding companies, that controlled the railroads, who controlled every foot of interstate track west of Chicago. President Roosevelt attempted to break up the combination via the Sherman Act. The company responded that it had nothing directly to do with interstate commerce—that it was only a holding company that owned common stock. This was the first time the justices were faced with the growing use of holding companies.

By another 5–4 vote the majority held that because of the nature of its holdings, the company did restrain trade, and therefore could be the subject of the act. In a bitter dissent, the minority argued that the majority had gone too far and now was allowing the government to regulate stock ownership. This case established the principle that holding companies could be regulated.

Then a year later, the meat packers tried an end run around the

6. For full details of *Plessy* v. *Ferguson*, see page 174–75.

Sherman Act. In *Swift & Company* v. *United States*, Swift and other meat packers argued that they did not fall under the Sherman Act because they bought their animals, did their own slaughtering, and sold their products all within one state, and thus they did not engage in interstate commerce. This argument was too much for any of the justices. Unanimously, they ruled that if a company restrains trade in many states, even though it does it one state at a time, it is still a restraint of trade and a violation of the Sherman Act.

Central to the conservatism of the Fuller Court's justices was their belief in the sanctity of a contract and the inability of the state to interfere with the absolute right to contract. This issue was certainly a holdover from earlier Courts, but now the justices saw the issue in terms more in keeping with the postindustrialized country. Freedom to contract was part of the right to buy and sell services and goods, unfettered by government regulation and subject only to the free market. The issue would begin to come up often in decisions around the turn of the century.

In 1897 †(*Allegeyer* v. *Louisiana*), the Court was asked to review a Louisiana law that limited the selling of insurance only to in-state companies who had been issued state licenses. Those licenses were issued only to politically favored companies, and an out-of-state insurance company sued. The Court struck down the law on the basis that it limited the rights of Louisiana residents to contract with any insurance company they wanted.

Louisiana did not pretend that this law had been put on the books for health or safety reasons. Had they, the Court might have had a great deal more difficulty reaching a decision. Health and safety was one area of social legislation the Fuller Court had great problems making up its mind about. Nothing in the Constitution explicitly allows Congress to undertake this sort of regulation. When the states tried it, the issue of private property was often raised. It was an issue that caused the Court no end of problems.

In 1898 (*Holden* v. *Hardy*), by a vote of 7–2, the justices upheld a Utah mine safety law that prohibited minors from working more than eight hours a day in underground mines. Where health and safety were at stake, said the majority, freedom to contract must take second place to the state's ability to regulate. But in 1905 †(*Lochner* v. *New York*), the Court revisited the same issue, and with the make-up of the Court now different, the majority reached an exactly opposite conclusion. By a vote of 5–4, the Court struck down a New York law that tried to set maximum hours for bakery workers for health and safety reasons. The majority ruled that the state was exceeding its police-power authority in interfering with the bakery workers' right to contract.

But the issue was not dead. Only three years later the Court again faced the exact same question in †*Mueller* v. *Oregon*, with the difference that the Oregon law in question dealt only with women. The Oregon measure sought to limit to ten hours a day, again for health and safety reasons, the workday of women in the laundries. Boston lawyer and justice-to-be Louis Brandeis represented Oregon, and filed with the Court what has become known as the Brandeis Brief—an argument of epic length—in which he gave a history of women in the labor movement and argued for the proposition that the Oregon law must be sustained if it sought to promote the general health and welfare of workers, which he called a valid exercise of the police power of the state. Reversing itself again, the Court agreed. The majority based its decision on what it saw as a distinction between men and women that might be offensive to feminists—"the inherent difference between the two sexes." But in doing so, the Court established the right of the state to use its legitimate police powers to attain a desired social end by interfering with the right to contract. And by inference, it found the right to contract not to be absolute. This did not end the issue; it comes up again and again.

In July 1910, Chief Justice Fuller died. For the first time a sitting justice, Edward D. White, was elevated to Chief Justice. His tenure would mark another new era for the Court.

# The White and Taft Courts

Historians have tended to divide the eras of the Supreme Court by the terms of service of the various Chief Justices. But from time to time in Court history, the Court's direction has been set, not by the Chief Justice, but by a president who appointed all or many of the justices. By most reckonings, the Taft Era did not begin until 1921, when the then ex-president became Chief Justice. But from 1909 to 1913, as president, Taft appointed six justices. So while this period is known as the White Court, Taft put his mark on it long before he actually assumed the center chair.

Taft's appointments started when Justice Peckham died in 1909. To replace him Taft selected Judge Horace Lurton, with whom he had served on the Sixth Circuit Court of Appeals. Then within a year, Taft was forced to name three new justices. First Justice Brewer died, and Taft—in what was viewed as a brilliant political move because it removed a potential rival for the presidential election of 1912—selected Charles Evans Hughes, the young governor of New York. In July, Chief Justice Fuller died, and Taft broke with tradition by elevating Justice Edward White. To replace White as associate justice, Taft chose a relatively unknown Georgia attorney, Joseph Lamar. Then before the year was out, in November, Justice Moody resigned and Taft replaced him with Willis Van Devanter of Wyoming. Finally, in 1911, the "Great Dissenter," Justice Harlan, died and was replaced by New Jersey Supreme Court judge Mahlon Pitney. The Court was almost completely remade. Only two justices remained from before the turn of the century: McKenna and Chief Justice White.

In terms of overall philosophy, the years before World War I were strange ones for the Court. Based on their past reputations, you would have expected the new justices to have been uniformly conservative, possibly even more conservative than the justices they replaced. But the White Court started out by taking a detour to the left, only to return to more familiar conservative ground with the approach of World War I.

White had already shown his strong views about the Sherman Act, and about how it should be applied to trusts. He saw the purpose of the law as not simply banning all combinations but rather a weapon to force trusts and combinations to work toward desirable social or economic ends. He was a major proponent of the so-called rule of reason that held that all trusts were not illegal under the Sherman Act, only "unreasonable" restraints of trade.

White was able to articulate this view in the first major decision of his tenure. In †Standard Oil v. United States—with White writing the opinion for an eight-member majority—the Court upheld the government's order that under the Sherman Act the huge Standard Oil Trust had to be broken up. But he ruled that the breakup was necessary not simply because the trust existed—that would have been a strict interpretation of the Sherman Act—but because the Standard Oil Trust had been shown to be guilty of unreasonable restraint of trade. Then only a few weeks later, in United States v. American Tobacco, the same majority agreed that the tobacco trust must be broken up, again not simply because it existed but rather because it acted as an unreasonable restraint of trade.

Although both these decisions supported the government's dismantling of the oil and tobacco trusts, they are looked upon as two of the most important decisions in the growth of corporate America, because they modified the seeming absoluteness of the Sherman Act with this new rule of reason.

While the new White Court was unified in its interpretation of the Sherman Act, one area the justices clearly had a growing difficulty with was defining the limits of police powers of the state. At first the justices had no problem approving an extension of police power by the federal government to regulate foods and drugs by upholding the new Pure Food and Drug Act (1911), mandating employer liability by upholding the Employers Liability Act (1912), and outlawing interstate prostitution by upholding the White Slave Act (1913). Then in 1914, in the Shreveport rate case, the justices upheld Congress's ability to empower the Interstate Commerce Commission to set intrastate rail rates under some circumstances. Finally, in 1917, in a pair of decisions, the justices upheld the government's power to set maximum hours and minimum wages for some classes of workers. Without specifically saying so, the Court seemed to have overruled the 1905 decision in *Lochner* v. *New York*, which had struck down such wage and hours regulations on the basis of the unfettered right to contract.

But now the Court staged a conservative reaction. In 1914 Justice Lurton had died, and to replace him President Wilson named his attorney general, James McReynolds. An arch-conservative and a highly opinionated man, McReynolds was certainly an anti-Semite who refused to have any dealings with the two Jewish justices with whom he would eventually serve, Louis Brandeis and Benjamin Cardozo.

The former was named to the Court the year after McReynolds. In Brandeis, Wilson could not have found a man more different in philosophy from his first appointee. Some have speculated that Wilson named Brandeis simply to goad Taft, who considered the Boston lawyer a dangerous radical. Whatever his motives, the choice generated a great deal of opposition in the Senate, which took six months to confirm the nominee. Then almost immediately, Justice Hughes resigned to run against Wilson for the presidency, and Wilson named federal judge John H. Clarke to replace him.

With McReynolds now on the Court, both 1915 decisions upholding wage and hour regulations had been by narrow one-vote majorities. It was clear that the four minority justices led by McReynolds were having a great deal of trouble with further extension of police powers, and that even the majority felt some limit had to be placed on their reach. That limit was arrived at in the 1918 case of *Hammer* v. *Dagenhart*. Congress had been trying to find a way to end child labor abuses in factories ever since the Court had ruled in 1895, in the sugar monopoly case (*Knight*), that manufacture was not a direct part of interstate commerce. By 1916 Congress thought it had found the way in the Court's expanding view of federal police power. It passed a law banning all products from interstate commerce that had been produced by workers under the age of fourteen. Ronald Dagenhart, who had two boys working in a North Carolina cotton mill, sued the local federal prosecutor, Willis Hammer, to prevent him from enforcing the new law. After Dagenhart won in the lower courts, Hammer appealed to the Supreme Court.

A sharply split Court ruled, 5–4, that Congress had finally overstepped its authority. Writing for the majority, Justice William Day declared the law unconstitutional based on the very questionable distinction that Congress could not forbid commerce from moving, but only regulate the means of movement. This was a hard distinction to now make stick because Congress had already banned many things from commerce—among them tainted foods, "white slaves" (prostitutes), and lottery tickets—and the Court had upheld these laws. So Day was forced to find another distinction in the fact that the already banned products, in and of themselves, produced harmful results. In the case of the North Carolina mill, its finished products produced no harmful results. Holmes wrote a bitter dissent, in which he said it should not make a difference whether the evil precedes or follows the transportation. But the "harmful results" doctrine would remain the law of the land until 1941.

The decision in *Hammer* seemed to mark the end of the Court's flirtation with liberalism. It had appeared that Hughes was going to become the philosophical center of the Court. He had helped craft opinions that had upheld the Sixteenth Amendment's establishment of a graduated income tax †(*Brushaber* v. *Union Pacific*), mandated the exclusion of evidence from federal trials that had been obtained as a result of illegal searches †(*Weeks* v. *United States*), and struck down a state law that made it very difficult for blacks to register to vote (*Guinn* v. *United States*). But Hughes left the Court to run for president. This left McReynolds to play a more important role, and the Court took a turn back to the right.

This conservative rebound was probably most clearly shown in the Court's attitude toward freedom of speech. Although the nation was in the second decade of the twentieth century, so far the Court had had little to say about the First Amendment and, more specifically, almost nothing about speech and press freedom. The Court had been insistent that the Bill of Rights did not apply to state law and state action. That made the First Amendment applicable only to federal law and action; by and large, neither Congress nor the federal government had infringed on free speech or free press rights. Thus the Court had been presented with few cases that raised free-speech and free-press issues. But that changed with the start of World War I.

Within days of war being declared, President Wilson introduced a tough law to make certain criticism of the government and the war effort a criminal offense. The Espionage Act of 1917 called for long imprisonment and steep fines for anyone found guilty of obstructing the military's enlistment program, attempting to cause mutiny or disloyalty within the armed forces, or conveying false information that hindered the war effort. If two or more people were found to have committed an individual act in concert, it was deemed a conspiracy and punishable as a separate crime. Then the next year Congress passed the Sedition Act of 1918, which effectively gave the government an almost unlimited power to censor publications or punish for "unpatriotic speech," and added to the list of original offenses in the Espionage Act any that would obstruct the sale of war bonds, or any which could be construed as bringing discredit or scorn on the government of the United States. Defeated during the debate was an amendment that had been offered by Senator Joseph France, R–MD, which had read: "Nothing in this act shall be construed as limiting the liberty or impairing the right of an individual to publish or speak what is true, with good motives and for justifiable ends."

In 1919, a series of four cases growing out of the initial Espionage Act reached the U.S. Supreme Court. Charles T. Schenck and Elizabeth Baer, two New York socialists, printed and distributed handbills decrying military conscription as "despotism arranged in the interest of Wall Street" and urging resistance to the draft. Arrested and convicted for violation of the Espionage Act, the pair found their appeal †(*Schenck* v. *United States*) finally before the Supreme Court.

Their lawyers argued that the First Amendment guarantees "absolutely unlimited discussion" of public matters and that includes "scrutiny and condemnation" of the government and its activities. But the government argued that it has a right of self-preservation that overshadows any First Amendment considerations, and that it alone should be the judge of what actions fall within that right of self-preservation.

Justice Holmes wrote the decision for a unanimous court. He rejected the defendants' First Amendment argument out-of-hand. But he also refused to go as far as the government wanted in its assertion that it alone had the ultimate right to determine what is necessary for its survival. In doing so, Holmes set up a test of the legitimacy of words spoken or printed

91

that has come to make *Schenck* one of the most famous of all Supreme Court opinions.

Holmes wrote:

> We admit that in many places and in ordinary times the defendants in saying all that was said in the circular would have been within their constitutional rights. But the character of every act depends upon the circumstances in which it was done. . . . The most stringent protection of free speech would not protect a man in falsely shouting fire in a theater and causing a panic. . . . The question in every case is whether the words used are used in such circumstances and are of such a nature as to create A CLEAR AND PRESENT DANGER that they will bring about the substantive evils that Congress has a right to prevent.

Prior to this, courts had used a test of whether the words or actions had a "tendency" or "reasonable tendency" to bring about the unwanted or prohibited result. That test had long been attacked by libertarians as so broad that almost any conduct or speech could fall within it. But now, having set up this more liberal "clear and present danger" test, Holmes had no trouble finding that Schenck and Baer's pamphlet clearly met the test. So he, and the court, affirmed their conviction.

Three other cases also reached the Court in 1919, brought by defendants who had been convicted under the Espionage Act, including one brought by Eugene Debs. Gene Debs was a major public figure and a major thorn in the side of the government. As a teenager he had started out working on the railroad for $6 a week and ended up as head of the American Railway Union. In 1895 he was arrested and jailed for leading what turned into a bloody strike and, as we have seen, that conviction was upheld by the Supreme Court. He came out of prison a hero of the labor movement, and in the four elections between 1900 and 1912, he was the Socialist party candidate for president. In the election of 1912 he received over a million votes—more than 8 percent of the total vote cast.

On June 16, 1918, Debs gave a speech in Canton, Ohio, in which he denounced the war as an instrument of the ruling classes and condemned the jailing of other socialists for their antiwar speeches. Debs was arrested and charged with violating the Espionage Act. Even though it was far from "clear" that Debs's words would lead to illegal actions, the Court found that was a "reasonably probable effect" and upheld his conviction.

But only eight months after the *Schenck* and *Debs* decisions, still another free-speech case brought the first break in the previously unanimous Court's thinking about the First Amendment, and started the Court on what would be a long road leading to the protections that speech and the press enjoy today.

In August 1918, Jacob Abrams and four other young Jewish Russian immigrants (all professed anarchists who had come to the United States less than a decade earlier as children) were arrested in New York for throwing Yiddish-language leaflets out a Lower East Side factory window. Although the four were denouncing the invasion of Vladivostok by U.S. troops during the Russian Revolution, they were tried and convicted of opposing the war with Germany (under a complex reasoning that the Bolsheviks had withdrawn from the war and thus were now said to be in league with Germany), and using language that sought to bring the United States into disrepute. Both were crimes under the expanded terms of the Sedition Act.

Their trial was a travesty. Spurred on by a judge who openly ridiculed the defense's attempt to put on a case, the jury quickly returned a guilty verdict and the defendants were sentenced to twenty years each. When the case reached the Supreme Court, the majority gave the same short shrift to the defendants' First Amendment arguments as it had in the previous four Espionage Act cases. But this time the Court was not unanimous. Holmes and Brandeis dissented in an opinion written by Holmes.

A number of things had happened in the intervening eight months between the decisions in *Schenck* and *Debs*, and the arguing of *Abrams* to begin to change Holmes's mind. His friend Judge Learned Hand (who many consider the greatest judge never to have sat on the Supreme Court) had gently chided him in a series of letters for overapplying the Espionage Act. Hand himself two years earlier, as a district court judge, had rejected the "bad tendency" test in a famous case in New York (*Masses Publishing Company* v. *Patten*), and had instead substituted a test of "direct incitement of violent resistance" in determining if sedition was present. Hand had been influenced to make this change by an article by one of the outstanding legal scholars of the day, Ernst Freud. (Hand's decision had been reversed by the appeals court and it never reached the Supreme Court.) Then another of the most prominent constitutional scholars of the day, Harvard's Zechariah Chafee, published a blistering condemnation of the three Espionage decisions in a *Harvard Law Review* article, "Freedom of Speech in Time of War."

In his dissent, Holmes referred back to his "clear and present danger" standard and found it lacking in *Abrams's* situation. "I think we should be eternally vigilant," Holmes wrote, "against attempts to check the expression of opinions that we loath and believe to be fraught with death, unless they so imminently threaten immediate interference with the lawful and pressing purposes of the law that an immediate check is required to save the country."

The *Abrams* decision is important to the development of both speech and press freedoms. Holmes effectively transformed his "clear and present danger" test from one used to limit the press and speech to a test that ultimately protected it. It also was the first of a decade of such dissents that eventually led to the majority adopting a progressively more libertarian view of the First Amendment.

Eventually the views of Brandeis and Holmes would become the majority view. But in 1921 they were still a minority view on a Court with a majority that seemed determined to adopt ever more conservative positions. That trend toward conservatism was accelerated by the unexpected death of Chief Justice White in May 1921. The new president was Warren G. Harding. He was only too happy to fulfill a fellow Republican's life-long dream by naming him to the Court. So he nominated former President William Howard Taft as Chief Justice. The Senate confirmed the nomination within minutes of receiving it on June 30, 1921, and Taft became the leader of the justices he himself had named to the Court.

Taft occupied the center chair for almost a decade, and proved to be one of the most conservative Chief Justices ever. For the most part, the decisions of his era were uniformly conservative. But during Taft's years, in the sharp and eloquent dissents of Brandeis and Holmes, a transformation began that would end with the many expansive decisions of the 1960s safeguarding individual liberties. More immediately, Taft was able—almost singularly through the force of his personality—to introduce administrative and jurisdictional changes that brought the Court fully into the twentieth century, and to successfully bargain with Congress to build the Court a new home. In looking back on Taft's tenure, we can have no doubt that he left the Court in decidedly better shape than he found it.

Taft's conservatism, and the sharp philosophical split between justices that would become a hallmark of his tenure, showed through in his first significant decision, †*Truax* v. *Corrigan*, decided in the middle of his first term. At issue was an Arizona law that prohibited judges from issuing injunctions to end strikes or picketing unless violence was endangering life or property. Writing for a 5–4 majority, Taft struck down the law as a violation of the Fourteenth Amendment because it deprived employers of free use of their property without due process. Brandeis authored a furious dissent in which he traced the evils of injunctions to end peaceful strikes. As with so many of his dissents in this period, his view eventually became the Court's majority view.

In another conservative decision (*Newberry* v. *United States*) from Taft's first term, the Court struck down a portion of the Federal Corrupt Practices Act of 1911, which had tried to set spending limits on primary elections. In a broad-based holding, the majority ruled that Congress had no power to regulate primary elections, that power resting entirely with the state. In doing so, the majority all but empowered Southern states to deny blacks the right to vote in primary elections.

Taft's conservative majority was bolstered at the end of his first term by the addition of three new Harding appointees. In quick succession, Justices Day, Clarke, and Pitney resigned. To replace them Harding chose Utah Senator George Sutherland, Minnesota attorney Pierce Butler, and Tennessee federal judge Edward T. Sanford.

The newly enlarged conservative majority faced its first real test in May 1922, when in *Baily* v. *Drexel Furniture Company*, the Court was asked to review yet another attempt by Congress to find a way to outlaw child labor. After the Court's 1918 ruling, which eliminated any commerce-clause method of getting at child labor by refusing to allow its products into interstate commerce, Congress tried to tax it to death. Following the Court's approval in 1919 (*United States* v. *Doremus*) of a high tax to try to limit narcotics sales, Congress passed the child labor tax, attaching a steep levy on all goods produced by child labor.

Having given its approval of the antinarcotics tax, the conservative majority was hard pressed to find a way to invalidate this anti–child-labor levy. But finally Taft and the other conservatives found a way in the Tenth Amendment.[7] They ruled that since child labor was not specifically mentioned in the Constitution, then by using its taxing power to try to outlaw it, Congress was infringing on rights left to the states. In a half-

---

7. "The powers not delegated to the United States by the Constitution, nor prohibited by it to the States, are reserved to the States respectively, or to the people."

dozen other situations over the next few years, the Taft Court's conservative majority would return to this Tenth Amendment argument to strike down attempts by Congress to regulate one activity or another.

The Taft conservatives showed they were willing to revisit areas of the law that seemed settled, and to overturn past decisions. Despite the several rulings that had upheld the federal government's right to regulate wages and hours, in *Adkins* v. *Children's Hospital*, the Court struck down a District of Columbia minimum wage law for women on the basis of the old right-to-contract argument. Then the Court struck down a Kansas law setting wages in the meat packing industry on the basis that the industry was not a public enough endeavor. This "not public enough" argument was used for years by the conservative majority to strike down various state attempts at wage and hour controls.

But at times the Taft Court's conservative majority was a group that could surprise. In 1925, in †*Gitlow* v. *New York*, the Court heard the appeal on Benjamin Gitlow, convicted under a New York State antisedition law modeled directly on the federal Sedition Act. The majority, in a decision written by Justice Sanford, had no trouble rejecting Gitlow's argument that New York's law was unconstitutional. But in doing so it dropped something of a bombshell. The majority said, almost matter-of-factly, that it was able to rule on the case because it now accepted that the Fourteenth Amendment's due process clause had extended the reach of the First Amendment to state laws and actions. This seeming offhand holding is a case upholding a state's right to limit speech, central to development of the First Amendment.

That same year, 1925, brought perhaps the most important administrative reform to the Court since the Judiciary Act of 1789. When Taft had assumed the Chief Justiceship in 1921, the Court was almost drowning in new cases. It was again falling way behind in any effort to keep its docket current. The Circuit Court of Appeals Act of 1891 had created a new level of appellate courts, and had given these mid-level courts final jurisdiction in matters of admiralty and noncapital crimes. But the Supreme Court was still obliged to hear cases involving constitutional questions, cases with a federal question on appeal from a state high court, and a whole slate of issues on direct appeal from federal district courts. Taft saw immediately that if things were allowed to proceed unchecked, the Court would become so overburdened that it would all but grind to a halt. So he proceeded to galvanize the entire federal judiciary to win general agreement on changes that were necessary.

He started in 1922 by convincing Congress to set up a governing board for the federal courts consisting of the senior circuit judges and justices of the Supreme Court.[8] He then named himself to head this board. Within a year the board had managed to win approval to streamline a number of procedures within the federal judicial system, which immediately resulted in speedier disposition of cases. At the same time, Taft introduced internal procedural reforms in the Supreme Court that speeded up the handling of cases by at least three months, and allowed the Court to dispose of a record number of cases in 1923.

But Taft realized that more basic reform was necessary. He lobbied Congress incessantly, until the Senate Judiciary Committee finally agreed to let Taft and the other justices draft a bill of structural changes they felt necessary to bring the Supreme Court into the modern age. That bill became the Judiciary Act of 1925, also called the "Judges Bill" because of who drafted it. Central to its reform was making most of the Supreme Court's reviews discretionary rather than mandatory. Henceforth, with the passage of the new law, virtually all decisions of the courts of appeal would be final unless a minimum of four Supreme Court Justices deemed the case, or the issues involved, important enough to merit review. On cases emerging from state high courts, the Supreme Court would be obligated to review only those cases in which a state law had been deemed invalid under federal law or the Constitution. In a few technical areas, such as when the government appealed an adverse antitrust decision at the district court level, the Court retained mandatory jurisdiction.

Taft's other major contribution to the Court was its building, which stands today across First Street from the Capitol.[9] It was Taft's vision, and his ability to maneuver Congress, that was responsible for its construction. The building stands today as one of his most enduring legacies. But he never lived to see it completed. Congress appropriated the money in 1929, and construction began in 1931. But in February 1930, Taft fell gravely ill and resigned from the Court. He was dead less than a month later. To succeed him, President Hoover asked Charles Evans Hughes to return to the Court as Chief Justice.

---

8. Today, this board has been enlarged and operates as the U.S. Judicial Conference. Its role, though, has remained the same—administrative supervision of the federal court system.

9. For a full account of the building of the Court's new home, see Section V.

# The Hughes, Stone, and Vinson Courts

Given that Charles Evans Hughes was a man of impeccable reputation, the assumption was that he would have little difficulty gaining confirmation. But it was just the opposite. Many western senators saw the Supreme Court as the last bastion of eastern elitism, an institution that protected business interests over the rights of the common man. To them, a corporate lawyer like Hughes—actually he was one of the richest lawyers in America—represented all that they saw as wrong with the Court. But in the end his reputation saved him, and he was confirmed 52–26. He also was confirmed because some in the Senate felt guilty about rejecting another Hoover nominee, whose confirmation came to a vote while the debate over Hughes continued. Justice Sanford had died within hours of Taft, and Hoover had selected North Carolina judge John Parker. But the Senate rejected him because of objections from organized labor and minority groups. Hoover then chose former federal prosecutor Owen Roberts, who was quickly confirmed. Then Hoover was able to make another appointment. Holmes, at age ninety the oldest man ever to serve, finally was persuaded to resign. To replace him Hoover chose New York judge Benjamin Cardozo. Although he would only serve six terms before his death in 1938, Cardozo would play a critical role in the development of the Court.

Initially, it appeared the Hughes Court was moving toward the left. In 1931, first in *Stromberg* v. *California* and then in *Near* v. *Minnesota*, narrow 5–4 majorities struck down for the first time state laws that violated the First Amendment. A year later, in the landmark †*Powell* v. *Alabama* (the first Scottsboro Boys case), a seven-man majority ruled that all defendants in state court actions are entitled to be represented by counsel. Then in 1934, in †*Nebbia* v. *New York*, the Hughes Court greatly expanded the states' ability to regulate any business for any reason, so long as the regulations were deemed reasonable.

But the Hughes Court era was dominated by the Great Depression. Its work load was light because few could afford the luxury of lawyers and protracted litigation. The issues it faced were born out the nation's needs and the government's response. It was the Depression, the Roosevelt administration's response to it, and the Court's reaction to this response that sparked perhaps the Court's greatest crisis.

The Court crisis of 1935–37 probably was caused by the simple fact that there has never been an older Supreme Court. Five of the justices were over seventy, with the other four all in their sixties. While the Court was philosophically not as conservative as the White or Taft Courts, still the justices were all men born in a much different era, when government intervention was something to be avoided at almost any cost. But now America was looking desperately to Washington for relief from the economic disaster that had befallen the nation. President Franklin Roosevelt and the Congress thought that desperate times called for desperate measures. So innovative legislation was passed to try to ease the country out of the depths of the Depression. Much of that legislation ran into the entrenched views of the septuagenarian Hughes Court.

On January 7, 1935, the Court struck down a major piece of New Deal legislation for the first time. In *Panama Refining Company* v. *Ryan*, the Court by a vote of 8–1 struck down a portion of the National Industrial Recovery Act (NIRA) as giving too much power to the president. Then a few weeks later the Court gave Roosevelt his only New Deal victory when it upheld, by a vote of 5–4 in the Gold Clause Cases, his moving the country away from the gold standard. But the dissent of Justices Van Devanter, Butler, Sutherland, and McReynolds was sharp and bitter. As they saw it, the Constitution was being jettisoned in this wave of New Deal legislation. They became the majority in early May when they were joined by Justice Roberts in striking down the Railroad Retirement Act and its mandated pension system for rail workers. Then only two weeks later, on May 27, 1935, in what was called "Black Monday," the majority struck down a farm relief program (*Louisville Bank* v. *Radford*), limited the president's power to fire independent agency board members who were fighting his New Deal reforms (*Humphrey's Executor* v. *United States*), and then struck down the entire NIRA (*Schecter Poultry* v. *United States*).

In *Schecter*, Chief Justice Hughes wrote: "Extraordinary conditions do not create or enlarge constitutional power." That was probably a correct constitutional statement. But given the tenor of the times, it was not something that America wanted to be told; and it was certainly not something that President Roosevelt wanted to hear. Roosevelt and the Congress tried to respond to the Court's rulings by replacing the rejected NIRA with a series of more narrowly crafted statutes such as the Social Security Act and the National Labor Relations Act.

The 1935–36 term was to prove one of the most important in Court history. It was the first term the Court was to spend in its magnificent new home. But it was to be a term that would rock the Court, as an institution, to its very foundations.

There has rarely been a Court as divided as the Supreme Court was in 1936. The four conservative justices—Van Devanter, Butler, Sutherland, and McReynolds—did almost everything together, from taking their lunches to riding to and from the Court, to spending their free time, to Sunday dinners. On the opposite end of the political spectrum, Justices Stone, Cardozo, and Brandeis became as close as the four conservatives. In the middle were Chief Justice Hughes and Justice Roberts, who did not feel they belonged with either bloc, but who were philosophically closer to the conservatives than to the three liberals.

It was clear that the new term was going to be critical to the future of the New Deal and to the nation's recovery. When the term started there were several cases already on the docket challenging New Deal laws, and before long others were added. The first of these decisions came down in January 1936 (*United States* v. *Butler*), with both Hughes and Roberts joining the conservatives to strike down the Agricultural Adjustment Act using the old, and by now largely discredited, argument that it violated rights delegated to the states under the Tenth Amendment. Then, in rapid order, the Court struck down the new Bankruptcy Act, then the Coal Act, and finally state minimum wage laws—all by identical 5–4 majorities.

In November 1936, Roosevelt was reelected by one of the great landslides in political history. He saw, quite correctly, the Court—called by almost everyone in America the "Nine Old Men"—as the major impediment for aggressive government action he thought necessary to put America back on its feet. He was clearly frustrated. His entire first term had passed without his being able to make a single Court appointment. The justices were getting older and older, but none seemed about to retire. Collectively their health was amazingly good, so Roosevelt decided to take action.

Roosevelt sent to Congress what he labeled his Judicial Reform Act, but it quickly became known as Roosevelt's court-packing plan. Its basis was the theory that as justices reach age seventy, they cannot be expected to keep up with the punishing work schedule that Court service requires. So Roosevelt asked Congress for authority to appoint a new justice for every justice on the Court over age seventy. When the older justice finally retired or died, the new appointee would take his place. Effectively, said Roosevelt, he was simply asking for the power to replace aging justices in advance— to allow other justices to be there to bear some of the burden of work.

Of course, everyone saw through the plan immediately. If passed it would have allowed Roosevelt to make six immediate appointments to what would have become a fifteen-member Court. Those six would have given him a pro–New Deal majority. Chief Justice Hughes lobbied furiously against the bill, but it had an immediate positive effect. The bill pointed out the lack of an equitable retirement system for justices. So immediately Congress passed a law allowing justices to retire at full salary, something that other federal judges had been able to do after fulfilling a certain term of service.

But what probably swung Congress against Roosevelt's plan was that the two swing justices had a change of heart. In *West Coast Hotel* v. *Parrish*, announced in late March on what has been called "White Monday" (but obviously decided well in advance of Roosevelt's introducing his court-packing plan), Hughes and Roberts joined with the liberal minority to form a five-member majority to uphold a state minimum wage law, and to reverse previous decisions that had struck them down. Then on the same day in other decisions, the same five justices also upheld a federal program to bail out bankrupt farmers, force government-mandated collective bargaining for rail workers, and offer gun control via special taxes on firearms. Then within a few weeks the same five-member majority voted to uphold the National Labor Relations Act, and seven justices voted to uphold key portions of the Social Security Act.

Those decisions took the steam out of the court-packing plan. With Hughes rallying the judiciary in opposition, the Senate Judiciary Committee reported the bill unfavorably. Then before it could go to the Senate floor, Justice Van Devanter announced that he was taking advantage of the new retirement system and was stepping down. The court-packing bill died, and the crisis ended.

As might have been expected given the age of the incumbent justices, Van Devanter's retirement started a wave of change in the Court. Over the next six years Roosevelt was able to make nine Court appointments. His first, replacing Van Devanter, was Alabama Senator Hugo Black, who took his seat in time for the 1937 term. The first major decision he participated in, *Palko* v. *Connecticut*, was seemingly another conservative reaction. The majority, including Black, held that the Fourteenth Amendment did not automatically extend all the guarantees of the Bill of Rights to all state actions. Rather, only those guarantees deemed "essential" to an ordered society were extended to the states. But the 1937 term was a turning point. The Court would slowly begin to change its focus and its priorities from matters of commerce to individual rights and freedoms. And in due course the ruling in *Palko* would have little impact because the justices would eventually, one by one, categorize virtually all conceivable rights as "essential."

The next of the septuagenarian justices to retire was Sutherland. Roosevelt named his solicitor general, Stanley Reed, to the seat. This meant that two of the Court's conservative bloc were now gone, and this showed up almost immediately when, in *DeJonge* v. *Oregon*, the Court ruled that the First Amendment right of freedom of assembly is equal to the rights of free speech and free press, and that in turn all are applicable to state laws and actions. Then in 1938, Justice Brandeis resigned. He was succeeded by the head of the Securities and Exchange Commission, William O. Douglas.

The year Douglas joined the Court at the start of his record 36-year tenure, the justices produced an opinion that was a complete reversal of all the earlier decisions striking down parts of the New Deal. In *United States* v. *Carolene Products Company*, a case involving federal standards for milk products, the Court ruled in favor of the government and in doing so said that from now on it would approach all economic legislation with the presumption that it was constitutional, and the burden would be on the challenger to prove otherwise.

In 1939 Justice Butler died, and Roosevelt replaced him with his attorney general, Frank Murphy. Now Roosevelt finally had a majority on the Court. Of the conservatives, only McReynolds was left. In fact, McReynolds seemed to mellow a bit in his final years on the Court. While he was the lone dissenter in *Carolene Products*, in 1939 he joined with the other eight justices in a unanimous decision, *Cantwell* v. *Connecticut*, which struck down a state breech-of-the-peace law as too vague to pass First Amendment muster and overturned the conviction of a preacher. In doing so the Court extended free exercise of religion protections to states.

Then in 1941, in Chief Justice Hughes's last major decision, the Court finally stuck a stake through the heart of child labor abuses. In †*United States* v. *Darby Lumber Company*, the Court unanimously sustained the Fair Labor Standards Act, which outlawed child labor and also regulated wages and hours of workers making products shipped in interstate commerce. In doing so the Court specifically overruled its 1918 decision in *Hammer*, and severely downgraded the importance of the Tenth Amendment—calling it a mere "truism" with little relevance to modern society.

Early in 1941, Justice McReynolds, the last of the conservatives, retired. But Roosevelt did not move quickly to replace him. Then at the end of the term in June, Chief Justice Hughes retired. Roosevelt chose to elevate associate justice Harlan Stone, and he nominated his attorney general, Robert H. Jackson, to fill Stone's seat. At the same time, he named Senator James Byrnes of South Carolina to fill McReynolds's still-empty seat. Byrnes only served a single term, resigning to play a more direct role in the war effort. As Byrnes's successor, Roosevelt chose federal judge Wiley Rutledge.

Probably the most important case of 1942 was †*Chaplinsky* v. *New Hampshire,* in which Justice Murphy placed "fighting words"—words so insulting they that almost surely will result in a physical response—outside the protection of the First Amendment in the same way that libel and obscenity are not protected speech.

Then also in 1942, another case stands out because of a new consti-tutional principle espoused by its author, Justice Douglas. In *Skinner* v. *Oklahoma,* the Court struck down a mandatory Oklahoma sterilization law for certain criminals. In striking down the law Douglas set forth for the first time what became known as the "fundamental interest test," in which he held that there were certain human rights so fundamental—marriage and procreation among them—that government may not regu-late them to any degree whatsoever, without an overwhelming showing of need. This theory later would become central to the finding within the Constitution of the implied right of privacy and the entire debate over the abortion issue.

As happened in World War I, the war years of the Second World War brought difficult times to the Court and its new Chief Justice. Various war measures were adopted limiting the First Amendment in one way or another. Most of the country supported these wartime limitations. In an unusual special Court session in July 1942, the Court revisited a Civil War issue and upheld Roosevelt's right, as commander-in-chief, to order accused German saboteurs tried by military courts rather than civilian. Then in later years of the war, the Court also upheld in several decisions the ability of the president to order the rights of Japanese Americans curtailed, and then to relocate them to detention camps for the balance of the war.

But in 1943 the new more liberal majority made a brave decision for wartime. In 1940, in *Minersville School District* v. *Gobitis,* the Court had upheld a state's mandatory flag-salute rule for schoolchildren. Walter Gobitis had objected on behalf of his two children, on the basis of their religious beliefs. Now three years later, in *West Virginia State Board of Education* v. *Barnette,* by a 6–3 vote, the Court reversed itself, with Justice Jackson expanding significantly the reach of the First Amendment. He wrote:

The very purpose of a Bill of Rights was to withdraw certain subjects from the vicissitudes of political controversy, to place them beyond the reach of majorities and officials and to establish them as legal principles to be applied by the courts. . . . No official, high or petty, can prescribe what shall be orthodox in politics, nationalism, religion, or other matters of opinion or force citizens to confess by word or act their faith therein.

On April 26, 1946, Chief Justice Stone was reading an opinion from the bench when he suffered a fatal stroke. He had served on the Court for twenty-one years, but had sat in the center chair only five. His unexpected death caused a minor crisis. Harry Truman was now president, and it was clear that his inclination was to elevate one of the sitting justices. Personally, he was closest to Justice Robert Jackson, whom he had asked to go to Germany to act as the U.S. prosecutor in the Nuremberg War Trials. Jackson was not well liked by his fellow justices. While Jackson lobbied Truman from Europe for the job, at least two, and possibly three, of the other justices told Truman they would resign if Roberts was elevated. Finally, Truman decided the only way to resolve the problem was to bring in an outsider, so he nominated Treasury Secretary Fred M. Vinson. The well-liked Vinson was quickly confirmed.

The Vinson Court was burdened with cases growing out of the limits on freedoms that had been imposed during the war, and problems growing out of the hunt for Communists that so preoccupied the nation in the early cold war years. As the war started, Congress had toughened the old Sedition and Espionage Acts by merging them into the new Alien Registration Act, known popularly as the Smith Act. The new law dealt mainly with the supposed Communist threat. It made it a crime to advocate or conspire to advocate the overthrow of the government. Its Section II read in part: "It shall be unlawful for any person . . . with the intent to cause the overthrow or destruction of any government in the United States, to print, publish, edit, issue, circulate, sell, distribute or publicly display any written or printed matter advocating, advising or teaching the duty, necessity, desirability or propriety of overthrowing or destroying any government in the United States by force or violence."

Even though this sweeping law was on the books, during the war years the Roosevelt administration resisted using and abusing it. Only two prosecutions were undertaken: one of a group of members of the Socialist Workers party (actually a Trotskyite faction of a Teamsters local in Minneapolis) that resulted in convictions upheld on appeal and which the Supreme Court refused to review; the other a group of thirty-one neo-Nazis who were never retried after a mistrial was declared when the judge died halfway through their long first trial.

But in 1948, the government prosecuted twelve leaders of the U.S. Communist party, including Eugene Dennis, its general secretary, in an epic year-long trial. It was in the appeal from Dennis's conviction (*Dennis v. United States*) that the Court eventually got a chance to pass judgment on the Smith Act. In the 1951 decision, Chief Justice Vinson upheld the law by rejecting the idea that there is under the Constitution some right to rebellion where peaceful means to change exist. "No one could conceive that it is not within the power of Congress to prohibit acts intended to overthrow the Government by force or violence."

But in so doing, Vinson also began to weaken Holmes's old "clear and present danger" formula. When the case had originally been appealed to the Second Circuit Court of Appeals, Judge Learned Hand had upheld the conviction and, in doing so, went into an analysis well beyond the old Holmes's test. Hand formulated a new test that might be termed the "gravity of the potential evil," discounted by the improbability of the defendant in bringing it about.

In some ways the new Hand test was a reversion to the old "bad tendency" test, and certainly fell far short of the idea contained in Brandeis's dissent in the *Whitney* case that speech can never be "clear and present" unless the danger is absolutely imminent. Vinson, however, liked this new formula, so he incorporated it into his decision, which had as its basis the reasoning that the Smith Act sought to regulate "advocacy," not "discussion"—a distinction that Justices Black and Douglas attacked in blistering dissents. They believed you might be able to legally distinguish between overt acts and speech, but not between discussion and advocacy. The decision emboldened the government, and in the next six years 145 indictments and 89 convictions were obtained under the Smith Act.

This was only one of a number of decisions the Vinson Court made upholding various anti-Communist laws. For instance, in *American Communications Association v. Douds*, a 5–3 majority upheld a provision of the Taft-Hartley Labor Act stripping union officials of their powers if they did not take an oath that they were not members of the Communist party. Here, as in *Dennis*, Vinson applied a balancing test instead of a "clear and present danger" test.

The Vinson Court is probably best remembered for a decision that went against the government and that permanently set limits on presidential power. Known as the great steel seizure case, †*Youngstown Sheet & Tube v. Sawyer* (1951) overturned President Truman's attempted seizure of steel plants to prevent a strike that he said would hurt the Korean War effort.

In other decisions the Vinson Court had its difficulties figuring out whether the Bill of Rights applied to the states. On several occasions it ruled that the First Amendment did not. But then on other occasions it ruled that the Fourth Amendment protection against unreasonable searches did (*Wolf* v. *Colorado*, 1949); that states could not segregate rail cars (*Morgan* v. *Virginia*, 1946); and that the Eighth Amendment protection against cruel and unusual punishment did apply to states (*Francis* v. *Resweber*, 1947).

The Vinson Court rejected several opportunities to overturn *Plessy* v. *Ferguson's* separate but equal holding. But what they did do in several different opinions was put teeth into *Plessy* by insisting that blacks be admitted to various schools unless it could be shown that, beyond any doubt, the alternative facilities were really equal. Then going further, in *McLaurin* v. *Oklahoma*, Vinson ruled that once a black is admitted to an institution, he must have equal access to all parts and facilities of it.

In the later years of Vinson's term, the National Association for the Advancement of Colored People (NAACP) began a concerted drive against the separate but equal doctrine. The NAACP began five lawsuits against school segregation, one each in South Carolina, Virginia, Delaware, Kansas, and the District of Columbia. Its argument in each was simply that separate is not equal, and thus *Plessy* v. *Ferguson* should be overturned.

Two cases emerged as the lead cases: †*Brown* v. *Board of Education of Topeka, Kansas*, brought by a black father on behalf of his daughter who had to walk twenty blocks to an all-black school because the neighborhood school was all white; and *Briggs* v. *Elliott*, a similar challenge to a South Carolina state-wide segregation plan. The Court heard the five cases together in December 1952. Justice-to-be Thurgood Marshall argued for the NAACP; former Solicitor General John Davis argued for the states. He was fresh off his victory in the steel seizure case, and was considered the nation's leading Supreme Court advocate. His main client, present in the courtroom, was South Carolina Governor, and former Associate Justice, James Byrnes.

The arguments were long and emotional. Davis argued strongly that the Fourteenth Amendment never intended states to forbid separate facilities according to race, only to forbid unequal facilities. Marshall countered by looking at the legislative history of the amendment and by arguing the evidence that being excluded made black children feel inferior. Six months passed without a decision. Then in June 1953, as the Court was about to recess for the summer, Chief Justice Vinson announced that the Court wanted the case reargued in December.

The summer was to become a very emotional one for the Court. As it was, several of the justices already were not getting along. Then came the final appeal of Julius and Ethel Rosenberg, accused of passing atomic secrets to the Soviets. On six occasions as their case progressed through the lower courts, the Rosenbergs had appealed their case to the Court. On all six occasions, no more than three justices had agreed to order a stay of execution until the fall term, when the full Court could decide whether to review the case.

The outcry was intense. There were calls for Douglas's impeachment. Vinson called the Court back into extraordinary session for only the second time in Court history. The justices fought for days over whether to continue the stay and hear the case in the fall. At one point there were four votes to continue the stay. But then under heavy pressure Justice Burton was prevailed upon to change his vote. The stay was lifted, and the Rosenbergs were executed. The fight left the justices bitterly divided.

Three weeks before the new term was to start, Chief Justice Vinson died in his sleep of a heart attack, at the relatively young age of sixty-three. President Eisenhower knew he could not promote one of the feuding justices, so he looked outside the Court. The years before, when Eisenhower was still fighting for the GOP nomination, the popular three-time Republican governor of California, Earl Warren, had endorsed him, and quite possibly ensured the former general of the nomination. At the time Warren said he wanted to be remembered if any Supreme Courts seats came open. It is likely that neither he, nor Eisenhower, ever had the Chief Justiceship in mind. But now that he needed an outsider, Eisenhower thought he could probably not go wrong with the low-keyed governor. Little did he realize it, but Eisenhower changed the face of the Court, perhaps forever. He would come to say that Warren's appointment was "the biggest damn fool mistake I ever made." That, of course, is a matter of perspective.

# The Warren Court

Warren received his appointment while the Senate was in recess, so he did not have to wait to be confirmed before beginning his tenure. He rushed to Washington and was in the center chair when the Court began its new term on the first Monday of October. The first sixty days passed quickly and uneventfully. Everyone's attention was focused on the upcoming rearguing of *Brown*. Relations between the justices had deteriorated to the point that most observers believed it would be virtually impossible to get all nine to agree to anything. So a split decision was expected in *Brown*, and supporters of the NAACP began to fear the worst after justices like Frankfurter seemed openly hostile to Thurgood Marshall in questioning, while seeming to ask Davis only encouraging questions.

Another six months passed, with the Senate taking its time before even bothering to start Warren's confirmation hearings. The nomination was considered noncontroversial, and finally in May the Senate Judiciary Committee turned its attention to the former governor of California and quickly confirmed him. It was only a few days later, on May 17, 1954, that Warren announced his first major opinion—the unanimous decision in *Brown*. This landmark that Warren had authored was unusual for its directness, for its eloquence, and for its brevity—thirteen paragraphs long in its entirety. After fifty-eight years, the Court was striking down *Plessy*. Warren did not bother trying to puzzle out the legislative intent behind the Fourteenth Amendment. Instead he simply agreed with Thurgood Marshall's argument, holding that "separate educational facilities are inherently unequal."

But the Court was not through with *Brown*. *Brown I*, as the May 1954 decision became known, made no mention of a remedy. So all five cases were ordered reargued yet again, on the question of what should be done to end educational segregation. A year later, on May 31, 1955, Warren announced another unanimous decision. In a ruling called *Brown II*, the justices decided that local federal courts would supervise local school board efforts to desegregate, and that all desegregation must be accomplished "with all deliberate speed." Under *Brown II*, some federal courts began more than thirty-five years of supervision of local school districts, some to the point that federal judges, de facto, actually took over the operation of school districts that resisted desegregation orders.

Since Taft, as president, had greatly influenced the direction of the Court with his six nominations, and then Roosevelt had eventually dominated it with his nine, Eisenhower now had his opportunity. A year after he appointed Warren, Justice Jackson died. To replace him, Eisenhower selected New York attorney John Marshall Harlan, grandson of the justice for whom he was named. Justice Minton retired in 1956, and Eisenhower named New Jersey Supreme Court judge William Brennan, Jr. Brennan became the first justice to serve on the court who was born in the twentieth century. Then Justice Reed retired, and Eisenhower named federal judge Charles Whittaker to succeed him. Finally, Eisenhower got to name his fifth justice when Justice Burton retired. To fill his seat, Eisenhower chose federal judge Potter Stewart.

What all five had in common were their generally moderate views. But compared to the conservative justices since the turn of the century, these Eisenhower appointments transformed the Court into a much more liberal body, with a much greater interest in civil rights and individual liberties. This showed clearly in numerous decisions that came out of the late 1950s.

On June 17, 1957, a day quickly dubbed "Red Monday" by conservative commentators, the Court handed down two controversial opinions. In *Yates* v. *United States*, the justices made it more difficult for the government to undertake Smith Act prosecutions by holding that an accused had to be directly involved in overt acts to overthrow the government, not simply to be abstractly advocating rebellion. Then in †*Watkins* v. *United States*, the Court struck down a congressional contempt citation against a union official who would not talk about alleged Communist activities of others. In doing so, Warren ruled that congressional hearings must have some legitimate legislative purpose and that Congress could not "expose for the sake of exposure."

Two weeks later, again on the same day, came two more controversial opinions. In *Mallory* v. *United States*, the Court reversed the conviction and death sentence of an accused rapist in the District of Columbia, on the grounds that he had been held in custody for an extended period before he was brought before a magistrate and told of his rights. In the second case, the famous †*Roth* v. *United States*, the Court placed obscenity as among those forms of speech outside the protection of the First Amendment, and then tried to adopt standards for judging what is obscene.

The next year, the Court unanimously threw out an attempt by the state of Alabama to get at the membership lists of the NAACP, and thereby strengthened the constitutional protection to the right of assembly.

By now the south was in full revolt against the desegregation orders flowing from federal courts as a result of *Brown II*. In August, the Conference of Chief Justices, made up of the heads of all the state courts, passed a motion at its annual meeting all but condemning Warren and the rest of the new, more liberal majority for their activism and "lack of judicial restraint." Completely unmoved by this act, Warren—less than a week later—called the Court into special session to quickly decide *Cooper* v. *Aaron*, a case growing out of the attempt by Little Rock, Arkansas, school officials to delay desegregation. In a unanimous opinion, signed by all nine justices for emphasis, the Court ruled that neither state officials nor state legislatures could directly or indirectly interfere with or attempt to nullify court-ordered desegregation plans. Then in 1964, in *Griffin* v. *Prince Edward County*, the Court struck down a plan by a southern Virginia county seeking to get around a desegregation order by closing its public schools and "donating" county funds to newly opened "private" schools that admitted only whites.

Between 1959 and 1961, the Warren Court seemed to pause to consider its actions, at least in the area of sedition and subversive activities. In something of a compromise on the subject of congressional investigations, the Court took a step backward from its position in *Watkins*, and introduced in *Barenblatt* v. *United States* a public interest versus private rights test to judge the legitimacy of congressional investigations. Then in *Communist Party* v. *Subversive Activities Control Board*, the Court ruled that it was not unconstitutional to require the Communist party, or any subversive organization, to register with the Justice Department and to be required to provide financial statements. Likewise, in *Scales* v. *United States* and *Noto* v. *United States*, the majority ruled that the First Amendment was not violated by a law penalizing active membership in specific subversive organizations. All these were identical 5–4 votes with Warren, Black, Douglas, and Brennan dissenting.

But in other areas during and after this period the Court extended individual rights. With Justice Stewart as the swing vote, the Court ruled 5–4 that evidence illegally obtained by state authorities could not be turned over to federal prosecutors for use in federal trials (the so-called silver platter rule). Then in the landmark *Mapp* v. *Ohio*, this time with Justice Tom Clark as the swing vote, a 5–4 majority voted to extend to state trials the prohibition on the introduction of evidence obtained in illegal searches as a violation of the Fourth Amendment.

In voting rights, the Warren Court took a much more activist stance in the area of state elections, and particularly in the area of reapportionment. Previously the Court had viewed the setting of voting districts as political questions not open to federal court review. But now the majority held that reapportionment is a Fifteenth Amendment matter. In *Gomillion* v. *Lightfoot*, the majority ruled it was unconstitutional for the state of Ala-

bama to exclude all blacks from a specific voting district. In the landmark
†*Baker* v. *Carr*, the Court greatly expanded the federal reach in state
apportionment matters as it struck down an attempt by Arkansas to concentrate black voters in a few districts by simply refusing, for most of the
twentieth century, to reapportion at all. With *Baker*, the Court gave a green
light to petitioners to use the federal courts to redress state apportionment
grievances; within two years lawsuits were being heard in forty-one states.
Then in 1965 the justices ruled in *Reynolds* v. *Sims* that both houses of a
state legislature must be apportioned according to the dictates of "one
man, one vote." Wrote Chief Justice Warren in this landmark decision:
"Legislators represent people, not trees or acres."

In 1962 President John Kennedy got the opportunity to replace two
of the justices who had tended to vote more conservatively: Whittaker and
Frankfurter. To succeed them he chose Deputy Attorney General Byron
White and Labor Secretary Arthur Goldberg. The latter was key because
all during his short tenure he almost always gave Warren the fifth vote he
needed to form a majority on most issues.

The Warren Court was now ready to make a very fundamental shift
in emphasis in constitutional jurisprudence. From the time of its ratification in 1868, the Court had continuously held that the Fourteenth Amendment's due process clause protected property and property rights, not
individual rights and personal freedoms. That emphasis had started to shift
slightly with decisions like *Powell* (1922) and *Palko* (1937). But now the
Warren Court, in a series of landmark decisions that have been called
nothing less than a "due process revolution," was ready to make a forceful
statement that the Fourteenth Amendment applied to all rights, not just
property rights.

This especially showed up in a series of criminal law decisions in
which the Court extended various federal constitutional protections to state
criminal proceedings and to state criminal defendants. In *Robertson* v.
*California*, the majority held that it was cruel and unusual punishment to
make narcotics addiction a crime.[10] Then in the landmark †*Gideon* v.
*Wainwright*, the majority ruled that states must provide all criminal defendants with attorneys if they are unable to pay for ones themselves. In
†*Malloy* v. *Hogan*, the majority extended the Fifth Amendment protection

---

10. Subsequent decisions upheld the constitutionality of laws making it illegal to possess narcotics
or controlled substances, even though addiction itself is not a crime.

against self-incrimination to state trials and courts; and in *Griffin* v. *California*, the Court ruled that a state prosecutor cannot make an adverse reference to a defendant's use of his Fifth Amendment rights. Then in †*Escobedo* v. *Illinois*, the justices ruled that any confession obtained in violation of a suspect's rights cannot be used in court.

The *Escobedo* ruling was rather vague, and it left unanswered some major questions—chiefly whether a suspect had to be appointed free counsel in every case; when in the process this right becomes mandatory; and whether, and how, a suspect can waive his right to counsel. Over the next two years more than 160 appeals were filed with the Court effectively seeking clarification of *Escobedo*. Sorting through these, the justices chose four to be argued. They were then combined into †*Miranda* v. *Arizona*, probably the most important criminal rights decision of the era. In *Miranda*, the Court ruled that suspects in police custody must be informed of their constitutional rights to remain silent, to have an attorney appointed and be present, and be told that anything they say may be used against them at trial before questioning by police can begin.

While many of the decisions of this period showed a sharp split by the Court, not all this era's decisions extending civil liberties had dissenting justices. Ever since the civil rights cases in 1883, the Court had placed private discrimination beyond any legal remedy. No more. In †*Heart of Atlanta Motel*, the Court unanimously ruled that under the commerce clause Congress can outlaw discrimination in any institution that is in, or affects, interstate commerce. In doing so, the justices upheld the Civil Rights Act of 1964; their definition of what is considered "in or affecting interstate commerce" was so broad as to include just about all forms of public accommodation.

In this period, in addition to the Civil Rights Act, Congress also passed the Voting Rights Act and later the Fair Housing Act. Both outlawed various forms of discrimination. As with the Civil Rights Act, the Warren Court quickly upheld them—the Voting Rights Act in *South Carolina* v. *Katzenbach*, and the Fair Housing Act in *Jones* v. *Alfred Mayer Company*.

In the mid-1960s, the Court underwent another significant membership change. President Lyndon Johnson wanted badly to make his mark on the Court, but given the justices' relative youth, he feared his time would pass. So he persuaded Justice Goldberg to accept the ambassadorship to the United Nations, and in his place Johnson appointed his friend and close adviser, the very liberal Abe Fortas. Then when Justice Tom Clark retired to avoid any conflict with his son Ramsey, who had been appointed attorney general, Johnson appointed NAACP lawyer Thurgood Marshall as the Court's first black justice.

In its quest to extend personal liberties, the Court struck down a state law that forbade married couples from using birth control. In †*Griswold v. Connecticut*, the seven-member majority—in six separate opinions of which Justice Douglas's is considered the lead—based its decision on a constitutionally guaranteed "zone of privacy" that is not specific, but which Douglas said can be implied from the First, Third, Fourth, Fifth, and Ninth Amendments. In a precursor to the abortion rights debate, in a blistering dissent, Justice Black said that a close reading of his copy of the Constitution could find no such implied right. Then in 1967, the justices agreed unanimously to strike down, in †*Virginia* v. *Loving*, a state law that prohibited interracial marriages.

Also without any dissenting justices, the Court made the most significant press-freedom ruling in Court history. In †*New York Times* v. *Sullivan*, the Court made it difficult for public officials to sue the news media for libel. In doing so the Court significantly extended First Amendment protections.

In June 1968, at the end of the 1967–68 term, Chief Justice Warren announced his intention to retire as soon as his successor was confirmed. Johnson immediately announced he was sending the name of Abe Fortas to the Senate for confirmation. That decision caused a fire storm of protest from both Republicans and southern Democrats. Johnson had announced that he was not running for reelection. Republicans were not about to give a lame duck president the right to name a Chief Justice when they suspected that Richard Nixon would capture the Oval Office in less than a year. The opposition to Fortas became so intense, that he asked Johnson to withdraw his name. The president did so, but those who opposed Fortas kept up their attacks. When opponents in the Senate began to call for his impeachment after news accounts accused him of unethical conduct, Fortas resigned his seat even while continuing to claim his innocence. In the meantime, Chief Justice Warren continued to serve for an additional eleven months.

In that term, the Court made one final ruling to complete the constitutional revolution it had started. In †*Benton* v. *Maryland*, the justices threw out the *Palko* decision and extended all Fifth Amendment rights—and specifically double jeopardy—to all state courts. By the time Warren left to return home to California, the Court had extended, one-by-one, virtually every protection of the Bill of Rights to the states.

# The Burger Court

In his 1968 presidential effort, Richard Nixon made bringing conservatives to the Court a major campaign promise. Once inaugurated in January 1969, Nixon announced that he had decided to allow Chief Justice Warren to serve out the term and would announce his successor in May, to give the Senate plenty of time to confirm his choice before the start of the new term in October. Probably no Supreme Court nomination has ever been made with more fanfare. Nixon was determined to show how important he considered the appointment. He made the announcement on nationwide television, in prime time, and with his entire cabinet present. His choice: Warren E. Burger of Minnesota, for the previous thirteen years a conservative judge on the Court of Appeals for the District of Columbia. The choice had not been an easy one for Nixon. He had considered and rejected his attorney general, John Mitchell. Then he was on the verge of offering to elevate Justice Potter Stewart, but Stewart declined and reportedly counseled Nixon to look outside the current Court. So Nixon ended up choosing Burger, most likely because of Burger's outspoken opposition to many of the rulings of the Warren Court, especially in the area of criminal rights.

But quite possibly no Chief Justice has come to the Court with a background as filled with contradictions. As a young lawyer in Minneapolis, Burger was known as a defender of individual rights, and at one time served as co-chairman of the Minnesota Commission on Human Rights. In his thirteen years on the court of appeals, he had developed a reputation as an expert in the area of court administration, and had exhibited a moderately conservative voting record. But he was also a sharp critic of the activism of the Warren Court. During his Senate confirmation, Burger put on his most moderate face and was easily confirmed. But it was clear he was Nixon's choice because the president believed Burger would move the Court back to the right.

Nixon was determined to give his new Chief Justice help right from the start. The Fortas seat was still empty, and Nixon nominated South Carolina appeals court judge Clement Haynsworth. Senate liberals were still outraged at the way Fortas had been hounded from the Court. They had accepted Burger without much of a fuss. But with Haynsworth, they drew the line. Using media reports of a conflict of interest as a pretext, the Senate rejected Haynsworth 55–45. So the seat remained empty into 1970, with Nixon still determined to name a conservative southerner. So his next choice was Florida Appeals Judge C. Harrold Carswell. It turned out that, given Carswell's racial attitudes and his undistinguished-at-best record on the appeals court, he had even more problems than Haynsworth. The Senate rejected him 51–45. Finally in May, Nixon accepted Burger's suggestion and nominated Harry Blackmun, an appeals court judge from Minnesota and an old friend of the Chief Justice. Blackmun was confirmed unanimously, and took his seat in time for the start of the 1971–72 term.

Because of changes in the Court's membership, the Burger years can roughly be divided into two parts, with election of Ronald Reagan in 1981 as the dividing line. It is clear that Burger came to the Court with restraint in mind, and in the pre-Reagan years of his tenure much of what the Court did was reactive to what the Warren Court had decided previously. But in its first decade—somewhat surprisingly—the Burger Court did not overturn any of the landmarks of the Warren years; rather, it narrowed and modified some of the focus of its predecessor. And in a number of areas, especially press and speech freedom, the Burger Court established its own landmarks.

After Burger and Blackmun were seated, the public and the legal community watched closely to see if the Court would begin to backtrack in a number of key areas. One was school desegregation, and Burger was quick to show that there would be no retreat from *Brown*. In *Swann* v. *Board of Education*, in Burger's first important opinion, a unanimous Court upheld the use of busing and racial quotas as a means of achieving desegregation.

But one area in which Burger was intent on taking at least a small step back was criminal procedure. Burger was known to think the Court had gone too far in *Miranda*. Now in his first term he authored *Harris* v. *New York*, in which he ruled on behalf of a narrow five-man majority that not all uses of an illegally obtained confession were barred. While such a confession could not be introduced as evidence directly against a defendant in trial court, it could be used to impeach a defendant if he chose to take the witness stand.

In Burger's first term, an important church-state issue was argued. Pennsylvania and Rhode Island had laws allowing the state to pay teachers of secular subjects in parochial schools. Writing for a unanimous Court in *Lemon* v. *Kurtzman*, Burger said that state aid to a church-sponsored school might be permissible if it did not lead to "an excessive government entanglement with religion." He established a three-part test to determine the degree of entanglement of any such aid, and in the case at hand the payments failed the test. Thus the two state laws were thrown out.

But Burger's big initial test came in one of the most famous cases to reach the Supreme Court in modern times. At issue in the Pentagon papers case (actually †*New York Times* v. *United States* and *United States* v. *Washington Post*) was whether the two newspapers should be allowed to print portions of a top-secret report on the origins of U.S. involvement in the Vietnam War. The case moved through the courts at a record pace. The Supreme Court received the case on June 24. It was argued the next day, and only four days later the justices struck a major blow to the Nixon administration by unanimously agreeing, in an unsigned order, that any prior restraint to publication bears a "heavy presumption against its constitutional validity." Then voting 6–3, in nine separate opinions, the justices ruled that the government had not met this burden in regard to this Vietnam report.

If Nixon was unhappy that in their first term Burger and Blackmun had not been able to turn the Court further to the right, he had an immediate chance to accelerate the process. Just before the opening of the 1971–72 term, both Justices Black and Harlan retired because of failing health. Black died just eight days later, and Harlan was dead before Christmas. To replace them, Nixon chose Lewis Powell, a Virginia lawyer and former president of the American Bar Association, and William Rehnquist, an assistant attorney general. Nixon chose both for their conservative views, but they were quickly confirmed by the Senate. Nixon had now been able, in only his first term, to keep his campaign pledge to bring conservatives to the Court. But despite there now being four Nixon justices voting, in the next term the Court continued to expand personal liberties by striking down nearly all uses of the death penalty (*Furman* v. *Georgia*); facing for the first time the issue of sexual discrimination and ruling (*Frontiero* v. *Richardson*) that any gender-based classification must be considered constitutionally suspect; and, in a stinging rebuke to the Nixon administration, holding that even in national security cases the government cannot wiretap without judicial approval.

It was the next term that brought the Burger Court its most famous case, and the Court's most controversial decision of the generation. Two pseudonymous plaintiffs, Jane Roe of Texas and Jane Doe of Georgia, both were seeking abortions that were against the laws of their respective states. In an opinion authored by Justice Blackmun, with only Justices Rehnquist and White dissenting, the Court struck down both state laws as violating the Constitution's implied right of privacy, the same implied right that Justice Douglas had first postulated in *Griswold* v. *Connecticut*.

But the Court during this period did continue to narrow some of the decisions of its predecessor. In *United States* v. *Calandra*, a six-man majority greatly narrowed the scope of the exclusionary rule by holding that the exclusion of illegally seized evidence is not a constitutional requirement but, rather, a judicial remedy created to deter police misconduct. That being the case, the majority ruled, a "cost-benefit" analysis must be undertaken to determine what permissible uses there might be for such evidence. In this case evidence obtained in an illegal search was allowed to be presented to a grand jury.

In the area of obscenity, in the landmark †*Miller* v. *California*, a narrow five-man majority led by Chief Justice Burger set out a new test for determining what is obscene, and in doing so allowed communities to develop their own locally based standards for what is obscene, rather than rely on a single national standard. This allowed for more widespread local obscenity prosecutions. Then in a major desegregation ruling, the Burger majority struck down a federal judge's plan to solve the massive segregation in Detroit's public schools by effectively merging them with surrounding, mostly white suburban school districts. The Court ruled that desegregation plans could not cross school district borders.

In an important free press ruling, *Branzburg* v. *Hayes*, the Court ruled, 5–4, that a reporter's notes could be subpoenaed and that a reporter could be held in contempt for refusing to answer a grand jury's questions. The result of this was the passage of state reporter shield laws. In the area of libel, the Court narrowed the definition of who is a public figure (*Gertz* v. *Robert Welch*). In a major church-state ruling, the justices held that a state could allow a parent to take tax deductions for parochial school expenses so long as all parents of all schoolchildren—public, private, and parochial—were allowed to take the same kind of deductions. In the area of sex discrimination, the Court struck down (*Craig* v. *Boren*) an Oklahoma law that set different drinking ages for men and women.

But if this was now the "Nixon Court," it had a funny way of showing it. Watergate Special Prosecutor Archibald Cox had subpoenaed tape recordings Richard Nixon had made in the Oval Office, and Nixon resisted turning them over, claiming executive privilege. After Federal District Judge John Sirica ordered the tapes surrendered, the Court received the White House's appeal—*United States* v. *U.S. District Court*. Unanimously, the justices ruled against the president. Going back all the way to

*Marbury* v. *Madison*, Chief Justice Burger found that while there might be a "preemptive privilege for Presidential communication," this privilege must be weighed against the needs of the criminal justice system.

In this period, Chief Justice Burger's greatest contribution may well have been internal to the operation of the Court. No Chief Justice since Taft was more intent on modernizing the Court. In Burger's first years, the Court was introduced to the computer age. Burger convinced his fellow justices to no longer read entire opinions from the bench, and to again shorten the time allotted to counsel to argue—from two hours per case to a single hour (one half-hour for each side). He also brought together a blue ribbon panel of legal experts to study the Court's case load and to make suggestions for greater efficiency. At the same time, more than any Chief Justice in memory, Burger was active in other Washington institutions, as a member of the boards of the Smithsonian and the National Gallery of Art.

In 1975 the Court's character changed further with the retirement of Justice Douglas, after serving a record thirty-six plus years. President Gerald Ford named appeals court judge John Paul Stevens to replace him; this would be the Court's only change for almost six years. Stevens was Gerald Ford's only appointment, and in an unusual happenstance, his successor, Jimmy Carter, became the only president to ever serve a full four-year term without being able to make at least one appointment to the Court.

The last half of the 1970s was a busy time for the Court, and a time when it began—slowly—to show its more conservative nature. In a 1976 decision, †*National League of Cities* v. *Usery*—in what seemed like a throwback to the 1920s—the Court limited Congress's use of its commerce power. The case involved an attempt to extend minimum wage protection to state and municipal workers. The Court struck it down on the basis of the long-neglected Tenth Amendment.[11] Then the new more conservative majority reinstated the death penalty based on new capital punishment statutes that states had drafted in the wake of the Court's 1972 ruling striking down all existing capital punishment laws. But while reinstating capital punishment, the Court also ruled separately, 5–4 (†*Gregg* v. *Geor-*

---

11. This actually remains a hot issue with the Court. In 1985, in *San Antonio* v. *Transit Authority*, a narrow five-member majority overturned Rehnquist's decision in *National League of Cities*. In a bitter dissent, the four dissenting justices, led by Rehnquist, said in effect that as soon as the proper case comes along it intends to revisit the subject of the relationship between Congress and state sovereignty.

*gia*), that the death penalty cannot be made mandatory. In every case, said the Court, there must be a separate sentencing hearing held, after guilt has been established, in which mitigating factors must be weighed. The Court also began to limit the use of affirmative action programs in professional schools †(*University of California* v. *Bakke*), but allowed widespread voluntary programs in industry (*Steelworkers* v. *Weber*).

The nature and makeup of the Court really began to change with the election of Ronald Reagan. Justice Stevens had long said that he would retire at age sixty-five. He waited until after the election, so within weeks of his inauguration President Reagan was able to make his first appointment to the Court. It was precedent shattering. Sandra Day O'Connor became the first woman named to the Court.

In the early 1980s the Burger Court continued to narrow further the rights of criminal suspects or defendants. In several exclusionary rule cases, the Court lowered the "probable cause" standards needed to obtain valid search warrants. In another, †*United States* v. *Leon*, it held a search to be valid because the police officer conducting it thought it was valid, even though it turned out he was using a technically invalid search warrant. This case established what is known as the "good faith exception." Then in *New York* v. *Quarles*, the Court established a "public safety exception" to the requirement that an arrestee must be immediately told of his constitutional rights. In situations "presenting danger," the Court ruled, police can ask questions first and issue *Miranda* warnings later. But in an exception to this narrowing of defendants' rights, in 1983 (*Solem* v. *Helm*), the Court ruled for the first time that a prison sentence of a fixed term of years can violate the Eighth Amendment's stricture against cruel and unusual punishment. Previously, the Court had made such rulings only in death penalty or life-sentence cases.

The early 1980s also brought a surprisingly strong reaffirmation of the Court's holding in †*Roe* v. *Wade*. In *Akron* v. *Akron Reproductive Health Center*, six justices, including Chief Justice Burger, strongly upheld the right of abortion based on the reasoning in *Roe*. Somewhat surprisingly, the Court's only woman, Justice O'Connor, did not agree and in a long dissent indicated that she favored at least modifying the trimester approach of *Roe*.

At the end of the 1985–86 term, in June 1986, Chief Justice Burger announced his intention to step down so he could concentrate on his leadership of the national commission to celebrate the 200th anniversary of the signing of the Constitution. Three days later, President Reagan announced his intention of elevating Associate Justice William Rehnquist to the center chair.

## The Rehnquist Court

The Reagan White House anticipated few problems in securing Rehnquist's confirmation. But various liberal, civil rights, and union groups mounted a strong campaign against him, and suddenly the White House found itself in a major fight. But in the end, Rehnquist prevailed 65–33. At the same time he elevated Rehnquist, Reagan named appeals court judge Antonin Scalia to take Rehnquist's seat. Scalia, a recognized scholar, was almost overlooked during the heat of the fight over Rehnquist's elevation. Scalia was quickly confirmed by the Senate despite being even more conservative then the new Chief Justice.

Then at the end of the 1986–87 term, Justice Powell announced his retirement. What ensued was the most intense confirmation battle of the 20th century. To replace Powell, Reagan chose Judge Robert Bork, like Scalia a member of the Court of Appeals of the District of Columbia. Bork was widely considered perhaps the most conservative jurist in the federal judiciary, and he had been extremely controversial during the Reagan years when, as solicitor general, he had fired Watergate Special Prosecutor Archibald Cox. Virtually every civil rights and liberal interest group opposed Bork. The battle over this confirmation raged through the summer of 1987. Finally, he was rejected 58–42. Reagan immediately named another conservative from the same appeals court, Douglas Ginsburg, to the seat. Again the nominee was opposed by liberal and civil rights groups. But even before the nomination was officially transmitted to the Senate, Ginsburg asked that his name be withdrawn after it was revealed that while a professor at Harvard Law School he had smoked marijuana. Finally Reagan named Judge Anthony Kennedy, from the Ninth Circuit Court of Appeals in San Francisco, to Powell's seat. He was confirmed without opposition.

Now only Brennan and Marshall remained from the liberal heart of the Warren Court. Ronald Reagan had appointed the Chief Justice and three other conservatives. Yet, he did not win any major victories from the Court during his last two years in office. It was not from lack of trying. Issues that were important to the conservatives in the White House and the Justice Department—a ban on abortion, eliminating affirmative action programs across-the-board, returning prayer to public school classrooms, went nowhere.

Moreover, the Reagan Administration lost the case that was possibly most important to it, a challenge to the special prosecutor law. In *Morrison v. Olson*, by a vote of 7–1 with only Justice Scalia dissenting, the Court upheld the law which authorizes a special three-judge panel to appoint a special prosecutor from outside the government to investigate government wrongdoing. In upholding the law, the Court effectively upheld the convictions of two Reagan administration officials who had been indicted by a special prosecutor.

In the 1989 term, the Rehnquist Court still continued to drift. In one of its two most important decisions, *Webster* v. *Reproductive Health*, it narrowed abortion rights somewhat, but stopped short of overturning *Roe* v. *Wade* and a woman's basic constitutional right to an abortion. Then in *Texas* v. *Johnson*, the Court came down strongly on the side of the First Amendment in upholding flag burning as a constitutionally protected political act.

Then in 1990 the first of the two remaining old-line liberals, Justice Brennan, retired. To replace him President George Bush selected a little known New Hampshire judge, David Souter, who had served only shortly on the Court of Appeals. A year later, Justice Marshall retired, and to replace him Bush named a conservative Republican black, Clarence Thomas, head of the Equal Employment Opportunity Commission. His confirmation was long and difficult, amid charges that he had been guilty of sexual harassment. In the end he was confirmed by two votes, the smallest margin of any justice in Court history.

With the appointments of Souter and Thomas, on paper at least, the Rehnquist Court became the most conservative since the Taft Court. But, as became apparent in the 1991–92 term, the Chief Justice still has not been able to fashion a dependable conservative majority to undo many of the Warren Court decisions. What emerged during the 1991–92 term was what some observers called a "cautious middle," comprised of justices Kennedy, Souter, and O'Connor. In his second year on the Court Souter emerged as the key swing vote, beginning to establish himself in the role so long occupied by Justice Potter Stewart. Kennedy, it seemed, was becoming less conservative. In the 1988–89 term he had voted with Scalia, the conservative benchmark of the Court, 93 percent of the time. By the 1991–92 term, that had dropped to 75 percent of the time.

The Rehnquist Court has been able to mount majorities to overturn some minor rulings of the Warren years, and even the Burger years, but there has only been further narrowing of more major areas. The Court especially continues to narrow criminal defendants' rights, and has been uniformly pro-prosecutorial. But it appears there continues to be deep splits among the justices, and no little personal animosity between some.

One result of this more cautious approach by the three justices in the middle was an unusual number of 5–4 votes in key cases. More than half the time in the fourteen such rulings in 1991–92, the three justices in the middle joined with the two justices on the left of the Rehnquist Court, Blackmun and Stevens. This was the lineup in the most important decision of the term, *Planned Parenthood* v. *Casey*, in which the Court upheld a Pennsylvania law putting some restrictions on abortion rights while also upholding a constitutionally based right for a woman to have an abortion at any point before the fetus becomes viable.

It remained clear from his increasingly strident dissents in cases like *Planned Parenthood*, that the activist Rehnquist would like to move aggressively to overturn many of the decisions of the past, especially those that limit government power. It is also clear that Justice Scalia sees himself as the philosophical center of this conservative counterrevolution. And it may still happen. In a concurring opinion in *Planned Parenthood*, Justice Blackmun pointed out that he is 83 and cannot stay on the Court forever. He noted that four justices—Rehnquist, Scalia, White, and Thomas—stood poised to overturn *Roe* v. *Wade*. All they lacked was a fifth vote. He pointed out that vote would be held by the justice who eventually replaced him.

As this is written, the future direction of the Court likely will be held by the president who emerges from the 1992 election. If George Bush wins reelection, it is likely he will continue to appoint conservatives who will finally give Rehnquist his dependable majority. In the meantime, the Rehnquist Court remains deeply divided and continues to drift.

# 3.

# The Decisions
# of the Court:
# The One Hundred
# Most Important Decisions

Ask any group of legal scholars, law professors, and historians to list what they believe are the U.S. Supreme Court's 100 most important decisions, and you likely will end up with very different lists. On each of the lists you would probably find forty or so of the same cases. These cases are so widely recognized as among the most important that there is now something approaching a consensus. But once you get beyond this consensus, you begin an exercise in the subjective.

As with much in life, the importance of a Supreme Court opinion is in the eye of the beholder. Ask a professor of taxation about the most important decisions, and you will likely get a list of opinions whose meaning, let alone worth, can be perceived only by someone knowledgeable about obscure portions of the U.S. Internal Revenue Code. Ask a criminal defense attorney, and the list might include decisions involving the intricacies of criminal procedure. Likewise, ask an historian and

the result might well be cases that helped the Court develop but that hold little relevance to modern society.

The problem is determining the criteria for importance. There have been cases of momentous importance on the day they were decided, but that quickly faded after an intervening act of Congress, a subsequent decision, or simply the passing of an era. There were decisions whose importance went largely unrecognized at the time, but that later grew in importance. Also, there are decisions whose specific cases have long since lost meaning, but that remain of vital importance to history and the development of the Court. And there are decisions of importance, not because of the majority opinion, but because a minority opinion was later adopted by the majority as the correct reasoning.

The following list attempts to satisfy everyone. It recognizes the consensus decisions, while also including decisions that helped develop the Court, our legal system, and its various bodies of law; decisions that had social impact in their day; and decisions that continue to have an impact.

As we have seen, it wasn't until well into this century that the justices turned their attention away from economic and commercial issues and toward individual and civil rights. It was also well into the twentieth century that the Court's case load began to grow—to the point that, in the last decade, the Court has reviewed more cases than it did in its entire first century. That is why three-fourths of these most important decisions are from this century, and more than half are from relatively modern times.

One last note: a certain amount of speculation was necessary in choosing very recent cases—say, from 1985 to the present. Some of these decisions may well be overturned soon or rendered moot by legislation. But right now, they represent issues that will only grow in importance as the years pass.

## 1. CHISLOM V. GEORGIA, 2 DALL. 419 (1793)[1]

Early in the Revolution, British merchant Robert Farquhar sold $170,000 worth of goods to the state of Georgia. After the war the state passed a law extinguishing all Tory debts, and refused to pay Farquhar. He died, and his executor, Alexander Chislom of South Carolina, filed suit in federal court in South Carolina, seeking to collect on the debt.

Georgia refused to answer the complaint, claiming both that federal courts had no jurisdiction over states and that state debts are unenforceable by federal courts. By a 4–1 vote the Supreme Court disagreed. Chief Justice Jay held that under Article III of the Constitution, if the federal court system is to be able to "establish justice," citizens of one state must have the right to sue another state.

The case is not important for the specific result, but rather because it was

---

1. The set of numbers and letters that often follow the name of a legal decision are citation numbers. They refer the reader to where the full opinion is recorded. Since 1875, the opinions of the U.S. Supreme Court are contained in the *United States Reports*, a series of volumes printed by the Government Printing Office.

Typically, you will see the following kind of citation: Smith v. Jones, 234 U.S. 111 (1918). This means that the Court's full opinion in the case of Smith versus Jones, decided in 1918, can be found on page 111 of volume 234 of the *U.S. Reports*.

There are also some commercial services that compile court decisions, including Supreme Court decisions. Typically, they take the complete decision and add other material, such as annotations or excerpts from the briefs on both sides. At times these alternative sources are used because they usually print opinions faster than the GPO. (It takes the GPO months to get its official volumes out.) These alternative sources are cited in various ways, including: L.Ed. (*Lawyers Edition*), S.Ct.—(*Supreme Court Reports*, from West Publishing Co.), or—L.W. (*Law Week*).

Prior to 1875, decisions were compiled and printed according to the last name of the official (or unofficial) court reporter at the time. So in this first case, the citation "2 Dall. 386" means the opinion can be found on page 386 of the second volume of Court opinions printed by Philadelphia lawyer Alexander J. Dallas.

one of the first times the Court applied the theory of federal supremacy, and the first time it exercised its power to invalidate a state law (Georgia's Tory debt law). That is why it is important, even though the verdict elicited rage in the states, with the result it was later (1798) reversed by the Eleventh Amendment, which specifically barred federal court jurisdiction over suits against states for debts and damages.

## 2. HYLTON V. UNITED STATES, 3 DALL. 171 (1796) WARE V. HYLTON, 3 DALL. 199 (1796)

These two cases, decided together, established some important provisions of the legal system. Congress had passed a law establishing a tax on carriages and said that it was to be a direct tax, which, under the Constitution the federal government is suppose to apportion back to the states, based on population. Secretary of the Treasury Alexander Hamilton disagreed, saying it was not a direct tax. Hamilton concocted a test case because he wanted a constitutional ruling on the federal government's taxing power, and especially what constituted a direct tax.

The justices agreed with Hamilton that direct taxes were not just any tax that Congress called direct, but, rather, had been limited by the Constitution to taxes on land or real property. This was the first time the Court struck down an act of Congress as unconstitutional.

In *Ware*, Virginia had passed a law allowing its residents to pay off old pre-Revolution debts to British creditors with depreciated currency or confiscated property. The Court struck down the law, ruling it in conflict with the terms of the treaty with Britain that had ended the war, which guaranteed full repayment of debts. In so holding, the justices ruled that the terms of any federal treaty take precedence over state laws.

## 3. MARBURY V. MADISON, 1 CRANCH 137 (1803)

In early 1801, outgoing president John Adams named William Marbury a District of Columbia justice of the peace. Marbury's commission papers were signed, but not "delivered" the day Adams left office. Therefore his successor, Thomas Jefferson, nullified the appointment. Marbury went to the Supreme Court to compel Jefferson, through Secretary of State James Madison, to install him in office.

Justice John Marshall delivered the opinion of the Court, which stated that although Marbury's right to the appointment was protected by the Constitution, the Court lacked the power to order its delivery. In so ruling, Marshall struck down as unconstitutional Section 13 of the Judiciary Act of 1789, which had authorized the Supreme Court to issue writs ordering federal officials to perform required actions.

This decision was critical to the development of the Court's powers, because it established the Court's right of judicial review for acts of Congress, and to declare them unconstitutional. This case clarified the jurisdiction of the Supreme Court and made its powers equal to the executive and legislative branches of government.

## 4. FLETCHER V. PECK, 6 CRANCH. 87 (1810)

Having held an act of Congress unconstitutional in *Marbury*, the Court now moved for the first time to strike down a state law as unconstitutional.

The Georgia legislature in 1795 was corrupt. Members took bribes to pass a land-grant law under which 35 million acres were sold off in state grants at about two cents an acre. The next year, a newly elected legislature came along and passed a new law nullifying the previous law and repealing all the grants made under it. Most of the grants had gone to insider speculators, who had resold the land to persons who had nothing to do with the bribery. So their titles were declared null and void, and they were losing their property. One such group filed suit in federal court.

Upon review, Chief Justice Marshall ruled that the Georgia repeal law was unconstitutional. He held that the new law, nullifying the land grants, was a clear violation of the Constitution's contract clause for a state act to impair the obligation of a contract. But what was important about the decision was the fact that the Court extended its authority to overturn a state law, on constitutional grounds, and for the first time used the contract clause to safeguard property.

## 5. MARTIN V. HUNTER'S LESSEE, 1 WHEAT 304 (1816)

This decision established the Supreme Court's supremacy in interpreting the Constitution and federal law.

Martin, a British subject, asserted that treaties between England and the United States had given him title to a parcel of land in Virginia. Hunter claimed ownership rights to the same land under a direct grant from Virginia. A state trial court found in favor of Martin's Crown grant, but then a Virginia state appellate court reversed that decision in favor of Hunter's state grant.

The U.S. Supreme Court ruled in favor of Martin and reversed the Virginia appellate court. But the state court refused to enter judgment in favor of Martin. Therefore, the Supreme Court received the case back to determine whether it had jurisdiction over federal law in state courts.

The Court held that the Constitution grants it power to hear all cases arising under federal law or under the Constitution, regardless of where the case was first considered. It also held constitutional Section 25 of the Judiciary Act of 1789, which gave it the power to review rejections by state courts of federally based challenges to state laws or actions.

## 6. McCULLOCH V. MARYLAND, 4 WHEAT 316 (1819)

This case came on a challenge of Congress's power to charter a new national bank. Treasury Secretary Alexander Hamilton had chartered the new United States' first national bank in 1798. Its charter expired in 1811. In 1816 President Madison and Congress chartered a new bank. McCulloch was the manager of the bank's branch office in Baltimore. The state of Maryland tried to impose a tax on the bank as if it were a state-chartered institution, and McCulloch refused to pay. A flurry of lawsuits ensued, with the bank calling the tax unconstitutional and the state calling the bank illegal.

The issue went far beyond the bank to exactly what were Congress's powers. The Court ruled that the creation of a bank fell within the "necessary and proper" clause of the Constitution. That clause gives Congress the prerogative to make "all laws which shall be necessary and proper for carrying into execution" its responsibilities—in this case, national fiscal management.

The Supreme Court held that state constitutions and state laws do not control federal law and the Constitution. The Court stated that federal law is supreme, but there must be a balance between federal supremacy and sovereignty as well as state autonomy and intrusion. This case represents the essence of Marshall's view of federalism.

## 7. COHENS V. VIRGINIA, 6 WHEAT 264 (1821)

The Cohens were arrested in Virginia for selling District of Columbia lottery tickets in violation of a state law. They claimed the lottery had been sanctioned by Congress, giving them the right to sell tickets anywhere. They were convicted. The Virginia Supreme Court refused to hear an appeal, so they brought a writ of error directly to the Supreme Court.

The critical issue was whether the Court had jurisdiction under Section 25 before there had been a final ruling by the highest court of a state. If it couldn't, then the supremacy clause could be rendered meaningless simply by a state avoiding a final ruling by its highest court. Using Justice Story's basic premise in *Martin*—that it is the case and not the originating court that determines jurisdiction—Marshall ruled that the Court has the power to issue writs of error to any state court at any level. This ruling was as important as *Marbury* in expanding the Court's authority.

Having ruled that the Court had jurisdiction, he then held against the Cohens, ruling that a state's police power was such it could prevent lottery sales.

## 8. GIBBONS V. OGDEN, 9 WHEAT 1 (1824)

This case represents the Court's first attempt to define exactly what the extent of Congress's power is to regulate interstate commerce.

Gibbons and Ogden operated ferry boats that ran between New York and New Jersey. They got into a dispute about who was licensed by what state to carry passengers where. Ogden claimed he had sole right to use the waterway because he had been given the grant to do so by the New York legislature. Gibbons argued that his federal license allowed him to pick up passengers anywhere, even if he did not have a state license.

The Court ruled that Gibbons's federal license, which was issued under Congress's powers via the commerce clause (Article 1, Section 8) did take precedent over Ogden's state license. In so ruling, the Court and Marshall gave an expansive definition of Congress's power, holding anything happening within a state that affects commerce between states, or in more than one state, can be federally regulated. Further, Marshall said, the federal power to regulate commercial "intercourse" is always superior to state power.

## 9. BARRON V. CITY OF
## BALTIMORE, 7 PETERS 515 (1833)

The city of Baltimore, while repaving streets near its docks, dumped sand and gravel into the Patapsco River. A strong current deposited most of it directly in front of John Barron's wharf, rendering it unusable. Barron sued, claiming the city's action constituted seizure of private property without compensation or due process, both in violation of the Fifth Amendment.

After six years of litigation, the case was heard by the Supreme Court. Baltimore was represented by Maryland's attorney general, Roger Brooke Taney, who would one day become Chief Justice. Taney argued simply that the Supreme Court had no jurisdiction because the Bill of Rights pertained only to the federal government, while the action involving Barron's wharf was a state action.

The Court agreed completely. Chief Justice John Marshall, writing his last opinion, dismissed the case, saying the Court had no jurisdiction because the Fifth Amendment—and by inference the entire Bill of Rights—"is intended solely as a limitation on the exercise of power by the government of the United States."

This remained a crippling limitation on individual rights, until the passage of the Fourteenth Amendment in 1868 and, through it, the gradual incorporation of the Bill of Rights into state laws and actions, a process that was not complete until 1925 (see *Gitlow* v. *New York*, number 41).

## 10. CITY OF NEW YORK V.
## MILN, 11 PETERS 102 (1837)

New York City had a law that required all ships entering its harbor to immediately report the names, dates of birth, place of previous residence, and occupation of everyone on board—passengers and crew—before the ship could unload either passengers or cargo. George Miln, owner of the *Emily*, challenged the law on the basis that it was an unconstitutional invasion by the state of the federal government's power to regulate interstate commerce.

This presented a substantial dilemma for the Taney Court. It was trying to back away from Marshall's all-encompassing definition of federalism, but clearly this state law did impinge upon commerce. So the Court searched for a way to uphold the law and thereby give states more power, without specifically limiting the power of the federal government. They found the answer in finding a "police power" for states contained in the Tenth Amendment. They held the New York law valid under the state's police power to control immigration.

This was the first of many cases in which the Taney Court would hold valid—as an exercise of police power— state laws that attempted to deal with social and economic problems, but were in areas of seeming federal jurisdiction.

## 11. RHODE ISLAND V. MASSACHUSETTS, 12 PETERS 657 (1846)

Article III of the Constitution gives the Supreme Court original jurisdiction over lawsuits by one state against another. Most states establish their borders with their neighbors through negotiated interstate compacts. But in this case, Rhode Island and Massachusetts could not agree on their common border, so each filed suit against the other. After sitting as a trial court, the justices resolved the case in favor of Massachusetts. This represents the first time the Court asserted its authority to resolve disputes between states.

## 12. THE PRIZE CASES, 2 BLACK 635 (1863)[2]

Just before the Civil War began, but after several Southern states had already seceded from the Union, President Lincoln—as commander-in-chief of the armed forces—declared a blockade of Southern ports. A lawsuit was brought, challenging whether a president could take such an action, absent a formal declaration of war by Congress.

Writing for a five-justice majority, Justice Robert Grier emphasized that a president may utilize the same powers in the face of a domestic threat as he would in the face of foreign aggression. "The president was bound to meet it in the shape it presented itself, without waiting for Congress to baptize it with a name." In so ruling, the majority not only expanded the definition of presidential power but also gave the stamp of legality to Lincoln's many wartime actions.

But four justices, led by Chief Justice Taney, disagreed sharply. Justice Nelson pointed out that the president has power over the military, but only Congress has the power to declare war. He said that even in time of emergency, Congress should be assembled, if necessary, to declare war or take immediate action. Had this minority been able to muster a fifth vote, Lincoln might have been powerless to carry on the war.

## 13. EX PARTE McCARDLE 7 WALL 560 (1869)

McCardle, a Mississippi newspaper editor, filed a claim after he was arrested and held for trial by a military commission, after being charged with writing inflammatory articles. He brought the claim to federal court under the terms of a post–Civil War law that gave federal courts the power to hear claims of individuals who were held in custody in former Confederate states. The federal circuit court refused the case, but the Supreme Court agreed to hear it on its merits.

But before it could rule, Congress repealed the part of the law that allowed Supreme Court review. Thus for the Court, the issue became, not settling McCardle's claim on its merit, but whether Congress had the power to change the Court's jurisdiction.

2. "Prize" as used in this context refers to the term in admiralty law meaning the capture of a vessel or cargo belonging or en route to a billigerent power by another made at sea or by ship.

In an opinion written by Chief Justice Chase, the Court agreed that Congress does have this power, and that it could no longer rule. Chase ruled that while the Court's appellate jurisdiction is conferred by the Constitution, it can be defined and limited by congressional act. The case became an early separation-of-powers test, and is important because the Court chose not to confront Congress.

## 14. THE LEGAL TENDER CASES (1869–1871): HEPBURN V. GRISWALD, 8 WALL 603 (1869) KNOX V. LEE, AND PARKER V. DAVIS, 12 WALL 457 (1871)

The Legal Tender Act was passed by Congress during the Civil War in order to make federally issued paper money, so-called greenbacks issued to pay for running the war, legal tender for most public and private debts. In *Hepburn*, by a vote of 5–3, the Court held the law was unconstitutional if applied to preexisting debt.

But in two consolidated cases decided together two years later, *Knox* v. *Lee*, and *Parker* v. *Davis*, the Court changed its mind and specifically overruled *Hepburn*. The vote was now 5–4. Knox and Parker were attempting to pay private debts with greenbacks, and the Court held that Congress had the authority to make U.S. treasury notes legal tender in satisfaction of obligations regardless of whether those obligations came into existence before or after the passage of the law. In doing so the Court strengthened Congress's ability to issue money.

## 15. THE SLAUGHTERHOUSE CASES, 16 WALL 36 (1873)

In 1869, Louisiana granted a twenty-five-year monopoly to a slaughterhouse company to operate in New Orleans. A number of butchers brought suit, claiming that the monopoly deprived them of the opportunity to earn a living, and thus was a violation of the Fourteenth Amendment's privileges and immunities clause, which says, in part, "[n]o state shall make or enforce any law which shall abridge the privileges or immunities of citizens of the United States." They lost in the Louisiana Supreme Court, and they appealed to the U.S. Supreme Court.

This was the first time the Court interpreted the Fourteenth Amendment. Writing for a five-member majority, Justice Samuel Miller ruled that the right to earn a living as a butcher was neither a right nor a privilege guaranteed by the amendment. The Fourteenth Amendment, said Miller, protects U.S. citizens against the unconstitutional exercise of state power to infringe on fundamental rights. But the right to exercise a specific trade is not such a right.

The list of what Miller said are fundamental rights was strikingly short, and included freedom to travel, petition for grievances, the privileges of habeas corpus, and the right of a citizen of the United States to become a citizen of a state.

## 16. MUNN V. ILLINOIS, 94 U.S. 113 (1877)

Again the Court was asked to interpret the Fourteenth Amendment, this time its due process clause. At issue was whether a state could enact legislation that regulates prices and rates, and set operating standards for certain types of businesses.

Ira Munn owned a grain elevator in Chicago. Illinois enacted the Warehouse Act, a statute that regulated grain warehouses and elevators, including setting prices and opening them to public inspection. Munn sued, claiming the law deprived him of the use of his personal property. The Illinois Supreme Court ruled that the state could regulate all matters pertaining to "public welfare."

Munn appealed to the U.S. Supreme Court, claiming the law violated due process. The Court said it did not. Chief Justice Waite held that grain warehouses served a quasipublic function, and laws setting maximum prices and standards are in the "public interest." Regulating such business property, ruled Waite, is within a state's police power.

In a debate that would consume the Court for decades to come, Justice Field dissented, holding that businesses are private property that should be protected from state regulation by the Constitution.

## 17. STAUDER V. WEST VIRGINIA, 100 U.S. 303 (1880)
## NEAL V. DELAWARE, 103 U.S. 370 (1880)

These two cases presented nearly identical facts. Stauder in West Virginia and Neal in Delaware—both criminal defendants—challenged the constitution-ality of their convictions because of racial discrimination. As blacks, they alleged they had been discriminated against because West Virginia and Delaware both had state laws excluding blacks from sitting on any jury.

The Supreme Court agreed. Justice Strong ruled a state may not discriminate against citizens because of their race in establishing qualifications or criteria. More broadly, he ruled that no citizen can be excluded from equal protection of the law under the Fourteenth Amendment, while the Fifteenth Amendment prohibits any type of state action that discriminates against blacks.

## 18. SANTA CLARA COUNTY V. SOUTHERN PACIFIC RAILROAD, 118 U.S. 394 (1886)

This case is important, not for the specific ruling in a tax dispute among a county, a state, and a railroad, but because, before delivering the Court's ruling, Chief Justice Waite announced that the Court was holding that the term *persons*, as used in the Fourteenth Amendment, includes corporate entities as well as natural persons.

He indicated the Court would, in the future, simply refuse to entertain arguments on the issue of whether a corporation or other legal entity was a "person" under the Fourteenth Amendment. Said Waite, "we are all of the opinion that it does."

This case marked the beginning of an era for the Court. In the next fifty years or so, the Court's attention would be devoted to protection of property rights and not civil rights, as it had been in the past.

## 19. WABASH, ST. LOUIS & PACIFIC RAILROAD V. ILLINOIS, 118 U.S. 557 (1886)

Can states control aspects of interstate commerce occurring within their borders? Here, for the first time, the Supreme Court said no, if Congress has acted.

Illinois had a law that said no railroad could charge a rate higher for moving passengers or freight a shorter distance. The Wabash was fined and ordered to cut its rates because it was charging less to carry freight from Peoria to New York than from Gilman to New York, an eighty-six-mile shorter trip.

By a 4–3 vote, the Court held that what this came down to was the Constitution versus state law, and that the Constitution—and its commerce clause—had to take precedent. The majority based its decision on the need for uniformity under the commerce clause.

The Court spoke to the burden that interstate regulation would cause on commerce because transportation is really part of a total intrastate scheme. This federal jurisdictional interest in uniform regulation of interstate commerce later came to be known as the Cooley Doctrine after Thomas Cooley, the major proponent of a laissez-faire approach to American law.

This decision spurred Congress to pass the Interstate Commerce Act the next year.

## 20. YICK WO V. HOPKINS, 118 U.S. 356 (1886)

Yick Wo, a Chinese immigrant, owned a San Francisco laundry housed in a wooden building. This violated a city fire code, so he was arrested and incarcerated.

His appeal presented the Court with several questions. Did San Francisco have the police power to enforce such a law? Did the fact that city officials were granted wide latitude in enforcing the law render it unconstitutional? Lastly, did Yick Wo have any constitutional rights because he was not a citizen?

In the end the Court ruled that while the fire code was a constitutional exercise of police power, it was rendered unconstitutional because placing such land-use policymaking totally in the hands of public officials was arbitrary and oppressive. In delivering the opinion, Justice Matthews also said that directing police power at individual groups violated the equal protection clause of the Fourteenth Amendment.

But more than that, *Yick Wo* stands for the proposition, in the words of Justice Stanley Matthews, that the equal protection clause "applies to all persons . . . without regard to any differences of race, of color or of nationality."

## 21. MUGLER V. KANSAS, 123 U.S. 623 (1887)

In an 1884 case, *Hurtado v. California,* the Court ruled as constitutional a California criminal procedure whereby a criminal prosecution could begin with a formal statement drawn up by a prosecutor, and reviewed by a magistrate, rather than an indictment by a formal grand jury. Justice Matthews ruled that the due process clause did not require states to emulate exactly the Bill of Rights in their criminal-law procedures. But he ruled that although the procedure did not have to mirror the Bill of Rights, it could not exceed "the limits of lawful authority" and did have to safeguard personal liberty and "further the general public good."

But Justice Harlan did not agree. He believed the Fourteenth Amendment limited state power in the same way the Fifth Amendment limited the federal government, and thus states also should be required to indict by grand jury.

Three years later, in *Mugler*, Harlan's view became the majority view. The case concerned the ability of a state to outlaw the manufacture and sale of liquor. While upholding the state's power to restrict liquor sales and dealers (and thus providing an early legal underpinning for what would become Prohibition), Harlan ruled that the due process clause does act as a curb to state police powers.

He said specifically that police powers are limited to matters of health, safety, and morals. Also, he said for the first time that the Court must look at the substance of laws it was being asked to review, not simply their form.

## 22. COUNSELMAN V. HITCHCOCK, 142 U.S. 547 (1892)

In 1887, Congress passed a law limiting immunity from self-incrimination in matters involving violation of interstate commerce laws. In cases arising under interstate commerce statutes, a witness was protected against self-incrimination

only to the extent that forced testimony could not be used directly against him at trial. The statute allowed for its indirect use, for its use in forfeitures, or for its use to discover other evidence that could be used against an accused.

Justice Blatchford, writing for a unanimous Court, struck down the law and ruled that only a grant of complete immunity against prosecution, or any other adverse use of self-incriminating evidence, is sufficient to waive protection against self-incrimination contained in the Fifth Amendment.

This decision began to define the protections available against self-incrimination under the Fifth Amendment.

## 23. UNITED STATES V. E. C. KNIGHT CO., 156 U.S. 1 (1895)

Since 1924 (*Gibbons* v. *Ogden*; see number 6), the Court had held fast to its view that the commerce clause gave Congress almost unlimited authority to regulate intrastate dealings that affected other states, or commerce to other states. In 1890, exercising this power, Congress passed the Sherman Antitrust Act, designed to curb monopolies and monopolistic trade practices.

One of the act's first targets was a trust that refined and sold more than 90 percent of the sugar in the United States. The company defended itself by claiming that the Sherman Act was unconstitutional.

In this first test of the Sherman Act, the court had no trouble finding the law itself constitutional. But then in a radical departure from its ruling in *Gibbons*, cal departure from its ruling in *Gibbons*, the majority established a distinction between what directly affects interstate commerce and what only indirectly affects it. It found that Congress had no power—and therefore neither did the Sherman Act—to regulate manufacture, even though the manufactured product was sold in interstate commerce and even though it might represent a virtual monopoly. The manufacture itself, said the Court, only indirectly affected interstate commerce.

Over the years this decision was gradually eaten away. But it represents the basis for complex commercial and economic arguments that involved the Court for the next thirty-five years.

## 24. IN RE DEBS, 158 U.S. 564 (1895)

Activist union leader Eugene Debs, and other leaders of the 1894 Pullman Rail Car strike, were convicted of violating a federal court injunction ordering them to end the strike. The injunction had been issued on behalf of President Cleveland, based on the Sherman Act, to prevent the strike from interfering with the movement of mail and interstate commerce.

The Court agreed that the injunction had been valid, and thus it upheld Debs's and the others' contempt convictions. But in so ruling, the Court went much further than the narrow grounds of the antitrust law. It ruled unanimously that, based on national sovereignty, the federal government had broad powers to remove obstructions to interstate commerce and the transporta-

tion of the mails, including outlawing strikes and arresting strikers.

For decades, this decision was used as the legal basis to force the end to strikes.

## 25. ALLEGEYER V. LOUISIANA, 165 U.S. 578 (1897)

Louisiana had a law that required any company wanting to insure property within the state to have a state license. This was a transparent subterfuge to limit insurance sales to politically favored local companies. Allegeyer was an out-of-state insurance company that claimed the law took away its freedom to contract without giving it due process of law.

The Supreme Court agreed. Justice Peckham wrote the opinion for a unanimous Court, saying the Constitution guaranteed a "freedom to contract" that was being denied Louisiana residents by the statute. In doing so the justices, for the first time, expressly stated that substantive due process protects fundamental economic rights. This concept of freedom to contract was to drive the Court in many of its upcoming opinions, especially those striking down early attempts at social reforms, like government regulation of minimum wages, hours, working conditions, and child labor.

## 26. CHAMPION V. AMES, 188 U.S. 321 (1903)

In this case, for the first time, the Court recognized a federal police power. At issue was the Federal Lottery Act, which outlawed, along with other related activities, the transporting of lottery tickets on an interstate basis. Ames asserted the law was unconstitutional. The Court, by a 5–4 vote, did not agree.

Justice Harlan, writing for the majority, agreed that the Constitution does not grant Congress any specific authority over public health, welfare, and morals. But he found that the federal government does have those types of police powers through its power to regulate interstate commerce. In the end, the debate came down to whether lottery tickets are articles of commerce.

Justice Fuller for the minority did not agree. He suggested that the Federal Lottery Act was actually a vehicle for carrying out general police powers (i.e., suppression of lotteries) and not the regulation of commerce. He said this was not permissible because they were powers never granted to Congress by the Constitution in the first place.

## 27. NORTH SECURITIES V. UNITED STATES, 193 U.S. 197 (1904)

In reaction to the Sherman Act, and to try to take advantage of the Court's ruling in *Knight* (see number 23), companies began using holding companies to evade antitrust laws. In this case, a holding company was formed for the express purpose of limiting competition between two railroads. By a very close 5–4 vote, the Court struck down the arrangement as a combination in restraint of trade.

At the heart of the ruling was the finding that a holding company, while itself technically not in interstate commerce, can sufficiently affect interstate commerce to force it within the scope of the Sherman Act. This ruling immediately changed the use of holding companies by businesses, and represented the first of many modifications to the *Knight* ruling.

## 28. MULLER V. OREGON, 208 U.S. 412 (1908)

In its 1897 ruling in *Allegeyer* v. *Louisiana* (see number 25), the Court held that a state could seek to attain certain social goals by limiting an individual's absolute right to contract. Then in 1905, in *Lochner* v. *New York*, the Court applied this theory to strike down a New York law that had sought to limit, for health and safety reasons, the daily hours of bakery workers.

Now the justices were faced with virtually the same question, but with a slightly different twist. In *Muller* they were being asked to rule on an Oregon law that sought to limit to ten hours a day, again for health and safety reasons, the workday of women in the laundries. Boston lawyer and justice-to-be Louis Brandeis represented Oregon, and filed with the Court what has become known as the Brandeis Brief—an argument of epic length—in which he gave a history of women in the labor movement and argued for the proposition that the Oregon law must be sustained if it sought to promote the general health and welfare of workers, which he called a valid exercise of the police power of the state.

Reversing itself, the Court agreed. The majority based its decision on what it saw as a distinction between men and women that might be offensive to feminists—"the inherent difference between the two sexes." But in doing so, the Court established the right of the state to use its legitimate police powers to attain a desired social end by interfering with the right to contract. And, by inference, found the right to contract not to be absolute.

## 29. LOEWE V. LAWLER, 208 U.S. 274 (1908)

A labor union, the United Hatters of North America, attempted to organize workers at the Danbury, Connecticut, hat plant of Loewe & Company by organizing a boycott of the company's products in stores in other states. The company sued.

A unanimous Court ruled that the secondary boycott organized by the union was a combination in restraint of trade, and therefore a violation of federal antitrust laws.

This decision led directly to the passage by Congress in 1914 of the Clayton Antitrust Act, one of the most important pieces of labor legislation ever enacted, in which labor unions were exempted from suits brought under antitrust laws.

## 30. EX PARTE YOUNG, 209 U.S. 123 (1908)

Minnesota passed a new law lowering the permissible rate a railroad could charge a passenger from three cents a mile to two cents. On the day before the law was to take effect, seven different lawsuits were filed against it by railroads or their stockholders. The federal district court issued an injunction, enjoining the attorney general of Minnesota from enforcing the new law until its constitutionality could be determined. He filed a writ of error with the Supreme Court, seeking a determination as to whether a federal court can enjoin the enforcement of a state law.

By an 8–1 vote the Court said that a temporary injunction can be issued against the enforcement of a state statute in order to give a federal court time to determine the constitutionality of the law. Such an injunction, the majority said, is not in conflict with the Eleventh Amendment.

Further, the Court said a specific state official could be enjoined from enforcing the challenged state law. Today, the state official has to be a named defendant in the suit, even though the state is the real party. This decision has become known as the Abstention Doctrine.

## 31. STANDARD OIL V. UNITED STATES, 221 U.S. 1 (1911)

On the basis of a massive antitrust suit that resulted in a trial record of twenty-three volumes, and over 12,000 pages, the federal circuit court ordered the holding company that controlled Standard Oil of New York and thirty-three other corporations dissolved, in violation of the Sherman Act. John D. Rockefeller appealed.

The Court considered for the first time the question of whether all trusts, or corporate combinations that had any effect on interstate trade, were illegal per se, and in violation of the Sherman Act. By a vote of 8–1, the Court said no, they are not.

The Court ruled that only undue restraints of interstate trade or commerce, or unreasonable combinations, are prohibited by the Sherman Act. The Court adopted "a rule of reason" to determine whether a combination unduly restrains trade. The key here is *unduly*, since previously the Court had looked upon any restraint caused by a combination to be illegal.

## 32. MINNESOTA RATE CASES, (SIMPSON V. SHEPARD, SIMPSON V. KENNEDY, SIMPSON V. SHILLABER), 230 U.S. 352 (1913)

The importance of these three cases (consolidated and argued as one) is shown by the fact that oral arguments took a full week and twenty-one states intervened as parties. The case resulted from suits brought by three shareholders of the Great Northern and the Minneapolis and St. Louis railroads against the head of the Minnesota Railroad Commission, seeking to prevent him from setting rates within Minnesota for freight in interstate commerce under the terms of a new state law.

The question presented to the Court was whether any law of a state is unconstitutional and void if it seeks to regulate interstate commerce, or if it burdens the rights of those involved in interstate commerce.

In an epic opinion that took him almost a year to write, Justice Hughes affirmed the absolute right of Congress alone to regulate interstate commerce, and for the first time he extended that power to regulate purely intrastate (within a single state) commerce when it is interwoven with interstate commerce. He said that states have a right to regulate to the extent that Congress is silent, but once Congress speaks, its laws and regulations are supreme.

## 33. WEEKS V. UNITED STATES, 232 U.S. 383 (1914)

Fremont Weeks was arrested in Kansas City and charged with transporting lottery tickets. He was arrested after police, without a warrant, searched his house after being told by a neighbor where a key was hidden. The search uncovered illegal materials, which were confiscated by police. At the start of his trial, Weeks asked that the materials be returned to him. The judge refused, and certain of the materials were later introduced into evidence. Weeks was convicted, and he appealed.

In a unanimous decision written by Justice Day, the Court ruled for the first time that material seized as part of a search in violation of an individual's Fourth Amendment rights must be excluded from use to incriminate him in a trial in federal court. This decision began what today is called the "exclusionary rule."

## 34. BRUSHABER V. UNION PACIFIC RAILROAD CO., 240 U.S. 1 (1916)

Congress passed an income tax for the first time in October 1913. Brushaber was a stockholder of the Union Pacific, and he sued the railroad to enjoin it from voluntarily complying with the new tax law, claiming that such a tax was unconstitutional.

The general issue facing the Supreme Court was whether an income tax was constitutional, and if so, whether under the Constitution it had to be apportioned back to the states. More specifically, the 1913 Tax Act was constitutionally challenged because it had been made retroactive, and it featured graduated tax rates.

The Court ruled that the Sixteenth Amendment could not have been much clearer in giving Congress the right to "lay and collect taxes on incomes from whatever source derived, without apportionment among the several states. . . ." Further, the Court said, Congress could establish any rate structure it deemed reasonable, and could make the effective date retroactive as far as some types of income are concerned.

This decision ended any doubt that income taxes were direct taxes that have to be apportioned, or that somehow the Sixteenth Amendment was defective because it conflicts with a person's Fifth Amendment rights or the due process clause of the Fourteenth Amendment.

## 35. SCHENCK V. UNITED STATES, 249 U.S. 47 (1919)

Charles T. Schenck and Elizabeth Baer, two New York socialists, printed and distributed handbills decrying military conscription as "despotism arranged in the interest of Wall Street." They urged resistance to the draft. They were arrested and convicted for violation of the Espionage Act.

They argued that the First Amendment guarantees "absolutely unlimited discussion" of public matters. The government, in turn, argued that it has a right of self-preservation that overshadows any First Amendment considerations.

Justice Holmes, writing for a unanimous Court, rejected Schenck and Baer's First Amendment argument. But he also refused to go as far as the government wanted in its assertion that it alone has the ultimate right to determine what is necessary for its survival.

## 36. SELECTIVE DRAFT LAW CASES, 245 U.S. 366 (1919)

On May 18, 1917, Congress passed the Selective Service Act, which for the first time established compulsory conscription. Many lawsuits were filed against the new law, claiming the draft was an unconstitutional violation of the Fourteenth Amendment, a violation of the Thirteenth Amendment's prohibition against involuntary servitude and slavery, an illegal delegation of Congress's war-making powers to the executive, and a violation of various other rights including religious freedom. Six of these cases were consolidated into this single action.

The Court unanimously disagreed. Congress, said the Court, has the power under the Constitution to raise armies for just and necessary causes. The draft, said the justices, is simply an exercise of that power and does not constitute involuntary servitude. Moreover, said the Court, military service can be said to be the obligation of a citizen in a "good and just government."

## 37. MISSOURI V. HOLLAND, 252 U.S. 416 (1920)

In 1916, Congress passed the Migratory Bird Treaty Act to codify into law an agreement between the United States and Britain, under which both guaranteed they would act to protect certain species of birds that migrated between the United States and Canada. Prior to the treaty, lower courts had thrown out a law seeking to protect certain kinds of birds as an unconstitutional invasion of states' prerogatives.

The state of Missouri brought suit to keep federal game wardens from enforcing the Migratory Bird Treaty Act inside Missouri, claiming that game laws are the exclusive right of the states.

Justice Holmes, writing on behalf of the Court, said that Congress, once the Senate has ratified a treaty, may enact whatever legislation is necessary to implement the provisions of the treaty, even if the provisions might otherwise be an unconstitutional infringement on the rights of a state. Such legislation, he said, is within Congress's treaty power and valid under the Tenth Amendment as a "necessary and proper" means of affecting the federal government's enumerated powers.

## 38. TRAUX V. CORRIGAN, 257 U.S. 312 (1921)

This is one of those cases where a dissent, and not the majority opinion, is of historical importance.

Traux owned a restaurant in Arizona and his employees went on strike. He filed for an injunction to end picketing in front of his establishment, but it was denied under an Arizona law that for-bade the issuance of injunctions in labor disputes. He appealed to the Supreme Court.

By a 5–4 vote the Court ruled the Arizona law unconstitutional because it served to deprive Traux of his property by refusing to end a "conspiratorial annoyance and obstruction." The majority also held that the law deprived a class of persons—employers—due process under the Fourteenth Amendment.

The four-justice minority did not agree. In a wide-ranging and eloquent dissent, Justice Brandeis argued that the realities of labor disputes, and of labor-management relations, coupled with the historic abuses of injunctions issued on behalf of employers to end strikes, more than justified the Arizona law. The minority argued that to prevent courts from enjoining peaceful picketing is a valid end, and the law should be allowed to stand.

Eventually this became the majority view of the Court, and the dissent in this case is viewed as a milestone in the development of labor law.

## 39. PIERCE V. SOCIETY OF SISTERS, 268 U.S. 510 (1925)

The state of Oregon enacted the Compulsory Education Act, which required all children between the ages of eight and sixteen to attend public school—except those physically unable, those who lived more than three miles from the nearest road, or those who had already completed the eighth grade. Public officials were interpreting the law literally: that children had to attend the public school in their district. So an order of Catholic nuns, who ran a series of elementary and high schools in Oregon, filed suit to allow parents to choose where they wanted their children to be educated.

For a unanimous Court, Justice McReynolds ruled that any law requiring children to attend public school, at the exclusion of private and parochial, is a violation of the Fourteenth Amendment's right of personal liberty of both student and parents. He did indicate that a state has a right to accredit and license schools under some reasonable scheme, but not to discriminate against nonpublic education.

## 40. MYERS V. UNITED STATES, 272 U.S. 52 (1926)

Myers was a Portland, Oregon, postmaster who, with the concurrence of President Wilson, was removed by the postmaster general. Previously, Congress had passed a law whereby postmasters were appointed by the president, confirmed by the Senate, and then held their appointments for four years unless they were removed by the president "with the advice and consent of the Senate." In this case, no Senate consent to Myers's removal had been sought.

In a decision that sought to define the breadth of the president's executive power to appoint and remove under Article II, Sections 1 and 3, Chief Justice (and former President Taft) ruled that the removal power is tied to and incidental to the power to appoint. He held that the law allowing removal only with the consent of the Senate is an unconstitutional excursion into the executive branch's authority.

And Taft went even further, indicating that a president's removal power was virtually unlimited, extending not only to people who worked for the executive branch but to independent agencies as well.

That issue came before the Court nine years later, in *Humphrey's Executor* v. *United States*, 295 U.S. 602 (1935). President Roosevelt was attempting to fire Humphrey, a Hoover appointee to the Federal Trade Commission. The question presented was whether a president's executive power allows him to remove individuals in quasijudicial or quasilegislative agencies. The Court again responded in the negative.

Justice Sutherland clarified that the president's removal powers are absolute with respect to government officials in positions that are within or subordinate to the executive branch. Because administrative agencies such as the Federal Trade Commission were created by Congress to fulfill specific mandates, while the president may have the power to appoint with Senate confirmation, he has no power of removal—only Congress does through impeachment.

## 41. GITLOW V. NEW YORK (1927)

Benjamin Gitlow was a Socialist party member during the early 1900s who wrote and distributed "The Left Wing Manifesto," a tract that advocated overthrow of the government. He was arrested under a New York State criminal anarchy statute, was convicted, and appealed to the Supreme Court.

The Court by a 7–2 vote, in rather routine fashion, upheld the constitutionality of the New York law, and Gitlow's conviction under it. In a decision written by Justice Edward Sanford, the majority ruled that states may suppress speech that has already been classified as dangerous to public welfare, or to the basic tenets of government.

What makes this case important is not the decision, which was conservative and predictable, but rather that the Court accepted the case for review. This was the first time the Court acknowledged that the First Amendment, through the Fourteenth, applies to state laws and actions. Wrote Sanford: "We may and do assume that the freedom of speech and of the press . . . are among the fundamental personal rights and liberties protected . . . from impairment by the States."

## 42. PATTON V. UNITED STATES 281 U.S. 276 (1930)

John Patton and two others were charged with attempting to bribe a federal agent. A twelve-member jury was empaneled, but during the course of the trial one became ill. The judge ordered the trial to continue with eleven jurors, after both sides agreed. The trial ended in the conviction of all three, and they were sentenced to jail. They appealed on the basis that they did not have the power to waive their constitutional right to a twelve-member jury.

The Court agreed with the three, and ordered a new trial. The justices said that the three elements of a constitutionally guaranteed "trial by jury" is trial in front of a jury of twelve persons, supervised by a judge who informs the jury of the law, and that a verdict of guilt is reached unanimously.

(Note: In *Williams* v. *Florida*, number 79, the Court later modified this ruling as to the number of required jurors).

## 43. NEAR V. MINNESOTA, 382 U.S. 679 (1931)

This was the era of yellow journalism. A weekly Minneapolis newspaper, the *Saturday Press*, was publishing a series of articles accusing the local police chief of being in league with a "Jewish gangster." The police chief filed a motion in state court against the newspaper, and its editor, Jay Near, under a Minnesota statute allowing abatement of publications deemed a public nuisance. As a result, the *Saturday Press* was enjoined from continuing publication.

This was the Court's first look at the issue of prior restraint on speech. By a vote of 5–4, a sharply divided Court threw out the Minnesota law. Justice Hughes wrote for the majority: "It is no longer open to doubt that the liberty of the press and of speech is within the liberty safeguarded by the due process clause of the Fourteenth Amendment from invasion by state actions." He made it clear that libel actions after publication are the proper legal recourse for false statements, and requiring the press to prove its motive prior to publication amounts to unconstitutional censorship.

## 44. NIXON V. CONDON, 286 U.S. 73 (1932)

The Fifteenth Amendment, ratified in 1870, established that the right to vote could not be abridged based on race or previous condition of servitude. In a series of decisions starting with *Ex parte Yarbrough*, 110 U.S. 651 in 1884, the Court consistently ruled that it was valid for Congress to establish laws to enforce the Fifteenth Amendment and to punish persons who attempted to keep persons from voting based on race.

The first major expansion of the right to vote came in 1927 when, in *Nixon v. Herndon*, 273 U.S. 536, the Court invalidated a Texas law that excluded blacks from voting in the Texas Democratic Party primary. In response, the Texas legislature passed a law that, henceforth, the political parties themselves would establish the rules under which their primaries would be conducted.

Now in this case, the Court was being asked to strike down the rule established by the Texas Democratic party, again barring blacks from voting in the primary. By a 5–4 vote, the majority held that neither states nor political parties can exclude persons from voting based on race. Justice Cardozo, writing for the majority, ruled that a political party acts as an agent for the state in holding party primaries, and therefore the Fifteenth Amendment is applicable.

## 45. RAILROAD RETIREMENT BOARD V. ALTON RAILROAD CO., 295 U.S. 330 (1935) SCHECHTER POULTRY CORP. V. UNITED STATES 295 U.S. 495 (1935)

These two cases, decided within two weeks of one another, invalidated two of the primary new agencies that President Franklin Roosevelt and the Democratic Congress had established to fight the Depression.

In *Railroad Retirement Board*, by a 5–4 vote, the majority struck down the Railroad Retirement Act of 1934, which had created a federally sponsored retirement system for railway workers. The majority ruled that pensions have nothing to do with interstate commerce, and that much of the new law violated due process.

In *Schechter*, a unanimous Court ruled that Congress had unconstitutionally delegated its legislative powers to the executive when it passed the National Industrial Recovery Act—a centerpiece of Roosevelt's New Deal. The Court also said the new law gave the president too much power, and that it sought to improperly regulate indirect aspects of interstate commerce.

These two rulings convinced Roosevelt that the Supreme Court was not going to allow him to go forward with his plan for economic recovery, and this led, in turn, to his court-packing plan.

## 46. POWELL V. ALABAMA, 287 U.S. 45 (1932)

Ozzie Powell and seven other black youths were charged with raping two white girls on a freight train near the town of Scottsboro, Alabama. The eight, who became known as the Scottsboro Boys, were divided into three groups, with each group tried separately in one day. Seven of the eight were convicted and sentenced to death. The trial record was unclear, but it appeared that a single appointed lawyer was present in the courtroom for all three trials, to render assistance to the defendants "if called upon." Later testimony was that none of the defendants had asked for help.

After the Alabama Supreme Court upheld their convictions, they appealed to the U.S. Supreme Court on two grounds: they had not been represented by counsel at their trials, and blacks had been systematically excluded from the juries that heard their cases.

The Court refused to rule on the second point. But by a vote of 7–2, the justices overturned the verdicts, ruling that the defendants had been denied adequate counsel.

Justice Sutherland, in delivering the opinion for the Court, indicated that under both state and federal law due process requires every trial judge to assign an individual attorney to each defendant who cannot afford to hire his or her own counsel.

The case was sent back for retrial of the seven youths who had been convicted. This time with each represented by his own lawyer, in a trial known as Scottsboro II, they were again convicted and sentenced to death. They again appealed, with the case now called *Norris* v. *Alabama*, 294 U.S. 240 (1935). This appeal was based on the grounds that the Supreme Court had refused to consider in Scottsboro I—exclusion of blacks from the jury pool.

Again, the Court threw out the convictions. A unanimous Court agreed that the systematic exclusion of jurors by race results in a violation of due process.

## 47. NEBBIA V. NEW YORK, 291 U.S. 502 (1934)

New York State had established a regulation scheme for the price of milk, setting the maximum and minimum prices that dairies could charge. In the challenge before the Supreme Court, dairy owners argued that this kind of scheme went well beyond the "public interest" rationale that the Court had enunciated in 1877 in *Munn* v. *Illinois* (see number 16).

The Court agreed that the price-setting scheme did go beyond the public-interest test, but a five-justice majority upheld the New York scheme and, in doing so, significantly expanded the rationale by which states could regulate business. The Court said that states have wide latitude to regulate almost any business, at any time, so long as the regulation is reasonable and is done through an appropriate means.

## 48. NLRB V. JONES & LAUGHLIN STEEL CORP. 301 U.S. 1 (1937)

The Jones & Laughlin Steel Corporation was a large enterprise with steel plants and manufacturing facilities in many states. It was involved in a labor dispute in one of its Pittsburgh-area plants, and was served with a cease-and-desist order by the National Labor Relations Board (NLRB). The order was based on the newly passed National Labor Relations Act of 1935, and charged the company with unfair labor practices.

Jones & Laughlin claimed its manufacturing plants were not involved in interstate commerce, and thus the NLRB had no jurisdiction. Moreover, it said the National Labor Relations Act itself was unconstitutional. An appeals court agreed, but the Supreme Court did not.

By a 5–4 vote, the Court held the new law constitutional. The majority did so by shifting, for the first time, from a narrow geographical definition of interstate commerce to a broader concept that any intrastate matter that directly or indirectly impacts on interstate commerce can be regulated by Congress and the federal government.

## 49. HAGUE V. CIO, 307 U.S. 496 (1939)

Jersey City, New Jersey, had passed a city ordinance that prohibited public meetings in the streets, parks, or other public places without a license signed by mayor and political boss Frank Hague. Hague apparently sharply limited his approvals to friends and favored organizations. The CIO, a labor organization, wanted to hold a rally but was denied a permit. It brought suit.

Mayor Hague argued that, as the mayor, he acted as trustee of public places for the citizenship, and that he could control access to them as he controlled access to his own private property. But the Court did not agree. For the first time, it ruled that the First Amendment requires public places "be open for assembly, communicating thought between citizens and discussing public questions." A city can establish reasonable regulations, said the justices, "but free speech must not, in the guise of regulation, be abridged or denied."

## 50. UNITED STATES V. DARBY LUMBER 312 U.S. 100 (1941)

The Fair Labor Standards Act of 1938 set minimum wages and maximum hours for workers producing goods for interstate commerce. Darby, a lumber manufacturer, was charged with violating the new law. But the trial court dismissed the charges, ruling that the law was an unconstitutional regulation of commerce within the states.

But now the Supreme Court, overturning almost a half-century of rulings, called the new law constitutional and said that Congress has the authority to prohibit from interstate commerce goods that are manufactured in violation of the new wage and hour laws.

The Court held that the federal commerce power includes regulation within a state, when what is being regulated affects interstate commerce. The Court reiterated that manufacturing per se is not in interstate commerce. But then it distinguished what Darby was doing by calling it "production for interstate commerce."

## 51. CHAPLINSKY V. NEW HAMPSHIRE, 315 U.S. 568 (1942)

Walter Chaplinsky, a Jehovah's Witness, while distributing literature on the streets of Rochester, New Hampshire, aggressively preached to persons he approached that mainstream Christian religions were a "racket," while also attacking various local officials, calling them fascists. He was arrested and convicted under a municipal ordinance proscribing speech that tends to annoy, harass, or deride others.

After state appeals failed, Chaplinsky appealed to the Supreme Court, claiming that his words and actions were protected by the First Amendment. A unanimous Court did not agree.

Justice Frank Murphy wrote that "it is well understood that the right of free speech is not absolute at all times and under all circumstances." Murphy went on to expand on those types of speech that are outside the protection of the First Amendment and included so-called fighting words—"those which by their very utterance inflict injury or tend to incite an immediate breach of peace."

Finding that what Chaplinsky was saying would have caused the "average addressee to fight," the justices ruled that Chaplinsky's arrest and conviction was constitutionally permissible.

## 52. MORGAN V. VIRGINIA, 328 U.S. 373 (1946)

A Virginia law required black and white passengers to be segregated from one another on both interstate and intrastate buses. Mrs. Morgan, a black woman, was riding on a bus from Glouchester County, Virginia, to Baltimore, Maryland, when she refused to obey the order of the driver to move to a "Negro seat" at the back of the bus. She was arrested, tried, and convicted. She appealed and the Supreme Court of Virginia upheld her conviction.

By a 7–1 vote, the U.S. Supreme Court threw out the Virginia law. Justice Reed based his decision on the need to require uniform seating requirements on buses in interstate commerce. Otherwise, theoretically, every time a bus

crossed a state line, the seating might have to be rearranged and this would be a burden on interstate commerce.

The Court avoided the issue of civil rights and the Bill of Rights, and resolved this case using the commerce clause. But the case is significant because, for the first time, the Court struck down a state-imposed discrimination scheme. This marked the start of an attack on discrimination that led to *Brown v. Board of Education* almost a decade later.

## 53. SHELLY V. KRAMER 334 U.S. 1 (1948)

In 1911, a group of thirty-nine St. Louis homeowners entered into an agreement that none could sell their property to a non-Caucasian. Shelly, a black man, bought one of the houses and received a title subject to the restrictive covenant. Kramer, an owner of one of the other houses, brought suit, seeking to hold Shelly to the restriction, to prevent him from taking occupancy, and to divest him of the title.

The district court refused to enforce the covenant. But the Missouri Supreme Court overruled it, and ordered that Shelly be stripped of the title. Shelly appealed the order to the U.S. Supreme Court, claiming that the state court could not enforce racially restrictive land agreements because they violated the equal protection clause of the Fourteenth Amendment. Kramer countered that the state was not involved in this private agreement between citizens.

Effectively the Supreme Court held that both were right. It ruled that private agreements to exclude persons of a designated race or color from the use or occupancy of real estate for residential purposes do not violate the Fourteenth Amendment. But at the same time it negated that ruling by also holding that it is a violation of the equal protection clause of the Fourteenth Amendment for federal, state, or local courts, or judicial officers in their official capacities, to enforce them.

This means that while the covenants might be legal, they are unenforceable, and therefore are effectively null.

## 54. TERMINELLO V. CHICAGO, 337 U.S. 1 (1949)

Inside an auditorium in Chicago, Terminello was giving a speech denouncing Jews and blacks. A crowd had gathered outside to protest the speech. This, in turn, led Terminello to also ridicule the protesters. In an attempt to avoid violence, police placed Terminello under arrest for violating a municipal ordinance that prohibited conduct leading to breaches of the peace. At his trial, the jury was instructed that Terminello should be found guilty if his speech "stir[red] the public to anger, invite[d] dispute, [or brought] about a condition of unrest." The jury found Terminello guilty of violating the ordinance.

The Court found, 5–4, that the ordinance was vague and that it was overbroad in its definition of breach of the peace, in that it inhibited constitutionally protected free speech. The Court found that allowing ordinances such as the one in Chicago would lead to a "standardization of ideas either by the legislatures, the court or by dominant political or community groups."

The Court's decision in Terminello was technical and tightly drawn. It was not a sweeping defense of the First Amendment. And it was a precursor to an era of control of speech that could be broadly defined as even potentially inciteful.

## 55. YOUNGSTOWN SHEET AND TUBE V. SAWYER, 343 U.S. 579 (1952)

What are the limits of a president's executive powers? In April 1952, the United Steelworkers of America gave notice of its intent to strike against various steel companies. Both Congress and President Truman had been involved in an attempt to avert the strike, owing to the need for continued steel production for the Korean War. Truman then issued an executive order commanding the secretary of commerce to seize the steel companies, ensuring that steel production would continue. The steel companies sued in federal court to have the seizures declared invalid.

The government argued that the president had the power as commander-in-chief to issue and enforce the order. The district court granted a preliminary injunction to stop the enforcement of the order, however the Court of Appeals stayed the injunction on the same day. The Supreme Court agreed to hear the arguments immediately.

The Court held that the president's executive power did not extend to taking private property to prevent a strike, even in time of war. Such an order constituted legislation, and the president's executive privilege cannot be enlarged to encompass law-making ability. The Court ruled that a president's powers in legislation are limited to recommending laws to Congress, and vetoing laws he finds inappropriate. Only Congress could have acted as Truman did in these circumstances.

## 56. BROWN V. BOARD OF EDUCATION, 347 U.S. 483 (1954) (BROWN I) BROWN V. BOARD OF EDUCATION, 349 U.S. 294 (1955) (BROWN II)

The Court had on its docket seventeen cases from Kansas, South Carolina, Virginia, Delaware, and the District of Columbia, all asking that state-mandated school segregation schemes be struck down as unconstitutional. Since the facts being presented were identical, sixteen of the cases were consolidated into *Brown.* The seventeenth, *Bolling* v. *Sharpe* concerning the school system of the District of Columbia, was decided separately because of the different nature of the federal district.

For a century, in Topeka, Kansas, black children had been denied access to public schools attended by white children under laws that required or permitted segregation according to race. In fact, all schools in the district were, or were in the process of being, equalized in respect to accommodations, classes, and faculty qualifications and salaries. But parents of the black children brought suit against the Board of Education to force integration of the schools.

The issue before the Court in *Brown I* was whether to overturn the 1896 decision of *Plessy* v. *Ferguson,* which allowed "separate but equal" facilities and accommodations for blacks. The issue raised now by the plaintiffs was whether the separation of black and white children in public schools was a denial of equal protection of the laws, even though the education and facilities were equal.

The Court held that segregation of public schools based on race was indeed an equal-protection violation. The Court stated that separating students leads inevitably to an interpretation that black children are inferior, and this sense of inferiority affects black children's motivation to learn.

The Court withheld any instructions for relief of segregation until its later decision in *Brown II,* when the justices chose to defer to lower federal courts the decision and oversight as to what methods should be used to desegregate specific school systems.

The Court's decision in *Brown* led to later cases, citing *Brown* as precedent, that desegregated parks, beaches, buses, golf courses, and other places of public accommodation.

## 57. ROTH V. UNITED STATES, 354 U.S. 476 (1957)

Roth was a publisher and seller of books, magazines, and photographs. He was convicted under a federal statute for mailing obscene materials. The issue before the Court was whether obscenity is protected under the First Amendment as freedom of speech.

The Court held that even though the

language of the First Amendment seems all encompassing, it does not protect every type of speech. While it does protect all ideas having even the slightest socially redeeming value, some types of "speech" lacking in this value fall outside the protection. Obscenity, said the Court, has been held to have no socially redeeming value, and is therefore outside Constitutional protection.

To determine if that value exists, material must be judged in its entirety, and the test should be whether, to the average person applying contemporary community standards, the material appeals to prurient interests.

Roth's materials failed this test and thus his conviction was upheld.

## 58. WATKINS V. UNITED STATES, 354 U.S. 178 (1957)

How far may Congress go to compel testimony? The House authorized investigation of alleged Communist activity by the House Un-American Activities Committee. Watkins, a trade union official, was subpoenaed to appear, after another witness linked him to the Communist party. Watkins denied all the allegations made against him, but did answer questions about himself and those he knew to be current members of the Communist party. But he refused to answer about past party affiliations of other persons. He was subsequently indicted, and convicted for statutory contempt for his refusal to answer all the committee's questions.

The Court ruled that even though Congress has a broad power to investigate, it must show that the investigation is tied directly to a legislative function. More specifically, in contempt for a nonanswering situation, it must show how questions asked at a hearing pertain to a valid legislative function, pertain to the person being asked the question, and pertain to the subject matter of the hearings.

The Court ruled that Watkins could not be forced to testify about another person's affiliations with the Communist party, and thus could not be held in contempt for failure to answer.

## 59. COOPER V. AARON, 358 U.S. 1 (1958)

The city of Little Rock, Arkansas, filed a motion in federal court to delay any court-ordered desegregation, citing the need for additional time to comply with the *Brown* decision. The school board asserted that it was acting in good faith, but that the education process would suffer if desegregation continued. It offered as proof, incidents of violence that had occurred at white schools elsewhere in the South, where black children had attempted to attend classes.

The Court held that, although it accepted the school board's claim that it was acting in good faith, the rights of black children should not be sacrificed because of the violence and disorder that had been created by the actions of state officials in their attempt to stop desegregation. The Court ordered that desegregation be moved forward with all deliberate speed.

## 60. NAACP V. ALABAMA EX REL. PATTERSON, 357 U.S. 449 (1958)

The state of Alabama brought legal action against the state chapter of the National Association for the Advancement of Colored People (NAACP) to forfeit its state charter for its failure to comply with a state statute governing foreign corporations. The NAACP claimed that it was exempt from complying with the statute.

A state court issued an order restraining the NAACP from engaging in any activities while the action was pending. As part of the pretrial discovery process, the state demanded the production of a complete membership list. The state court granted the motion and ordered the production of the list. The NAACP refused to produce the list, and was held in civil contempt. The NAACP appealed that decision.

The Supreme Court held that a state may not compel an organization to reveal its membership list, without demonstrating a justification for the deterrent effect such a disclosure would have on the right to free association. The Court found a direct relationship between the right of association guaranteed by the First Amendment, and a right to privacy in those associations. The Court found that revealing the names and addresses of the NAACP's members could result in economic reprisals, loss of employment, and threat of physical coercion, thus inhibiting their right to associate.

## 61. BARENBLATT V. UNITED STATES, 360 U.S. 109 (1959)

Lloyd Barenblatt was a young Vassar College instructor who had been called before the House Un-American Activities Committee in 1954 to answer whether he had ever been a member of the Communist party. He refused to answer on First Amendment grounds, and was eventually tried and sentenced to six months in jail for contempt of Congress. By a vote of 5–4 the Court upheld the conviction.

Writing for the majority, Justice Harlan said, "Where First Amendment rights are asserted to bar governmental interrogation, resolution of the issue always involves a balancing by the courts of competing private and public interests. . . . We conclude that the balance between the individual and the governmental interests here at stake must be struck in favor of the latter, and that therefore the provisions of the First Amendment have not been offended."

The majority said that this case differed from *Watkins* (see number 58) in that Barenblatt was being asked whether he personally was a member of the Communist party, where Watkins had been asked about the past activities of others.

What makes this case of significant historical importance to the development of the Court is that it represents the first time the four-member minority of Justices Black, Brennan, Douglas, and Chief Justice Warren came together and formed what eventually became the core of a strong pro–First Amendment majority.

Thus this case has become known for Black's bitter dissent, in which he said in part:

> I cannot agree with the Court's notion that the First Amendment must be abridged in order to "preserve" our country. That notion rests upon the unarticulated premise that this nation's se-

curity hangs upon its power to punish people because of what they think, speak or write about, or because of those with whom they associate for political purposes. . . . I challenge this premise, and deny that ideas can be proscribed under our Constitution.

## 62. MAPP V. OHIO, 367 U.S. 643 (1961)

Dollree Mapp and her daughter lived on the top floor of a two-family dwelling in Cleveland. Police came to her door and demanded entry, saying they were searching for a man wanted in connection with a bombing. She refused to admit them without a warrant, and they left. Three hours later they, and four additional officers, returned and when Miss Mapp did not immediately answer their knock, they forced the door open. They entered, holding up a piece a paper they claimed to be a warrant. Miss Mapp grabbed the paper and placed it in her bra. A struggle ensued in which the police recovered the paper, and handcuffed Miss Mapp. The paper was not a warrant.

In the course of their search, they did not find the man they wanted, but did find materials they seized as being obscene. Eventually Miss Mapp was charged with their possession, and was convicted under an Ohio law for possessing "lewd and lascivious books, materials and photographs." The Supreme Court of Ohio upheld her conviction.

The U.S. Supreme Court held that the search and seizure of evidence from Miss Mapp's home was unlawful, and a violation of her Fourth Amendment

right against unreasonable search and seizure. The Court recognized the right to privacy embodied in the Fourth Amendment to be applicable against the states, and that any individual should be secure against "rude invasions of privacy by state officers."

And because the search was unlawful, the Court ruled, any evidence that was seized was tainted and could not be used in either a state or federal trial. This overturned the 1949 decision in *Wolf* v. *Colorado*, in which the Court had ruled that a state could determine what evidence is admissible in its courts.

## 63. ENGEL V. VITALE, 370 U.S. 421 (1962)

In 1960, the Board of Education of Union Free School District No. 9, New Hyde Park, New York, ordered the principal to have a prayer read aloud in each class at the beginning of each school day. The prayer, which started "Almighty God we acknowledge our dependence upon Thee, . . ." had been approved by the State Board of Regents. A group of parents objected, and brought suit against the school board. New York state trial and appeals courts upheld the prayer.

The Supreme Court held that the use of even a nondenominational prayer in school, written by a government authority, violated the establishment clause of the First Amendment. The fact that students did not have to participate in the reading of the prayer did not alter the fact that the reading of any prayer is a violation of the separation of church and state.

## 64. BAKER V. CARR, 369 U.S. 186 (1962)
## REYNOLDS V. SIMS, 377 U.S. 533 (1964)

Baker claimed that because of population growth and redistribution in Tennessee since 1900, the 1901 Apportionment Act, which outlined voting districts in Tennessee, was obsolete and should be declared unconstitutional. Baker also claimed that the Tennessee legislature refused to reapportion itself. The issue before the Court was whether a constitutional challenge to a state apportionment act was a political question and not subject to judicial review.

The Court answered by laying out a six-part test to determine whether an issue is a political question. The Court refused to find the issues a political question in this case, ruling that what Baker was alleging was a violation of the equal-protection clause, which is not a political question.

Then two years later, in *Reynolds*, the Court was presented with a substantive apportionment question. The federal district court in Alabama had ruled that the existing and proposed legislative plans for voting districts in Alabama violated the equal-protection clause. It ordered into effect a temporary reapportionment plan made up of a combination of the proposed plans.

The issue before the Supreme Court this time was to determine if the equal-protection clause requires that seats in both houses of a state legislature be apportioned based on population. The Court held that, in order to achieve fair representation for all its citizens, and because the Constitution's guarantee of equal participation of voters, seats in both houses must be based on population. The ruling was based on the premise that overvaluing the votes of persons living in one area has the effect of diluting the value of votes in other areas. Such a practice violates the Fourteenth Amendment right to equal protection.

## 65. GIDEON V. WAINWRIGHT, 372 U.S. 335 (1963)

Clarence Earl Gideon was charged with breaking and entering a poolroom with the intent to commit a misdemeanor. The law in the state of Florida did not allow for appointing counsel for indigents, unless a capital case. Since Gideon could not afford an attorney, he conducted his own defense before a jury. The jury found him guilty. Gideon then appealed his conviction, claiming that he had been denied his Sixth Amendment right to counsel.

In an unusual move, the Supreme Court not only granted certiorari to Gideon but also appointed an attorney to represent him. The Court held that the Sixth Amendment guarantees that "in all criminal prosecutions, the accused shall enjoy the right . . . to have assistance of counsel in his defense."

Previously, the Court had held that counsel must be provided in federal court for defendants unable to afford their own counsel, unless the right is voluntarily and intelligently waived. Now the Court extended this right to state proceedings.

In doing so, the Court reiterated that certain rights granted under the Bill of Rights were fundamental, and as such should be incorporated into the Fourteenth Amendment to apply to the states. Such rights include freedom of speech, press, assembly, and religion. The Court increased this list by determining that the guarantee of counsel is also a fundamental right and is essential to a fair trial.

## 66. MALLOY V. HOGAN, 378 U.S. 1 (1964)

William Malloy, who was on probation for a gambling misdemeanor, was again arrested in a gambling raid on a Hartford pool hall. He was ordered to testify in an investigation of gambling and other criminal activities. He refused to answer questions pertaining to the circumstances of his arrest, and to identify who owned the pool hall, on the grounds that the answers might incriminate him. He was found in contempt by a Hartford County superior court judge, and was sent to the city jail until he answered. His writ of habeas corpus was denied by the Supreme Court of Connecticut.

In ruling for Hogan, 5–4, the U.S. Supreme Court held for the first time that the constitutionally protected right against self-incrimination found in the Fifth Amendment is applicable to the states through the Fourteenth Amendment. The Court ruled that in applying the privilege against self-incrimination, the same standards should apply in state and federal courts. Malloy's contempt violation was overturned.

## 67. HEART OF ATLANTA MOTEL V. UNITED STATES, 379 U.S. 241 (1964)

Can the federal government's commerce-clause powers over interstate commerce be used to prohibit racial discrimination in privately owned public accommodations? The Court said no in 1883, in the civil rights cases, but Congress had now attempted to overturn that decision with the passage of the Civil Rights Act of 1964. Was the law constitutional?

The Heart of Atlanta Motel refused to rent rooms to blacks. The motel was located near two interstate highways, advertised nationwide, and approximately 75% of its visitors were from out-of-state. The government brought suit against the motel, holding it in violation of the 1964 Civil Rights Act. The motel claimed that as an in-state operation it was not subject to federal statute.

The Court held that Congress, under its commerce power, can prohibit discrimination in public accommodations. The test as to whether Congress can exercise this power is whether the activity to be regulated concerns or impacts more than one state. In this case, the Court found that since the motel catered to out-of-state visitors and advertised widely, it was subject to federal law.

## 68. NEW YORK TIMES V. SULLIVAN, 376 U.S. 254 (1964)

Sullivan was a city commissioner in Montgomery, Alabama, whose job included overseeing city police. During a series of civil rights disturbances in 1960, the *New York Times* published an ad from a civil rights group charging the Montgomery Police Department with various illegal acts. Certain of the statements in the ad ended up being false. Sullivan, even though his name did not appear in the ad, sued the *Times* for defamation and won a judgment for $500,000 under an Alabama law that held that no damages need be proved whenever a defamatory falsehood is shown to have injured its subject in his public office or have imputed misconduct to him in his official duties.

The Court held that, in cases where libel is alleged by a public official or "public figure," the plaintiff must prove that the falsehoods made against him were done so with "actual malice." That, in turn, was defined as knowing that what was about to be published is false, and then proceeding with reckless disregard as to whether it was false or not.

The Court's reasoning was that public figures have access to media outlets to refute charges against them. Since there was no evidence of actual malice on the part of the *New York Times*, the decision was reversed and remanded back to the lower court.

## 69. ESCOBEDO V. ILLINOIS, 378 U.S. 478 (1964)

Danny Escobedo was arrested and brought in for questioning in the death of his brother-in-law. He had been arrested previously, shortly after the shooting, but had made no statement and had been released. At the second arrest,

Escobedo made several requests to see his lawyer, who, though present in the building, was not allowed to see him. Escobedo also was not advised of his right to remain silent; during questioning he made certain incriminating statements that were later admitted at his trial. He was convicted of murder, and the Illinois Supreme Court upheld the conviction.

The Court held that after police questioning stops being a general inquiry, and becomes an interrogation of a particular crime, a suspect must be given the right to consult with counsel, and must be advised of his right to remain silent. If not, as was the case with Escobedo, he is denied his constitutional rights under the Sixth and Fourteenth Amendments, and no statement he subsequently makes during questioning may later be admitted at trial.

## 70. GRISWOLD V. CONNECTICUT, 381 U.S. 479 (1965)

Griswold was executive director of the Planned Parenthood League of Connecticut. Both he and Dr. Buxton were convicted under a Connecticut law that made it illegal to counsel persons, single or married, to use contraceptives.

The issue before the Court was whether a constitutionally protected privacy right exists in the marital relationship, despite the absence of any specific language in the Constitution. The justices ruled that protected zones of privacy exist under various amendments in the Bill of Rights. The Court found that the Connecticut law forbidding the use of contraceptives had a destructive impact on the marital relationship, and thus violated this implied right of privacy.

It must be noted that the justices did not agree on exactly where, in the Constitution or Bill of Rights, this right of privacy is contained.

## 71. MIRANDA V. ARIZONA, 384 U.S. 436 (1966)

The issue before the Court was the admissibility of statements obtained while in police custody. Ernesto Miranda was convicted of kidnapping and rape, based on a confession he made to police during two hours of questioning. He was never told of his right under the Fifth Amendment to remain silent, or of his Sixth Amendment right to have counsel present. Miranda sought to have his conviction overturned owing to failure of the police to inform him of his rights.

The Court found that interrogation can lead to coerced confessions and violate an accused's Fifth Amendment right not to incriminate himself. Therefore, the Court said, prior to any questioning, a suspect must be warned that (1) he has a right to remain silent; (2) that any statement may be used as evidence against him; (3) that he has a right to the presence of an attorney; and (4) if he cannot afford one, one will be appointed for him. Any of the above rights can be waived if done so voluntarily and intelligently. But if at any time a suspect indicates that he wishes to consult with an attorney, all questioning by police must cease.

## 72. SOUTH CAROLINA V. KATZENBACH, 383 U.S. 436 (1966)

South Carolina sought to find certain sections of the Voting Rights Act of 1965 unconstitutional, and requested an injunction against their enforcement. The state had a long history of voting-rights violations, having, among other things, long required passage of a literacy test as a precondition for voting. The federal government had suspended many of South Carolina's voting tests and rules, and now the Voting Rights Act was requiring that any new rules be first approved by the U.S. attorney general.

The Court held the Voting Rights Act was a proper exercise of Congress's power to combat racial discrimination in voting, and thus was constitutional. As for Justice Department actions regarding South Carolina, the Court ruled that considering its past history of voting-rights violations, the requirement for judicial review of any new voting regulations was warranted and constitutional.

## 73. LOVING V. VIRGINIA, 388 U.S. 1 (1967)

Virginia had a law banning interracial marriages. In June 1958, Richard Loving, a white man, married Mildred Jester, a black woman, in the District of Columbia. They moved to Caroline County, Virginia, and were indicted by a local grand jury. On January 6, 1959, they plead guilty and were sentenced to a year in jail, but the sentence was stayed on their agreement to leave the state and not return for twenty-five years. They moved to the District of Columbia, and eventually filed suit both in federal court and in the Virginia state courts, seeking to invalidate the Virginia law. The law was upheld by the highest court in Virginia. The Lovings appealed to the U.S. Supreme Court.

The Court unanimously struck down the Virginia law, holding it violated both the equal-protection and the due process clauses. Chief Justice Warren noted that the Fourteenth Amendment demands that any law involving a racial classification meet the most rigorous test that it seeks to accomplish some vital state objective. Preventing miscegenation, he ruled, is clearly not a valid objective.

Taken more broadly, this case is the first in which the Court specifically said that any scheme involving racial classifications is "inherently suspect."

## 74. TINKER V. DES MOINES SCHOOL INDEPENDENT COMMUNITY SCHOOL DISTRICT, 393 U.S. 503 (1969)

Mary Beth Tinker, age thirteen, and a friend and her brother wore black arm bands to school to protest the Vietnam War. They were suspended pursuant to a two-day-old school policy. The federal district court denied their request for injunctive relief on the grounds that school officials acted reasonably in order to prevent a disturbance on school grounds. The students appealed.

In a decision that impacted both on the right of free speech and students'

rights generally, the Court upheld the students' right to wear the armbands as a symbolic political speech protected by the First Amendment. Writing for the majority, Justice Abe Fortas said "It can hardly be argued that either students or teachers shed their constitutional rights to freedom of speech or expression at the schoolhouse gate."

But the decision was a close one. Justice Black wrote a furious dissent blasting the majority for limiting the ability of administrators to run their schools. This, in turn, has gradually become the majority position. More recently, the Court has tended to limit the rights of public school students, including their free-speech rights, by limiting their rights to a free student press through allowing administrative control of school newspapers and allowing unannounced searches of student lockers. All these actions would be unconstitutional outside the public school setting.

## 75. BRANDENBERG V. OHIO, 395 U.S. 444 (1969)

In 1940, the Alien Registration Act, known popularly as the Smith Act, was passed. In part it outlawed the advocacy of, or teaching about, the overthrow of the government by force or violence, or the organizing of people to do so.

Eugene Dennis was a leader of the Communist party. In 1951, in *Dennis v. United States*, the Court upheld the constitutionality of the Smith Act and Dennis's conviction on the basis that the government's interest in limiting the speech of a group intent on overthrowing the government outweighed the group or its members' right to free speech.

Then in 1957, in another Smith Act case—*Yates* v. *United States*—the Court for the first time modified its stance in *Dennis*. The now more liberal Court held that the Smith Act did not outlaw the mere advocacy or teaching of the overthrow of government as an abstract concept; rather, it outlawed only direct incitement to immediate action.

Now twelve years after *Dennis*, the Court received the case of *Clarence Brandenberg*, the head of the Ohio Ku Klux Klan. He was arrested after giving a rabble-rousing speech in which he talked generally about the people being "revengent" against the president, Congress, and Supreme Court if changes were not made in society. He was convicted under an Ohio law that duplicated the Smith Act. Although the case was brought under the Ohio law, the Court used the decision to finally strike down the Smith Act as unconstitutional.

## 76. POWELL V. McCORMACK, 395 U.S. 486 (1969)

The Court was faced with two questions: what right does Congress have to exclude its own members? And is the issue a political question, and thus out-of-bounds to the courts?

Representative Adam Clayton Powell, D–NY, was reelected to the 90th Congress. He met all the age and residency requirements, but a congressional subcommittee reported that he was guilty of all sorts of misconduct, filed false official reports, and misused federal funds. The House passed a resolution calling for his exclusion, and House Speaker McCormack refused to swear him in.

When Powell filed suit, McCormack argued that the issue was a political question and not entitled to judicial review.

The Court did not agree. Chief Justice Warren, writing for a seven-member majority, ruled that the Court could decide this issue since the action against Powell was an exclusion, rather than an expulsion. (An expulsion would have been a political question, and not reviewable.)

Having ruled that the Court had jurisdiction, Warren ruled that Congress could not exclude Powell because its power was limited to determining if a member met the constitutional qualifications of age and residence. It was up to the voters to decide if a candidate should be elected or reelected.

## 77. BENTON V. MARYLAND, 395 U.S. 784 (1969)

In a 1937 decision, *Palko* v. *Connecticut*, the Court had ruled that a Connecticut law, which permitted the state to appeal when a criminal was convicted of a lesser crime than originally indicated, did not constitute double jeopardy. More broadly, the decision held that federal double-jeopardy standards did not apply to states.

Now the Court was hearing the case of John Benton, who had been tried in Maryland charged with burglary and larceny, and found not guilty to larceny, but guilty of burglary. An appeals court later threw out the burglary conviction and ordered a new trial.

The state retried Benton on both burglary and larceny, with the judge denying his motion that he should not be tried on a charge to which he had previously been acquitted. In the second trial he was found guilty on both counts, and he appealed.

The Court threw out the larceny conviction. It ruled that the Fifth Amendment's guarantee against double jeopardy is fundamental and should apply to all state actions through the Fourteenth Amendment. In so ruling, the Court specifically overturned *Palko*.

## 78. IN RE WINSHIP, 397 U.S. 358 (1970)

Under the New York Family Court Act, for a juvenile to be found guilty of a crime, all that was required was that he be proven guilty by a "preponderance of the evidence."

Applying this standard, twelve-year-old Winship was found to have committed an act that "if done by an adult, would constitute the crime . . . of larceny." The New York Court of Appeals affirmed the conviction, upholding the constitutionality of the statute.

The Supreme Court was asked to decide whether in any criminal case, regardless whether the accused is a juvenile or an adult, the due process clause requires the standard to be "proof beyond a reasonable doubt." It answered in the affirmative, ruling that a lesser standard of proof for juveniles is not constitutional. All criminal defendants, regardless of age or in what kind of a proceeding, must be found guilty beyond a reasonable doubt.

## 79. WILLIAMS V. FLORIDA, 399 U.S. 78 (1970)

This case was significant in establishing two important rules of criminal procedure. Johnny Williams was arrested in Dade County (Miami), charged with robbery, and eventually convicted by a six-man jury. He appealed on the basis that criminal actions must be tried by twelve-member juries.

Not so, said the Supreme Court. Partly overturning *Patton* v. *United States* (see number 42), the justices held that in noncapital cases, being tried by a jury of less than twelve is not a violation of the Sixth Amendment guarantee of a fair trial. But at the same time the justices did hold that, while using fewer than twelve is constitutional, no fewer than six may be used.

In addition, Florida had a rule requiring defendants to disclose the names of alibi witnesses to the prosecution, as well as for the prosecution to disclose to the defense any alibi rebuttal witnesses. Failure to comply with the rule could have resulted in the exclusion of alibi evidence at trial, or the exclusion of rebuttal witnesses.

Williams complied with the rule after failing in his effort to avoid its application. Now Williams claimed that his Fifth Amendment rights were violated by his having to furnish the prosecution with information useful in convicting him.

The Court held that a notice-of-alibi rule does not violate the Fifth Amendment. The Court found that the discovery rule was designed to facilitate the search for the truth in criminal trials, by giving both sides the chance to investigate crucial facts. The Court held the rule only accelerated the defendant's alibi defense, but did not violate his right against compelled testimony.

## 80. NEW YORK TIMES CO. V. UNITED STATES, 403 U.S. 713 (1971) (PENTAGON PAPERS CASE)

The *Washington Post* and the *New York Times* were about to publish the contents of a classified study entitled "History of U.S. Decision-Making Process on Viet Nam Policy." The U.S. government filed for an injunction to stop the publication on the grounds of national security. The federal district court denied the government's request for the injunction, and the government appealed to the Supreme Court.

The issue before the Court was what burden of proof the government must meet in order to justify a prior restraint. The Court ruled that the government would be held to a higher standard of proof because any attempt at prior restraint of expression comes with the strong presumption that it is unconstitutional. Here, the government did not meet that burden, and the denial of the injunction was upheld.

The publication of the papers began on June 17 and 18, 1971. The government immediately brought legal action to stop the publication through a temporary restraining order. Between June 15 and 28, two district courts and two courts of appeal heard the arguments. On June 25, the Supreme Court granted certiorari. The restraining order remained in effect until a final decision was handed down on June 30, 1971, allowing publication.

## 81. MILLER V. CALIFORNIA, 413 U.S. 15 (1973)

Marvin Miller conducted a mass-mailing campaign to advertise the sale of adult materials. The advertising brochures themselves were found obscene by the lower court. The brochures were sent to individuals who had not requested them. Miller was convicted of violating a California statute that prohibited the knowing distribution of obscene matter, after the trial judge instructed the jury to apply a local community standard in determining if the brochures were obscene.

The central question before the Court was whether a local or a national standard must be applied in determining obscenity. Must the materials be, as set forth in *Roth* (see number 57), "utterly without redeeming social value," or can a lesser local community standard be applied?

The Court held that a local community standard can be applied, and then set forth a new three-part test of obscenity:

1. Whether the average person, applying community standards, would find that the work, as a whole, appeals to the prurient interest.

2. Whether the material depicts in a patently offensive way sexual conduct specifically defined by the applicable state law.

3. Whether the work lacks serious literary, artistic, political, or scientific value.

The Miller tripartite test of obscenity is the most current one. If the three requirements are met, then the material in question is considered obscene and outside the protection of the First Amendment.

## 82. ROE V. WADE, 410 U.S. 113 (1973)
## DOE V. BOLTON, 410 U.S. 179 (1973)

*Roe*, a Texas case, and *Doe*, a Georgia case, were heard together. The Texas law being challenged in *Roe* was typical of laws in most states. The plaintiff was a single pregnant woman who sought to have the laws in Texas changed to allow her to obtain a legal abortion in the state. Texas argued that the fetus was a person within the meaning of the Fourteenth Amendment, and as such was entitled to a right to life. Although Roe terminated her pregnancy in 1970, the case was found not to be moot, as the court held that pregnancy was "capable of repetition."

The Georgia law attacked in *Doe* allowed a physician to perform an abortion only if the mother's life was in danger, if the fetus was likely to be born with birth defects, or if the pregnancy had resulted from a rape.

The issue before the Court was whether the Constitution guarantees a right to privacy that extends to a woman's decision to obtain an abortion.

The Court held that the state does have a legitimate interest in preserving the health of a pregnant woman, and in protecting potential life. It also found that while the Constitution does not explicitly mention a right to privacy, it had previously found such a right to exist, and that right was broad enough to cover this situation.

In balancing the states' rights against the privacy interests of the mother, Justice Blackmun, writing for the majority, developed a trimester analysis, holding that the state's interests increase as the pregnancy progresses. The point after which the fetus gains rights as an individual was determined to be the point of viability, or when the fetus could survive outside of the mother. That was determined to be approximately twenty-four weeks. Prior to this point in the pregnancy, the mother is free to decide whether her pregnancy should be terminated. After viability, the state may regulate and even prohibit abortion.

By one count, Blackmun's opinion has been cited more than 3,700 times by district courts, appeals courts, and Supreme Court decisions involving a very wide range of social issues: a patient's right-to-die, the rights of the mentally ill, the regulation of the newly emerging science of genetic research, and a state's power to regulate social conduct.

Most recently in *Planned Parenthood v. Casey* (1992), a narrow five justice majority continued to uphold the central tenant of *Roe*, that a woman's right to an abortion is constitutionally protected. But the majority did narrow the Roe holding by throwing out the specific trimester test and replaced it with a rule that after a fetus reaches the point of viability it is presumed the state has an interest in the unborn life and even before can regulate abortions so long as the regulation is reasonable and does not place an "undue burden" on the right.

## 83. FRONTIERO V. RICHARDSON, 411 U.S. 677 (1973)
## CRAIG V. BOREN, 429 U.S. 1124 (1977)

In *Frontiero*, the issue was that female military personnel were not allowed to claim their spouses as dependents for purposes of obtaining increased quarters allowances and medical and dental benefits. Males could automatically claim their wives as dependents, regardless of actual dependency, whereas women had to show that their husbands were actually dependent upon them.

In a wide-ranging opinion, the Court used the case to strike down most gender-based discrimination. The Court held that it was a violation of the due process clause to treat men and women differently. Gender, said the Court, is always a suspect classification. Whenever men and women are treated differently, the Court said it would look very closely to determine if the interest of the government in making gender-based distinctions outweighs equal-protection rights. In this case, the Court held that the government's interest in administrative expediency was not enough to warrant the discrimination. In fact, the Court found no proof that the classification saved the government any money. The government failed to show that the classification actually achieved a legitimate government objective.

Then in *Craig*, the Court was asked for the first time to apply its reasoning in *Frontiero*. It was to review an Oklahoma statute that prohibited the sale of 3.2 percent beer to males under the age of twenty-one, and to females under the age of eighteen. Craig, twenty, challenged the statute on the grounds that the classification denied males aged eighteen to twenty equal protection of the law.

The Court held that the government had failed to show that the classification supported any legitimate government interest. The state claimed that the statute supported the government's interest in traffic safety, but statistics showed that arrests of eighteen- to twenty-year-old males for alcohol-related traffic offenses was only 2 percent higher than for females. The Oklahoma statute was found unconstitutional.

## 84. UNITED STATES V. U.S. DISTRICT COURT, 418 U.S. 94 (1974)

Following the Watergate break-in, and subsequent indictment of seven defendants for various offenses related to the break-in, the special prosecutor assigned to the case issued a subpoena to obtain Watergate-related tapes and documents from then-president Nixon. Nixon turned over some materials, but then moved to have the subpoena quashed, claiming both that the need for the confidentiality of high-level communication within the executive branch required his refusal to obey the subpoena, and that the separation-of-powers doctrine precluded the judicial branch from reviewing his executive decision not to turn over the remainder of the documents.

The Court held that the president does not possess absolute immunity from judicial review. Referring to its holding in *Marbury v. Madison*, the Court reiterated that "it is emphatically the province of the Judicial Department to say what the law is," and that this was also true in respect to determining claims of executive privilege. Although the need for confidentiality does justify a presumptive privilege, said the Court, the need of the criminal justice system for all of the facts, and the special prosecutor's demonstration of a specific need for the material sought, outweigh any such privilege.

Nixon was ordered to turn over the materials to the special prosecutor.

## 85. GREGG V. GEORGIA, 428 U.S. 153 (1976)
## PROFFITT V. FLORIDA, 428 U.S. 242 (1976)
## JUREK V. TEXAS, 428 U.S. 262 (1976)
## WOODSON V. NORTH CAROLINA, 428 U.S. 280 (1976)
## ROBERTS V. LOUISIANA, 428 U.S. 325 (1976)

All five cases, decided at the same time, dealt with the constitutionality of the death penalty as punishment in murder cases. Taken together, they represent the Court's view of capital punishment.

In *Gregg, Proffitt*, and *Jurek*, the Court held that the death penalty as punishment for murder does not violate the Eighth Amendment prohibition against cruel and unusual punishment. But in saying that, the Court did hold that the Eighth Amendment does require a sentencing judge to take into consideration the individual character of the defendant and the specific circumstances of the crime.

Thus, what is constitutionally required is a two-part process: to assess guilt or innocence, and to determine the sentence.

In *Woodson* and *Roberts*, their juries were instructed that the death penalty was mandatory punishment for the crimes of which the defendants were convicted. The Court reversed and remanded both cases, holding that a mandatory death penalty allowed for no consideration of mitigating factors in deciding whether the death penalty is warranted.

## 86. COKER V. GEORGIA, 433 U.S. 584 (1977)

While serving time for murder, rape, kidnapping, and aggravated assault, Coker escaped from prison. Later, while committing an armed robbery, he raped a woman. He was subsequently convicted of rape, armed robbery, and other offenses, and then was sentenced to death on the rape charge. The Georgia Supreme Court affirmed the conviction and the sentence.

The Court reversed the death-penalty ruling, and remanded the case back to the Georgia court for resentencing, finding that a death sentence for rape is "grossly disproportionate and excessive punishment," which violates the Eighth Amendment guarantee against cruel and unusual punishment.

## 87. REGENTS OF THE UNIVERSITY OF CALIFORNIA V. BAKKE, 438 U.S. 265 (1978)

The University of California at Davis Medical School had an admissions policy that required at least sixteen out of every hundred students be admitted from specified minority groups. Bakke, a Caucasian, alleged that his application for admission was denied in 1973 and 1974, while less qualified minority applicants were admitted. He brought action under Title VI of the Civil Rights Act of 1964, and under the state and federal equal-protection clauses.

The California Supreme Court held that, although there was a compelling state interest to increase the number of minority doctors, there were less intrusive methods available. Bakke was ordered admitted into the medical program, since the university could not meet its burden of proof that he would not have been admitted had the special admissions program not been in existence. The university appealed the decision.

The issue before the U.S. Supreme Court was whether the equal-protection clause prohibits discrimination aimed at promoting the welfare of minorities. The Court held that the equal-protection clause prohibited discrimination against persons of any race, and was designed to equally protect both minorities and whites. When any classification is based on race, the courts must use strict scrutiny in determining the justification for the discrimination. In order to justify discrimination, it must be established that the classification is necessary for the

accomplishment of its goals and constitutionally permissible and substantial.

The Court held that the state's interest in correcting general societal discrimination and to aid undeserved communities was not sufficient to justify using racially based admissions criteria. The system was declared unconstitutional, and the California Supreme Court's order admitting Bakke was upheld.

## 88. UNITED STEELWORKERS V. WEBER, KAISER ALUMINUM V. WEBER, UNITED STATES V. WEBER, 443 U.S. 193 (1979)

In 1974, the United Steelworkers Union and Kaiser Aluminum entered into a collective-bargaining agreement covering wages and conditions at Kaiser plants. The agreement included provisions to eliminate racial imbalances in the work force. Weber, a white production worker, filed a class-action suit in federal court alleging that junior black employees were being promoted in preference to senior white employees, thus violating Title VII of the Civil Rights Act of 1964, which made it unlawful to discriminate on the basis of race. The district court found for Weber, and the court of appeals affirmed.

The Court overturned the lower courts' judgments. The justices interpreted Title VII to permit "voluntary" race-conscious affirmative-action programs, after looking at the legislative history of the act and determining Congress's concern with discrimination against minorities and the fact that Congress had not prohibited such programs.

The Court held that there was no limitation on employers or unions from seeking to remedy racial imbalances in traditionally segregated job categories.

## 89. RICHMOND NEWSPAPERS V. VIRGINIA, 448 U.S. 555 (1980)

A fourth murder trial for George Stevenson was about to begin. The first had resulted in a conviction, but had been subsequently reversed. Two retrials had ended in hung juries. Now at the fourth trial, the defense requested that the trial be closed to the press and public, and the trial judge granted the request. A newspaper and two of its reporters filed a motion to vacate the order for the closed trial. The trial judge denied the motion, and he was upheld by the Virginia Supreme Court.

The U.S. Supreme Court held that the right of the public and the press to attend criminal trials is guaranteed under the First and Fourteenth Amendments. Absent some overriding interest (national security might be one), and none was found in this case, criminal trials must be opened to the public and the press.

## 90. CHANDLER V. FLORIDA, 449 U.S. 560 (1981)

Noel Chandler and Robert Granger were arrested in Florida and charged with burglary. They were convicted in a trial that was televised under a pilot program in Florida that allowed television cameras in the courtroom. They objected at the time, and now were appealing their convictions under the theory that televising their trial live deprived them of a fair trial. A state appeals court affirmed their conviction, and the Florida Supreme Court denied review.

The U.S. Supreme Court held there was no constitutional prohibition against the state of Florida providing for radio, television, and photographic coverage of a criminal trial. The justices said a constitutional ban on broadcasting of trials cannot be justified because of a danger that, in some cases, a jury's ability to make an impartial decision may be impaired. The safeguard against juror prejudice, the Court stated, is the defendant's right to demonstrate that the media coverage prejudiced his or her particular jury.

## 91. BOARD OF EDUCATION V. PICO, 102 S.CT. 2799 (1982)

The Board of Education of the Island Trees Union Free School District No. 26, in New York, removed nine books from the shelves of its high school and junior high school libraries. The board claimed the books were "anti-American, anti-Christian, anti-Semitic and just plain filthy." Pico, along with other students, brought legal action alleging the removal of the books was due to the personal tastes of the board members, and not because the books lacked any educational value. This, they alleged, constituted a denial of their First Amendment rights. The district court ruled in favor of the board, but the court of appeals reversed and remanded the case for further evidence on the board's motivation. The board petitioned the Supreme Court for reinstatement of the district court's order.

The Supreme Court ruled that there is no absolute discretion on the part of the school board to remove materials from school libraries. The Court also found that there was a significant issue of fact as to the matter of the board's motivations that needed to be decided at the lower court level.

Justice Brennan stated in his opinion: "We are . . . in full agreement with petitioners that local school boards must be permitted to establish and apply their curricula in such a way as to transmit community values and that there is a legitimate and substantial community interest in promoting respect for authority and traditional values. . . ." However, he went on to say that such action must be reconciled with the First Amendment.

## 92. UNITED STATES V. LEON 468 U.S. 897 (1984)

Pursuant to information gained from confidential informants, and from their subsequent investigation, police prepared an affidavit and a request for a search warrant. The application was reviewed by several deputy district attorneys, and a search warrant was issued by a state court judge. The search produced large quantities of drugs and other evidence. Respondents were indicted, and filed motions to suppress the evidence found during the search on the basis that the search warrant was invalid. The trial court judge agreed, finding that the affidavit on which the warrant was based was insufficient to establish probable cause. The state appealed.

The Supreme Court held that the Fourth Amendment's exclusionary rule, which prevents evidence obtained in an illegal search from being introduced at trial, should not apply in instances where the police were acting in reliance on a search warrant issued by a detached and neutral judicial officer, even if the warrant was later found to be defective. The Court reiterated that the exclusionary rule should continue to apply in those situations where the violation has been substantial and deliberate, but that a balancing approach must be used in determining the application of the rule.

## 93. TENNESSEE V. GARNER, 471 U.S. 1 (1985)

A Tennessee statute provided that if, after a police officer has given notice of his intent to arrest an individual, the individual should flee, "the officer may use all the necessary means to effect the arrest." A Memphis police officer shot and killed Garner's son, who after being told to stop, jumped over a fence in an attempt to flee. The officer admitted that he used deadly force even though he suspected Garner was a minor, was of slight build, and that he was reasonably sure that the suspect was unarmed.

The father brought an action in federal district court seeking damages for violations of his son's constitutional rights. The court found the Tennessee statute constitutional. But the court of appeals reversed.

The Supreme Court ruled that the Fourth Amendment's guarantee against unreasonable search and seizure prohibits the use of deadly force against suspects unless police authorities who use force have probable cause to believe the suspect poses a threat of serious physical harm to the police or to other persons.

## 94. GARCIA V. SAN ANTONIO METRO TRANSIT AUTHORITY, 469 U.S. 528 (1985)

In 1974, Congress passed amendments to the Fair Labor Standards Act (FLSA) that extended its minimum wage and maximum hour provisions to employees of the state and local governments, and all their political subdivisions. In a 1976 ruling, *National League of Cities* v. *Usery*, the Court held that was an unconstitutional use of Congress's commerce power, in that it forced choices upon the states as to how to conduct their governmental functions.

Now in *Garcia*, the San Antonio Transit Authority (which received substantial federal assistance) was told by the U.S. Department of Labor that it was not immune from the minimum wage and overtime regulations of the Fair Labor Standards Act. It filed suit in federal district court for a declaratory judgment, citing the decision in *National League of Cities*. The district court held that the Transit Authority was a traditional governmental function, and thus was exempt, based on the previous Court decision.

But now the Supreme Court no longer agreed. The Court overturned *National League of Cities* by finding that there was nothing in the wage and overtime regulations of the FLSA that would be destructive to state sovereignty or violate the Constitution. The Court

also stated that the attempts to draw boundaries based on whether an activity was a traditional governmental function were unworkable and inconsistent with the principles of federalism.

## 95. LOCKHART V. McCREE, 476 U.S. 162 (1986)

McCree was charged with felony murder. At his trial, the judge removed for cause, over McCree's objection, those prospective jurors who stated that they could not under any circumstances vote for the death penalty. McCree was convicted, and the jury sentenced him to life without parole. The conviction was affirmed on appeal. So McCree now sought federal habeas corpus relief, claiming that the removal of the prospective jurors violated his rights under the Sixth and Fourteenth Amendments to trial by an impartial jury.

The Court held that the Constitution does not prohibit the removal, for cause, of prospective jurors who oppose the death penalty. The purpose of the exclusion was to serve the state's legitimate interest in obtaining a single jury that could properly and impartially apply the law to the facts of the case.

## 96. FORD V. WAINWRIGHT 477 U.S. 399 (1986)

Alvin Ford was convicted in a 1974 trial of murder, and was sentenced to death. After being jailed, he began exhibiting symptoms of severe mental disorder. Upon examining him, two psychiatrists came to the conclusion that he was no longer mentally competent. The question presented to the Supreme Court was whether an insane man can be executed.

By a 5–4 vote, the Court said no. Writing for a four-member plurality, Justice Marshall said that the Eighth Amendment prohibits an insane man from being executed. Justice Powell agreed, but added that, as he saw it, the basis for judging insanity was not mental illness generally, but whether the prisoner is aware that he is going to be executed and can comprehend why. In this case he agreed with the majority because he thought that Ford could not.

The justices who dissented did so on the basis of a Florida procedure that had been used to examine Ford during the appeal process, and which had found him sane. The majority had dismissed the finding of that three-member panel, saying the procedure it had used had been defective.

## 97. BOWERS V. HARDWICK, 478 U.S. 186 (1986)

In August 1982, Bowers was charged with violating a Georgia sodomy statute by performing a sex act with another adult male in the bedroom of his home. After a preliminary hearing, the district attorney decided not to present the matter to a grand jury without further evidence. Respondent brought suit anyway in federal district court, challenging the constitutionality of the statute insofar as it criminalizes sexual acts between consenting adults. He claimed that the continued existence of the statute placed him, as a practicing homosexual, in constant fear of arrest. The district court

dismissed the case for failure to state a claim, but the court of appeals reversed.

The Supreme Court, by a vote of 5–4, found the Georgia law constitutional. It refused to extend the right of privacy to cover even consensual sodomy in the home. The Court found that no fundamental right is involved, and held that the presumed belief by society that certain sex acts are immoral and unacceptable is a rational basis for the statute.

## 98. SCHOOL BOARD OF NASSAU COUNTY V. ARLINE, 480 U.S. 273 (1987)

Gene Arline taught school in Nassau County, Florida, from 1966 until 1979. She was discharged in 1979 after suffering her third relapse in three years of tuberculosis she originally contracted in 1957. After failing to win her job back through the school system's internal administrative process, she filed suit in district court alleging her firing violated Section 504 of the Rehabilitation Act of 1973. That law prohibits any program receiving federal funds from discriminating against a handicapped individual, solely by reason of or because of his handicap. The question in this case came down to whether a medical illness can be deemed a "handicap," for the purposes of the statute.

The district court found Arline was not a handicapped person under the act. But even if she was, the trial court judge ruled she was no longer "qualified to teach elementary school" because of the possibility of giving the disease to one of her students. The court of appeals reversed, holding that persons with diseases are covered by the law, and then ordered the case sent back to the trial court to take expert testimony to determine the medical question of contagion.

The Supreme Court agreed with the appeals court that a person with a contagious disease is "handicapped," and thus is covered by the Rehabilitation Act of 1973. The Court addressed the issue of qualification to teach, by stating that findings as to the risk of transmittal of the disease should be addressed by expert public health officials, and remanded the case to the lower court for further determination.

This case has come into prominence lately owing to the AIDS epidemic. Teachers who have been dismissed because of their illness are citing *Arline* in their arguments.

## 99. TEXAS V. JOHNSON, 491 U.S. 397 (1989)

At the 1984 Republican National Convention in Dallas, Johnson allegedly doused an American flag with kerosene and set it afire. He was the only one out of 100 demonstrators arrested, and he was subsequently charged and convicted of violating a Texas statute that prohibited the desecration of a venerated object. A person violated the state law if they intentionally or knowingly desecrated (1) a public monument, (2) a place of worship or burial, or (3) a state or national flag.

The issue before the Court was whether the act of burning an American flag constitutes expressive conduct that should be protected under the First Amendment; and if so, does the Texas statute unconstitutionally suppress expression? The Court held that the burning of the flag is expressive conduct constituting political speech, and thus is protected by the First Amendment. The Court refused to create an exception to the First Amendment to prohibit flag burning.

## 100. PACIFIC MUTUAL LIFE INSURANCE COMPANY V. HASLIP, 111 S. CT. (1991)

This case involved a constitutional challenge to a punitive damage award in a tort case. The Supreme Court had previously held that the Eighth Amendment's excessive-fines clause does not apply to punitive damage awards between private parties. However, the Court agreed to review this case under the due process clause.

The Court held that the traditional process of allowing a jury to determine the amount of punitive damages was tempered by the subsequent review of that award, by both trial and appellate courts, to ensure its reasonableness. The Court held that proper jury instructions, accompanied by the jury's discretion in exercising reasonable constraints, ensures that any punitive damage awards do violate the due process clause.

# 4.
# The Supreme Court's Ten Worst Decisions

If reaching any sort of consensus on the Court's 100 most important decisions is difficult, choosing a list of its ten worst decisions is even more daunting. As with the forty or so decisions almost universally recognized as among the Court's most important, there are a handful of opinions that almost anyone would agree should live in infamy. In most cases this is true because we can now look at these long past issues dispassionately, and because now we know the course of history, and how socially destructive these opinions were.

But once you get beyond this mere handful of consensus worst decisions, picking a "ten worst" list inevitably becomes largely an excursion into subjectivity. One person's bad decision is another's logical finding; it all depends upon the observer's own views. Then, too, what might have seemed a wise decision in its own time now in hindsight looks wrong-headed, if not outrageous.

It should also be recognized that some of the Court's worst decisions are among its most important. Of the cases that follow, certainly *Dred Scott*, *Plessy* v. *Ferguson*, and the *Civil Rights Cases*, as well as some of the others, would be included among any list of the Court's most important decisions. But in light of history, these opinions now seem so wrong and so socially destructive that they must head any list of the worst decisions in Court history.

Of the ten that follow, some appear to be accidents of history or products of the inflamed social passions of their day. Others tend to fall into a common category: situations in which a probably valid constitutional principle has simply been stretched too far.

Finally, as with trying to include recent decisions in the list of 100 most important cases, the difficulty in assessing recent decisions to include as among the Court's worst, we do not yet know the long-term effects of more recent decisions. They might simply fade into obscurity. Or they might lead to significant displacements within society, and go on to affect the lives and practices of many. That is for some future Court or social historian to determine.

## 1. [DRED] SCOTT V. SANDFORD, 19 HOW. 393 (1856)

Dred Scott was born a slave, the property of wealthy Virginia farmer Peter Blow. In 1827, Blow moved to St. Louis, taking with him Scott and several of his other slaves. In 1832 Blow died and Scott was sold to Dr. John Emerson, an army physician. The army transferred Emerson to the Wisconsin Territory, where slavery was outlawed under the Missouri Compromise. But Scott stayed with Emerson, marrying another slave owned by him, and started to raise two daughters. In 1843 the Scotts returned to St. Louis with Emerson, and when he died several years later, they became the property of his widow. Eventually she moved back to her original home in New York, leaving Scott and his family in the service of Henry Blow, Peter Blow's son.

Henry Blow, who was something of an abolitionist, especially opposed the advancement of slavery into the new territories and states. He wanted to make Scott a free man, but under Missouri law that was extremely difficult absent a release signed by his owner, who was technically still Mrs. Emerson. For some reason, now lost in history, she refused to sign emancipation papers even though she had abandoned the Scotts. So on Dred Scott's behalf, Blow filed a suit in the Missouri state court seeking to have him declared a free man.

The case had much wider ramifications than simply the freedom of one slave and his family. The suit was based on the fact that Scott had resided for a time in the free Wisconsin territory. If this made Scott free, than any slave getting to a nonslave state could claim emancipation.

The trial court ruled in favor of Scott. But the Missouri Supreme Court reversed that ruling. It ruled that under Missouri law, once Scott had reentered the state, he had again become a slave. But in losing his case, Scott became a symbol for abolitionists who a year later filed a new lawsuit on his behalf, this time in federal court in St. Louis. Before the federal suit was filed, Mrs. Emerson sold Scott to her brother, John Sandford, so the suit became known as *Dred Scott* v. *Sandford.*

In the federal district court, the all-white jury quickly found for Sandford, declaring that Scott and his family remained his property. An appeals court agreed, but certified the question to the Supreme Court. The Supreme Court realized this was no ordinary case. The abolitionist movement was growing stronger and was being countered by a progressively more violent movement by slave owners who wanted slavery in the new territories to be the subject of popular referendum. The Court realized this was going to be the final judicial attempt to mediate this growing tension.

The Court ended up hearing oral arguments twice. The second time, the arguments lasted four days during December 1856. So split were the justices that they did not even meet to discuss the case for two months. Finally they ruled in an extraordinary manner with all nine justices writing separate opinions. When they were tallied, seven of the justices had ruled that Scott was still a slave.

As Chief Justice, Roger Taney is considered to have had the lead opinion, and his is the one most remembered. He ruled that whether or not Scott had resided for a time in a free state was inconsequential since neither a Negro, nor his descendants, could ever become a citizen of the United States. Thus his rights were determined solely by the laws of the state in which he was currently residing—Missouri. Moreover, in what came to be looked upon as one of the principal causes of the Civil War, Taney held that the Missouri Compromise was unconstitutional, and that slavery could not be prohibited in the territories. Taney's ruling meant that only a constitutional amendment could outlaw the expansion of slavery. That was politically impossible, so the only recourse left was war.

Only Justices John McLean and Benjamin Curtis argued that Scott was a citizen, and as such his freedom was not determined by Missouri law and that Congress had a constitutional right to prohibit slavery in the newly forming territories.

In an interesting footnote, John Sandford died before the Court announced its verdict. Ownership of the Scotts transferred back to Mrs. Emerson, who then retransferred ownership to Blow. In 1857, just weeks after the decision, Blow freed Scott, who remained in St. Louis working as a hotel porter until his death only a year later from tuberculosis.

## 2. MINOR V. HAPPERSETT, 21 WALL 162 (1875)

Virginia Minor was a social activist. Although brought up in the state of Virginia, she and her lawyer husband supported the Union in the Civil War and moved to St. Louis where she became active in the Ladies Aid Society.

When the war ended and her relief work was finished, Virginia Minor turned her attention to women's rights. Missouri was about to adopt a new state constitution that included a provision allowing Negro males to vote. She circulated a petition to the legislature demanding that since voting rights were being extended to Negro males, women too should be allowed to vote. The state assembly brought her proposal up for a vote and it was defeated 90–5. In response, Minor formed the Women's Suffrage Association and became its first president.

On October 15, 1872, Virginia Minor attempted to register to vote in St. Louis. The city's registrar refused to allow her name to be entered on the voting rolls, citing the newly adopted state constitution, which restricted voting to males. Under Missouri law, a married woman could not file a lawsuit unless she were joined in it by her husband. In this case, Francis Minor not only approved of his wife's efforts but he and several other lawyers marshaled an array of legal arguments in support of women's suffrage.

In their suit the Minors relied on three arguments: (1) that laws prohibiting women from voting were "bills of attainder"—laws aimed at specific groups of individuals; (2) that the "privileges and immunities" clause of the Constitution—"Citizens of each state shall be entitled to all privileges and immunities of citizens in the several states"—applies equally to men and women because women are not specifically denied its protections; and (3) that not allowing women to vote violates the equal protection provision of the Fourteenth Amendment. But the Missouri Supreme Court did not agree. It ruled against the Minors on each of their three legal arguments, holding among other things that the continued denial of a right showed that right had never been established.

The Supreme Court agreed to hear the case. Its ruling was quick and unanimous. It said that while there could be no question that a woman is a citizen, the mere fact of citizenship did not automatically confer the right of suffrage. Just as the right to vote could be limited to property owners, or persons of a certain age or intelligence, it could also be limited to men only.

Actually the ruling was in keeping with several others limiting women's rights that were of the same era. Two years earlier, in *Bradwell* v. *Illinois*, the Court had ruled that a woman had no right to practice law. A year later, in *United States* v. *Reese* (1876), the Court ruled that although the Fifteenth Amendment forbad the states from denying the right to vote because of race, color, or previous condition of servitude, it did not actively confer on anyone the right to vote. Using convoluted reasoning, the Court held that it simply guaranteed a right be exercised free of racial discrimination if that right were extended, but that extension was up to

state law and thus the federal government had no power to punish a state official who denies blacks the right to vote or who refuses to count votes cast by blacks.

A year after the Minor decision denying women the right to vote, famed suffragette Susan B. Anthony convinced a member of the U.S. Senate to introduce a constitutional amendment allowing women the vote. It was defeated 34–6. It was reintroduced almost every year thereafter, and on those rare occasions it made it out of committee it was easily defeated. Finally, forty-one years after first being introduced, the Nineteenth Amendment was finally approved and sent to the states for ratification. It became a part of the Constitution in 1920.

## 3. UNITED STATES V. CRUICKSHANK, 92 U.S. 542 (1876)

After the Civil War, Congress set up a special committee to seek ways to unify the divided country. That committee determined that a new constitutional amendment covering a range of issues—from limits on the public debt to the qualification of former Confederate officials and officers to hold public office—was now necessary. Included in the new amendment, which was passed and ratified by the states in 1868, was a provision that has become known as the due process clause:

No State shall make or enforce any law which shall abridge the privileges or immunities of citizens of the United States nor shall any State deprive any person of life, liberty, or property, without due process of law; nor deny any person within its jurisdiction the equal protection of the laws.

This clause had been drafted by Representatives John A. Bingham of Ohio and Jacob Howard of Michigan. When they presented their handiwork to the House for its consideration, they said clearly that the clause would make all the guarantees of the Bill of Rights applicable to state laws and actions. The House adopted the language for that very purpose.

But this was a period in which a staunchly pro-Southern and conservative Court was clearly bent on preventing too many disruptions from occurring in the post-Civil War South, despite Congress's clear intention that such change must occur. The main method the Court used was an extraordinarily formal review of cases presented to it. And at the heart of all these rulings was the basic determination that nothing in the 14th Amendment specifically required the protections and sanctions of the Bill of Rights be applied to the states or state actions.

As we saw in the two 1873 decisions that have become known as the slaughterhouse cases, the Court rejected the doctrine of "incorporation," and denied that the fourteenth Amendment extended to state laws and actions the guarantees of the Bill of Rights. Using this same reasoning the next year, the Court rendered what might be its most appalling ruling ever.

In 1871, a large group of blacks had gathered in a Louisiana church for a political meeting. They were set upon by a large number of heavily armed whites, and in the ensuing melee, over 100 blacks were killed. Eventually more than 100 whites were federally indicted for murder. The federal indictments were necessary because, under Louisiana law, it had been the blacks who were committing a crime by gathering, and it was argued that their attackers had undertaken legal self-help to protect the community.

William Woods, an Alabama judge who would later serve six years on the U.S. Supreme Court, potentially gave the justices the opening they should have been looking for to extend the Bill of Rights to the states. Judge Woods ruled that the newly passed Fourteenth Amendment extended First Amendment protections to the states, and therefore the mob had violated the free speech and assembly rights of those at the political meeting.

But again, despite the seemingly clear wording of the amendment and its ample and unambiguous legislative history, the Court refused to extend not only the First Amendment but any of the Bill of Rights to states and state actions.

In his opinion, Chief Justice Waite started out by lionizing the right of assembly and right of petition guaranteed by the First Amendment. But then he "had" to rule that the amendment and its protections only apply to the right to petition the federal government. Then, since the Fourteenth Amendment had not given the federal government police powers formerly held by the states, and since the meeting was to petition the state government and thus not covered by the First Amendment, the indictments were defective and could not be sustained.

## 4. THE CIVIL RIGHTS CASES, 109 U.S. 3 (1883)

In 1875, Congress was determined to implement the Thirteenth and Fourteenth Amendments. So it passed the Civil Rights Act of 1875, making it a crime for one person to deprive another, based on color or previous condition of servitude, of "the full and equal enjoyment of the accommodations, advantages, facilities and privileges of inns, public conveyances on land or water, theaters and other places of public amusement."

William R. Davis, Jr., was not thinking about this law when he showed up at New York City's Grand Opera House for a November 23, 1879, matinee performance of Victor Hugo's *Ruy Blas*. Davis had been born a slave in South Carolina, but had come to New York after gaining his freedom after the Civil War and was working as a reporter on a newspaper advocating advancement for colored people. According to an account in the *New York Times*, the well-dressed Davis and his light-skinned girlfriend (who had actually purchased the two tickets) were turned away at the door by usher Sam Singleton, who told them "these tickets are no good." Later, Davis's girlfriend, who was only one-eighth black and who could pass for white, was admitted at another door without question using her disputed ticket. Davis was not, nor was he admitted when he attempted to use another ticket bought for him at the box office by a white patron.

Davis immediately complained to a policeman. The policeman was not sympathetic and said that the management of the theater did not admit colored people and that was their right. Davis knew better and went to the U.S. attorney and filed a criminal complaint against usher Singleton. On December 9, 1879, a grand jury indicted Singleton, and on January 14, 1880, the usher became the first person in New York ever tried under the Civil Rights Act of 1875.

Singleton's lawyer argued that the 1875 law was unconstitutional because it interfered with private citizens and their unfettered use of private property. The trial judge said that he was unable to reach a verdict on the issue and forwarded the case to the circuit court of appeals. It too said it was unable to reach a verdict, and certified the case to the Supreme Court, where it was joined to several others, all seeking to test the constitutionality of the Civil Rights Act.

By an 8–1 vote, with only Justice John Marshall Harlan dissenting, the Court agreed that the law was unconstitutional. It held that neither the Thirteenth nor the Fourteenth Amendment empowered Congress to enact a statute that could control the way a person used his private property. Writing for the majority, Justice Joseph Bradley ruled that the Thirteenth Amendment does not bar private acts of discrimination "because such an act of refusal has nothing to do with slavery or involuntary servitude." As for the Fourteenth Amendment, Bradley ruled it only prohibited state-sponsored discrimination and not private acts.

Bradley ruled that a law like the Civil Rights Act was "repugnant to the Tenth Amendment . . . which declares that powers not delegated to the United

States by the Constitution, nor prohibited by it to the States, are reserved to the States respectively or to the people." Bradley developed a theory of "legal rights" versus "social rights," and argued that what the Constitution protects are legal rights while what the Civil Rights Act of 1875 covered were social rights.

Justice Harlan delivered a historically scathing dissent in response to the majority's opinion. He pointed out that any legislation can target not only the institution of slavery but "the badges and incidents of slavery and servitude." He held up racial discrimination exercised by public and quasipublic entities as a "badge of servitude" that Congress could proscribe under the Thirteenth Amendment. He said that through the equal protection clause of the Fourteenth Amendment, Congress affirmatively can ensure blacks the right of full citizenship, legislating citizen action on both federal and state levels, especially if they act as instruments of the state. "Today, it is the colored race which is denied," he wrote. "At some future time it may well be some other race that will fall under the ban of race discrimination. . . . There cannot be in this republic, any class of human beings in practical subjection to another class."

At the same time as it decided the Civil Rights Cases, the Court also decided another even more outrageous "private" discrimination case. In *United States* v. *Harris* the Court held that persons who participated in the lynching of blacks, but were not connected with government or interfering with federal rights, could not be indicted under the Civil Rights Act.

It now seems amazing that Justice

Bradley's civil rights decision, which constitutionally protected private discrimination, remained the law of the land for more than fifty years. It ended for more than five decades any congressional attempt to protect individual rights in a private setting. It was not until well into the modern era that Congress passed the Civil Rights Act of 1964, which outlawed private discrimination in public accommodations and which the Supreme Court upheld in *Heart of Atlanta Motel* v. *United States* (see number 67, One Hundred Most Important Decisions).

## 5. PLESSY V. FERGUSON, 163 U.S. 537 (1896)

After the Civil War, many Southern states were determined to try to limit the rights of former slaves. Their biggest fear was that emancipation would bring a mixing of the races—something they vowed to stop. Their answer was the segregation laws, such as one passed by Florida in 1887 that required railroads operating in the state, or passing through, to house blacks in separate cars from whites. Other states soon followed suit, and within a short time "separate car" laws were in force in most of the South.

A group of New Orleans black businessmen vowed to fight these laws. They were joined by the railroads, who considered the laws cumbersome and expensive to comply with. The group decided on a test case, and Homer Plessy volunteered to break the law. Plessy boarded an East Louisiana Railroad train in New Orleans, and took a seat in a whites-only car. He was asked to move and refused. He was then arrested and brought before New Orleans Parish Judge John Ferguson. Thus was Plessy versus Ferguson joined.

Plessy, through his attorney Albion Tourgee, a North Carolina judge and also a black man, argued that the separate-car laws violated his civil rights. But Judge Ferguson found him guilty and fined him $25.

The case then went to the Louisiana Supreme Court, whose chief justice at the time was former Governor Francis Nicholls, who had signed the separate-car legislation into law. The court, not surprisingly, quickly found the law to be constitutional, unanimously ruling that any scheme of "separate but equal facilities" was proper under the Fourteenth Amendment.

Plessy appealed to the Supreme Court. The case ended up being argued twice, and after almost two years of deliberation, the Court ruled 8–1 that Louisiana was correct: separate but equal was all the Constitution required. Writing for the majority, Justice Henry Billings Brown relied on the fact that governments in the North had themselves set up segregated institutions, especially school systems, and he pinpointed the fact that Congress itself supported a segregated school system in that it controlled the government of the District of Columbia, which had a completely segregated school system. Wrote Justice Brown:

> The [Fourteenth] Amendment . . . could not have been intended to abolish distinctions based upon color, or to enforce social, as distinguished from political, equality, or a commingling of the two races upon terms unsatisfactory

to either. Laws permitting and even requiring their separation in places where they are liable to be brought into contact do not necessarily imply the inferiority of either race to the other. . . .

Only Justice John Harlan objected. In what is considered his finest opinion he said in part:

> Our Constitution is color-blind, and neither knows nor tolerates classes among citizens. In respect to civil rights, all citizens are equal before the law. The humblest is the peer of the most powerful. The law regards man as man, and takes no account of his surroundings or of his color when his civil rights . . . are involved.

"Separate but equal" remained the law of the land for fifty-eight years, until 1954 when the Court held in *Brown* v. *Board of Education* that separate is "inherently unequal."

## 6. DEBS V. UNITED STATES, 249 U.S. 211 (1919)
## ABRAMS V. UNITED STATES, 250 U.S. 616 (1919)

As noted in the discussion of *Schenck* v. *United States* (number 35, One Hundred Most Important Decisions), Justice Oliver Wendell Holmes established his "clear and present danger" standard in 1919. Before that year was out, the Court would decide three more cases brought by defendants who had been convicted under the Espionage Act. This was the Court's first opportunity to apply its new standard. In the first case, *United States* v. *Debs*, the result was extreme. In the second, *Abrams* v.

*United States*, the result was so extreme that taken together these two cases form a single entry in our list of ten worst Court decisions.

Eugene Debs was a major public figure of his era, and a substantial thorn in the side of the government. As a teenager he had started out working on the railroad for $6 a week and ended up as head of the American Railway Union. In 1895 he was arrested and jailed for leading what turned into a bloody strike, and his conviction was upheld by the Supreme Court. He came out of prison a hero of the labor movement, and in the four elections between 1900 and 1912 he was the Socialist party candidate for president. In the election of 1912 he received over a million votes— more than 8 percent of the total vote cast.

On June 16, 1918, Debs gave a speech in Canton, Ohio, in which he denounced the war as an instrument of the ruling classes and condemned the jailing of other socialists for their antiwar speeches. Debs was arrested and charged with violating the Espionage Act.

Eventually his case ended up on appeal in the Supreme Court. Even though it was far from "clear" that Debs's words would lead to any illegal actions, the Court found that was a "reasonably probable effect" and upheld his conviction.

More than one commentator has mused that had the Espionage Act been in existence, with the same attitude prevailing in 1972, Democratic presidential contender Senator George McGovern would likely have ended up in jail for his anti-Vietnam views.

Two months after Gene Debs's speech, in August 1918, Jacob Abrams and four other young Jewish-Russian immigrants (all professed anarchists who had come to the United States less than a decade earlier as children) were arrested in New York for throwing out of a lower East Side factory window some Yiddish-language leaflets denouncing the invasion of Vladivostok by U.S. troops. Although the four were protesting the invasion of their homeland during the Russian Revolution, they were actually tried and convicted of opposing the war with Germany (under a complex reasoning that the Bolsheviks had withdrawn from the war and thus were now said to be in league with Germany) and using language that sought to bring the United States into disrepute, both crimes under the expanded terms of the Sedition Act.

The trial was a travesty. The government argued what would have happened if one of these leaflets had found its way into a munitions factory (none did) and had been read by workers who could speak Yiddish and then would walk off their jobs, leading within days to the stopping of the entire U.S. war effort. Spurred on by a judge who openly ridiculed the defense's attempt to put on a case, the jury quickly returned a guilty verdict and the defendants were sentenced to twenty years each.

When the case reached the Supreme Court, the majority gave the same short shrift to the defendants' First Amendment arguments as it had in the *Debs* case. But this time the Court was not unanimous. Holmes and Justice Lewis

Brandeis dissented in an opinion written by Holmes.

Holmes had come to listen and agree with critics such as Judge Learned Hand and legal scholars like Ernst Freud and Zachariah Chafee that he was over-applying the Espionage Act. So as he wrote in his famous dissent in the Abrams case:

> In this case sentences of twenty years have been imposed for the publishing of two leaflets I believe the defendants had as much right to publish as the Government has to publish the Constitution of the United States now vainly invoked by them. . . . I think we should be eternally vigilant against attempts to check the expression of opinions that we loath and believe to be fraught with death, unless they so imminently threaten immediate interference with the lawful and pressing purposes of the law that an immediate check is required to save the country.

## 7. GALLAGHER V. CROWN SUPER MARKET, 366 U.S. 617 (1961)
## BRAUNFELD V. BROWN, 366 U.S. 599 (1961)

Both these cases contain essentially the same fact situations and both were decided together with several other "blue law" cases on the same day. The Crown Kosher Super Market operated in Springfield, Massachusetts, while Braunfeld was one of a number of Orthodox Jewish merchants doing business in Philadelphia. At the time both Pennsylvania and Massachusetts had very similar Sunday closing laws, forbidding certain types of stores from operating on Sunday while limiting the kinds of merchandise that could be sold by stores that were allowed to open.

In both cases the Jewish plaintiffs argued that the rules of their faith required them to refrain from all work from sundown on Friday through Saturday, and thus the Sunday closing law meant they were allowed to operate only four and a half days a week, including requiring them to be closed for the entire weekend. This, they argued, put them at an economic disadvantage with non-Jewish merchants, which meant the Sunday closing law was actually working in support of non-Jewish faiths.

Not so, said the Court, by a vote of 6–3. Sunday closing laws were in no way religiously compulsive; they didn't call on or force the Jewish merchants to do anything of a religious nature, such as force them to open on Saturday. Said the Court: "If the purpose or effect of a law is to impede the observance of one or all religions or is to discriminate invidiously between religions, that law is constitutionally invalid even though the burden may be characterized as being only indirect." The fact that these Orthodox merchants felt they could not open on Saturday, the majority reasoned, was their personal decision. Even though, as the Court noted, Sunday closing laws have their origin in Christian religious practice and actually speak in terms of "the Lord's day," in today's society they do not attempt to regulate religious practice; rather, they regulate a secular activity (selling) for a public purpose (to guarantee a uniform day of rest and relaxation for workers). In fact, said the Court, for the state to recognize the observance of the Jewish sabbath and provide exemptions from the Sunday closing law for those who observe a Saturday sabbath, would amount to state support of the Jewish faith, because it would put them at an economic advantage over merchants who had to close on Sundays.

As Justice Potter Stewart noted in a strong dissent in the *Crown Super Market* case, "Massachusetts has passed a law which compels an Orthodox Jew to choose between his religious faith and his economic survival. That is a cruel choice. That is a choice which I think no State can constitutionally demand."

Almost immediately after this decision the politicians acted. In Massachusetts and Pennsylvania, laws were changed to allow kosher markets but not general businesses operated by Orthodox Jews to open on Sundays. Gradually, the issue became moot as more and more states repealed their Sunday closing laws, allowing any kind of business to open when it wanted, seven days a week.

## 8. GINZBURG V. UNITED STATES, 383 U.S. 463 (1966)

For the next case we rely on no less an authority than Justice Potter Stewart, who at a law school seminar once said that as far as he was concerned, the two worst decisions in Supreme Court history were the *Dred Scott* case and *Ginzburg* v. *United States*.

In 1873, Congress passed the Obscene Literature and Articles Act, which for all time has been known as the Comstock Act, after anti-obscenity crusader Anthony Comstock who forced its passage. The statute made it an unlawful act to advertise, sell, disseminate through the mails, or import "any obscene book, pamphlet, paper, writing, advertisement circular, print, picture drawing or other representation . . . any article of an immoral nature . . . any drug or medicine or any article whatsoever to prevent conception, or for causing an unlawful abortion."  .

Almost ninety years later, New York publisher Ralph Ginzburg was found guilty by a federal judge (he was so sure he would win he had waived a jury trial) of violating the Comstock Act, by the sending through the mails his publications *Eros*, *Liaison*, and *The Housewife's Handbook on Selective Promiscuity*, a clinical study on sexuality he had sold only to health professionals. The trial court judge found Ginzburg guilty and sentenced him to five years in prison, and the appeals court affirmed the conviction—this, despite the fact that both magazines contained numerous scholarly articles and important works of fiction by some of the finest writers of the day, and despite the fact that neither the pictures nor the text of either publication was sexually explicit by almost any stretch of the definition.

When the Supreme Court received the case it was faced with a major problem. In order to uphold the lower court's finding that Ginzburg's publications violated the Comstock Act, the Court had to find the publications legally obscene under a three-prong test for obscenity that it had recently approved in another decision. Almost without a doubt, that simply would not have been possible. So instead, the

Court, by a vote of 5–4, effectively found Ginzburg guilty of a crime with which he had never even been charged.

Writing for the majority Justice William Brennan, who later called the decision the worst of his career, ruled that the material that Ginzburg was selling did not even have to face the tripartite test. Rather, the conviction for violation of the Comstock Act could be upheld simply by looking at the means Ginzburg used to sell his two publications. In his advertising Ginzburg had what Brennan called "the leer of the sensualist," all but calling his own material pornographic. Basically, what Brennan said was that if Ginzburg calls it obscene, who are we to argue? He ruled that material can be considered obscene if it is "advertised as if the material appeals to the prurient interest."

Actually, to be technical, Brennan found Ginzburg guilty of the crime of pandering—employing sexually suggestive advertising to sell a product. That may in fact have been the case, but as four justices noted in a blistering dissent, Ginzburg had never been charged with such a crime, never convicted in a trial court, and never was allowed to defend himself on the charge in clear violation of his due process rights. Brennan, though, gave the reason away for his decision. At one point he referred to Ginzburg's "sordid business," and noted in a footnote that many in the country were trying to take advantage of the Court's recent obscenity decisions— "this new freedom of expression," he called it. He implied that Ginzburg was guilty of pushing the window too far.

Four separate dissents were written by Justices Black, Douglas, Harlan, and Stewart. The latter was considered the leading dissent and one of the best Stewart ever wrote in his long career. At one point he wrote: "There was testimony at his trial that these publications possess artistic and social merit. Personally, I have a hard time discerning any. Most of the material strikes me as both vulgar and unedifying. But if the First Amendment means anything, it means that a man cannot be sent to prison merely for distributing publications which offend a judge's aesthetic sensibilities, mine or any other's."

## 9. ANDERSON V. CREIGHTON, 483 U.S. 635 (1987)

On November 11, 1983, Robert Creighton, a black St. Paul, Minnesota telephone company employee, was sitting in his comfortable middle-class living room on West Minnehaha Road— within sight of the state capitol dome— watching television with his wife, Sarisse, and their two young daughters. Suddenly he heard a commotion on his front porch, and upon opening the door found himself staring down the barrels of at least five shotguns wielded by who would later be identified as seven police officers led by an FBI agent.

They immediately burst into Creighton's home, identifying themselves as "federal officers." When Creighton asked if they had a warrant, their response was they didn't need one. "You watch too much television," one officer reportedly said.

Sarisse Creighton did not know what was going on. So she told her children to run for safety at a neighbor's house. One of the officers ran after them, grabbing one of the children by the neck and dragging her screaming back into the house. The child later had to be taken to an emergency room to be treated for injuries.

In turned out that Sarisse Creighton's brother, Vadaain Dixon, was a suspect in a bank robbery that had occurred that afternoon. The FBI agent, identified later as Russell Anderson, was searching for him and said that he believed he did not need a warrant to enter any premises because he was "searching for a fugitive" and had probable cause to enter the home of any relative of Dixon's.

Greatly angered by the intrusion, the Creightons filed a damage suit against both the local police and the Justice Department, claiming violation of their civil rights, assault and battery, and false imprisonment. It was clear that the officers had no right to enter the Creightons' house without a warrant. But the lawyers for the state argued that the suit should be dismissed because the officers believed what they were doing was correct. The trial judge agreed, and dismissed the suit before trial.

The court of appeals disagreed. It found that there was no reason to believe the fugitive was in the Creighton home, and that no "hot pursuit" situation existed since there was no chase involved. Without a search warrant, said the appeals court, what the officers had done seemed clearly out of bounds. The appeals court ordered the matter back to the district court for trial.

Instead, the government appealed the case to the U.S. Supreme Court. It is almost unheard of for the Supreme Court to accept a case without a trial record having been established: it is done usually only in situations of overriding constitutional need. This did not seem such a case. But observers were surprised when the Court agreed to hear the case, and some were even more surprised when by a vote of 6–3 agreed that the lawsuit should be dismissed because the officers thought they were in the right.

Writing for the majority, Justice Antonin Scalia had a problem. The Fourth Amendment seems clear: "The right of the people to be secure in their persons, houses, papers and effects, against unreasonable searches and seizures shall not be violated. . . ." So what Scalia did was judicially rewrite the Fourth Amendment. As he viewed it, the Founding Fathers had simply made a poor choice of words. They didn't really mean "unreasonable." Here in this situation the police believed, wrongly but honestly, that what they were doing was correct. Thus they were reasonable. But a reasonable person can't do something unreasonable. What the Founding Fathers meant to say, reasoned Scalia, was that persons should be secure in their persons and homes against "undue" searches, which this was not because the officers were acting reasonably since they believed what they were doing was right.

Justices John Paul Stevens, William Brennan, and Thurgood Marshall pointed out, in a bitter dissent authored by Stevens, that Scalia and the majority "announces a new rule of law that protects federal agents who make forcible nighttime entries into the homes of innocent citizens without probable cause, without a warrant, without any valid reason. . . ." But more than this, said Stevens, what the majority was proposing is a rule that would allow a policeman to do anything just so long as he thinks what he is doing is correct. "The Court stunningly restricts the constitutional accountability of the police," wrote Stevens.

## 10. EMPLOYMENT DIVISION, DEPARTMENT OF HUMAN RESOURCES OF OREGON V. ALFRED L. SMITH (AKA OREGON V. SMITH), 494 U.S. 872 (1990)

Two Native Americans, Alfred Smith and Galen Black, were fired from their jobs at an Oregon antidrug counseling center because they used peyote, a hallucinogen, as part of the ceremonies of their Native American Church. The sacramental use of peyote is so central to the rites of the Native American Church that more than half the states, and the federal government, list it as an approved use of a controlled substance. Oregon, while not approving the use, admits it does not enforce the law against its use as part of church ceremonies. But the state refused unemployment benefits to the two on the basis they had been fired from their previous job for cause. They brought suit against the state for denying them unemployment benefits and the case reached the Supreme Court.

Both sides argued the case as an unemployment benefits case. But Justice Antonin Scalia used it to issue a sweeping opinion on the subject of religious freedom. Scalia began the decision by reviewing what he believed the free-exercise clause means, based on various past Court decisions:

> The free exercise of religion means, first and foremost, the right to believe and profess whatever religious doctrine one desires. Thus the First Amendment obviously excludes all "governmental regulation of religious beliefs as such." The government may not compel affirmation of religious belief, punish the expression of religious doctrines it believes to be false, impose special disabilities on the basis of religious views or religious status, or lend its power to one or the other side in controversies over religious authority or dogma.

## Then he went on to say:

> But the exercise of religion often involves not only belief and profession but the performance of (or abstention from) physical acts; assembling with others for a worship service, participating in sacramental use of bread and wine, proselytizing, abstaining from certain foods or modes of transportation. It would be true, we think (though no case of ours has involved the point) that a state would be "prohibiting the free exercise of religion" if it sought to ban such acts or abstentions only when they are engaged in for religious reasons, or only because of the religious belief that they display.

Had he stopped here and ruled that the state was within its rights to ban the use of a hallucinogen, and had done so generally and not simply within the context of its use within the Native American Church, the opinion would only have represented a departure in the

181

way governmental interests have been balanced in free-exercise cases. But Scalia went further, much further. He held: "We have never held that an individual's religious beliefs excuse him from compliance with an otherwise valid law prohibiting conduct the State is free to regulate."

He then continued: "Respondents urge us to hold, quite simply, that when otherwise prohibitable conduct is accompanied by religious convictions, not only the convictions but the conduct itself must be free from governmental regulation. We have never held that, and decline to do so now."

Scalia held that when a valid criminal law, not specifically aimed at a religious practice, causes a burden on any religious practice, the criminal law will prevail—automatically and every time. And since it does always prevail, no balancing test is necessary to determine whether there is a compelling governmental interest. "Our conclusion that generally applicable religion-neutral laws that have the effect of burdening a particular religious practice need not be justified by a compelling governmental interest, is the only approach compatible with these precedents."

The Court was bitterly divided, 5–4. In what is technically a concurring opinion (because she eventually reached the same bottom-line conclusion that Oregon was justified in refusing the unemployment compensation claim), Justice Sandra Day O'Connor took Scalia sharply to task, calling the decision "incompatible with our nation's fundamental commitment to an individual's religious liberty." She especially disagreed with the majority's dis-

missing out of hand the need for any kind of balancing test when looking at a valid criminal statute not specifically aimed at religious practice. "To reach this sweeping result," she wrote, "the Court must not only give a strained reading of the First Amendment but must also disregard our consistent application of free exercise doctrine to cases involving generally applicable regulations that burden religious conduct."

O'Connor went on to say: "[a] law that prohibits certain conduct—conduct that happens to be an act of worship for someone—manifestly does prohibit that person's free exercise of his religion. A person who is barred from engaging in religiously motivated conduct is barred from freely exercising his religion." In order to do this, she said, the government must be required to make a showing of compelling interest.

Justice Harry Blackmun wrote an unusually bitter and personal dissent:

> This Court over the years painstakingly has developed a consistent and exacting standard to test the constitutionality of a state statute that burdens the free exercise of religion. . . . Until today I thought this was a settled and inviolate principle of this Court's First Amendment jurisprudence. The majority, however, perfunctorily dismisses it as a "constitutional anomaly." As carefully detailed in Justice O'Connor's concurring opinion the majority is able to arrive at this view only by mischaracterizing this Court's precedents. . . . This distorted view of our precedents leads the majority to conclude that strict scrutiny of a state law burdening the free exercise of religion is a "luxury" that a well ordered society cannot afford. . . .

# 5.

# The Justices of the Court

In October of 1992, when Clarence Thomas took his judicial oath to begin his service on the Supreme Court, he became the 106th person to do so. Actually, his was the 111th time the oath was administered, because five associate justices—John Rutledge,[1] Edward D. White, Charles Evan Hughes, Harlan F. Stone, and William Rehnquist— were elevated from associate justice to Chief Justice, and were thus twice administered the oath.

Of the 106 who have served on the Court, 105 have been men. Associate Justice Sandra Day O'Connor is the only woman ever to have served. Of the 106, 104 have been white. Only Associate Justice Thurgood Marshall and the man who succeeded him, Clarence Thomas, have been black. Almost all

the justices have been Protestant—92 of the 106. The first Catholic member of the Court was Chief Justice Roger B. Taney, who was nominated by President Andrew Jackson in 1835. But it was not until thirty years after Taney's death that the second Catholic was nominated—Edward D. White, in 1894. Other Catholic justices have been Joseph McKenna (1897), Pierce Butler (1922), Frank Murphy (1939), William Brennan (1956), Antonin Scalia (1987), and Anthony Kennedy (1988).

With Kennedy and Scalia sitting together, the Rehnquist Court is the first to have two Catholics sitting at the same time. The fear that was often expressed is that Catholic justices would allow their religious convictions to color their decisions, or that somehow they would

---

1. Rutledge was nominated and confirmed as an associate justice, took his oath of office, and was carried on the roster of the Court from 1789 to 1791. But he never actually sat with the Court (although his name did appear as taking part in two decisions), before he resigned to become the chief justice of the South Carolina Supreme Court. He returned to the U.S. Supreme Court in 1795, after being named Chief Justice.

be "controlled by Rome." In retrospect, this charge now seems almost silly. Look at the issue of abortion. Scalia is bitterly opposed, but this is in keeping with his overall conservative philosophy. Kennedy has voted to limit abortion rights, but also to retain its constitutional basis. The Catholic justice who preceded them—William Brennan—was a champion of abortion rights during his tenure on the Court. That, too, fit into his generally liberal philosophy.

There have also been six Jewish justices. The first, Louis Brandeis, was not nominated until 1916. His nomination was so controversial that his fellow justice, James McReynolds, refused to speak to him for the three years the two sat on the Court together. Actually, once Brandeis was seated, his became the "Jewish chair." When Brandeis left the Court in 1932, President Hoover nominated Felix Frankfurter to replace him. Frankfurter was followed by Arthur Goldberg (1962), and he by Abe Fortas (1969). The practice of having a Jewish justice was broken when Harry Blackmun was nominated to replace Fortas. No Jews sit on the Rehnquist Court.

Nominated justices have ranged in age from thirty-two—William Johnson (1804) and Joseph Story (1812), with Story the youngest by three months, to age sixty-five—Horace Lurton (1910) and Chief Justice Edward White (1910). Both Chief Justices Harlan Stone, at age sixty-eight, and Charles Evan Hughes, at age sixty-seven, were older when they were sworn in. But both had previously served on the Court as associate justices. Two other justices were under the age of forty when appointed—Bushrod

Washington (1799) and James Iredell (1790). Obviously these youthful appointments were made in the early days of the Republic, when life expectancy was much shorter and men were put into positions of trust at a much younger age. But even in modern time, a number of justices who went on to play significant roles on the Court received their nominations while still in their forties. These included John McLean (1830), John Marshall Harlan (the first, 1877), Charles Evans Hughes (1910), William O. Douglas (1939), Potter Stewart (1958), and Byron White (1962).

Eight justices have served past their eightieth birthdays, with Justice Oliver Wendell Holmes the oldest ever to have served. Holmes finally retired at age ninety. Chief Justice Taney died still in office, at age eighty-eight. Justice Thurgood Marshall retired at age eighty-three, Justices Louis Brandeis and Gabriel Duval at age eighty-two, Justices Joseph McKenna and Stephen Field at age eighty-one, and Justice Samuel Nelson at age eighty. By contrast, five justices left the Court before age fifty. James Iredell, who had been appointed at age thirty-eight, died when only forty-eight. Benjamin Curtis, Alfred Moore, John Jay, and John Campbell all retired from the Court to accept other positions while still in their forties.

The longest-serving justice was William O. Douglas, who had served 36 years, seven months, when he retired in 1975. In all, eleven justices have served tenures longer than thirty years. After Douglas, the next longest-serving justice was Stephen J. Field, who served thirty-four years, nine months. Then in order come William J. Brennan, thirty-three years, seven months; John Marshall, thirty-four years, five months; Hugo L. Black, thirty-four years, one month; John Marshall Harlan (the first), thirty-three years, one month; Joseph Story, thirty-three years; James Wayne, thirty-two years, four months; John McLean, thirty-one years, five months; William Johnson, thirty years, two months; Bushrod Washington, thirty years; and for good measure, Oliver Wendell Holmes, twenty-nine years, eleven months, eleven days.

The justice with the shortest tenure had so short a tenure he is officially not considered to have been a justice. In 1869, President Ulysses S. Grant nominated former Secretary of War Edwin Stanton. Stanton was confirmed by the Senate on December 20, 1869, but died four days later before taking his oath of office. Of the justices who actually sat, two served terms of less than two years: Thomas Johnson, who had served less than fourteen months when he died in 1793, and James F. Byrnes, who resigned to serve in the war effort in 1942 after serving only sixteen months on the Court.

An appointment to the Supreme Court is for life, and for 50 of the 106 justices, that has been exactly how long they served. The fifty died while still in office. Of the rest, the vast majority died within a few years of retirement. But several went on to have significant careers after their Supreme Court service. Byrnes, who quit after less than two years because of World War II, went on to hold several cabinet positions and the governorship of South Carolina. Two—Benjamin Curtis and John Campbell—both retired before age fifty after short tenures

to return to long and successful law practices. Two others in more modern times—Arthur Goldberg and Abe Fortas—also had successful law practices after leaving the Court. Tom Clark heard cases on lower courts for a decade after retiring in 1967 to avoid a conflict of interest with his son, who had been appointed attorney general. David Davis was elected to the Senate in 1877. John Jay, the first Chief Justice, resigned to become governor of New York. Owen Roberts became dean of the University of Pennsylvania Law School. Former Chief Justice Warren Burger has headed presidential commissions since retiring in 1986.

The two justices who lived the longest in retirement—George Shiras, who retired in 1903 at age seventy-one and lived another twenty years, and John H. Clarke, who retired in 1922 at age sixty-five and lived another twenty-four years—both enjoyed their retirements at leisure.

Historically, the two most prevalent reasons for selection to the Court have been politics and personal friendship with the nominating president. With only a very few exceptions, presidents have chosen justices whose politics and political philosophies match their own. In many cases justiceships were given out as a reward for personal service to a president or, more often, as a reward for long service to the president's political party.

In the first century of the Court, geography played a major role in the selection of justices. When George Washington made his original six selections, he was very careful to ensure that there was one each from the four most important states of the time: New York, Massachusetts, Pennsylvania, and Virginia; and that the south was represented in James Iredell from North Carolina and John Rutledge from South Carolina. For the next hundred years this pattern continued to the point that most presidents looked upon the Court as having a New York seat, a New England seat, and a Maryland-Virginia seat. Then, too, when justices still road circuit, appointments had to be balanced to ensure that a justice lived in the judicial circuit over which he would be presiding.

The six men whom George Washington selected for the first Supreme Court were lawyers. Although the Constitution or the Judicial Act of 1789 does not specify that a justice be a lawyer, Washington thought it mandatory and made admission to a state bar a criterion for the six he selected. This established a precedent that has continued to this day. Every Supreme Court justice, and nominee, has been a lawyer.

But it is interesting to note that it was not until modern times—1957—that the Court was composed entirely of law school graduates. In 1957, Charles Whittaker replaced Stanley Reed on the Court. Although Reed had studied law at the University of Virginia and Columbia University, he never graduated. The last justice to never have attended any law school was James Byrnes, who served from 1941 to 1942.

It has to be remembered that what we understand today to be a law school did not exist before 1870, when the Harvard University Law School was established. Prior to that, a few colleges taught law courses and some even offered what

they called a law degree. Benjamin Curtis, who was nominated in 1851, for instance, was the first justice to have received a university law degree—from Harvard College. It was not until 1902, when Oliver Wendell Holmes was sworn in, that any Supreme Court justice possessed a modern law degree from what today we would recognize as a law school. Holmes had graduated from Harvard Law School with an LL.B. in 1869.

For the first hundred years of the Supreme Court, by and large, young men (and in a very few instances young women) who wanted to become lawyers would pay established lawyers a fee to be an apprentice in their offices and to act as their teachers. After a year or two of "reading the law," as the process was known, the lawyer would certify that his apprentice was ready for admission to the state bar; upon successfully passing an examination, the person would be a lawyer.

George Washington also believed that some prior judicial experience would be valuable for members of his first Supreme Court. Therefore, four of the six men he chose had some state court experience. However, the next Court nomination of a man with previous judicial experience did not occur until District Judge Robert Trimble was appointed in 1826. From that date until Circuit Judge William Wood was elevated to the High Court in 1880, only two other former judges were nominated—Philip Barbour (1836) and Peter Daniel (1841). But since 1880 a majority of justices have been judges. Today, all nine justices were sitting judges when elevated to the Court. In total now, 47 of the 106 justices have been lower court judges.

Many Supreme Court appointees had held appointed or elected political office. Among the justices, fourteen had served at some point as U.S. attorney generals or deputy attorney generals; four had served as solicitor general; twenty-three others have served in various cabinet positions including secretaries of state, treasury, war, commerce, navy, labor, and interior. At some point in their careers, twenty-eight had been congressmen and seven had been U.S. senators. Five were still sitting in the Senate when nominated: John McKinley (1837), Levi Woodbury (1846), Edward White (1894), Hugo Black (1937), and Harold Burton (1945). One—James Wayne in 1835—went directly from the U.S. House to the Supreme Court. Six justices served previously as state governors, and three served as governors after leaving the Court.

Most every Supreme Court appointee was involved in the private practice of law at some point in his or her careers. But only twenty-six were in private practice when selected for the Court. Almost two dozen justices taught in law schools at some point, but only three were either deans or law professors at the time of their nomination.

In their personal lives, justices have been the marrying kind. Of the 106 justices, only nine have been bachelors. The remaining have had 126 wives and one husband. Justice William O. Douglas had four wives, while Henry Livingston, Benjamin Curtis, and Samuel Chase each had three. But it must be noted that well into the nineteenth century women tended to die young, often from childbirth or complications. Many of the early justices were widowed two or even three times in their lifetimes.

Justices have also had a large number of children. Both John Marshall and John Rutledge had ten children; current Justice Antonin Scalia has nine; Justices William Johnson, Thomas Todd, and Stanley Matthews each had eight; while six justices have each had seven children.

## JUDICIAL PERFORMANCE

Which justices have been great, and which have been failures? Any such compilation by an individual would be highly subjective, subject to the prejudices of the compiler. But in the early 1970s, two law professors—Albert P. Blaustein of Rutgers University Law School and Roy M. Mersky of the University of Texas Law School—tried to approach the problem scientifically. They circulated a list of all justices—those past and those still serving in 1970—to a panel of sixty-five distinguished law professors, historians, and political scientists. They asked the panel to rate every justice as either great, near great, average, below average, or a failure, with corresponding letter grades of A, B, C, D, and F. The result was both surprising and not so surprising.

Not surprising was the fact that Chief Justice John Marshall received a unanimous vote from all sixty-five rates as "great." Among the other chief justices, those receiving "great" ratings were Roger Taney, Charles Evans Hughes,

Harlan Stone, and Earl Warren. This means that the raters felt that fully one-third of all the Chief Justices who had served up to 1970 should be rated at the very top. Among the associate justices who were also rated "great" were Joseph Story, John M. Harlan (first), Oliver Wendell Holmes, Louis Brandeis, Benjamin Cardozo, Hugo Black, and Felix Frankfurter. Brandeis and Holmes fell just short of being named "great" on all sixty-five ballots.

Fifteen justices received the next highest rating of "near great." They were William Johnson, Benjamin Curtis, Samuel Miller, Stephen J. Field, Joseph Bradley, Morrison R. Waite, Chief Justice William Howard Taft, George Sutherland, William O. Douglas, Robert Jackson, Wiley Rutledge, John Harlan (second), William Brennan, and Abe Fortas. The last is somewhat surprising, given that he left the Court in some disgrace after only four years of service.

At the other end of the scale, the panel rated six justices as "below average." They were Alfred Moore, Thomas Johnson, Robert Trimble, Philip Barbour, William Woods, and Howell Jackson. In describing the way voters tended to look at these justices, the authors noted that most of these justices were obscure and simply unimportant, as opposed to actual failures.

But in the "failure" category were eight justices who, in the opinion of a large majority of the reviewing panel, had done a demonstratively poor job. Somewhat surprisingly, on the list is Chief Justice Fred M. Vinson. Also something of a surprise in the lowest

grouping is Willis Van Devanter, who in his day was viewed as a highly competent justice. Less surprising in the final group are Pierce Butler, James Byrnes, Harold Burton, Sherman Minton, and two justices who received almost perfect negative scores: James McReynolds and Charles Whittaker. It is worth noting that three of the four considered failures—Butler, McReynolds, and Van Devanter—were part of the four-member conservative anti–New Deal bloc of justices in the 1930s.

In the center, "average" category were fifty-five of the ninety-six justices being rated. Included in the group were four Chief Justices: John Rutledge, Oliver Ellsworth, Salmon P. Chase, and Melville Fuller. Among the associate justices rated "average" were Potter Stewart, Byron White, and Thurgood Marshall, who were all still early in their tenures on the Court.

In early 1992, Professor Mersky indicated that he and Professor Blaustein were looking at updating the ratings to include all the justices through those now serving on the Rehnquist Court. He also indicated that it would be his personal opinion, in any new survey, that Justice William Brennan would likely be moved into the top "great" category, and that Justices Stewart and Marshall might fair better now that their careers have ended.

Since the Blaustein-Mersky study was published in the *Journal of the American Bar Association* in November 1972, its results have been vindicated in a half-dozen law journal articles and doctoral dissertations using more scientific methods. One of the most interesting uses it has been put to is a 1991 study authored by University of Pennsylvania Professor Emeritus of Sociology E. Digby Baltzell and Layette College sociologist Howard Schneiderman.[2] The two wanted to examine the justices who have served on the Supreme Court to see if there are any common sociological factors that could explain good and bad performance. So they grouped all the justices into three social stratas: upper, upper-middle and middle, and lower. They assumed that all in the first two categories can be considered privileged. Those in the lowest category, while not necessarily underprivileged, are clearly less privileged, although about half of the thirty-two justices in the bottom social category came from solid families in small towns or farming communities. The results were interesting, to say the least.

What the two social scientists determined was that of the twelve justices rated by the Blaustein-Mersky panel as "great," five came from the lowest socioeconomic class. Of the fourteen who rated "near great," seven came from the lowest class. This means that of the twenty-six justices in the top two categories, almost half came from the lowest socioeconomic class.

What adds significance to this finding is the fact that before the middle of the nineteenth century, virtually everyone who rose to the Supreme Court almost by definition had to have come from a privileged class. They were the only families who could afford to give their sons the education that would have re-

sulted in careers that could lead one day to the Supreme Court. In fact, the authors categorize the period in America between 1789 and 1850 as the Age of Aristocracy. It was not until almost the middle of the nineteenth century that education became sufficiently universal as to be readily available to children from the less privileged classes.

So if you look at the justices rated "great," you find that nine began serving in the latter part of the nineteenth century. Of these nine, five—or more than half—came from the lowest socioeconomic grouping. Of the "near greats," twelve began their careers after education became widely available. Of the twelve, seven had underprivileged beginnings. So in the categories "great" and "near great," of twenty-one justices so rated, twelve—57 percent—came from the lowest socioeconomic background.

The conclusion? Humble beginnings often breed great Supreme Court justices.

## JUDICIAL SUCCESSION

The size of the Court has varied from six to nine justices. Historically the progression has been as follows:

| | |
|---|---|
| 1789–1807 | 6 justices |
| 1807–1837 | 7 justices |
| 1837–1863 | 9 justices |
| 1863–1869 | 6 justices |
| 1869–today | 9 justices |

But while there have never been more than nine justices actually autho-

---

2. See *Society*, May-June 1991, pp. 47–54.

rized by statute, a strange situation grew out of the Civil War era that resulted in ten justices serving on the Court from 1863 to 1865, and a tenth seat created that has actually continued to today. Thus, when Court historians trace the succession of justices from Washington's first Court in 1789 to the current Rehnquist Court, they must talk about the ten seats in Court history.

The original Court was composed of a Chief Justice and five associate justices. They are, therefore, arranged in order across the six seats in the order that they were named by Washington. From that point on, as each resigned or died, his successor was listed in that seat. As new seats were added—the first being seat seven in 1807 (Thomas Todd)—the first occupant is listed along with his successors. In 1837 the Court was increased to nine, and so seats eight and nine began with their first occupants: John Catron and John McKinley.

The confusion started at the height of the Civil War. John Catron occupied the eighth seat, but was in Tennessee unable to return to Washington. So in 1863 President Lincoln nominated Stephen Field to the Court. In confirming him, the Senate indirectly created a tenth seat. Officially, both Catron and Field served on the Court from 1863 until May 30, 1865, when Catron died in Tennessee. But at no time did ten justices ever sit at the same time. After Catron died, the Senate extinguished the seat. But technically, it extinguished seat eight; and seat ten, occupied by Field, continued. So today, again technically, Justice Antonin Scalia sits on the Court's tenth seat.

## BIOGRAPHIES OF THE JUSTICES

### John Jay, 1789–1795

*Personal Data* Born: December 12, 1745, New York City. Education: graduated King's College (now Columbia University), 1764; read the law under Benjamin Kissam and admitted to the New York Bar, 1768. Married Sarah Livingston, 1774, seven children. Died: May 17, 1829, Bedford, New York.

*Career Data* Practiced law, 1768–74. Delegate, Continental Congress, 1774–77; President of Congress, 1778–79. Chief Justice, New York State, 1777–78. Ambassador to Spain, 1779. Secretary of State, 1784–89. Ambassador to Great Britain, 1794–95; Governor of New York, 1795–1801.

*Supreme Court Data* Nominated Chief Justice by George Washington on September 24, 1789. Resigned June 29, 1795.

Jay was among the most important of the Founding Fathers. He represented New York at both the first and second Continental Congress, and was elected its president in 1778. He took a leave the next year to become special envoy to Spain, and in 1783 helped negotiate the Treaty of Paris, ending the Revolutionary War. He declined membership in the Constitutional Convention for health reasons, but supported the new Constitution as one of the authors of the Federalist Papers. He received significant support in the first presidential election in 1789.

Washington wanted Jay to be his secretary of state. But Jay declined, so Washington named him the first Chief

*All photos courtesy of the collection of the Supreme Court of the United States*

The Supreme Court Building

(ABOVE:) Construction on the Supeme Court's home began in 1932.

(AT RIGHT:) Justices Brandeis, Van Devanter, Taft, Holmes, Butler, Sutherland and Stone survey the model for the Supreme Court building designed by Cass Gilbert.

(ABOVE:) The current Supreme Court chambers. The Court held its first session here on October 7, 1935.

(AT RIGHT, TOP:) The old Supreme Court Chambers where the court met from 1801 to 1860.

(AT RIGHT, BOTTOM:) The Court used the old Senate chamber from 1860 to 1935.

John Marshall

Roger B. Taney

The first meeting of the United States Supreme Court: Justices James Irendell, John Jay, John Blair and James Wilson

The Taney Court: *Seated:* Levi Woodburg, Philip P. Barbour, Roger B. Taney,
Peter Vivian Daniel, Samuel Nelson *Standing:* Robert C. Grier, Benjamin Curtis,
John A. Campbell, John McKinley

The Chase Court: D.W. Middleton (clerk), David Davis, Noah H.Swayne,
Robert Grier, James Moore Wayne, Salmon P. Chase, Samuel Nelson, Nathan
Clifford, Samuel Miller and Stephen Miller

The Waite Court: *Seated:* Horace Gray, Samuel F. Miller, Morrison R. Waite, Stephen J. Field, John M. Harlan *Standing:* William B. Woods, Joseph P. Bradley, Stanley Mathews, Samuel Blatchford

The Fuller Court: *Seated:* Joseph Bradley, Samuel Miller, Melville Fuller, Stephen Field, Lucius Q. C. Lamar *Standing:* Stanley Mathews, Horace Gray, John Marshall Harlan, Samuel Blatchford

The White Court: *Seated:* Oliver W. Holmes, John Marshall Harlan, Edward D. White, Joseph McKenna, William R. Day *Standing:* Willis Van Devanter, Horace H. Lurton, Charles E. Hughes, Joseph R. Lamar

The Taft Court: *Seated:* James McReynolds, Oliver Wendell Holmes, William Howard Taft, Willis Van Devanter, Louis D. Brandeis *Standing:* Edward T. Stanford, George Sutherland, Pierre Butler, Harlan Fiske Stone

The Hughes Court: *Seated:* Louis D. Brandeis, Willis Van Devanter, Charles Evan Hughes, James McReynolds, George Sutherland *Standing:* Owen J. Roberts, Pierre Butler, Harlan Fiske Stone, Benjamin Cardozo

The Stone Court: *Seated:* Stanley F. Reed, Owen J. Roberts, Harlan F. Stone, Hugo L. Black, Felix Frankfurter *Standing:* Robert H. Jackson, William O. Douglas, Frank Murphy, Wiley B. Rutledge

The Vinson Court: *Seated:* Felix Frankfurter, Hugo L. Black, Fred Vinson, Stanley Reed, William O. Douglas. *Standing:* Tom C. Clark, Robert Jackson, Harold Burton, Sherman Minton

The Warren Court: *Seated:* Tom C. Clark, Hugo L. Black, Earl Warren, William O. Douglas, John Marshall Harlan
*Standing:* Byron R. White, William J. Brennan, Jr., Potter Stewart, Abe Fortas

The Burger Court: *Seated:* John Marshall Harlan, Hugo L. Black, Warren E. Burger, William O. Douglas, William J. Brennan, Jr., *Standing:* Thurgood Marshall, Potter Stewart, Byron R. White, Harry A. Blackmun

(ABOVE:) The Rehnquist Court: *Standing:* David H. Souter, Antonin Scalia, Anthony M. Kennedy, Clarence Thomas *Seated:* John Paul Stevens III, Byron R. White, William H. Rehnquist, Harry A. Blackmun, Sandra Day O'Connor

(AT LEFT:) Warren Burger delivers the oath of office to Sandra Day O'Connor, the first woman to serve on the Supreme Court.

Justice. A firm advocate of separation of powers, Jay left his mark on Court history with his decision in *Chisholm* v. *Georgia* (1793), the first major decision of the Court. Although the decision sustaining the rights of citizens of one state to sue another state was ultimately overturned by the ratification of the Eleventh Amendment, its importance has endured to the present.

While still Chief Justice, Jay was sent to England by Washington to try to calm growing tensions. The resulting Jay Treaty outraged many who felt Jay gave up too much. Jay returned to find that he had been elected governor of New York. So he resigned from the Court and served two three-year terms.

In 1800, President Adams nominated Jay for a second term as Chief Justice, and he was immediately confirmed by the Senate. But upon learning of the nomination, Jay refused the appointment telling the president that the Court was not being shown the dignity he considered essential for it to function. He lived out his almost three-decade-long retirement farming his large Westchester, New York, estate. He also helped found the American Bible Society, and was elected its president.

John Rutledge, 1789–1791

*Personal Data* Born: September 1739, Charleston, South Carolina. Education: privately tutored; studied law at the Inns of Court in London and was admitted to the Bar of England, 1760. Married Elizabeth Grimke, 1763, ten children. Died: July 18, 1800, Charleston, South Carolina.

*Career Data* Member, South Carolina Assembly, 1761–76. South Carolina Attorney General, 1764–65. Member, Continental Congress. President, South Carolina General Assembly, 1776–78. Governor, South Carolina, 1779–82. Judge, Court of Chancery of South Carolina, 1784–89. Chief Justice, South Carolina Supreme Court, 1791–95.

*Supreme Court Data* Nominated by George Washington on September 24, 1789. Resigned March 5, 1791, to return to South Carolina. Was later nominated Chief Justice on August 12, 1795, and served until December 15, 1795, when the Senate refused to confirm.

With his English legal education, a very young Rutledge became one of South Carolina's leading lawyers and a powerful local figure. In 1774, he led the state's delegation to the Continental Congress, where he became one of the leaders opposing separation from Britain. In 1775 he returned to South Carolina to help form a new state government, and was elected the first president of the new state assembly. In 1779 he was elected governor, but fled in 1780 when South Carolina fell to the British.

At the Constitutional Convention in 1787, Rutledge was deeply involved in producing the first draft of the Constitution. In 1789 he accepted nomination to the Supreme Court, but never actually took his seat because of its inactivity. Then in 1791, he resigned to accept what he considered the more important post of chief justice of the South Carolina Supreme Court. But he came to regret the decision, and he eventually convinced Washington to allow him to succeed John Jay as Chief Justice. But his nomination was rejected by the Senate because of his opposition to the Jay Treaty. Rutledge's reaction to the news was to attempt suicide, and he reportedly lived on the edge of sanity until his death four years later.

## William Cushing, 1789–1810

*Personal Data* Born: March 1, 1732, Scituate, Massachusetts. Education: Graduated Harvard, 1751; read the law under Jeremiah Gridley and was admitted to the bar, 1755. Married Hannah Phillips, 1774, no children. Died: September 13, 1810, Scituate, Massachusetts.

*Career Data* Practiced law, 1755–60. Judge, Lincoln County (Mass.) Probate Court, 1760–61. Judge, Superior Court, 1772–77; Chief Justice, 1777–80. Justice, Supreme Judicial Court of Massachusetts, 1780–89.

*Supreme Court Data* Nominated by George Washington on September 24, 1789. Resigned September 13, 1810.

The Cushings were one of the oldest and most prominent families of Massachusetts. After an undistinguished start as a lawyer and lower court judge, he succeeded his father as judge of the Superior Court. He became an early supporter of the Revolution, and was almost impeached for his stance. He was a key supporter of the new Constitution in Massachusetts, and served as a delegate to the electoral college that elected Washington in 1788.

As a result, Cushing was one of Washington's original appointees to the Supreme Court in 1789. Then in 1794, while still sitting on the Court, he ran for governor of Massachusetts but lost. The next year he turned down the Chief Justiceship, but remained on the Court until his death in 1810, making him the longest serving of the original members.

## James Wilson, 1789–1798

*Personal Data* Born: September 14, 1742, Caskardy, Scotland. Education: graduated St. Andrews University (Scotland); read the law under John Dickinson in Philadelphia and admitted to the Pennsylvania Bar, 1767. Married Rachel Bird, 1771, six children; married Hannah Gray, 1793, one child. Died: August 21, 1798, Edenton, North Carolina.

*Career Data* Law practice and business owner, 1767–89. Delegate, Continental Congress, 1775–87. Delegate, Constitutional Convention, 1787. Delegate, Pennsylvania convention to ratify Constitution, 1787.

*Supreme Court Data* Nominated by George Washington on September 24, 1789. Resigned August 21, 1798.

After completing his education in Scotland, young Wilson sailed to the Colonies to teach at the College of Philadelphia. He tired of teaching, and started to study law under the city's outstanding lawyer, John Dickinson. He was admitted to the bar, and quickly earned the reputation as an outstanding legal scholar. He soon built a large law practice, but devoted most of his time to speculative business ventures that landed him deeply in debt.

He became a prominent member of the Continental Congress, where he was one of the leaders against separation. But he ended up signing the Declaration of Independence. During the Revolution he was forced into hiding because of his pro-British views. But then, strangely, he became one of the activists at the Constitutional Convention and was responsible for inserting in the Constitution the sections on the popular election of the president and members of the new Congress. He also authored sections on the judiciary and backed the principle of judicial review. He wanted to be the first Chief Justice and lobbied Washington for the job. But Washington appointed John Jay instead, and named Wilson a justice.

Of the original appointees, Wilson was the most accomplished legal scholar. But his debts and shoddy business practices caught up with him in 1796. While riding circuit in the south, his creditors had him thrown in jail. Released because of his judicial status, he hid in Edenton, North Carolina, the hometown of fellow justice James Iredell. He was found and again jailed, and forced to resign from the Supreme Court. Eventually released for ill health, he remained in Edenton, where he died in a cheap boardinghouse.

## John Blair, Jr., 1789–1796

*Personal Data* Born: 1732, Williamsburg, Virginia. Education: graduated College of William and Mary, 1754; studied law at the Inns of Court, London, and was admitted to the Bar of England, 1756. Married Jean Balfour, no children. Died: August 31, 1800, Williamsburg, Virginia.

*Career Data* Practiced law, 1757–1770. Member, Virginia House of Burgesses, 1766–70. Secretary, Virginia Governor's Council, 1770–1775. Delegate, Virginia Constitutional Convention, 1776. Judge, Virginia General Court, 1777–78; Chief Justice, 1779. Judge, Virginia Court of Appeals, 1780–1789. Delegate, Constitutional Convention, 1787. Judge, Virginia Supreme Court, 1789.

*Supreme Court Data* Nominated by George Washington on September 24, 1789. Resigned January 27, 1796.

Blair's father was among Virginia's wealthiest and most important colonial officials. Given his family background, Blair was a conservative who became a major opponent of Patrick Henry in the Virginia House of Burgesses. But his views modified, and he became a supporter of the Revolution and eventually was one of Virginia's three signers of the Constitution. He was serving on Virginia's newly reconstructed Supreme Court of Appeals when he was appointed to the U.S. Supreme Court. However, because of his wife's long illness, and the Court's inactivity, he attended few sessions before his resignation in 1796. In failing health he retired to his home in Williamsburg, where he died four years later.

## James Iredell, 1790–1799

*Personal Data* Born: October 5, 1751, Lewes, England. Education: English public schools. Read the law under Samuel Johnston of North Carolina and admitted to the Bar of North Carolina, 1770. Married Hannah Johnston, 1773, three children. Died: October 20, 1799, Edenton, North Carolina.

*Career Data* Collector of Customs, Edenton, North Carolina, 1768–74, Port of North Carolina, 1774–76. Judge, Superior Court, 1778; North Carolina Attorney General, 1779–81.

*Supreme Court Data* Nominated by George Washington on February 8, 1790. Resigned October 20, 1799.

Iredell's family was able to secure for him a tax collector's job in the North Carolina Colony. While holding that position he read the law, was admitted to the bar, and started a law practice in 1770. Although he was still a British citizen, he became a vocal supporter of the Revolution. After the war he became a leader of the faction that supported a strong central government, and he became a Federalist and an outspoken proponent of the new U.S. Constitution. In 1787, the North Carolina legislature gave him the task of completely rewriting state law. While not one of Washington's first choices for the Supreme Court, he was appointed after Robert Harrison declined to serve, and because Washington needed an appointee from North Carolina.

Iredell ended up being one of the more influential of the early justices. Possibly his most famous opinion was his dissent in *Chisholm* v. *Georgia*, in which he argued that a state cannot be sued in federal court by a citizen of another state—a position added to the Constitution by the Eleventh Amendment. He also set an earlier precedent for *Marbury* v. *Madison* in arguing (*Calder* v. *Bull*) that courts have the right to strike down laws as unconstitu-

tional. He resigned from the Court in failing health, and died soon afterward at age forty-eight.

Thomas Johnson, 1791–1793

*Personal Data* Born: November 4, 1732, Calvert, Maryland. Education: privately tutored; read the law under Stephen Bordley and was admitted to the Maryland Bar, 1760. Married Ann Jennings, 1766, seven children. Died: October 26, 1819, Frederick, Maryland.

*Career Data* Practiced law, 1760–74, 1780–90. Delegate, Maryland Assembly, 1762–74. Member, Continental Congress, 1774–77; General, Maryland Militia 1776–78. First governor of Maryland, 1777–79. Member, Maryland House of Delegates, 1780–87. Chief Judge, General Court of Maryland, 1790–91. Board of Commissioners of the Federal City, 1791–1794.

*Supreme Court Data* Nominated by George Washington on November 1, 1791, to replace Justice John Rutledge, who resigned. Resigned February 1, 1793.

One of twelve children, Johnson had no formal education but became an apprentice in the office of the clerk of the Maryland provincial court in Annapolis. He then read the law and was admitted to the bar. From these humble beginnings he rose quickly. In 1775 he placed Washington's name in nomination before the Congress for the position of commander-in-chief of the Continental Army and two years later, as brigadier-general of the Maryland Militia, led a force to Washington's relief in

Trenton. The two became close friends, and after the war he and Washington organized the Potomac Company to improve navigation along the River.

Johnson was hesitant to accept appointment to the Supreme Court because of his health and because justices had to ride circuit. After assuring him it would not be a problem, Chief Justice Jay assigned him to the southern circuit, which included everything south of the Potomac. When Jay would not change the assignment, Johnson resigned after serving only a year on the Court. Washington then appointed him to serve on the commission planning the new national capital. It was his idea to name it Washington. In 1795, he refused Washington's offer to serve as secretary of state. He retired to his large estate in Frederick, Maryland, where he died at the age of eighty-six.

William Paterson, 1793–1806

*Personal Data* Born: December 24, 1745, Antrim, Ireland. Education: graduated Princeton, 1763, M.A., 1766; read the law under Richard Stockton and was admitted to the New Jersey Bar, 1769. Married Cornelia Bell, 1779, three children; married Euphemia White, 1785, no children. Died: September 9, 1806, Albany, New York.
*Career Data* Practiced law, 1769–76. Member, New Jersey Provincial Congress, 1775–76. New Jersey Attorney General, 1776–83. Delegate, Constitutional Convention, 1787. Member, U.S. Senate, 1789–90. Governor, New Jersey, 1790–93.
*Supreme Court Data* Nominated by George Washington on March 4, 1793,

to replace Thomas Johnson, who resigned. Resigned September 9, 1806.

Paterson emigrated to America as an infant, with his family finally settling in Princeton, New Jersey. In 1776, he helped write the New Jersey state constitution, and was chosen its first attorney general. Paterson headed the New Jersey delegation to the Constitutional Convention, where he was the chief advocate of the New Jersey Plan, which called for a unicameral legislature in which each state would have an equal vote. Even after its failure, Paterson signed the Constitution and was a leader of the adoption movement in New Jersey. As New Jersey's first U.S. senator, Paterson chaired the judiciary committee and was a chief author of the Judiciary Act of 1789. He resigned the next year to become governor of New Jersey, where he became a close ally of Alexander Hamilton of New York.

Paterson was appointed to the Supreme Court in 1793. He gained a reputation as a proponent of the Federalist cause in several sedition trials. His opinion in *Hylton* v. *United States* (1796) has been revered as the most authoritative elaboration of the legality of direct taxes. In 1800, when Oliver Ellsworth resigned as Chief Justice, President Adams refused to elevate Paterson because of his relationship with Hamilton. His health began to fail around 1804, and he died in 1806, less than a month after resigning from the Court.

Samuel Chase, 1796–1811

*Personal Data* Born: April 17, 1741, Somerset, Maryland. Education: home tutored; read the law in several Annapolis law offices and was admitted to the Maryland Bar, 1761. Married Anne Baldwin, 1762, no children; married Hannah Giles, 1784, four children. Died: June 19, 1811, Baltimore, Maryland.

*Career Data* Practiced law and business investments, 1761–78. Member, Maryland Assembly, 1764–84. Delegate, Continental Congress, 1774–78, 1784–85. Judge, Baltimore Criminal Court, 1788–96. Chief Judge, General Court of Maryland, 1791–96.

*Supreme Court Data* Nominated by George Washington on January 26, 1796. Served until June 19, 1811.

Chase was an avowed rebel who was a signer of the Declaration of Independence, and then was a revolutionary leader. In 1778, he was a major figure at the Continental Congress, and was sent along with Benjamin Franklin to Canada to try to get Canada to join the rebellion. His service in the Congress, however, was suspended because of his shady financial dealings and in 1789 he was forced to declare bankruptcy.

Eventually he became a radical Federalist and actually was appointed to the Supreme Court as a political reward. He has been hailed as the most turbulent individual ever to serve on the Court. On the Court he still was an active politician, one of the prime movers of the Alien and Sedition Acts, and was opposed to the Constitution. Chase has the distinction as the only Supreme Court Justice impeached by the House and tried in the Senate on charges of "high crimes and misde-

meanors." The Senate vote fell a few votes short of the majority required. But after his Senate trial, he attended few Court sessions even though he continued to hold his seat until his death in 1811.

Oliver Ellsworth, 1796–1800

*Personal Data* Born: April 29, 1745, Windsor, Connecticut. Education: graduated Princeton, B.A., 1766; read the law and qualified for the Connecticut Bar, 1788. Married Abigail Wolcott, 1771, seven children. Died: November 26, 1807, Windsor, Connecticut.

*Career Data* Member, Connecticut Assembly, 1773–76; County Attorney, Hartford County, 1777–85. Delegate, Continental Congress, 1777–84. Member, Governor's Council, 1780–85, 1801–07. Judge, Connecticut Superior Court, 1785–89. Delegate, Constitutional Convention, 1787. Member, U.S. Senate, 1789–96. Ambassador to France, 1799–1800.

*Supreme Court Data* Nominated Chief Justice by George Washington on March 3, 1796, to replace Justice John Jay, who resigned. Resigned September 30, 1800.

Ellsworth began studying for the ministry after graduating from Princeton. But he soon turned to the law, and after admission to the bar began to practice. As a young lawyer, he supported his family as a working farmer. Soon his practice grew and he prospered. In 1773 he was elected to the Connecticut General Assembly and then was a Connecticut delegate to the Continental Congress.

In 1787 Ellsworth was elected a member of the Connecticut delegation to the Constitutional Convention. Although he was back in Connecticut arguing a legal case the day the new Constitution was signed, Ellsworth is among the most important of the Founding Fathers. He devised the Connecticut Compromise that ended the dispute between large and small states over size of state representation in the new Congress, and it was his idea to name the new country the United States.

In 1789 Ellsworth became one of Connecticut's first U.S. senators and was a driving force in designing the new government. He was responsible for setting up the new army, the new judiciary, and the new postal system. He was responsible for the conference report that resulted in the drafting of the Bill of Rights. When John Jay resigned as Chief Justice in 1795, Washington appointed John Rutledge. When the Senate refused to confirm, Washington tried to elevate Associate Justice William Cushing. When Cushing declined, the nomination went finally to Ellsworth.

Ellsworth only sat on the Court for two years. In that period, the Court had little to do, although he was busy organizing the lower court system. In 1798 Washington sent Ellsworth to France to repair relations between the two countries. It was a long and difficult mission and his health began to fail. Even before he returned from France, Ellsworth notified Adams of his resignation as Chief Justice. He returned to his estate in Connecticut, where he lived until his death in 1807.

## Bushrod Washington, 1798–1829

*Personal Data* Born: June 5, 1762, Westmoreland County, Virginia. Education: graduated College of William and Mary, 1778; read law under James Wilson and was admitted to the Virginia Bar, 1783. Married Julia Ann Blackburn, 1785, no children. Died: November 26, 1829, in Philadelphia, Pennsylvania.
*Career Data* Practiced law, 1783–98. Member, Virginia House of Delegates, 1787.
*Supreme Court Data* Nominated by John Adams on December 19, 1798, to replace Justice James Wilson, who died. Resigned November 26, 1829.

Bushrod Washington's father, John, was George Washington's brother. At the College of William and Mary, he was a founding member of Phi Beta Kappa. After college he fought in the Revolution, then read the law in Philadelphia under James Wilson, the man he would eventually succeed on the Supreme Court.

Washington established a law practice that prospered almost immediately. At his uncle's urging he ran for and won a seat in the Virginia House of Delegates. He soon became one of Virginia's most successful lawyers. When his uncle died childless in 1799, Bushrod was left Mount Vernon, and all his uncle's public and private papers.

During thirty-one years on the Court, Washington was often allied with Chief

Justice Marshall and Justice Story. He differed with Marshall only three times in twenty-nine years.

## Alfred Moore, 1799–1804

*Personal Data* Born: May 21, 1755, New Hanover, North Carolina. Education: tutored in Boston; read the law under his father and was admitted to North Carolina Bar, 1775. Married Susanna Eagles, no children. Died: October 15, 1810, Bladen, North Carolina.

*Career Data* Practiced law and farmed, 1778–82. Member, North Carolina legislature, 1782, 1792. North Carolina Attorney General, 1782–91. Judge, North Carolina Superior Court, 1799.

*Supreme Court Data* Nominated by John Adams on December 6, 1799, to replace Justice James Iredell, who died. Resigned January 26, 1804.

Moore's father was a famed Colonial judge. During the Revolution, Moore served as an officer in a regiment that was involved in many battles. After the war, he returned to run the family plantation and also to practice law. In 1792 Moore was again elected to the state legislature, and lost a race for the U.S. Senate by a single vote. Instead, he became North Carolina attorney general. In 1799 he was appointed a judge on the North Carolina Superior Court.

When Justice James Iredell died in 1799, Adams wanted to replace him with another North Carolinian. When his first choice was not available, he turned to Moore. In five years on the Court, Moore did little. He wrote only a single opinion, and was often absent from Court sessions. When he did attend, he refused to render opinions.

## John Marshall, 1801–1835

*Personal Data* Born: September 24, 1755, Germantown, Virginia. Education: home tutored, attended law lectures at College of William and Mary; was admitted to the Virginia Bar, 1780. Married Mary Willis Ambler, 1783, ten children. Died: July 6, 1835, Philadelphia, Pennsylvania.

*Career Data* Practiced law, 1780–97. Member, Virginia House of Delegates, 1782–85, 1787–90, 1795–96. Member, Executive Council of State (Va.), 1782–84. U.S. Minister to France, 1797–98. Member, U.S. House, 1799–1800. U.S. Secretary of State, 1800–01.

*Supreme Court Data* Nominated Chief Justice by John Adams on January 20, 1801, to replace Chief Justice Oliver Ellsworth, who resigned. Served until July 6, 1835.

The eldest of fifteen children, Marshall was tutored by several local ministers and by his father. In the Revolution he was a captain in the Third Virginia Regiment. In 1780, he was admitted to the Virginia Bar and quickly built up a lucrative law practice in Richmond. He was elected to the Virginia House of Delegates in 1782 and was the leader in the fight for the ratification of the new U.S. Constitution in Virginia.

Marshall was asked to take numerous appointments in the Washington and Adams administrations, including a Supreme Court justiceship in 1798, but he refused. The next year, after a year as a special envoy to France, Marshall as a favor to Washington won a seat in the U.S. House of Representatives where he served only a single term. In 1800 he finally agreed to serve as Adams's secretary of state, and when Adams took ill, Marshall served almost a year as unofficial de-facto president. When Oliver Ellsworth resigned as Chief Justice in 1800, Adams first offered the job to John Jay. When Jay declined, Adams nominated Marshall.

Marshall has become known as the Father of the Supreme Court. He went on to serve the longest tenure of any Chief Justice—thirty-four years—and completely changed the course of American law. He participated in more than 1,000 decisions, authoring half personally. His legal philosophy was rooted in the belief that freedom lay in the absolute right to private property. He was a strident Federalist, who believed in federal supremacy over the states. His visions encompassed a Constitutional framework that was flexible enough to leave room for judicial interpretation within the confines of individual disputes. His goal was to lay a broad foundation that future generations could refine into more explicit Constitutional doctrines.

Marshall died while still in office and only three months short of his eightieth birthday. The Liberty Bell cracked as it tolled in mourning for Marshall. It was the last time the Bell was rung. (For a fuller examination of the Marshall Court, see pages 45–60).

William Johnson, 1804–1834

*Personal Data* Born: December 17, 1771, Charleston, South Carolina. Ed-

ucation: graduated Princeton, 1790; read the law under Charles Pinckney and was admitted to the South Carolina Bar, 1793. Married Sarah Bennett, 1794, eight children. Died: August 4, 1834, Brooklyn, New York.
*Career Data* Practiced law, 1793–94. Member, South Carolina House, 1794–98, Speaker, 1798. Judge, Court of Common Pleas, 1799–1804.
*Supreme Court Data* Nominated by Thomas Jefferson on March 22, 1804, to replace Justice Alfred Moore, who resigned. Served until August 4, 1834.

A year after starting his law practice, Johnson was elected to the South Carolina House of Representatives, and four years later he was elected its Speaker. In 1799, Johnson was selected as one of three judges of the state's top court. Within four years he had been named the first Republican nominee to the Supreme Court.

Reportedly, he initially was not happy on the Court and tried to convince Jefferson to give him another top-level appointment. But none was forthcoming and he ended up serving almost thirty years until his death in 1834. On the Court he had the distinction of being the only justice willing to stand up to Chief Justice Marshall. In doing so, Johnson helped establish the tradition of dissenting opinions.

Henry Brockholst Livingston, 1806–1823

*Personal Data* Born: November 25, 1757, New York City. Education: graduated Princeton, 1774; read the law under Peter Yates and admitted New York Bar, 1783. Married Catharine Keteltas,

1783, five children; married Ann Ludlow, 1795, three children; married Catharine Kortright, 1812, three children. Died: March 18, 1823, Washington, D.C.

*Career Data* Practiced law, 1783–1802. Member New York Assembly, 1786–1802. Judge, New York State Supreme Court, 1802–1807.

*Supreme Court Data* Nominated by Thomas Jefferson on December 13, 1806, to replace Justice William Paterson, who died. Served until March 18, 1823.

After graduating from Princeton, Livingston served in the Continental Army as an aide to General Benedict Arnold. After the war, he served as aide to his brother-in-law John Jay while Jay served as envoy to Spain. Livingston returned to New York, read the law, and was admitted to the bar in 1783. Three years later he was elected to the New York Assembly in 1786.

In Spain, Livingston had come to intensely dislike Jay. This led him to become an anti-Federalist and to oppose his brother-in-law's election as governor of New York. When the anti-Federalists came to power in 1802, Livingston and two close relatives were named to the New York Supreme Court. Two years later, Livingston was almost appointed to the U.S. Supreme Court, but the position went to William Johnson. Finally in 1806 he was named to the Court.

In his sixteen years on the Court, Livingston went through another political conversion, this time back to conservative, Federalist views. None of his opinions were of lasting constitutional value, but he did make significant contributions in the areas of commercial and maritime law. Upon his retirement, he returned to New York where he was a cofounder of the New York Historical Society, treasurer of Columbia University, and one of the founders of the New York public school system.

Thomas Todd, 1807–1826

*Personal Data* Born: January 23, 1765, Kings County, Virginia. Education: graduated Washington and Lee University, 1783; read law under Harry Innes and was admitted to the Virginia Bar in 1788. Married Elizabeth Harris, 1788, five children; married Lucy Payne, 1812, three children. Died: February 7, 1826, Frankfort, Kentucky.

*Career Data* Practiced law, 1788–92. Clerk, Kentucky State House, 1792–99. Clerk, Kentucky Supreme Court, 1799–1801; Judge, 1801–06; Chief Justice, 1806–07.

*Supreme Court Data* Nominated by Thomas Jefferson on February 28, 1807, to fill a new seat. Served until February 7, 1826.

When Todd was still reading the law, he followed his mentor, Judge Harry Innes, to Danville, Kentucky—then still part of Virginia—where he was admitted to the Virginia Bar. He served as clerk to the Kentucky statehood convention, and then as secretary to the new state legislature. When the Kentucky Supreme Court was created, Todd became its first clerk and two years later was appointed a judge, and five years later its chief justice. In 1807, a new federal circuit consisting of Kentucky,

Ohio, and Tennessee was created, and Jefferson chose Todd to preside over it as the Supreme Court's new sixth associate justice.

Although he served on the Court for nineteen years, Todd missed five full sessions because of illness and delivered only fourteen opinions during his entire tenure. As a member of the Marshall Court, Todd generally conformed with the economic conservatism and belief in a strong union that Marshall advocated. In Washington, the Todds became part of the social scene. In 1811 Todd's first wife Elizabeth died, and a year later he married Dolley Madison's sister, Lucy Payne, in a White House ceremony.

## Gabriel Duval, 1811–1835

*Personal Data* Born: December 6, 1752, Buena Vista, Maryland. Education: preparatory school; read the law privately and was admitted to the Maryland Bar, 1778. Married Mary Bryce, 1787, one child; married Jane Gibbon, 1795, no children. Died: March 6, 1844, Prince George's, Maryland.

*Career Data* Clerk, Maryland House of Delegates, 1777–87; Member, 1787–94. Member, U.S. House, 1794–96. Chief Justice, General Court of Maryland, 1796–1802. Comptroller of the U.S. Treasury, 1802–11.

*Supreme Court Data* Nominated by James Madison on November 15, 1811, to replace Justice Samuel Chase, who died. Resigned January 14, 1835.

A soldier in the Revolution, Duval became the clerk of the Maryland Convention that formed its first state government, and then clerk to the House of Delegates. He was also chosen a member of the Maryland delegation to the Constitutional Convention, but the delegation chose to boycott the sessions. Elected to Congress, he resigned after a single term to become chief justice of the Maryland high court. In 1802 President Thomas Jefferson chose Duval to be the first comptroller of the U.S. Treasury, a position he held until his elevation to the Court.

Duval was a relatively old fifty-eight when he took his Court seat, yet he served twenty-four years. Duval is probably best known for his dissent against the opinion of Chief Justice Marshall in the famous *Dartmouth College* v. *Woodward* (1819). It was the first time any justice stood up to Marshall's dominance, and was important in establishing the principle of judicial dissent on the Court. By the time he retired in 1835 at age eighty-two, he was almost completely deaf and was absent from most Court sessions.

## Joseph Story, 1811–1845

*Personal Data* Born: September 18, 1779, Marblehead, Massachusetts. Education: graduated Harvard University, 1798; read the law under Samuel Sewall and was admitted to the Massachusetts Bar, 1801. Married Mary Oliver, 1804, no children; married Sarah Wetmore, 1808, seven children. Died: September 10, 1845, Cambridge, Massachusetts.

*Career Data* Practiced law, 1801–08, 1809–11. Member, Massachusetts House, 1805–08. Member, U.S. House, 1808–09. Speaker of the Massachusetts House, 1811.

*Supreme Court Data* Nominated by James Madison on November 15, 1811, to replace Justice William Cushing, who died. Served until September 10, 1845.

A Republican, Story served two terms in the Massachusetts legislature before winning a seat in Congress. But during his first term he had numerous clashes with President Jefferson and was not renominated. So he returned to the Massachusetts legislature and was elected its Speaker. But within a matter of months, Madison—after his first choice was rejected—appointed Story.

At age thirty-two, Story was the youngest justice ever and one of its great legal minds. Through his opinions, he became central to the development of American business, corporation, and patent law. His most famous opinion, *Swift* v. *Tyson* (1842), held that federal courts did not have to take notice of state court decisions in the area of commercial law. For almost a century, his holdings controlled interstate commercial transactions.

There was general agreement that when Chief Justice Marshall died in 1835, Story should have been elevated. But Andrew Jackson disliked him, and instead appointed Roger Taney. Story's nine years as a member of the Taney Court were filled with dissents, and gradually he simply lost heart.

While a member of the Court, Story was elected to the Harvard Board of Overseers and then a director of the Harvard Corporation. He also became a professor of law and helped form the Harvard Law School. He also authored one of the major early works on the developing American legal system, his *Nine Commentaries*.

## Smith Thompson, 1823–1843

*Personal Data* Born: January 17, 1768, Stanford, New York. Education: graduated Princeton, 1788; read the law under James Kent and admitted to the New York Bar, 1792. Married Sarah Livingston, 1798, four children; married Eliza Livingston, 1815, three children. Died: December 18, 1843, Poughkeepsie, New York.

*Career Data* Practiced law, 1793–1802. Member, New York legislature, 1800. Member, New York State Constitutional Convention, 1801. Judge, New York Supreme Court, 1802–14; Chief Justice, 1814–18. Secretary of the Navy, 1819–23.

*Supreme Court Data* Nominated by James Monroe on December 8, 1823, to replace Justice Henry Brockholst Livingston, who died. Served until December 18, 1843.

Having married into the powerful Livingston family, Thompson's political future was guaranteed. First he served in the state legislature. Next came an appointment as district attorney. But even before he could assume that job, the new state supreme court was formed; and he was offered a seat along with two of his brothers-in-law including Henry Brockholst Livingston, whom he eventually succeeded on the U.S. Supreme Court.

Thompson was appointed Secretary of the Navy by President Monroe in 1819. While navy secretary, Thompson actually spent most of his time involved in New York politics, and promoting himself for a possible presidential bid. But when his brother-in-law died in 1823, Thompson was immediately offered his Supreme Court seat. He delayed accepting still hoping to mount a presidential challenge. But when it became clear that his old friend Martin Van Buren had outfoxed him and would get the presidential nomination, he accepted the Supreme Court appointment.

Thompson has the distinction of being perhaps the most politically active justice ever to serve. On the Court he continued to harbor political ambitions. In 1828 he ran for governor of New York, losing to Van Buren in a bitter contest. On the Court he often found himself at odds with Marshall and the Chief Justice's strong federal views. This was shown strikingly in his bitter dissent against Marshall in *Cherokee Nation* v. *Georgia* (1831), when he tried to uphold the view that an Indian tribe is a "foreign state" under the Constitution.

*Supreme Court Data* Nominated by John Quincy Adams on April 11, 1826, to replace Justice Thomas Todd, who died. Served until August 25, 1828.

Trimble began private practice in Paris, Kentucky. In 1807 he was appointed a justice of the Kentucky Court of Appeals, but resigned because of the low pay. The need to support his large family made Trimble refuse numerous positions, including the U.S. Senate in 1812. But by 1817 he had become financially well off, so he accepted the position of federal district judge for Kentucky.

Trimble's death only twenty-seven months after taking his seat ended what appeared destined to be a distinguished career. John Quincy Adams chose him because of his strong federal views. Thus he agreed with Chief Justice Marshall in almost every case. The majority of the cases in which Trimble issued the Court's opinion dealt with technical land ownership and procedural matters.

## Robert Trimble, 1826–1828

*Personal Data* Born: November 17, 1776, Augustus, Virginia. Education: Kentucky Academy; read the law under George Nicholas and admitted to the Kentucky Bar, 1800. Married Nancy Timberlake, 1803, eleven children. Died: August 25, 1828, Paris, Kentucky.
*Career Data* Practiced law, 1800–07, 1808–13. Member, Kentucky Assembly, 1802. Judge, Kentucky Court of Appeals, 1807–09. U.S. Attorney for Kentucky, 1813–17. Judge, U.S. District Court, 1817–26.

## John McLean, 1829–1861

*Personal Data* Born: March 11, 1785, Morris, New Jersey. Education: privately tutored; read the law under Arthur St. Clair and was admitted to the Ohio Bar, 1806. Married Rebecca Edwards, 1807, seven children; married Sarah Garrard, 1843, no children. Died: April 4, 1861, Cincinnati, Ohio.
*Career Data* Member, U.S. House, 1813–16. Judge, Ohio Supreme Court, 1816–22. Commissioner, U.S. Land Office, 1822–23. U.S. Postmaster General, 1823–29.
*Supreme Court Data* Nominated by

Andrew Jackson on January 6, 1829, to replace Justice Robert Trimble, who died. Served until April 4, 1861.

After being admitted to the bar, McLean moved to Lebanon, Ohio, where he opened a printing office and published the *Western Star*, a weekly newspaper. Three years later he turned the paper over to his brother-in-law, and built up his law practice. Two years later he was elected to Congress, where he served two terms. In 1816 he resigned from the House to run for a judgeship on the Ohio Supreme Court. He became a major supporter of James Monroe, and in 1822 Monroe appointed him to head the U.S. Land Office, and a year later made him postmaster general. Under McLean, the post office system was greatly expanded, and he was reappointed by John Quincy Adams. When Andrew Jackson became president in 1829, Adams had not filled a long vacant Supreme Court seat because of a fight with the Senate. McLean was well respected, and became the compromise appointee.

McLean's thirty-three-year tenure on the Court is filled with contradictions. Despite his long tenure, what he really wanted was to be president. In 1856, he received the most votes on the first ballot at the first Republican national convention in Philadelphia, but eventually lost the nomination to John Freemont. He tried again four years later, only to lose to Abraham Lincoln. He died of pneumonia the next year. As an antislavery proponent, he earned distinction as a champion of freedom. His dissent in the *Dred Scott* case has been hailed as the most important opinion in the case, and

his views were eventually put into the Constitution in the Fourteenth Amendment.

Henry Baldwin, 1830–1844

*Personal Data* Born: January 14, 1780, New Haven, Connecticut. Education: graduated Yale College, 1797; read the law under Alexander J. Dallas and admitted to the Pennsylvania Bar, 1800. Married Marianna Norton, 1802, one child; married Sally Ellicott, 1805, no children. Died: April 21, 1844, Philadelphia, Pennsylvania.
*Career Data* Practiced law, 1800–16, 1823–30. Member, U.S. House, 1817–22.
*Supreme Court Data* Nominated by Andrew Jackson on January 4, 1830, to replace Justice Bushrod Washington, who died. Served until April 21, 1844.

After graduation from Yale, Baldwin read the law under Alexander Dallas, a prominent Philadelphia attorney. After being admitted to the bar, he moved to Pittsburgh to establish a law practice. His law practice flourished and he became a power in the Republican party of western Pennsylvania. Eventually he became possibly the most popular figure in Pittsburgh, and was called by local newspapers the "Pride of Pittsburgh."

Also a businessman, Baldwin decided to run for Congress in 1817 to support higher tariffs. Forced to resign for health reasons in 1822 he returned to Pittsburgh, and after regaining his health assumed the role of political leader of Allegheny County. He became an adviser to Andrew Jackson and worked on his presidential campaign. When Bushrod Washington died in 1829, Jackson nominated Baldwin to the seat, setting off a major battle with Vice-President John C. Calhoun, who had his own candidate.

Despite fourteen years on the Court, Baldwin served with little distinction. He did not feel strongly that the Court must be a harmonious unit and spent much of his time writing concurring opinions that offended his colleagues. Baldwin also suffered from bouts with mental infirmity throughout his tenure.

## James Moore Wayne, 1835–1867

*Personal Data* Born: June 10, 1790, Savannah, Georgia. Education: graduated Princeton, 1808; read the law under Judge Charles Chauncey of New Haven, Connecticut, and then Samuel Bond of Savannah; admitted to Georgia Bar, 1810. Married Mary Johnston Campbell, 1813, three children. Died: July 5, 1867, Washington, D.C.

*Career Data* Practiced law, 1810–16. Member, Georgia State House, 1815–16. Mayor of Savannah, 1817–19. Judge, Savannah District Court, 1820–22. Judge, Georgia Superior Court, 1822–28. U.S. Representative, 1829–35.

*Supreme Court Data* Nominated by Andrew Jackson on January 7, 1835, to replace Justice William Johnson, who died. Served until July 5, 1867.

Shortly after Wayne started to practice law in Savannah with his brother-in-law, the War of 1812 broke out. He served as an officer in the Georgia militia. Returning, he resumed his law practice and then was elected, in 1815, to the Georgia legislature. Two years later,

at age twenty-seven, he was elected mayor of Savannah. From there he became first a judge on the Savannah Court of Common Pleas, then the superior court. He won a seat in Congress in 1829, and served three terms during which he became a valuable ally on Capitol Hill for Andrew Jackson. Jackson rewarded him with a Supreme Court nomination in 1835.

It was in the area of admiralty law and, more broadly, corporate business, that Wayne displayed his expertise. In *Dodge* v. *Wollsey* (1856), Wayne upheld a generous tax exemption for a state-chartered bank, which the state legislature had repealed, marking the first time a state Constitutional provision was found invalid. He served all through the Civil War. He was the only Southern justice not to leave his seat. Although believing Negroes should not be allowed citizenship, Wayne was, in fact, a strong Union supporter. He was disowned by Georgia, labeled an enemy of the state, and all his property was seized. After the war, Wayne became a strong opponent of Reconstruction, but he died before his opposition could have any effect.

## Roger Brooke Taney, 1836–1864

*Personal Data* Born: March 17, 1777, Calvert, Maryland. Education: graduated Dickinson College (Pa.), 1795; read the law under Judge Jeremiah Chase of Annapolis and admitted to the Maryland Bar, 1799. Married Anne Key, 1806, seven children. Died: October 12, 1864, Washington, D.C.

*Career Data* Practiced law, 1801–16, 1821–27. Member, Maryland House of Delegates, 1799–1800. Member, Maryland State Senate, 1816–21. Maryland Attorney General, 1827–31. U.S. Attorney General, 1831–33. U.S. Secretary of War, 1831. U.S. Secretary of the Treasury, 1833–34.

*Supreme Court Data* Nominated Chief Justice by Andrew Jackson on December 28, 1835, to replace Chief Justice John Marshall, who died. Served until October 12, 1864.

Taney's political career got off to a rough start. He served a single term in the Maryland legislature and was defeated for reelection. He moved to Frederick, Maryland, where he started a twenty-year law practice. He finally returned to politics in 1816, winning a State Senate race, and eventually he became a power in state politics. After a term in the Senate, Taney moved to Baltimore, where he resumed his law practice. He served as state attorney general from 1827 to 1831, and he ran Jackson's presidential campaign in Maryland. As a reward, Jackson brought him to Washington in 1831 as U.S. attorney general.

Almost immediately, Taney became deeply involved in Jackson's fight over the rechartering of the Bank of the United States. When Treasury Secretary William Duane refused to withdraw federal deposits from the bank, Taney replaced him. His actions angered the Senate, which then refused to confirm him in the new position. So Jackson removed him, and immediately offered him the Supreme Court seat of retiring Associate Justice Gabriel Duval. The still angry Senate refused to vote his confirmation, Jackson refused to withdraw it, and a year-long stalemate ensued. Jackson then proposed Taney for the Chief Justiceship after Marshall's death. A bitter confirmation battle followed, but in the end Taney was confirmed by a narrow margin.

Labeled a proponent of Jacksonian reform, Taney's tenure was saddled with the burden of overcoming the shadow of his predecessor, John Marshall. His philosophy did not prove as radical as many had feared. Taney undertook change within the broad confines of Marshall's ideas, rather than completely destroying them. This change began with a shift to states' rights; the states were granted more autonomy in commerce. Taney is remembered for upholding his basic belief in dual sovereignty without departing significantly from the Marshall legacy of a federal government that possesses significant powers under the Constitution. (For a fuller examination of the Taney Court, see pages 60–70.)

## Philip Pendleton Barbour, 1836–1841

*Personal Data* Born: May 25, 1783, Orange, Virginia. Education: home tutored; attended legal classes at the College of William and Mary, 1801, and was admitted to Virginia Bar, 1803. Married Frances Johnson, 1804, seven children. Died: February 25, 1841, Washington, D.C.

*Career Data* Member, Virginia House of Delegates, 1812–14. Member, U.S. House, 1814–30, Speaker, 1821–23. Judge, General Court of Virginia, 1825–27. Judge, U.S. District Court, 1830–36.

*Supreme Court Data* Nominated by

Andrew Jackson on February 28, 1835, to replace Justice Gabriel Duval, who resigned. Served until February 25, 1841.

Barbour was elected to the Virginia House of Delegates in 1812 and two years later he won a seat in the U.S. House. There he had a significant career, including serving one term (1821–23) as Speaker, but was defeated for reelection as Speaker by Henry Clay. Angered by this defeat, he declined to run for reelection, and became a judge instead. In 1827 he again returned to Congress, but again he lost the Speaker's race. He again declined to run for reelection and accepted a federal judgeship in 1830. In 1832 he was favored to become vice-president, but Jackson persuaded him to withdraw in favor of Martin Van Buren. As a reward, Jackson named him to the Court at the relatively old age of fifty-four.

Barbour was a strict constructionist, firmly supportive of states' rights. In his short tenure on the Court, only five years, he generally followed the lead of Chief Justice Taney. He died of a heart attack after attending a late-night conference with other justices.

John Catron, 1837–1865

*Personal Data* Believed born in Pennsylvania about 1786. Education: self-educated. Believed married, but wife's name unknown. Died: May 30, 1865, Nashville, Tennessee.
*Career Data* Practiced law, 1815–24, 1834–37. Judge, Tennessee Supreme Court, 1824–31, Chief Justice, 1831–34. *Supreme Court Data* Nominated by

Andrew Jackson on March 3, 1837, to fill a new seat. Served until May 30, 1865, after which his seat was abolished by Congress.

Historians know little about John Catron's early life. Poor and self-educated, he settled in the Cumberland Mountains of Tennessee and served as a junior officer under Andrew Jackson in the War of 1812. He read law for a year and was admitted to the Tennessee Bar in 1815. In 1818 he moved to Nashville, where he quickly developed a law practice specializing in land law.

In 1824, when Tennessee created the new State Supreme Court of Errors (Appeals), Catron was elected to fill one of its seats. He became the court's first chief justice, but the court was abolished in 1834 in a judicial reorganization. He returned to his law practice and ran Martin Van Buren's presidential campaign in the western states. As a reward, on his last day in office, Jackson named him to one of two newly created seats on the Court.

As a member of the Taney Court, Catron believed that preservation of the Union was of paramount importance. Labeled a Jacksonian jurist, he was adamant in protecting the rights of the states against individuals of wealth and privilege. He played an integral part in the *Dred Scott* case as a member of the pro-Southern majority.

John McKinley, 1837–1852

*Personal Data* Born: May 1, 1780, Culpepper, Virginia. Education: home tutored; read the law privately and was admitted to the Kentucky Bar, 1800.

Married Juliana Bryan, no children; married Elizabeth Armistead, no children. Died: July 19, 1852, Louisville, Kentucky.

*Career Data* Practiced law, 1801–20. Member, Alabama State House, 1820–26, 1831–33. Member, U.S. Senate, 1826–31, 1837. Member, U.S. House, 1833–35.

*Supreme Court Data* Nominated by Martin Van Buren on September 18, 1837, to fill a new seat. Served until July 19, 1852.

After being admitted to the Kentucky bar, McKinley practiced for several years in Frankfort and Louisville. He then moved to the Alabama Territory, figuring correctly it would soon become a state and would be in need of lawyers. He settled in Huntsville and soon developed a large law practice. He then entered politics and was elected to the new Alabama legislature in 1820, and in 1822 fell one vote short of winning a U.S. Senate seat. Four years later he won the seat, and served one term. He returned to the state legislature for a term, and then was elected to the U.S. House in 1832, where he served until again elected to the Senate in 1837. He never got a chance to serve. Before the Senate convened, he was offered the Supreme Court seat by his friend, Van Buren.

McKinley's fifteen years on the bench were unremarkable. He primarily sided with the majority, dissenting only when in the company of at least one other justice. His most famous dissent came in *Bank of Augusta* v. *Earle* (1839), in which he ruled that a corporation chartered in one state could not operate in another. His position was based on a belief in compact government. He stood by his states' rights and proslavery views to the last.

## Peter Vivian Daniel, 1841–1860

*Personal Data* Born: April 24, 1784, Stafford, Virginia. Education: attended Princeton, 1802; read the law under Edmund Randolph and was admitted to the Virginia Bar, 1808. Married Lucy Randolph, 1809, no children; married Elizabeth Harris, 1853, two children. Died: May 31, 1860, Richmond, Virginia.

*Career Data* Member, Virginia House of Delegates, 1809–12; Member, Privy Council, 1812–35. Lieutenant Governor, 1818–35; Judge, U.S. District Court, 1836–41.

*Supreme Court Data* Nominated by Van Buren on February 26, 1841, to replace Justice Philip Barbour, who died. Served until May 31, 1860.

From a prominent family and married into another, Daniel had a privileged life. He was first elected to the House of Delegates and then to the Privy Council, a kind of state executive board. Then in 1818 he was chosen lieutenant governor and served in that office and on the Privy Council for the next seventeen years. He supported Jackson and as a result was thrown out of his positions in 1835. But Jackson rewarded him with a district judgeship. Daniel received his Supreme Court seat in a maneuver between Van Buren and the Democratically controlled Senate in the final hours of Van Buren's term. When Justice Philip Barbour died, Van Buren had promised the incoming Whigs he would leave the seat open. But he suddenly named Daniel, who was quickly confirmed by the Senate.

Daniel ended up serving for the next nineteen years. He was known for his unwavering support of states' rights, his advocacy of a weak central government, and a rigid proslavery stance. His views led him to a most extreme position, taken in *Searight* v. *Stokes* (1845), in which he dissented, rejecting the power of the federal government to undertake any internal improvements including roads and canals.

## Samuel Nelson, 1845–1872

*Personal Data* Born: November 10, 1792, Hebron, New York. Education: graduated Middlebury College, 1813; read the law under several lawyers in Salem, New York, and was admitted to the New York Bar, 1817. Married Pamela Woods, 1819, one child; married Catherine Ann Russell, 1826, three children. Died: December 13, 1873, Cooperstown, New York.
*Career Data* Postmaster, Cortland, New York, 1820–23. Judge, Circuit Court of New York, 1823–31. Judge, New York Supreme Court, 1831–37; Chief Justice, 1837–45.
*Supreme Court Data* Nominated by John Tyler on February 4, 1845, to replace Justice Smith Thompson, who died. Retired November 28, 1872.

Nelson established a law practice in Cortland, New York, and entered local politics as a Democrat. Through his political connections he became the local postmaster, and then a judge on the New York district court. From there he was elevated to the state supreme court, and six years later became its chief justice.

Nelson was the first career jurist to be named to the U.S. Supreme Court. President Tyler had been having great difficulty filling a vacant seat. First several leading contenders turned down the nomination, and then the Senate rejected the next two. So Tyler looked for someone completely noncontroversial and found Nelson.

Nelson ended up serving twenty-seven little noticed years on the Court. Almost always, he could be found voting with the majority. He had a deep respect for the power of the legislature, and thus embraced the notion of judicial restraint with fervor. He believed that the Supreme Court should follow lower courts decisions, and should defer to state law. His one act of real note came in 1860, when he and Justice John Campbell tried to mediate a compromise between the North and South to avoid the Civil War.

## Levi Woodbury, 1846–1851

*Personal data* Born: December 22, 1789, Francestown, New Hampshire. Education: graduated Dartmouth College, 1809; attended Tapping Law School, 1811; admitted to the New Hampshire Bar, 1812. Married Elizabeth Clapp, 1819, five children. Died: September 4, 1851, Portsmouth, New Hampshire.
*Career Data* Clerk, New Hampshire Senate, 1816. Judge, New Hampshire Superior Court, 1817–23. Governor of New Hampshire, 1823–24. Speaker, New

Hampshire State House, 1825. Member, U.S. Senate, 1825–31, 1841–45. Secretary of the Navy, 1831–34. Secretary of the Treasury, 1834–41.

*Supreme Court Data* Nominated by James K. Polk on December 23, 1845, to replace Justice Joseph Story, who died. Served until September 4, 1851.

Woodbury was the first Supreme Court justice to have attended a formal law school. He established a law practice in Portsmouth, and became involved in politics. For a year he was clerk of the State Senate, then served six years as a judge, and in 1823 won the state governorship. He was defeated for reelection, but then ran for the state's House, where he was elected Speaker. From there he went to the U.S. Senate for a single six-year term and then left to become Andrew Jackson's Secretary of the Navy in 1831. Three years later Jackson made him treasury secretary—a position he held through the Van Buren administration. From there it was back to the Senate, where he was sitting when he was selected for the Supreme Court.

Woodbury's six years on the Court can be characterized by his desire to seek a balance between private rights and public interest. He tried to please both Southerners and the northern Constitutional conservatives. He was a leading contender for the Democratic presidential nomination in 1848, but lost to Lewis Cass.

Robert Cooper Grier, 1846–1870

*Personal data* Born: March 5, 1794, Cumberland County, Pennsylvania. Education: graduated Dickinson College (Pa.), 1812. Married Isabella Rose, 1829, no children. Died: September 25, 1870, Philadelphia, Pennsylvania.

*Career Data* Practiced law, 1817–33. Chief Judge, Allegheny County Court, 1833–46.

*Supreme Court Data* Nominated by James K. Polk on August 3, 1846, to replace Justice Henry Baldwin, who died. Retired January 31, 1870.

After college, Grier began to teach at the Northumberland Academy, where he succeeded his minister father as principal in 1815. But he soon lost interest in teaching and began to privately read the law. After passing the bar, he moved to Danville, Pennsylvania, where he soon developed a large law practice and began to dabble in Jacksonian Democrat politics. This led to an appointment as chief judge of the District Court of Allegheny County in 1833, a position he was to hold for the next thirteen years.

When Justice Henry Baldwin died in 1844, one of the most complicated searches for a new justice ensued. Twice, President Tyler—a Whig—sent names to the Democratic-controlled Senate, who simply ignored them. Then Tyler was replaced by Polk, who quickly named James Buchanan, but the future president turned the nomination down to remain in politics. Then Polk sent a nomination to the Senate, and it too was rejected. So Polk set out to find an absolutely nonpolitical, noncontroversial nominee, and he came up with Grier. The Senate, grown weary of fighting over nominees, easily confirmed him.

Grier served on the Court for nearly a quarter of a century. He wrote many opinions in cases involving Constitutional issues. His most noteworthy contribution took place in the prize cases (1863), in which he displayed his commitment to the preservation of the Union. Grier's final years on the Court were hampered by mental infirmity that eventually led to his resignation in January 1870. He died seven months later.

Benjamin Robbins Curtis, 1851–1857

*Personal Data* Born: November 4, 1809, Watertown, Massachusetts. Education: graduated Harvard University, 1829; Harvard Law School, 1832. Married Eliza Woodward, 1833, five children; married Anna Curtis, 1846, three children; married Malleville Allen, 1861, four children. Died: September 15, 1874, Newport, Rhode Island.
*Career Data* Practiced law, 1832–51, 1857–74. Member, Massachusetts State House, 1849–51.
*Supreme Court Data* Nominated by Millard Fillmore on December 11, 1851, to replace Justice Levi Woodbury, who died. Resigned September 30, 1857.

Curtis was one of the first graduates of the new Harvard Law School. After two years practicing law in Northfield, Massachusetts, he moved to Boston, where he became one of the city's leading lawyers. He served only a single term in the Massachusetts House, but during those two years chaired a committee that reorganized the state judiciary. He was a conservative Whig and a close supporter of Daniel Webster. Webster was serving as secretary of state under Millard Fillmore, when Fillmore was trying to find a replacement for Justice Woodbury, who had died. Webster recommended his friend Curtis.

Curtis ended up serving six turbulent years on the Court. One of the best legal minds of his age, he possessed a vast knowledge of admiralty and commercial law, as well as Constitutional law, and this did not set well with his colleagues. He was one of the two dissenters in the *Dred Scott* decision, and the only one to reject the notion that a Negro is not a citizen, and that federal agreements could not take away a Negro's citizenship. His battles with Chief Justice Taney became so bitter that finally he simply resigned at age forty-seven and returned to his law practice in Boston. In 1868 Curtis represented President Andrew Johnson during his impeachment and afterward was offered the position of attorney general, which he declined.

John Archibald Campbell, 1853–1861

*Personal Data* Born: June 24, 1811, Washington, Georgia. Education: graduated University of Georgia, 1825; U.S. Military Academy, 1825–28. Married Anna Goldthwaite, 1833, five children. Died: March 12, 1889, Baltimore, Maryland.
*Career Data* Practiced law, 1830–53, 1866–89. Member, Alabama State House, 1837–45. Assistant Secretary of War, Confederate States of America, 1862–65.
*Supreme Court Data* Nominated by Franklin Pierce on March 21, 1853, to replace Justice John McKinley, who died. Resigned April 30, 1861.

Campbell was a child prodigy, graduating college at age fourteen and then attending West Point. He was forced to leave just short of graduation to return home to support his family after his father died. At age eighteen, without any formal legal training, he was admitted to the Georgia Bar by a special act of the state legislature.

Almost immediately he moved west to Montgomery, Alabama, where he set up a law practice. In short order Campbell was considered one of the top lawyers in the state. Twice he declined appointment to the Alabama Supreme Court. Then in 1850 he became a delegate to the Nashville Convention, a meeting of Southern states to plan action against the Northern states. At this convention, Campbell almost single-handedly pushed through moderate resolutions and prevented secession that would have started the Civil War a decade early.

Campbell may have had the oddest selection to the Supreme Court in history. The Democratic Senate had ignored three nominees from Whig president Fillmore. When Pierce took office in 1853, the sitting justices, aware of Campbell's reputation as perhaps the nation's leading lawyer, sent a delegation to Pierce to ask that he nominate Campbell. He agreed.

Given his obvious brilliance and relative youth, Campbell might have changed the course of judicial history, but the Civil War intervened. Although he was against secession, he still believed in the South. He attempted to act as a moderator between the Southern states and President Lincoln. Personally against slavery, he argued that it would

gradually disappear. But his efforts failed, and when the war began he resigned his Court seat to return to New Orleans, where he became the Confederates' assistant secretary of war. After the war he was held in prison for a time and then returned to New Orleans, where he became that city's leading attorney. He also developed a reputation for winning arguments before the Supreme Court, where he appeared often.

## Nathan Clifford, 1858–1881

*Personal Data* Born: August 18, 1803, Rumney, New Hampshire. Education: home tutored; read the law under Josiah Quincy and was admitted to the New Hampshire Bar, 1827. Married Hannah Ayer, 1829, six children. Died: July 25, 1881, Cornish, Maine.

*Career Data* Practiced law, 1827–34, 1843–46, 1849–57. Member, Maine State House, 1830–34. State Attorney General, 1834–38. Member, U.S. House, 1839–43. U.S. Attorney General, 1846–48. Ambassador to Mexico, 1848–49.

*Supreme Court Data* Nominated by James Buchanan on December 9, 1857, to replace Benjamin Curtis, who resigned. Served until July 25, 1881.

After being admitted to the bar, Clifford moved to Newfield, Maine, to begin practice. He won a seat in the Maine legislature, where he served three one-year terms, two as Speaker. He was elected state attorney general for four years, and then went to Congress for two terms. After his defeat for a third term, he returned to Maine and his law practice. Three years later President

Polk needed a New Englander in his cabinet, so he offered Clifford the attorney generalship. In that job Clifford ended up being the mediator between the president and James Buchanan, his secretary of state who opposed the war with Mexico. In 1848, at Buchanan's insistence, Clifford was sent to Mexico to negotiate a peace treaty and he stayed a year as ambassador. In 1849, Clifford returned to Maine to resume his law practice, which prospered over the next eight years.

When a Supreme Court vacancy occurred in late 1857, President Buchanan chose his old friend Clifford to fill it. A bitter Senate fight ensued, with Clifford winning confirmation by a narrow 26–23 vote. Clifford opposed federalism and the Republicans with equal fervor. On the Court he became its expert in the areas of commercial, patent, and admiralty law as well as Mexican land titles.

In 1877, while still on the Court, Clifford chaired the special commission to decide the disputed presidential election of 1876 between Samuel J. Tilden and Rutherford B. Hayes. Clifford supported Tilden, and when Hayes won Clifford denounced him and refused to enter the White House during his presidency. In 1880 Clifford suffered a severe stroke, but refused to leave the Court until a Democrat could be elected to name his successor. But he died before that happened.

## Noah Haynes Swayne, 1862–1881

*Personal Data* Born: December 7, 1804, Frederick, Virginia. Education: home tutored; read the law privately and was admitted to the Virginia Bar, 1823. Married Sarah Ann Wager, 1832; five children. Died: June 8, 1884, New York City.

*Career Data* Practiced law, 1825–26, 1841–62. Coshocton County (Ohio) Prosecuting Attorney, 1826–30. Member, Ohio State House, 1830 and 1836. U.S. Attorney for Ohio, 1830–41.

*Supreme Court Data* Nominated by Abraham Lincoln on January 21, 1862, to replace John McLean, who died. Retired January 24, 1881.

After being admitted to the bar in Virginia, Swayne moved to Ohio because of his opposition to slavery. Soon after starting his law practice, Swayne was elected prosecuting attorney of Coshocton County, and then as a member of the Ohio legislature. In 1830 he won a seat in Congress, but before leaving he resigned to accept appointment as U.S. attorney for Ohio. After 1836, Swayne dropped out of politics to concentrate on his law practice, but he remained deeply involved in the antislavery movement and this brought him to the attention of Abraham Lincoln, who rewarded his abolitionist work by granting the death-bed wish of Justice John McLean that his close friend Swayne be given his seat.

While on the Court, Swayne maintained a strong nationalist stance that continued into the post–Civil War years. As a result of his solid reputation, Swayne was expected to eventually gain the Chief Justiceship. In 1864 when Roger B. Taney died, he lost out to Salmon P. Chase. Then in 1873, when Chase died, his quest was again destroyed when Morrison Waite was selected instead. Overall, despite his initial promise, Swayne's Court performance fell short. His opinions lacked quality, and he fell out of favor with his colleagues, who grew tired of his obsessive quest for the Chief Justiceship.

## Samuel Freeman Miller, 1862–1890

*Personal Data* Born: April 5, 1816, Richmond, Kentucky. Education: graduated with medical degree, Transylvania University, 1838; read the law privately and was admitted to the Kentucky Bar, 1847. Married Lucy Ballinger, 1838, three children; married Elizabeth Reeves, 1857, two children. Died: October 13, 1890, Washington, D.C.
*Career Data* Practiced medicine, 1838–50. Practiced law, 1850–62.
*Supreme Court Data* Nominated by Abraham Lincoln on July 16, 1862, to replace Justice Peter Daniel, who died. Served until October 13, 1890.

After graduating with a medical degree, Miller started a rural practice in Kentucky's Knox County. But he developed an interest in the law, studied privately, and passed the bar exam. He was against slavery, and when the new Kentucky constitution strengthened the position of slave owners, he moved west to the new state of Iowa. Miller settled in Keokuk and started practicing law instead of medicine. He got interested in politics and was one of the founders of the Iowa Republican party. He then became a strong supporter of Abraham Lincoln's bid for the Republican presidential nomination. When Congress established a new judicial circuit west of

the Mississippi, members of Congress pressed Lincoln for someone from the region to be named to the Supreme Court seat. Lincoln chose Miller.

During his twenty-eight years on the Court, Miller wrote more opinions than any Justice preceding him. While Constitutional law was his focus, his pragmatism and statesmanship enabled him to put forth thoughtful input in many areas of jurisprudence. Miller felt that the Supreme Court was the weakest branch of the tripartite system, maintaining that the Court's power was derived solely from the public. He was respected by his brethren, and was often referred to as the strongest member of the Court. Twice Miller was considered for Chief Justice—in 1873 and 1888—but was passed over both times.

## David Davis, 1862–1877

*Personal Data* Born: March 9, 1815, Cecil County, Maryland. Education: graduated Kenyon College, 1832; Yale Law School, 1835. Married Sarah Woodruff, 1838, no children; married Adeline Burr, 1883, two children. Died: June 26, 1886, Bloomington, Illinois.
*Career Data* Practiced law, 1835–48. Member, Illinois House, 1845–47. Judge, Illinois Circuit Court, 1848–62. Member, U.S. Senate, 1877–83.
*Supreme Court Data* Nominated by Abraham Lincoln on December 1, 1862, to replace Justice John A. Campbell, who resigned. Resigned March 4, 1877.

After being admitted to the bar, Davis moved west to Illinois, settling in Bloomington where he established a law practice and became involved in Whig politics. He won a seat in the State House in 1844, where he met and became close friends with another young Illinois lawmaker, Abraham Lincoln. In 1848 he was elected a state judge and held that position until nominated by Lincoln to the Supreme Court. He and Lincoln were very close, and when the Whig party fell apart in Illinois the two helped form the Republican party. Later Davis served as Lincoln's presidential campaign manager.

On the Court, Davis remained very political. In 1872 he received the presidential nomination of a minor third party—the Labor Reform party. His quest for the presidency clearly hampered what potentially could have been a promising judicial career. He is remembered for his forceful opinion in *Ex parte Milligan* (1866), in which he held that if civil courts were available to try civilians during the Civil War, presidentially appointed military commissions were unconstitutional. By 1877 he had grown tired of the infighting on the Court and accepted election to a U.S. Senate seat. Interestingly, his timing was awful. If he had remained on the Court he would have been a member of the commission to decide the Tilden-Hayes election and his vote for Tilden would have denied Hayes his one-vote victory. Davis served one term in the Senate, serving as president pro tem for two years. He then retired to his home in Illinois.

### Stephen Johnson Field, 1863–1897

*Personal Data* Born: November 4, 1816, Haddam, Connecticut. Education: graduated Williams College, 1837; read the law privately and was admitted to the New York Bar, 1841. Married Virginia Swearingen, 1859, no children. Died: April 9, 1899, Washington, D.C.

*Career Data* Practiced law, 1841–47, 1850–57. Alcalde (Mayor) of Marysville, California, 1850. California State Representative, 1850–51. Justice, California Supreme Court, 1857–63.

*Supreme Court Data* Nominated by Abraham Lincoln on March 6, 1863, for a newly created seat. Retired December 1, 1897.

Field studied law with his brother Dudley and with John Van Buren, son of President Martin Van Buren. The three set up a law practice in New York, but after seven years Field got tired and took a long trip to Europe. During this trip he decided to change his life completely, and upon returning to New York packed his bags and set out for the California goldfields. He settled in Marysville, and within a year had been appointed alcalde—effectively mayor—under the Spanish system of government. In 1850 he was elected to the California state legislature, where he wrote a new civil and criminal codes for the state. Defeated in an attempt for the state Senate, he returned to Marysville and his legal practice. Then in 1857 he was elected to the California Supreme Court.

In 1863 Congress authorized another judicial circuit for the fast-growing western states. Members of the congressional delegations from the region wanted someone to head it who was familiar with local issues, particularly with land and mining issues. The California delegation recommended Field, who had become the state's leading expert on land law. Lincoln agreed.

Field's tenure on the Court is the second longest ever by a justice—thirty-four years. During that time, he participated in 640 opinions, 220 of which were dissents. Described as a loyal Democrat and prominent jurist who moved into the tenth position created on the Court, Field left his mark as one of the most ardent judicial proponents of laissez-faire capitalism displaying his unwavering pro-business stance. His name was mentioned for the Democratic presidential nomination in 1880 and again in 1884, but his candidacy did not advance very far. He aspired to be Chief Justice in 1888 when Morrison Waite died, but President Cleveland picked Melville W. Fuller instead. In the 1890s Field's mental powers declined and he missed many Court sessions. Finally, the other justices strongly hinted it was time he retire.

Salmon Portland Chase, 1864–1873

*Personal Data* Born: January 13, 1808, Cornish, New Hampshire. Education: graduated Dartmouth College, 1826; read the law under U.S. Attorney General William Wirt and was admitted to the bar 1829. Married Katherine Garniss, 1834, no children; married Eliza Ann Smith, 1839, no children; married Sara Ludlow, 1846, six children. Died, May 7, 1873, New York City.

*Career Data* Practiced law, 1829–49. Member, U.S. Senate, 1849–55, 1861. Governor of Ohio, 1856–60. Secretary of the Treasury, 1861–64.

*Supreme Court Data* Nominated Chief Justice by Abraham Lincoln on December 6, 1864, to replace Chief Justice Roger B. Taney, who died. Served until May 7, 1873.

When his father died in 1817, Chase went to live with his uncle in Ohio. After graduation from Dartmouth, Chase went to Washington, D.C., where he opened and taught at a private school while studying law. After admission to the bar he moved to Cincinnati to begin a law practice.

Chase became an abolitionist, and one of the most prominent lawyers representing runaway slaves. In 1849 he was elected to the U.S. Senate, where he became a leader in the antislavery movement. In 1855 he returned to Ohio to become governor, and after serving two terms was again elected to the U.S. Senate. But he never served, instead accepting Lincoln's offer to become treasury secretary. During the Civil War he became perhaps the most important member of Lincoln's cabinet, the man responsible for financing the war and redesigning the federal banking system.

Chase and Lincoln did not get along personally. Chase ended up heading a faction of the Republican party that twice tried to dump the president. When these efforts failed, Chase resigned. But despite the bad blood between them, when Chief Justice Taney died in October, Chase was Lincoln's choice to replace him.

As Chief Justice, Chase had to preside over the problems and excesses of Reconstruction. At one point he refused to allow justices to ride circuit until the Congress reestablished the authority of civilian courts over military courts. The high point of his career, however, came when in 1868, he presided at the impeachment trial of Johnson, and fought with the radical Republicans for his rights as presiding officer of the trial. One of the most political of chief justices, Chase continued in his quest for the presidency, losing attempts for a nomination both in 1868 and again in 1872. (For a fuller examination of the Chase Court, see pages 70–76.)

William Strong, 1870–1880

*Personal Data* Born: May 6, 1808, Somers, Connecticut. Education: graduated Yale University, B.A. 1828, M.A. 1831. Studied law one year at Yale Law School, and was admitted to the Pennsylvania Bar, 1832. Married Priscilla Mallery, 1836, three children; married Rachel Davis Bull, 1849, four children. Died: August 19, 1895, New York.
*Career Data* Practiced law, 1832–47, 1851–57, 1868. Member, U.S. House, 1847–51. Judge, Pennsylvania Supreme Court 1857–68.
*Supreme Court Data* Nominated by Ulysses S. Grant on February 7, 1870, to replace Robert C. Grier, who retired. Retired December 14, 1880.

Strong began practicing law in Reading, and soon built a large practice in part because of his ability to speak German. He became an active antislavery Democrat, and in 1847 won a seat in the U.S. House. After two terms he returned to law practice, then in 1857 was elected to a fifteen-year term on the Pennsylvania Supreme Court. In 1864,

when Chief Justice Roger B. Taney died, Lincoln considered Strong before naming Salmon P. Chase. In 1868, Strong resigned from the Pennsylvania court for financial reasons and returned to law practice. The next year a vacancy occurred on the Court. Again Strong was considered, but instead Grant named former Secretary of War Edwin M. Stanton. But when Stanton died four days after being confirmed, Grant turned to Strong.

During his ten years of Court service, Strong was a model justice. He got along well with his colleagues, worked hard, wrote a large number of well-crafted opinions, and was highly respected by the bar. Yet he toiled in relative obscurity perhaps because the areas of the law at which he excelled—admiralty, revenue, and common law—were not of great popular interest. He rarely was spotlighted in important Constitutional cases. But having said this, Strong wrote one of the Court's most important civil rights decisions, holding in *Strauder* v. *West Virginia* (1880) that Negroes are entitled to "all the civil rights enjoyed by the white race."

Joseph P. Bradley, 1870–1892

*Personal Data* Born: March 14, 1813, Berne, New York. Education: graduated Rutgers University, 1836; read the law under Archer Gifford and was admitted to the New Jersey Bar, 1839. Married Mary Hornblower, 1844, seven children. Died: January 22, 1892, Washington, D.C.
*Career Data* Practiced law, 1839–70.
*Supreme Court Data* Nominated by Ulysses S. Grant on February 7, 1870,

succeeding James Wayne, who died. Served until January 22, 1892.

Bradley quickly built a booming law practice representing railroads, and his career was helped greatly when he married the daughter of the chief justice of the New Jersey Supreme Court. He dabbled in politics from time to time, first as a Whig and then as a Republican. Several times he ran for elective office, but lost each time. Grant nominated him for a seat on the Court in part because of his staunch Republican politics and in part because of his legal reputation.

In his twenty-two years on the Court, Bradley developed a reputation for solid scholarship and, at times, innovative legal thinking especially in the area of interstate commerce. He held, for instance, that a state could tax products arriving from another state. One important early decision he wrote, *Railroad Company* v. *Lockwood* (1873), held that a railroad or coach company could not require a passenger to sign a contract relinquishing his legal rights in order to accept transport.

Ward Hunt, 1873–1882

*Personal Data* Born: June 14, 1810, Utica, New York. Education: graduated Union College, 1828; read the law under Judge Hiram Denio and admitted to the New York Bar, 1831. Married Mary Ann Savage, 1837, no children; married Marie Taylor, 1853, two children. Died: March 24, 1886, Washington, D.C.
*Career Data* Practiced law, 1831–66. Member, New York Assembly, 1839.

Mayor of Utica, 1844. Chief Judge, New York Court of Appeals, 1866–69. New York Commissioner of Appeals, 1869–73.
*Supreme Court Data* Nominated by Ulysses S. Grant on December 3, 1872, to replace Justice Samuel Nelson, who retired. Retired January 27, 1882.

Hunt quickly built a lucrative practice in partnership with the judge he had read the law with. He then got involved in politics, and was elected to the New York Assembly and then as mayor of Utica. Against slavery, he broke with the Democratic party in 1848, and backed Martin Van Buren's antislavery presidential bid. He tried to return to the Democratic party in 1855, but when it refused to back him for a judgeship, he helped found the New York Republican party. In 1865 Hunt was elected to the New York court of Appeals and three years later became its chief judge. When the court system was changed, he became state commissioner of appeals. When Justice Nelson died, New York Republican politicians persuaded Grant to name Hunt.

There may never have been a justice with a lower profile than Hunt in the Court's history. He authored few opinions and almost always voted with the majority. In early 1879 he suffered a stroke that left him largely incapacitated. But he did not resign, wanting to wait until he had served long enough to get a pension. After a three-year absence from the bench, Congress finally gave in and passed a special bill granting Hunt a pension at full pay if he retired within twenty-four hours. He did.

Morrison Remick Waite, 1874–1888

*Personal Data* Born: November 29, 1816, Lyme, Connecticut. Education: graduated Yale University, 1837; read the law under Samuel D. Young and was admitted to the Ohio Bar, 1839. Married Amelia Warner, 1840, five children. Died: March 23, 1888, Washington, D.C.

*Career Data* Practiced law, 1839–74. Member, Ohio State House, 1850–52.

*Supreme Court Data* Nominated Chief Justice by Ulysses S. Grant on January 19, 1874, to replace Salmon P. Chase, who died. Served until March 23, 1888.

After graduating from Yale, Waite moved to Ohio, where he read the law and set up a practice in Maumee City. In 1850, he moved to Toledo, where his practice expanded quickly. Twice he attempted to run for the U.S. House, but lost both times. He did serve one term in the Ohio state legislature. During the Civil War, Waite was a strong public advocate of the Union cause. He was offered a seat on the Ohio Supreme Court, but declined for financial reasons. He eventually came to President Grant's attention when he was chosen for his admiralty expertise to represent the U.S. in an international claims case against Great Britain for allowing Confederate vessels to use British ports during the Civil War. Waite became something of a hero in Washington when he was able to win a $15.5 million judgment. He was serving as president of the Ohio Constitutional Convention when word came that Grant had chosen to submit him as Chief Justice. The choice was a shock, but Grant was look-

ing for a noncontroversial nominee after the Senate had rejected his first two choices.

Court historians call Waite one of the least known men ever to serve on the Court, and certainly the least known Chief Justice. He got off to a poor start because other members of the Court felt he had too little experience to be Chief Justice. But by the time he retired he was held in generally high esteem by his colleagues, not because of the legal scholarship he had brought to the Court, but because he had always handled affairs with courtesy and finesse. In the end Waite is remembered for his contract law decisions and especially for *Munn* v. *Illinois* (1877), which held that states could regulate grain storage prices for the benefit of farmers. (For a fuller examination of the Waite Court, see pages 76–81.)

John Marshall Harlan, 1877–1911

*Personal Data* Born: June 1, 1833, Boyle, Kentucky. Education: graduated Centre College, A.B. 1850; studied law at Transylvania University, 1851–53, and then under his father, James Harlan; was admitted to the Kentucky Bar, 1853. Married Malvina Shanklin, 1856, six children. Died: October 14, 1911, Washington, D.C.

*Career Data* Practiced law, 1853–58, 1859–60, 1867–77. Judge, Franklin County Circuit Court, 1858. State Attorney General, 1863–67.

*Supreme Court Data* Nominated by Rutherford B. Hayes on October 17, 1877, to replace Justice David Davis, who resigned. Served until October 14, 1911.

The first of two justices with the same name (his grandson and namesake would serve 1955–71), Harlan came from a politically powerful family whose connections helped him win a term as Franklin County judge in 1858. He than ran for Congress, losing a close contest, and returned to the practice of law. His problem was that he was a slaveholder from an old Southern family. But surprisingly, when the Civil War started he fought as a Northern officer. In 1863 he returned to Kentucky upon the death of his father and then ran for attorney general as pro-Union. But he fought against the postwar constitutional amendments ending slavery and guaranteeing civil rights to former slaves. He eventually became a Republican and lost one attempt for governor of Kentucky in 1875.

His breakthrough in national politics came in 1876, when he headed the Kentucky delegation to the Republican national convention. With the convention deadlocked, he swung Kentucky's delegates to Hayes and the future president was very grateful. At first he considered Harlan for attorney general. Instead, he named him to head a commission to resolve the Louisiana land dispute. Then when Supreme Court Justice Davis resigned to enter the U.S. Senate, Hayes nominated Harlan.

His eventual tenure, almost thirty-four years, was one of the longest in Court history. One of his biographers has calculated that he took part in reviewing 14,226 cases. He ended up writing majority opinions in 745 cases, plus 100 concurring opinions and 316 dissents. It was the latter that gained him fame. He became famous for delivering long, emotional, and usually extemporaneous dissents that earned him the title of the "Great Dissenter."

## William Burnham Woods, 1880–1887

*Personal Data* Born: August 3, 1824, Newark, Ohio. Education: Western Reserve College; graduated Yale University, 1845; read the law under S. D. King and was admitted to the Ohio Bar, 1847. Married Anne Warner, 1855, two children. Died: May 14, 1887, Washington, D.C.

*Career Data* Practiced law, 1847–58, 1866–68. Mayor Newark, Ohio, 1856. Speaker, Ohio State House, 1858–60, minority leader, 1860–62; Chancellor, Middle District of Alabama, 1868–69. Judge, U.S. Circuit Court of Appeals, 1869–80.

*Supreme Court Data* Nominated by Rutherford B. Hayes on December 15, 1880, to replace Justice William Strong, who retired. Served until May 14, 1887.

Woods returned home to Newark, Ohio to read the law after graduation from Yale. He joined the law practice of his mentor, S. D. King, one of the region's most prominent lawyers. Very popular, Woods was elected mayor, and the following year was elected to the state legislature, where he was chosen Speaker. When the Civil War broke out he joined the Union Army, rising to the rank of brigadier general under Sherman. After the war, instead of returning to Ohio, he remained in the South, becoming a plantation owner and investor, and eventually reestablishing a law practice. He was soon elected a local judge as a Republican, and when the Republicans came to power, President Grant quickly named him a federal judge. He moved to Atlanta and developed a national reputation for honesty and enlightened decisions. In 1880, President Hayes felt he needed a Southerner on the Court. So he turned to Hayes, who despite his birth in the north, was widely admired throughout the southern circuit.

Because of illness his tenure on the Court was relatively brief. In his six years of service, Woods wrote more than 200 opinions, but most were in dry cases having to do with equity, and they were little noticed by the public.

## Stanley Matthews, 1881–1889

*Personal Data* Born: July 21, 1824, Cincinnati, Ohio. Education: graduated Kenyon College, A.B. 1840; read the law privately and was admitted to the Tennessee Bar, 1842. Married Mary Ann Black, 1843, eight children; married Mary Theaker, 1887, no children. Died: March 22, 1889, Washington, D.C.

*Career Data* Practiced law, 1842–48, 1865–81. Editor, *Cincinnati Morning Herald*, 1845–48. Clerk, Ohio House of Representatives, 1848–49. Judge, Hamilton County Court, 1851–53. Member, Ohio Senate, 1855–58. U.S. Attorney, 1858–61. Judge, Superior Court of Cincinnati, 1863–65. Counsel, Hayes-Tilden electoral commission, 1877. Member, U.S. Senate, 1877–79.

*Supreme Court Data* Nominated by Rutherford B. Hayes on January 26, 1881, to replace Noah Swayne, who

retired. After the Senate refused to consider the nomination, he was renominated by James A. Garfield, March 14, 1881. Served until March 22, 1889.

After reading the law in Ohio, Matthews moved to Maury County, Tennessee, where he passed the bar. At the age of eighteen he started to establish a law practice and also to edit the weekly *Tennessee Democrat*. Two years later Matthews returned to Cincinnati, and within less than eighteen months had been appointed assistant prosecuting attorney for Hamilton County, and editor of the *Cincinnati Morning Herald*. He was then elected clerk of the Ohio House of Representatives and, three years later, a judge on the Hamilton County Court. Matthews resigned from the court to serve in the Ohio State Senate and then was appointed U.S. attorney for southern Ohio. In the Civil War he commanded troops in the Ohio Twenty-third Regiment, resigning his commission to return to Cincinnati and election to the Superior Court. Two years later he returned to his private practice.

Matthews campaigned for his close friend Rutherford B. Hayes (the two had been college classmates, practiced law together at one point, and served in the war together), and was one of his lead counsels before the 1877 electoral commission. When Ohio Senator John Sherman was appointed secretary of the treasury by Hayes, Matthews was elected to serve out his term. When John Swayne resigned from the Court and Hayes nominated Matthews, a major political battle ensued. The nomination was seen as a reward for work on Hayes's behalf on the election commission. The Senate refused to take up the nomination. Matthews was renominated by Garfield, Hayes's successor, but the Senate opposition did not diminish. Finally the Senate agreed to put the nomination to a vote. Matthews won confirmation, 24–23.

Despite his relatively short eight years on the Court, before he died Matthews had developed a reputation as one of the leading legal thinkers of his day, whose opinions were usually models of scholarly research. But despite this reputation, Matthew played a relatively minor role in the conservative court on which he served. He authored none of the more famous decisions of the time with one exception, *Yick Wo v. Hopkins* (1886), in which he ruled that laws cannot be unequally applied because of race.

## Horace Gray, 1881–1902

*Personal Data* Born: March 24, 1828, Boston, Massachusetts. Education: graduated Harvard University, A.B. 1845; Harvard Law School, 1849; admitted to the bar, 1849. Married Jane Matthews, 1889, no children. Died: September 15, 1902, Nahant, Massachusetts.
*Career Data* Practiced law, 1849–64. Reporter, Massachusetts Supreme Court, 1854–73; Chief Justice, 1873–81.
*Supreme Court Data* Nominated by Chester A. Arthur on December 19, 1881, to replace Justice Nathan Clifford, who died. Served until September 15, 1902.

Gray wanted to become a scientist, but family financial reversals forced him to choose a better paying profession, the law. After graduating from Harvard Law School, he joined a Boston law firm, where he remained for the next thirteen years. Gray's only attempt at elective office came in a try for state attorney general, in which he failed to obtain the Republican nomination. But this brought him to the attention of Governor John A. Andrews, who named Gray the youngest ever (age thirty-six) justice on the state Supreme Court. Nine years later he was elevated to chief justice. Gray was probably the nation's outstanding state court jurist. When Justice Nathan Clifford died, President Garfield was about to name Gray, when he died. His successor, Chester A. Arthur, made the appointment.

Gray was another justice known for his scholarship. But in his twenty years of service, he seemed never to develop a consistent philosophy. He often issued contrary opinions on the same general points of law. For example, he voted to strike down the Civil Rights Act of 1875, but then wrote the majority opinion in *Ex parte Yarbrough*, which held that the federal government could enforce the voting rights of Negroes. About halfway through his tenure, Gray began to become ill frequently, and his contributions to the Court lessened considerably.

## Samuel Blatchford, 1882–1893

*Personal Data* Born: March 9, 1820, New York City. Education: graduated Columbia College, A.B. 1837; read the law under New York Governor William

H. Seward and was admitted to the New York Bar, 1842. Married Caroline Appleton, 1844, no children. Died: July 7, 1893, Newport, Rhode Island.

*Career Data* Practiced law, 1842–67. Judge, U.S. District Court, 1867–72. Judge, Second Circuit Court of Appeals, 1872–82.

*Supreme Court Data* Nominated by Chester A. Arthur on March 13, 1882, to replace Justice Ward Hunt, who retired. Served until July 7, 1893.

Blatchford, from a powerful political family, graduated from Columbia College at the age of seventeen. He then read the law while working as the private secretary to New York Governor William H. Seward. He began to practice law, first with his father's law firm and then with Seward's, after the governor left office. Nine years later he and Seward's nephew established the New York City law firm of Blatchford, Seward, and Griswold. In 1855 he turned down an appointment to the New York State Supreme Court. Blatchford was one of the outstanding reporters of federal court decisions of his day. He was also a legal historian of some note. This led to his appointment as a federal judge, first in the district court and then in the court of appeals.

Blatchford was not President Arthur's first choice for replacing Justice Ward Hunt. Roscoe Conkling, a famed New York lawyer and political figure, was actually nominated and confirmed before turning down the appointment. When Arthur's second choice, Vermont Senator George F. Edmunds, also said no, Arthur took Conkling's advise and named Blatchford.

In his eleven years on the Court, Blatchford developed a reputation for solid, if unimaginative work. He was an expert in patent law, and wrote many of the Court's decisions in this area. But as he neared the end of his career, he issued several controversial civil liberties rulings, including probably his most lasting opinion—*Councilman* v. *Hitchcock* (1892)—which liberally interpreted the Fifth Amendment right against self-incrimination.

Lucius Quintus Cincinnatus Lamar, 1888–1893

*Personal Data* Born: September 17, 1825, Eatonton, Georgia. Education: graduated Emory College, A.B. 1845; read the law privately and was admitted to the Georgia Bar, 1847. Married Virginia Longstreet, 1847, four children; married Henrietta Holt, 1887, no children. Died: January 23, 1893, Vineville, Georgia.

*Career Data* Practiced law, 1847–57, 1865–73. Member, Georgia State House, 1853. Member, U.S. House, 1857–60, 1873–77. Member, U.S. Senate, 1877–85; Secretary of the Interior, 1885–88.

*Supreme Court Data* Nominated by Grover Cleveland on December 6, 1887, to replace William Woods, who died. Served until January 23, 1893.

After graduating from Emory College in 1845 and being admitted to the bar two years later, L. Q. C. Lamar, as he would always be known, wed the daughter of Emory's president, the Reverend Augustus B. Longstreet. Immediately the newlyweds accompanied Reverend

Longstreet to Oxford, Mississippi, where he became the president of the University of Mississippi. Lamar taught at the university and started to practice law. After five years Lamar returned to Georgia and established a growing law practice in Covington and began to get involved in local politics. But his failure to win a congressional nomination resulted in a move back to Mississippi. A proponent of states' rights and secession, Lamar won a U.S. House seat in 1857, but resigned in protest before his term expired to return to Mississippi to work for secession. During the war, Lamar served as a colonel in the Eighteenth Mississippi Regiment, then as a Confederate envoy to Russia, and finally as a military judge advocate for the Confederate Army. At war's end, he returned to Mississippi to practice law and teach at the university.

After being pardoned, Lamar was reelected to Congress in 1872. His advocacy of reconciliation won him the title of the "Great Pacificator," and he was elected to the U.S. Senate in 1877. He then resigned from a second term to become the first Southerner since the war to sit on a presidential cabinet as Grover Cleveland's secretary of the interior. Justice William Woods's death in 1887 gave President Cleveland a chance to show the nation was healing by naming a Southerner to the Court. He chose Lamar. Despite his sterling reputation, it was a controversial nomination and a bitter Senate fight ensued. In the end Lamar was confirmed 32–28.

Lamar served on the Court for only five years. In his four active years, because of his Interior experience, Lamar was the Court's leading expert in boundary and land-use cases. His work load consisted of these kinds of matters, which filled the Court's docket in this era. Generally, though, Lamar brought with him a deep suspicion of executive power, and this colored many of his votes and opinions. In the end he became most noted for a series of powerful dissents in cases arising out of the exercise of political power.

## Melville Weston Fuller, 1888–1910

*Personal Data* Born: February 11, 1833, Augusta, Maine. Education: graduated Bowdoin College, A.B. 1853; attended Harvard Law School, 1853–55; was admitted to the Maine Bar, 1855. Married Calista Reynolds, 1858, two children; married Mary Coolbaugh, 1866, six children. Died: July 4, 1910, Sorrento, Maine.

*Career Data* Practiced law, 1855–88. Member, Illinois House of Representatives, 1863–64.

*Supreme Court Data* Nominated Chief Justice by Grover Cleveland on April 30, 1888, to replace Chief Justice Morrison Waite, who died. Served until July 4, 1910.

After being admitted to the bar, Fuller began to practice in Augusta and became an editor of *The Age*, a local Democratic daily newspaper. Two years later, he was elected president of the Augusta Common Council and was appointed city counsel. But he thought he could do better in the west, so in 1850 he moved to Chicago, where he started a railroad law and real estate practice.

In Chicago, Fuller became involved in politics. He managed Stephen Douglas's presidential campaign against Abraham Lincoln. He was elected to the Illinois House of Representatives. As his law practice grew he was introduced to Grover Cleveland, who was impressed by his wealth and legal talent. When he became president, Cleveland offered Fuller several appointments including solicitor general. Fuller said no. But when he was offered the Chief Justiceship, he jumped at the opportunity. The press called the nominee the most obscure man ever appointed Chief Justice, which was probably true. The Senate took its time in confirming him, but in the end did so.

He ended up serving as Chief Justice for twenty-two years. Not a great legal mind, he was a good administrator and was well liked. He hated dissent on the Court and worked tirelessly to fashion compromises if at all possible. He ended up writing 840 opinions, but fewer than 30 dissents. President Cleveland at one point asked him to resign to accept the position of secretary of state, but Fuller refused, saying a Chief Justice, once confirmed, must serve for life. (For an expanded examination of the Fuller Court era, see pages 81–87.)

David Josiah Brewer, 1889–1910

*Personal Data* Born: June 20, 1837, Asia Minor (now Turkey). Education: Wesleyan University, 1852–53; graduated Yale University, A.B. 1856; Albany Law School, LL.B. 1858; admitted to the New York Bar, 1858. Married Louise Landon, 1861, no children; married Emma Mott, 1901, no children. Died: March 28, 1910, Washington, D.C.

*Career Data* Clerk, U.S. Circuit Court,

1861–62; Judge, Leavenworth County Criminal Court, 1863–64. Judge, Kansas District Court, 1865–69. Leavenworth City Attorney, 1869–70. Judge, Kansas Supreme Court, 1870–84. Judge, U.S. Circuit Court of Appeals, 1884–89.

*Supreme Court Data* Nominated by Benjamin Harrison on December 4, 1889, to replace Justice Stanley Matthews, who died. Served until March 28, 1910.

Brewer's father was a missionary, and then the family returned to the United States to settle in Connecticut. After graduating from law school, young Brewer decided to go west and chose Kansas. He began a law practice in Leavenworth, and was soon named commissioner of the local circuit court. Two years later he was nominated a criminal courts judge and then served as the city attorney. At age thirty-three he was elected to the Kansas Supreme Court, where he served for fourteen years until named to the federal appeals bench. Upon the death of Justice Matthews, Brewer was highly recommended for the appointment, but President Benjamin Harrison hesitated. What won him over, it is said, was a letter of recommendation Brewer sent him recommending his Yale classmate, Judge Henry Billings Brown.

During his twenty years on the Court, Brewer was known for his long hours, hard work, and prolific output. At times a contradiction, he was an avid supporter of women's rights but otherwise almost ultraconservative on most economic and social issues. His holdings ranged from believing that the state has few rights to restrict contracts or the free use of private property to the deep-seated belief that all men are not in fact equal.

## Henry Billings Brown, 1890–1906

*Personal Data* Born: March 2, 1836, South Lee, Massachusetts. Education: graduated Yale University, A.B. 1856; studied at both Yale and Harvard Law Schools; admitted to the Michigan Bar, 1860. Married Caroline Pitts, 1864, no children; married Josephine E. Tyler, 1904, no children. Died: September 4, 1913, New York City.

*Career Data* Practiced law, 1860–63, 1868–75. Deputy U.S. Marshal, 1861. Assistant U.S. attorney, 1863–68. Judge, Circuit Court of Wayne County, 1868. Judge, Federal District Court, 1875–90.

*Supreme Court Data* Nominated by Benjamin Harrison on December 23, 1890, to replace Justice Samuel Miller, who died. Retired May 28, 1906.

Brown left law school to move to Detroit, read Michigan law for a year, and was admitted to the bar. He avoided the Civil War by buying his way out of military service, an option available to the rich in the cash-strapped Union. He established a law practice, and then was appointed deputy U.S. marshal for Detroit, an important position in the war era. Two years later he was promoted to assistant U.S. attorney, a position he held for five years. He then was appointed circuit judge for Wayne County, but failed to convince voters to make the appointment permanent. He returned to law practice and tried twice,

unsuccessfully, to run for Congress. Finally, President Grant appointed him to a federal judgeship. During his fourteen years on the district court, Brown developed a national reputation in admiralty law. Upon the death of Justice Samuel Miller, several judges recommended Brown. President Harrison also remembered the glowing recommendation that David Brewer had submitted a year earlier, so he nominated Brown.

Shortly after taking his seat, Brown suffered a severe attack of neuritis that left him blind in one eye. But despite this handicap he eventually served fifteen years, until his health declined to the point he was forced to retire. His most famous decision was *Plessy* v. *Ferguson* (1896), which established the doctrine of "separate but equal" that for fifty years provided the legal underpinnings for segregation in America. This has colored the historical view of Brown as being a social conservative. But a close examination of his record shows he was more of a pragmatist who was generally a moderate.

## George Shiras, Jr., 1892–1903

*Personal Data* Born: January 26, 1832, Pittsburgh, Pennsylvania. Education: Ohio University, graduated Yale University, B.A. 1853; studied law at Yale and under Pittsburgh Judge Hopewell Hepburn and was admitted to the Allegheny County Bar, 1855. Married Lillie Kennedy, 1857, two children. Died: August 2, 1924, Pittsburgh, Pennsylvania.

*Career Data* Practiced law, 1855–92.

*Supreme Court Data* Nominated by

Benjamin Harrison on July 19, 1892, to replace Justice Joseph P. Bradley, who died. Retired February 23, 1903.

After admission to the bar, Shiras settled in Iowa where he practiced law for several years with his brother. He then moved back to Pittsburgh and practiced with his mentor, Judge Hepburn, and inherited Hepburn's law practice when he died in 1862. He ran it very successfully for the next thirty years. Shiras held no elective or appointed office until his Supreme Court nomination at age 60. On one occasion he turned down an appointment to the U.S. Senate, and on another occasion a seat on Pennsylvania's high court. When he was nominated by President Harrison, he had the backing of the Pennsylvania congressional delegation and such as Andrew Carnegie, whom he had long represented. He was quickly confirmed.

In some ways Shiras is as much remembered for how he retired as for his service on the Court. From the day he took his seat he always said that he would retire on his seventy-first birthday and he did. He was perhaps the first justice to retire (as opposed to taking another position) in good health and to live for almost twenty years beyond retirement. In his ten years on the Court he was considered something of a legal technician, writing solid if slightly unimaginative opinions, and always shouldering his portion of the work load.

Howell Edmunds Jackson, 1893–1895

*Personal Data* Born: April 8, 1832, Paris, Tennessee. Education: graduated

West Tennessee College, A.B. 1849; legal studies at University of Virginia, 1851–52 and Cumberland (Tenn.) University, 1856; admitted to the Tennessee Bar, 1856. Married Sophia Malloy, 1859, four children; married Mary Harding, 1874, three children. Died: August 8, 1895, West Meade, Tennessee.

*Career Data* Custodian of Property for Confederate States, 1861–65. Judge, Court of Arbitration, 1875–79. Member, State House, 1880. Member, U.S. Senate, 1881–86. Judge, Sixth Federal Circuit Court, 1886–91. Judge, Court of Appeals, 1891–93.

*Supreme Court Data* Nominated by President Benjamin Harrison on February 2, 1893, to replace Justice Lucius Lamar, who died. Served until August 8, 1895.

After admission to the bar, Jackson settled in Memphis and opened a law partnership. After he married, he moved to his wife's home near Nashville. By now the Civil War had started, and although Jackson had been opposed to secession, he became a Confederate legal officer. After the war his service was not held against him and he was twice appointed to the court of arbitration for western Tennessee. His law practice flourished, and in 1881 he was elected to the state legislature. The following year he was elected to the U.S. Senate. At President Grover Cleveland's request, Jackson resigned his Senate seat to accept a seat on the federal court of appeals for the Sixth Circuit, where he served with distinction for two years.

When Justice Lucius Lamar died,

newly elected Benjamin Harrison remembered his former Senate colleague and friend, and nominated him for the seat. One year after he began his tenure, Jackson contracted tuberculosis. He tried to recuperate, leaving Washington in October 1895 to go to a better climate, but he had to return to hear several key cases and never recovered from the trip. He returned to his home in Nashville, where he died.

## Edward Douglass White, 1894–1921

*Personal Data* Born: November 3, 1845, Lafourche, Louisiana. Education: Georgetown University, 1861; read the law under Edward Bermudez and was admitted to the Louisiana Bar, 1868. Married Virginia Kent, 1894, no children. Died: May 19, 1921, Washington, D.C.

*Career Data* Practiced law, 1868–78, 1880–91. Member, Louisiana State Senate, 1874. Judge, Louisiana Supreme Court, 1878–80. Member, U.S. Senate (D), 1891–94.

*Supreme Court Data* Nominated by Grover Cleveland on February 19, 1894, to replace Justice Samuel Blatchford, who died. Nominated Chief Justice by William Howard Taft on December 12, 1910, to replace Chief Justice Melville Fuller, who died. Served until May 19, 1921.

White's father was a judge, congressman, and governor of Louisiana. White was a student at Georgetown when the Civil War broke out, and he left school to join the Confederate Army. He spent much of the war in a Union prison after being captured in 1863. After the war he remained in New Orleans and began reading the law under a prominent local lawyer. Then after being admitted to the bar, he quickly established a growing law practice and began to get involved in Democratic politics.

White was elected to the Louisiana State Senate at age twenty-nine. Through his political connections he was able to secure a state Supreme Court judgeship four years later. But after three years he was removed from office when a political opponent became governor and pushed through the state legislature a minimum-age requirement for judges that White could not meet. He returned to private practice, and eleven years later, when his wing of the Democratic party recaptured the governorship, White was given a U.S. Senate seat.

White had only been in Washington a few years when Justice Samuel Blatchford died. There ensued a major tug-of-war between President Grover Cleveland and the Senate. For political reasons the Senate rejected Cleveland's first two choices. Then Cleveland, assuming that the Senate would not reject one of its own, surprisingly nominated White, who was quickly confirmed.

White's sixteen-year tenure as an associate justice is marked with changes in his views on a number of areas of the law including substantive due process and federal regulation. The longer he was on the Court, the more conservative he became. Early in his career he seemed unsure or even hostile to many aspects of federal regulation. But as the years passed, and the Court was faced with problems arising from the rapid industrialization of the nation, his attitude changed to one highly supportive of strong federal controls. He eventually began to believe the most liberal interpretation of the commerce clause and the powers of the Interstate Commerce Commission.

In 1910, Chief Justice Melville Fuller died, and President William Howard Taft surprised almost everyone by elevating, for the first time, an associate justice to the Chief Justiceship. Some say Taft nominated White, a Catholic, because he wanted to lessen the anti-South and anti-Catholic bias still rampant in the nation. A less charitable view is that Taft himself had always wanted to be Chief Justice, and he figured the job would open up more quickly if he appointed the sixty-five-year-old White rather than several potential younger candidates, most notably forty-eight-year-old Charles Evans Hughes.

White probably outlived Taft's expectations, serving as Chief Justice for a decade. Finally, at age seventy-five, he took ill in May 1921, and died within a matter of days. He was replaced by William Howard Taft. (For a fuller examination of the White Court years, see pages 87–94.)

Rufus Wheeler Peckham, 1895–1909

*Personal Data* Born: November 8, 1838, Albany, New York. Education: Albany Academy; read the law under his father, also Rufus Peckham, and was admitted to the New York Bar, 1867. Married Harriette Arnold, 1866, two children. Died: October 24, 1909, Altamont, New York.
*Career Data* Practiced law, 1867–83.

District attorney, Albany County, 1869–72. Corporation counsel, City of Albany, 1881–83. Judge, New York Supreme Court, 1883–86. Judge, New York Court of Appeals, 1886–95.
*Supreme Court Data* Nominated by Grover Cleveland on December 3, 1895, to replace Justice Howell Jackson, who died. Served until October 24, 1909.

Peckham's father was a New York State Supreme Court Justice. After being privately educated and traveling, he read the law under his father and, after being admitted to the bar, joined his father's Albany law firm. Soon, he was appointed Albany County district attorney, a post his father had once held. Then he became corporation counsel of Albany, and continuing almost exactly in his father's footsteps, was elected to the State Supreme Court and then to the New York Court of Appeals.

Growing up in New York politics, Peckham had been a long-time supporter and friend of fellow New York politician Grover Cleveland. So now when Justice Jackson died, President Cleveland nominated Peckham, who surprised most observers by being quickly confirmed. The surprise was brought about by the fact that the Senate had only three months earlier rejected Peckham's older brother Wheeler for Justice Blatchford's seat. But in the interim, a dispute between Cleveland and Senator David B. Hill (D–NY) had ended, and Rufus Peckham was Hill's friend.

Peckham, while still on the New York bench, had accepted a new legal theory greatly expanding on the concept of liberty in commercial transactions and limiting the ability of government to regulate many aspects of business. He brought this view with him to the Supreme Court, and beginning with *Allegeyer* v. *Louisiana* (1897), made it the majority view. In a whole line of cases he limited the ability of the state to regulate business and commercial transactions, even for reasons of health and safety. He also wanted to limit the scope of the Sherman Antitrust Act and did so in a number of decisions.

Joseph McKenna, 1898–1925

*Personal Data* Born: August 10, 1843, Philadelphia, Pennsylvania. Education: graduated Benicia Institute, 1865; read the law privately and was admitted to the California Bar, 1866. Married Amanda Bornemann, 1869, three children. Died: November 21, 1926, Washington, D.C.

*Career Data* Practiced law, 1870–85. District Attorney, Solano County, 1866–70. Member, California Assembly, 1875–76. Member, U.S. House, 1885–92. Judge, U.S. Circuit Court, 1892–97. U.S. Attorney General, 1897.

*Supreme Court Data* Nominated by William McKinley on December 16, 1897, to replace Justice Stephen J. Field, who retired. Retired January 5, 1925.

The McKenna family moved to California when Joseph was an infant. While still in college, young McKenna had become active in the new Republican party and almost as soon as he was admitted to the bar, he was elected district attorney of Solano County. His political career, however, was filled with disappointment. Elected to the state assembly, he lost a race for the speakership. He then twice ran for the U.S. Congress and lost before he finally won on the third try. He served four terms and then was appointed a judge on California's ninth Circuit. After five years, his friend William McKinley made him attorney general, and a year later nominated him to the Supreme Court.

McKenna ended up serving twenty-six years on the Court. His first years were very difficult because—as he readily admitted—he did not know much law. He had gone back to Columbia University Law School for six months before hearing his first Court case, but it was several years before he reportedly felt comfortable writing an opinion. Slowly he began to emerge. His first opinions were filled with references to past precedents. But gradually he began to gain the confidence to interpret the law. But even then, his mind could be easily changed. As he grew older his thought process began to deteriorate. At times it was clear that he simply did not comprehend arguments being made to the Court. Finally, Chief Justice Taft got agreement that the Court would not report any case in which McKenna was the swing vote. Eventually, Taft and the other justices convinced McKenna, eighty-two and in failing health, to step down.

Oliver Wendell Holmes, Jr., 1902–1932

*Personal Data* Born: March 8, 1841, Boston, Massachusetts. Education:

graduated Harvard University, A.B. 1861; Harvard Law School, LL.B. 1866; admitted to the Massachusetts Bar, 1867. Married Fanny Bowdich Dixwell, 1872, no children. Died: March 6, 1935, Washington, D.C.
*Career Data* Practiced law, 1867–82. Justice, Massachusetts Supreme Court, 1882–99; Chief Justice, 1899–02.
*Supreme Court Data* Nominated by Theodore Roosevelt on December 2, 1902, to replace Horace Gray, who died. Retired January 12, 1932.

Holmes's father was a doctor, a professor at Harvard Medical School, and one of the outstanding poets of his day. After graduating from Harvard at the top of his class, young Holmes immediately enlisted as a second lieutenant in the Massachusetts Volunteers and went to fight in the Civil War. He was wounded three times and highly decorated, and was released from his enlistment as a captain. He returned to Boston and Harvard Law School.

After graduation, Holmes practiced in Boston for fifteen years, developing into a legal scholar with an international reputation. He taught constitutional law at Harvard, where he was quickly made a full professor, and he edited the *American Law Review*. In 1882, he was persuaded to become an associate justice on the Massachusetts Supreme Court, where he ended up serving for twenty years, the last four as chief justice. He was among the nation's most progressive jurists and was the odds-on choice to fill what was called the "Massachusetts seat" on the Supreme Court, when Horace Gray (of Boston) retired.

Although Holmes was sixty-one when nominated, he ended up serving twenty-nine years on the Court. He became one of the most influential justices in Court history, although some of that influence was not felt until years later when more liberal courts took Holmes's reasoning in dissents and made it the majority view. Holmes was a man ahead of his time, a liberal on a conservative Court. Somewhat surprising, Holmes also had some very conservative views on the subject of the First Amendment and free speech. It was only in his later years on the Court that his free-speech views began to become more liberal.

## William Rufus Day, 1903–1922

*Personal Data* Born: April 17, 1849, Ravenna, Ohio. Education: graduated University of Michigan, A.B. 1870; University of Michigan Law School, 1872; admitted to the Ohio Bar, 1873. Married Mary Schaefer, 1875, four children. Died: July 9, 1923, Mackinac Island, Michigan.
*Career Data* Practiced law, 1870–86, 1890–97. Judge, Court of Common Pleas, 1886–90. Assistant U.S. Secretary of State, 1897–98; Secretary of State, 1898. Judge, U.S. Court of Appeals, 1899–1903.
*Supreme Court Data* Nominated by Theodore Roosevelt on February 19, 1903, to replace Justice George Shiras, who resigned. Resigned November 13, 1922.

Day's father and grandfather were judges; his father, Luther Day, was chief justice of Ohio. Day always assumed that he, too, would be a lawyer and after graduation from the University of Michigan he returned to set up a law practice in Canton, Ohio. There he worked closely with another young lawyer, William McKinley, and the two worked in local Republican politics. Day was elected to the Court of Common Pleas, and three years later was appointed to the U.S. District Court. But ill health prevented him from serving, and he returned to his law practice until his old friend McKinley was elected president.

McKinley appointed him assistant secretary of state to the aged secretary, John Sherman. When the Spanish-American War broke out, Sherman was quickly retired and Day became secretary of state. He served less than six months, and then was named by McKinley to head the commission for peace negotiations with Spain. It was Day's idea to buy the Philippines. When this task was completed, Day was named by McKinley in 1899 to the U.S. Court of Appeals. Four years later he was named to the Supreme Court by McKinley's successor, Theodore Roosevelt.

Day served on the Supreme Court for eighteen years. For a number of years he became the swing vote on a court sharply divided on government control of commerce. He basically sided with "conservatives" who disagreed with any government interference, no matter the reasoning. In one famous case, *Hammer* v. *Dagenhart* (1918), he ruled that although it was right for the government to try to stamp out child labor, the government could not forbid goods made with illegal child labor from entering interstate commerce.

## William Henry Moody, 1906–1910

*Personal Data* Born: December 23, 1853, Newbury, Massachusetts. Education: graduated Harvard University, A.B. 1876; attended Harvard Law School, 1877; read the law under Boston lawyer Richard Dana and was admitted to the Massachusetts Bar, 1878. Never married. Died: July 2, 1917, Haverhill, Massachusetts.

*Career Data* Practiced law, 1878–90. City Solicitor, Haverhill, 1888–90. U.S. Attorney, 1890–95, Member, U.S. House (R), 1895–1902. Secretary of the Navy, 1902–04. U.S. Attorney General, 1904–06.

*Supreme Court Data* Nominated by Theodore Roosevelt on December 3, 1906, to replace Justice Henry B. Brown, who retired. Retired November 20, 1910.

Moody established a private law practice in Haverhill, became heavily involved in local Republican politics, and ten years later became the city solicitor. He was then named U.S. attorney and became famous when he prosecuted ax murderer Lizzie Borden. He used this fame to win a House seat in 1895, and he served with distinction for four terms. In Washington, he became a good friend of Theodore Roosevelt, and when Roosevelt became president, Moody was one of his first cabinet choices. He served as secretary of the navy and then attorney general. Then Roosevelt named him to the Supreme Court.

Moody's Supreme Court career was short because of illness. He served five years but was frequently absent because of a crippling form of arthritis. He wrote only sixty-seven opinions, most in the 1907 and 1908 terms. He was a moderate liberal nationalist, and his vote was influential in a number of important 5–4 decisions. Finally his illness caused his retirement in 1910.

Horace Harmon Lurton, 1909–1914

*Personal Data* Born: February 26, 1844, Newport, Kentucky. Education: graduated University of Chicago, 1860; Cumberland Law School, LL.B. 1867. Married Mary Owen, 1867, four children. Died: July 12, 1914, Atlantic City, New Jersey.
*Career Data* Practiced law, 1867–75, 1878–86. Court Chancellor, 1875–78. Judge, Tennessee Supreme Court, 1886–93. Judge, U.S. Court of Appeals, 1893–1909.
*Supreme Court Data* Nominated by William Howard Taft on December 13, 1909, to replace Justice Rufus Peckham, who died. Served until July 12, 1914.

Lurton returned to Tennessee after graduating from the University of Chicago, to join the Confederate Army. He was captured by Union forces, but escaped and became one of the most highly decorated Confederate officers before being captured again. When he contracted tuberculosis in prison, his mother went to President Lincoln personally and convinced him to pardon her son and to let her take him home.

After his recuperation, Lurton went to law school, set up a law practice in

Clarksville, and became involved in Democratic politics. His practice grew and he also acted as a local bank president. In 1886 he was elected to the Tennessee Supreme Court, where he served for seven years. Then he was appointed to the U.S. Court of Appeals for the Sixth Circuit, where William Howard Taft was the presiding judge. When he left, Lurton succeeded him. While on the court he was also a professor and dean at Vanderbilt University Law School.

In 1906 Roosevelt tried to elevate Lurton to the Supreme Court. He was opposed by one senator for geographic reasons, and the nomination went to Moody. No other openings occurred until Taft became president. When an opening came, he quickly elevated Lurton to the High Court at the relatively advanced age of sixty-five. Lurton served only five years on the Court. During that period he usually followed the majority in a moderate liberal nationalist view. He also had a conservative view of antitrust as a supporter of the Sherman Act.

Charles Evans Hughes, 1910–1916, 1930–1941

*Personal Data* Born: April 11, 1862, Glens Falls, New York. Education: graduated Brown University, A.B. 1881, A.M. 1884; Columbia Law School, LL.B. 1884. Married Antoinette Carter, 1888, three children. Died: August 27, 1948, Osterville, Massachusetts.
*Career Data* Practiced law, 1884–1905, 1917–21. Counsel, New York

Investigating Commission, 1905–06. Governor of New York, 1907–10. U.S. Secretary of State, 1921–25. Member, Permanent Court of Arbitration and Judge, Permanent Court of International Justice, 1926–30.

*Supreme Court Data* Nominated by William Howard Taft on April 25, 1910, to replace Justice David Brewer, who died. Resigned June 10, 1916. Nominated Chief Justice on February 3, 1930, by Herbert Hoover, to replace Chief Justice Taft, who retired. Retired July 1, 1941.

Hughes passed the bar and joined the Wall Street law firm of Chamberlin, Carter, and Hornblower; he married the daughter of the managing partner and remained for twenty years. In 1905 Hughes became counsel for a state investigation of racketeering, and immediately developed such a reputation that he was supported by President Theodore Roosevelt in a race for governor, in which he defeated the newspaper king, William Randolph Hearst. After his second term was completed, President William Howard Taft appointed Hughes to the Supreme Court.

Hughes's six years on the Court as an associate justice were rather low keyed. His views were relatively conservative in areas of personal liberties, but quite liberal regarding federal regulatory power. As such, he fit in well with the majority. In his six-year tenure, Hughes wrote only thirty-two dissents.

Hughes resigned to run for president in 1916, with the nominations of both the Republican and Progressive parties. He lost to Woodrow Wilson by only twenty-three electoral votes. He re-

turned to New York and his law practice. When Warren G. Harding became president, he appointed Hughes secretary of state. That was followed by a term as judge on the Permanent Court of International Justice. He was then nominated Chief Justice by President Herbert Hoover.

Hughes served eleven years as Chief Justice. He served during a period of severe economic and political crisis that sorely tested the Court's ability to answer the challenges of modern society. Hughes became perhaps the most important Chief Justice since Marshall, and many of the 283 opinions he personally wrote helped shape the growth of modern American jurisprudence. In this period Hughes was much more socially liberal than he had been in his previous tenure, and the era was marked by constant, sharp divisions on the Court. (For a fuller examination of the Hughes Court, see pages 98–102.)

### Willis Van Devanter, 1910–1937

*Personal Data* Born: April 17, 1859, Marion, Indiana. Education: graduated Indiana University, A.B. 1878; University of Cincinnati Law School, LL.B. 1881. Married Dellice Burhans, 1883, no children. Died: February 8, 1941, Washington, D.C.

*Career Data* Practiced law, 1881–87, 1890–97. City Attorney, Cheyenne, 1887–88. Member, Wyoming territorial legislature, 1888. Chief Justice, Wyoming Territory Supreme Court, 1889–90. Assistant U.S. Attorney General, 1897–1903. Judge, U.S. Court of Appeals, 1903–10.

*Supreme Court Data* Nominated by

William Howard Taft on December 12, 1910, to replace Justice Edward White, who was elevated to Chief Justice. Retired June 2, 1937.

After receiving his law degree in 1881, Van Devanter joined his father's law firm in Marion, Indiana. Three years later, he heeded the call to "go west young man" and settled in Cheyenne, in the Wyoming Territory. There he established a law practice and became involved in Republican politics, becoming a close adviser to Governor Francis Warren. In 1886, Van Devanter helped rewrite the territory's statutes. Then he was appointed city attorney in Cheyenne, and the following year was elected to the territorial legislature. The next year, at age thirty, he was named chief justice of the Wyoming Territory Supreme Court but he served only a year before returning to private practice.

He remained politically active including membership on the Republican National Committee. Republican President William McKinley then named him as assistant attorney general in charge of public lands and Indian affairs. In 1903 President Theodore Roosevelt appointed him to the U.S. Court of Appeals, where he developed a national reputation for his work on land claims and railroad law cases. President Taft then named him to the Supreme Court.

Van Devanter served twenty-six years. He kept a low profile both on the Court and in public. He usually voted with the majority. He was long considered the Court's expert in land matters and Indian affairs, and usually wrote

these opinions. He also was important in the reshaping of corporate law. A militant dry, Van Devanter wrote the Court's opinion upholding the Eighteenth Amendment and Prohibition.

## Joseph Rucker Lamar, 1910–1916

*Personal Data* Born: October 14, 1857, Elbert County, Georgia. Education: graduated Bethany College, A.B. 1877; read the law under Henry Clay Foster and was admitted to the Georgia Bar, 1880. Married Clarinda Pendleton, 1879, three children. Died: January 2, 1916, Washington, D.C.

*Career Data* Practiced law, 1880–86, 1890–93, 1905–10. Member, Georgia legislature, 1886–89. Judge, Georgia Supreme Court, 1903–05.

*Supreme Court Data* Nominated by William Howard Taft on December 12, 1910, to replace Justice William Moody, who retired. Served until January 2, 1916.

Lamar came from an old Southern family who numbered among its members the governor of Texas and Supreme Court Justice Lucius Quintus Cincinnatus Lamar. He lived in Augusta where his father was a minister, and he became close friends with another minister's son in town, Woodrow Wilson. He began a law practice in Augusta that lasted nearly three decades. He spent two years on the Georgia Supreme Court before resigning and resumed his law practice. It was a national shock when five years later President William Howard Taft nominated him to the Supreme Court. Taft had come to know him during vacations to Augusta.

Lamar only had a short five-year tenure, dying of a heart attack at age fifty-eight. He almost always voted with the majority, dissenting only seven times in his career. He helped form a consistent majority for upholding and increasing the police powers of the state, and for expanding the powers of the executive branch. Because of his short tenure and his low profile, Lamar has not fared well among historians. But he was highly liked by his colleagues, who thought him a very valuable member of the Court.

## Mahlon Pitney, 1912–1922

*Personal Data* Born: February 5, 1858, Morristown, New Jersey. Education: graduated Princeton, A.B. 1879, A.M. 1882; read the law under his father and was admitted to the New Jersey Bar, 1882. Married Florence T. Shelton, 1891, three children. Died: December 9, 1924, Washington, D.C.

*Career Data* Practiced law, 1882–94. Member, U.S. House, 1895–99. Member, New Jersey State Senate, 1899–1901; president, 1901. Judge, New Jersey Supreme Court, 1901–08. Chancellor of New Jersey, 1908–12.

*Supreme Court Data* Nominated by William H. Taft on February 19, 1912, to replace Justice John Marshall Harlan, who died. Retired December 31, 1922.

After being admitted to the bar, Pitney practiced in Dover for seven years. Then when his father became vice-chancellor of New Jersey in 1889, he moved back to Morristown to take over his father's practice. He became involved in politics and was elected to Congress in 1894. He resigned his seat in Congress to accept a seat in the New Jersey State Senate, to position himself to run for governor. But that goal changed in 1901, when he was named to the New Jersey Supreme Court, and then named chancellor.

Pitney was shocked that President Taft nominated him for the Supreme Court. His only meeting with the president had been a week earlier at a dinner, when they discussed the qualifications of another New Jersey Supreme Court justice for the opening. But the conversation so impressed Taft, he named Pitney.

Pitney served ten years in which he formed a central part of a strong majority. Of 268 opinions he wrote, only nineteen were dissents. He wrote many of his decisions in the area of labor law, where his views were conservative and traditional, usually granting business protection from unions. He was far from a civil libertarian, voting consistently to allow the state to limit individual rights.

## James Clark McReynolds, 1914–1941

*Personal Data* Born: February 3, 1862, Elkton, Kentucky. Education: graduated Vanderbilt University, B.S. 1882; University of Virginia, LL.B. 1884. Never married. Died: August 24, 1946, Washington, D.C.

*Career Data* Practiced law, 1884–1903, 1907–13. Assistant U.S. Attorney, 1903–07. U.S. Attorney General, 1913–14.

*Supreme Court Data* Nominated by Woodrow Wilson on August 19, 1914, to replace Justice Horace H. Lurton, who died. Retired January 31, 1941.

After graduating from law school, McReynolds returned to Nashville to practice law. He practiced there for twenty years, while also teaching law at Vanderbilt University. He made two attempts at Congress, but lost both races. As a reward for the last loss, he was appointed an assistant U.S. attorney by Theodore Roosevelt. He became an expert at antitrust prosecutions, and after four years resigned to become a partner in a New York law firm. He also became an adviser to Wilson, and when he won the presidency, he named McReynolds attorney general. Less than a year later, Wilson named McReynolds to the Supreme Court because McReynolds was coming under fire from a number of senators whom he had angered.

McReynolds ended up serving twenty-seven rather contradictory years. A doctrinaire conservative, he often took conflicting positions from case to case. He wrote many of the Courts most important opinions in the area of educational freedom, but could also readily vote to limit civil liberties if he saw a national self-interest to be protected. He was an ardent trust buster who almost always supported a strong interpretation of the Sherman Act. But he also opposed expanded powers for the Federal Trade Commission. McReynolds was not a prolific justice, authoring only 503 opinions in his twenty-seven years. A man of deep prejudices, some Court historians rate him among the worst justices ever to have served a long tenure.

Louis Dembitz Brandeis, 1916–1939

*Personal Data* Born: November 13, 1856, Louisville, Kentucky. Education: graduated Harvard Law School, LL.B. 1877. Married Alice Goldmark, 1891, two children. Died: October 5, 1941, Washington, D.C.
*Career Data* Practiced law, 1887–1916.
*Supreme Court Data* Nominated by Woodrow Wilson on January 28, 1916, to replace Justice Joseph Lamar, who died. Retired February 13, 1939.

Brandeis enrolled in Harvard Law School at age eighteen. He graduated in one year with the highest average in the school's history. He went into a law partnership with Samuel D. Warren, Jr., that lasted forty years. Brandeis lived simply and devoted much of his energy to litigating cases in the public interest. He also developed a reputation for one of the nation's finest legal minds, and was a founder of the *Harvard Law Review*.

President Wilson was a long-time admirer of Brandeis, who advised him on legal issues, so he nominated him to the Court in 1916. The appointment set off a firestorm in the Senate, mainly ignited by corporations who had lost cases to Brandeis. For almost five months the confirmation battle raged and finally he was confirmed by a vote of 47–22. He became the first Jewish justice.

At eighty-two, after twenty-two years on the bench, Brandeis resigned. One of the great liberals in Court history, he often found himself in dissent from the majority that Chief Justice Taft had assembled around the idea that the state could not limit an individual's fundamental right to contract and to own property. Brandeis believed that the state could limit these rights to remedy a number of social ills. He also became one of the foremost protectors of free speech and press rights and, above all, freedom of religion. Although his fame came in dissent, actually during his tenure 454 of his 528 opinions were majority opinions.

## John Hessin Clarke, 1916–1922

*Personal Data* Born: September 18, 1857, Lisbon, Ohio. Education: graduated Western Reserve University, A.B. 1877, A.M. 1880; read the law under his father and was admitted to the Ohio Bar, 1879. Never married. Died: March 22, 1945, San Diego, California.

*Career Data* Practiced law, 1879–1914. Judge, U.S. District Court, 1914–16.

*Supreme Court Data* Nominated by Woodrow Wilson on July 14, 1916, to replace Charles Evans Hughes, who resigned. Resigned September 18, 1922.

Clarke began to practice law with his father after being admitted to the Bar. In 1880 Clarke moved to Youngstown, where he established a law practice and became publisher of the local newspaper, *The Vindicator*. Then after seventeen years he moved again, this time to Cleveland, where he became a partner in the firm of William and Cushing, and counsel to the Nickel Plate Railroad. In his thirty-five-year legal career, Clarke developed a national reputation for his progressive views. In 1894 he ran for the U.S. Senate but lost. He ran again in 1914, but withdrew to accept a judgeship on the U.S. District Court. Two years later he was named to the Supreme Court by Wilson, who wanted a progressive voice on the Court.

Clarke is perhaps better known for his resignation than for his five-year tenure on the Court. He has the distinction of being the only justice ever to resign while relatively young, and in good health, to devote himself to a social cause. In Clarke's case it was to tour the nation to drum up support for the U.S. entry in the League of Nations. On the Court, Clarke had been something of a progressive, with a legal theory before its time. He was pro-labor, against trusts, and had a special interest in immigration cases. But at the same time he held a rather narrow view of the First Amendment.

## William Howard Taft, 1921–1930

*Personal Data* Born: September 15, 1857, Cincinnati, Ohio. Education: graduated Yale University, A.B. 1878; Cincinnati Law School, LL.B. 1880. Married Helen Herron, 1886, three children. Died: March 8, 1930, Washington, D.C.

*Career Data* Practiced law, 1880–81, 1883–87. Assistant Prosecuting Attorney, Hamilton County (Ohio), 1881–83; Assistant County Solicitor, 1885–87. Judge, State Superior Court, 1887–90. U.S. Solicitor General, 1890–91. Judge, U.S. Circuit Court, 1892–1900. Governor of the Philippines, 1901–04. Secretary of War, 1904–08. President of the United States, 1909–13. Professor, Yale University, 1914–21. Chairman, National War Labor Board, 1918–19.

*Supreme Court Data* Nominated Chief Justice by Warren G. Harding on June

30, 1921, to replace Chief Justice Edward White, who died. Retired February 3, 1930.

While in law school, Taft became a reporter on the *Cincinnati Commercial*. He graduated and started to practice law and became involved in Republican politics. This led to his appointment as an assistant prosecutor and then assistant county solicitor and, still short of his thirtieth birthday, as a judge on the Ohio Superior Court. On the Republican fast track, three years later he was named by President Benjamin Harrison as U.S. solicitor general and two years later a judge on the Sixth Circuit.

Taft likely would have been happy to remain a judge the rest of his life. He served eight years on the Sixth Circuit and only left because President McKinley implored him to head the transition of the Philippines to a civilian government after the Spanish-American War. He remained in the Philippines for four years, until President Theodore Roosevelt brought him back to Washington as secretary of war.

Taft soon emerged as Roosevelt's chief adviser. With Roosevelt's support he won the Republican presidential nomination and the election in 1908. But even while he served in the White House, he made it clear to friends that the job he really coveted was the Chief Justiceship. That is believed why he nominated the relatively elderly Edward D. White as Chief Justice. Taft tried to win reelection in 1912, but the Republican party had split, and Democrat Woodrow Wilson was elected. Wilson in the White House, coupled with White's continued good health, kept Taft from the job he coveted. After leaving the White House, Taft taught at Yale Law School, lectured, and wrote. He served as chairman of the National War Labor Board, 1918–19, and then campaigned for approval of the League of Nations. Finally White passed away, and with a Republican back in the White House, Taft realized his life-long dream. He became the only man in U.S. history to be both president and Chief Justice.

Taft's philosophy was conservative. He seemed to have a fear of progressives. He believed that the only restraints on national government should be political, not legal or judicial. In case after case he supported the most expansive powers of the government except, contradictorily, in the taxing power, which he viewed as relatively limited. He also brought to the Court a depth of administrative ability not often seen in a Chief Justice, and devoted considerable time to making the Court work more efficiently and saving money. (For a fuller examination of the Taft Court, see pages 94–97.)

## George Sutherland, 1922–1938

*Personal Data* Born: March 25, 1862, Buckinghamshire, England. Education: Brigham Young School, 1876–81; University of Michigan Law School, 1883. Married Rosamund Lee, 1883, three children. Died: July 18, 1942, Stockbridge, Massachusetts.
*Career Data* Practiced law, 1883–96, 1918–21. Member, Utah State Senate, 1896–1900. Member, U.S. House,

1900–02. Member, U.S. Senate, 1905–17. U.S. Representative, Norway-United States arbitration, The Hague, 1921–22.

*Supreme Court Data* Nominated by Warren G. Harding on September 5, 1922, to replace Justice John H. Clarke, who resigned. Retired January 17, 1938.

Sutherland was brought to the United States as an infant, and in 1863 his family settled in the Utah Territory. After a year at the University of Michigan Law School, Sutherland returned to Provo to begin law practice and to marry. After Utah became a state in 1896, Sutherland—a Republican—was elected a state senator. Four years later, in 1900, he was elected to the U.S. House, but served only a single term. He returned to Utah, where he ran for and won a U.S. Senate seat in 1904.

Sutherland's Senate career was not particularly distinguished, and it ended abruptly in 1916, when he was not renominated by his party. He remained in Washington, practiced law, and became a close adviser to his former Senate colleague, Warren Harding. He worked on Harding's successful presidential campaign, and was rewarded with several appointments and finally with his seat on the Supreme Court.

Sutherland's tenure on the Court was filled with contradictions. A staunch conservative who bitterly opposed Roosevelt's New Deal, he became the intellectual leader of the Court's conservatives. Yet he is best remembered for his firm dedication to individual rights, and as one of the most significant civil libertarians of his era. His most famous

opinion, *Powell* v. *Alabama* (1932), incorporated the right to counsel as part of the due process clause of the Fourteenth Amendment and extended that right to all state trials.

## Pierce Butler, 1922–1939

*Personal Data* Born: March 17, 1866, Northfield, Minnesota. Education: graduated Carleton College, A.B. and B.S. 1887; read the law with the St. Paul law firm of Pinch and Twohy and was admitted to the Minnesota Bar, 1888. Married Annie Cronin, 1891, eight children. Died: November 16, 1939, Washington, D.C.

*Career Data* Practiced law, 1888–93, 1897–1922. County attorney, 1893–97. Regent, University of Minnesota, 1907–24.

*Supreme Court Data* Nominated by Warren G. Harding on November 23, 1922, to replace Justice William R. Day, who retired. Served until November 16, 1939.

Butler practiced law in St. Paul all his life, acting also as county attorney for four years. He established a national reputation representing big corporations, especially railroads, in antitrust actions and acted as special counsel for the U.S. both in trial cases and several international arbitrations. The latter, as well as his conservative views, brought him to the attention of Chief Justice Taft. When Justice Day resigned, Taft recommended Butler to President Harding, who agreed because Butler would be a Catholic replacing the Catholic Day. He was confirmed despite considerable opposition from one of his home-state senators, who felt with his corporate background he would be too reactionary.

Butler served seventeen years on the Court. During that time he remained unrelentingly conservative, holding absolutely to the view that government should not be able to limit the rights of property and commerce. This traditional conservatism carried through to a libertarian approach to civil liberties, in which he held that government should not limit personal freedoms without significant reason. He was, for instance, against Prohibition. But his libertarianism did not extend to patriotism. If Butler did not believe in the cause being espoused, he would extend little protection to the individual espousing it.

### Edward Terry Sanford, 1923–1930

*Personal Data* Born: July 23, 1865, Knoxville, Tennessee. Education: graduated University of Tennessee, B.A. 1883; Harvard, B.A. 1884, M.A. 1889; Harvard Law School, LL.B. 1889. Married Lutie Woodruff, 1891, two children. Died: March 8, 1930, Washington, D.C.
*Career Data* Practiced law, 1889–1905. Special assistant to the U.S. Attorney General, 1906–07. Assistant U.S. Attorney General, 1907–08. Judge, U.S. District Court, 1908–23.
*Supreme Court Data* Nominated by Warren G. Harding on January 24, 1923, to replace Mahlon Pitney, who retired. Served until March 8, 1930.

Sanford started his law career relatively late, not graduating from Harvard Law School until age thirty-four. He returned to Knoxville and began a pri-

vate practice. In 1905 he was brought to Washington to prosecute antitrust cases as a special assistant to the attorney general, and then was named assistant attorney general. A year later President Roosevelt named him a federal district judge, and he remained on the district court bench for fifteen years until named to the Supreme Court.

In his seven years on the Court, Sanford specialized in business cases, especially those relating to government regulation. He always tried to strike a balance between the needs of government and commerce. From his long service on the district court, he was also an expert on bankruptcy. But Sanford is probably best remembered in the area of civil liberties, where he extended the First Amendment to state actions. But at the same time, he took an expansive view on the state's ability to limit freedom of speech. Sanford might well have developed into one of the more significant justices of his era, but he died suddenly of a heart attack at age sixty-four. His passing went almost unnoticed because Taft also died only minutes later.

### Harlan Fiske Stone, 1925–1946

*Personal Data* Born: October 11, 1872, Chesterfield, New Hampshire. Education: graduated Amherst College, A.B. 1894, M.A. 1897; Columbia University Law School, LL.B. 1898. Married Agnes Harvey, 1899, two children. Died: April 22, 1946, Washington, D.C.
*Career Data* Practiced law, 1899–1924. Dean, Columbia University Law School, 1910–23. U.S. Attorney General, 1924–25.
*Supreme Court Data* Nominated by

Calvin Coolidge on January 5, 1925, to replace Joseph McKenna, who retired. Elevated to Chief Justice by Franklin D. Roosevelt, June 12, 1941, to replace Chief Justice Hughes, who retired. Served until April 22, 1946.

After graduating from Columbia Law School, Stone began to practice with the Wall Street firm of Sullivan and Cromwell, where he remained for the next twenty-five years while also teaching law, and then spent almost a decade as Dean of Columbia University Law School. In 1924 President Coolidge, his Amherst classmate, appointed Stone attorney general. A year later Coolidge named Stone to the High Court.

Over the next sixteen years, Stone rose to become the most senior associate justice. During this period the moderate Stone was frequently at odds with the conservatives on the Taft and Hughes Courts. As such, many of Stone's most memorable opinions were dissents. He often found himself allied with Holmes and Brandeis, but he also thought the two went too far in their liberalism in the area of civil liberties. When Chief Justice Hughes retired, Roosevelt wanted a Chief Justice who would not wreck his programs. By this time Stone had become the ideological center of the Court and its spokesman for judicial restraint. He was exactly what Roosevelt was looking for. His elevation was met with nearly universal approval.

Stone ended up serving only six years as Chief Justice. Whereas he often fought with the conservatives of the Taft and Hughes Courts, now he often found himself at odds with the liberals that Roosevelt had appointed. Stone ended up presiding over a Court that did much to advance civil liberties, but Stone still saw himself as a moderating influence on that Court. His watchword was always "judicial restraint." He died in a manner befitting a justice, while reading an opinion from the bench. (For a fuller look at the Stone Court, see pages 102–04.)

## Owen Josephus Roberts, 1930–1945

*Personal Data* Born: May 2, 1875, Germantown, Pennsylvania. Education: graduated University of Pennsylvania, A.B. 1895, LL.B. 1898. Married Elizabeth Rogers, 1904, no children. Died: May 17, 1955, Vincent, Pennsylvania.

*Career Data* Practiced law, 1900–30. Dean, University of Pennsylvania Law School, 1948–51.

*Supreme Court Data* Nominated by Herbert Hoover on May 9, 1930, to replace Justice Edward Sanford, who died. Resigned July 4, 1945.

Roberts was named a university fellow at the University of Pennsylvania, where he taught for several years after graduation. He then started a private practice in Philadelphia, which continued for thirty years. During his legal career he acted as a special prosecutor for the United States (1918–19) in a number of Espionage Act cases. In 1924 he was named a special U.S. attorney to investigate Harding administration scandals. His success earned him national attention. In May 1930, President Hoover was having trouble filling a Supreme Court vacancy. The Senate had rejected his first choice, and was threatening to reject his second. So instead he nominated Roberts, who was quickly confirmed.

Roberts served a decade and a half on the High Court. He is mainly remembered for his work in the area of civil liberties and business regulation. In his early years on a sharply divided Court, Roberts provided the fifth vote to form majorities expanding the rights of free speech and protections against government infringement of personal liberties. But from time to time, on a given case, Roberts might vote with the conservatives, giving him a reputation for vacillation. Later, Roberts became a supporter of almost all the New Deal legislation and was the critical swing vote in upholding its validity. In addition to his Court duties, Roberts oversaw an investigation of the attack on Pearl Harbor.

Benjamin Nathan Cardozo,
1932–1938

*Personal Data* Born: May 24, 1870, New York City. Education: graduated Columbia University, A.B. 1889, A.M. 1890; attended Columbia University Law School, 1891. Never married. Died: July 9, 1938, Port Chester, New York.
*Career Data* Practiced law, 1891–1914. Judge, New York Supreme Court, 1914. Judge, New York Court of Appeals, 1914–26, Chief Judge, 1926–32.
*Supreme Court Data* Nominated by President Herbert Hoover, on February 15, 1932, to replace Justice Oliver Wendell Holmes, who retired. Served until July 9, 1938.

Cardozo started Columbia University at age fourteen. After receiving bachelor's and master's degrees with high honors, he attended Columbia Law School for only a year before passing the bar examination. He began a law practice with his brother, which continued for twenty-three years. In 1914 he ran as a reform candidate for a seat on the New York Supreme Court (the state's trial court) and in less than a year he had been elevated to the New York Court of Appeals, serving there for eighteen years, the last six as chief judge. Cardozo earned the reputation as perhaps the leading state court jurist and a legal scholar of international repute. His Yale Law School lectures and his legal texts became required reading in the nation's law schools.

After all this, Cardozo came close to not being named to the High Court. At the time of Holmes's retirement, two New Yorkers—Hughes and Stone— and one other Jew, Brandeis, were already sitting on the Court. Hoover hesitated, but after both Hughes and Stone offered to resign to make way for Cardozo, he relented.

Cardozo only served on the Court for six years. As the junior justice he did not get many major opinions to write. He also found himself in the minority more often than not, on this still conservative Court. But his brilliance and clarity of legal thought showed in his dissents. His tenure marked the start of the Court's interest in expanding the protection of civil liberties. Cardozo took the lead in a number of key areas, especially on the question of how much of the Bill of Rights should be extended to state actions.

Hugo Lafayette Black, 1937–1971

*Personal Data* Born: February 27, 1886, Harlan, Alabama. Education: Birmingham Medical College, 1903–04; graduated University of Alabama Law School, LL.B. 1906. Married Josephine Foster, 1921, three children; married Elizabeth DeMeritte, 1957, no children. Died: September 25, 1971, Washington, D.C.

*Career Data* Practiced law, 1906–27. Member, U.S. Senate, 1927–37.

*Supreme Court Data* Nominated by Franklin D. Roosevelt on August 12, 1937, to replace Justice Willis Van Devanter, who retired. Retired September 17, 1971.

After law school, Black returned to his home in Ashland, Alabama, and set up a law practice. The next year he moved to Birmingham, where he quickly developed a reputation for labor law and personal-injury cases. He got involved in Democratic politics and joined the Ku Klux Klan, resigning to run for the Senate in 1927. In the Senate he developed a liberal reputation for reform measures, labor rights, and for his support of Roosevelt's New Deal. The latter caused Roosevelt to name him to the Court, upon the retirement of Willis Van Devanter.

In his more than three decades on the High Court, Black served with more than a quarter of all the justices who had served and a third of the Chief Justices. In that time he became one of the most influential justices ever to sit on the Court. Given the length of his service, and the depth of his influence, it is impossible to categorize his tenure in a few words. He was the central figure in the evolution of civil liberties and minority rights, criminal defendant's rights, and First Amendment rights. He was central to the Court's abandoning its rejection of legislation, based on the Court's test of its reasonableness. He led the way for approval of federal power to regulate commerce for social ends and expansion of governmental antitrust powers. Black retired from the Court on September 17, 1971, after suffering an impairing stroke. He died eight days later.

Stanley Forman Reed, 1938–1957

*Personal Data* Born: December 31, 1884, Minerva, Kentucky. Education: graduated Kentucky Wesleyan University, A.B. 1902; Yale University, A.B. 1906; University of Virginia Law School, Columbia University Law School (no degree); University of Paris, 1909–10. Married Winifred Elgin, 1908, two children. Died: April 2, 1980, New York City.

*Career Data* Practiced law, 1910–19, 1960–78. Member, Kentucky General Assembly, 1914–18. Counsel, Federal Farm Board, 1929–32. Counsel, Reconstruction Finance Corporation, 1932–35. Solicitor General, 1935–38. Chairman, U.S. Civil Rights Commission, 1958–59.

*Supreme Court Data* Nominated by Franklin D. Roosevelt on January 15, 1938, to replace Justice George Sutherland, who retired. Retired February 25, 1957.

Reed practiced law in Maysville, Kentucky, from 1910 to 1929, with time out to serve in World War I. Among his clients was the Burley Tobacco Company, where he gained experience in commodity sales. This expertise was recommended to President Herbert Hoover, who named Reed counsel to the Federal Farm Board. Two years later he was promoted to head the Reconstruction Finance Corporation. In 1935 Roosevelt asked him to prepare and argue a case before the Supreme Court defending the administration's monetary policies, and when he won Roosevelt named him solicitor general. In the position Reed successfully argued the constitutionality of most New Deal legislation.

When Justice Sutherland retired in 1938, Roosevelt quickly moved to name Reed. He served nineteen years, during which he wrote 339 opinions, 231 majority, 20 concurrences, and 88 dissents. During almost his entire tenure he sat exactly in the middle of the Court philosophically. He was a moderate who believed in the states' power to regulate for the social good, but also espoused judicial restraint. He was pro-labor, but also favored limited antitrust enforcement. Reed was not generally considered a civil libertarian—he was a strong supporter of government action against suspected subversives—but he was a defender of free speech and First Amendment rights, and an opponent of censorship.

Reed retired in 1957 for health reasons. But he ended up with one of the longest retirements in Court history—twenty-three years. He first served as head of the newly created Civil Rights Commission and then returned to private practice, arguing cases before the Supreme Court and courts of appeal.

## Felix Frankfurter, 1939–1962

*Personal Data* Born: November 15, 1882, Vienna, Austria. Education: graduated City College of New York, A.B. 1902; Harvard Law School, LL.B. 1906. Married Marion Denman, 1919, no children. Died: February 22, 1965, Washington, D.C.

*Career Data* Assistant U.S. attorney, 1906–09. Counsel, War Department, 1910–14. Assistant to the Secretary of War, 1917–18. Chairman, War Labor Policies Board, 1918. Professor, Harvard Law School 1914–17, 1919–39.

*Supreme Court Data* Nominated by Franklin D. Roosevelt on January 5, 1939, to replace Justice Benjamin Cardozo, who died. Retired August 28, 1962.

Because of his high academic record at Harvard Law School, Frankfurter came to the attention of Henry L. Stimson, the U.S. attorney for the southern district of New York, who recruited him to work in his office. When Stimson was named secretary of war by William Howard Taft, he brought Frankfurter with him. In 1914 Harvard Law School asked him to return to teach, and he remained three years before returning to Washington as assistant to Secretary of War Newton D. Baker and as chairman of the War Labor Policies Board. He returned to Harvard, where he remained until being named to the Supreme Court in 1939. He developed an international reputation as both a scholar and a liberal activist. At one point he declined a seat on the Massachusetts Supreme Court and Franklin Roosevelt's offer to become solicitor general. While at Harvard, Frankfurter helped found the American Civil Liberties Union and the National Association for the Advancement of Colored People.

As with Black, Frankfurter's quarter-century on the Court represents such a prodigious body of work, it is impossible to adequately categorize in a few words. His opinions stand as among the most scholarly ever crafted. Given his background, many assumed he would be the most liberal of justices. But he was quite moderate in most of his views. Most of all he approached each case on its own merits and often decided by balancing one right against another.

Frankfurter remained on the Court until he suffered a debilitating stroke in 1962.

## William Orville Douglas, 1939–1975

*Personal Data* Born: October 16, 1898, Maine, Minnesota. Education: graduated Whitman College, B.A. 1920; Columbia University Law School, LL.B. 1925. Married Mildred Riddle, 1923, divorced 1954, two children; married Mercedes Hester, 1954, divorced 1963, no children; married Joan Martin, 1963, divorced 1966, no children; married Cathleen Heffernan, July 1966, no children. Died: January 19, 1980, Washington, D.C.

*Career Data* Practiced law, 1925–27. Law professor, Columbia University, 1928; Yale Law School, 1929–36. Member, Securities and Exchange Commission, 1936–37; Chairman, 1937–39.

*Supreme Court Data* Nominated by Franklin D. Roosevelt on March 20, 1939, to replace Justice Louis D. Brandeis, who retired. Retired November 12, 1975.

Following law school, Douglas started to practice law in New York, decided he didn't like practice, and accepted a teaching position at Columbia University Law School. The next year he moved to Yale, where he quickly developed a reputation as the nation's outstanding academic authority on securities law. When Roosevelt created the Securities and Exchange Commission, it was almost natural he would call on Douglas, who became the SEC's chairman in 1937. He remained in that position for three years, until being named to the Court by Roosevelt.

Douglas was only on the Court for four years when he was approached by Roosevelt about whether he would serve as vice-president. He was not enthusiastic and for that and other reasons Roosevelt chose Senator Harry Truman. Douglas could well have become president if he had said yes to Roosevelt.

By the time he retired, Douglas had served thirty-six years and seven months—to that point longer than any other justice in history. He was among the most liberal of justices to ever serve, an iron-willed proponent of individual liberty and especially of free speech. But at the same time he was an outspoken foe of world communism. His years of service on the Court were often stormy. Three times he faced the threat of impeachment, although only in 1970 did the move gain any real support. In the end a special House Judiciary Subcommittee found no grounds for impeachment.

Francis William Murphy, 1940–1949

*Personal Data* Born: April 13, 1890, Harbor Beach, Michigan. Education: graduated University of Michigan, A.B. 1912, LL.B. 1914. Never married. Died: July 19, 1949, Detroit, Michigan. *Career Data* Practiced law, 1915–18, 1920–23. Assistant Attorney General (Mich.), 1919–20. Judge, Recorder's Court, Detroit, 1923–30. Mayor of Detroit, 1930–33. Governor General of the Philippines, 1933–36. Governor of Michigan, 1937–39. U.S. Attorney General, 1939–40. *Supreme Court Data* Nominated by Franklin D. Roosevelt on January 4, 1940, to replace Justice Pierce Butler, who died. Served until July 19, 1949.

After graduating from law school, Frank Murphy clerked for a Detroit law firm and then joined the army to fight in World War I. After the war he stayed in London to take advanced law classes and then returned to Michigan, where he became an assistant state attorney general and then went into private practice. In 1923 he became a criminal courts judge in Detroit, and seven years later was elected the city's mayor. He was a supporter of Franklin Roosevelt and was rewarded by being made governor general of the Philippines. He returned to Michigan to successfully run for governor, but two years later he was defeated for reelection. He begged Roosevelt to name him secretary of war. But that job was taken and so Roosevelt told him to come to Washington temporarily as attorney general.

Murphy assumed he would get the secretary of war position quickly. But the next year Justice Pierce Butler died and suddenly Roosevelt needed an Irish Catholic nominee. Murphy did not want the job, but finally agreed to take it. To show where his heart was, he accepted a reserve commission and spent all the Court recesses serving at Fort Benning, helping train soldiers for the war.

Murphy's almost ten-year tenure on the Court has been devalued by historians because he wrote few important opinions. Murphy's problem was that he was not liked, or held in high esteem by Chief Justice Stone, because Stone thought him too dependent on his clerks. As a result he was not assigned many cases of note. He was mainly kept busy writing technical tax opinions, or other highly technical opinions dealing with arcane aspects of federal regulation. One area of the law where Murphy did have an impact was criminal procedure—specifically the area of search and seizure, where he broadened the right of search incident to an arrest.

James Francis Byrnes, 1941–1942

*Personal Data* Born: May 2, 1879, Charleston, South Carolina. Education: left secondary school before graduation; read the law and was admitted to the South Carolina Bar, 1903. Married Maude Busch, 1906, no children. Died: April 9, 1972, Columbia, South Carolina. *Career Data* Editor, *Aiken* (S.C.) *Journal and Review*, 1903–08. Solicitor, Second Circuit of South Carolina, 1908–10. Member, U.S. House (D), 1911–25. Member, U.S. Senate, 1931–41. Director, Office of Economic

Stabilization, 1942–43. Director, Office of War Mobilization, 1943–45. U.S. Secretary of State, 1945–47. Practiced law, 1947–50. Governor of South Carolina, 1951–55.

*Supreme Court Data* Nominated by Franklin D. Roosevelt on June 12, 1941, to replace Justice James McReynolds, who retired. Resigned October 3, 1942.

The son of poor Irish immigrant parents, Byrnes left school at age fourteen to help support his widowed mother. A law clerk, he learned shorthand and became a court stenographer. While serving as the official court reporter for the Second Circuit, he read the law with the help of several of the judges, and was admitted to the bar in 1903. At the same time he bought a local newspaper and became its editor. Then he became the district attorney for South Carolina's Second Circuit, and two years later won a U.S. House seat. He served eight terms before moving on to the U.S. Senate. A good friend of Roosevelt, he was twice the leading contender for the vice-presidency, but was passed over out of fear that voters might reject a Catholic. Instead, Roosevelt rewarded Byrnes by nominating him to the Supreme Court in June 1941. But in one of the oddest nominations ever, Roosevelt kept the nomination secret for almost seven months to allow Byrnes to finish his Senate session, in which he was acting as point man for many of Roosevelt's bills.

Roosevelt soon realized that he almost could not afford to have Byrnes on the Court while the war was on; he needed him elsewhere. Byrnes ended up serving only sixteen months before resigning to head, first, the Office of Economic Stabilization, and then the Office of War Mobilization. But he was more than that. Byrnes has been called the assistant president during the war years, and in 1945 was Roosevelt's chief aide at the Yalta Conference with Stalin and Churchill. The next year he became secretary of state, and then after practicing law in Washington, was elected governor of South Carolina in 1950.

Brynes's one full year on the Court—1941—was among its most contentious. There were 162 opinions and 160 dissents. Brynes ended up writing four important civil liberties decisions for the Court, including one striking down a state statute requiring compulsory sterilization of "habitual criminals."

## Robert Houghwout Jackson, 1941–1954

*Personal Data* Born: February 13, 1892, Spring Creek, Pennsylvania. Education: local schools; Albany (N.Y.) Law School, 1912. Married Irene Gerhardt, 1916, two children. Died: October 9, 1954, Washington, D.C.

*Career Data* Practiced law, 1912–34. Counsel, Internal Revenue Service, 1934–36. Counsel, Securities and Exchange Commission, 1935. Assistant U.S. Attorney General, 1936–38. U.S. Solicitor General, 1938–39. U.S. Attorney General, 1940–41. Chief Prosecutor, Nuremberg War Crimes Trial, 1945–46.

*Supreme Court Data* Nominated by Franklin D. Roosevelt on June 12, 1941, to replace Justice Harlan F.

Stone, who was elevated to Chief Justice. Served until October 9, 1954.

After a year studying at Albany Law School, Jackson began a lucrative general practice. He dabbled in Democratic politics, but was turned off by what he saw. But the experience brought him into contact with Franklin Roosevelt, who remembered the young lawyer and brought Jackson to Washington in 1934 for a "temporary" assignment as counsel to the Internal Revenue Bureau. He made a quick rise through the Roosevelt administration, first to assistant attorney general and then solicitor general, finally to attorney general in 1940.

In June 1941 Roosevelt named Jackson to the Supreme Court, where he served for thirteen years. In his first years on the Court, Jackson was unhappy. The war effort was going on that he wanted to be a part of. On the Court, the liberal Jackson was involved in sharp clashes with a number of his fellow justices and the atmosphere was tense. Reportedly, he was considering leaving the Court by 1946, when President Truman approached him with the offer to take a leave from the Court to be chief prosecutor at the Nuremberg Trials. When he returned to the Court in 1947, relations between him and his fellow justices improved considerably, and he is said to have enjoyed the next four years.

## Wiley Blount Rutledge, 1943–1949

*Personal Data* Born: July 20, 1894, Cloverport, Kentucky. Education: graduated University of Wisconsin, A.B. 1914; University of Colorado, LL.B. 1922. Married Annabel Person, 1917,

three children. Died: September 10, 1949, York, Maine.

*Career Data* Practiced law, 1922–25. Law professor and dean, 1926–39. Judge, U.S. Court of Appeals, 1939–43.

*Supreme Court Data* Nominated by Franklin D. Roosevelt on January 11, 1943, to replace Justice James Byrnes, who resigned. Served until September 10, 1949.

After college, Rutledge began to teach and go to law school at night. He developed tuberculosis, and moved first to New Mexico and then Colorado, where he eventually resumed his legal studies. He began to practice in Boulder before returning to the law school to teach. Over the next decade and a half he taught at Colorado, Washington University (St. Louis), and the University of Iowa, where he became dean. In the latter position he supported Roosevelt's court-packing plan. In thanks Roosevelt appointed Rutledge to the court of appeals, and four years later to the Supreme Court.

Rutledge's tenure came to an end after only six years, with his sudden death on September 10, 1949. In this short time he had developed a reputation as among the most strident civil libertarians ever to have served on the Court; he especially was a champion of the Bill of Rights. Given the generally conservative tenor of the Court he served on, many of his most famous and impassioned opinions were dissents.

## Harold Hitz Burton, 1945–1958

*Personal Data* Born: June 22, 1888, Jamaica Plain, Massachusetts. Education:

graduated Bowdoin College, A.B. 1909; Harvard University, LL.B. 1912. Married Selma Florence Smith, 1912, four children. Died: October 28, 1964, Washington, D.C.

*Career Data* Practiced law, 1912–16, 1919–29. Member, Ohio State House, 1929. Counsel, City of Cleveland, 1929–32. Mayor of Cleveland, 1935–40. Member, U.S. Senate (R), 1941–45. *Supreme Court Data* Nominated by Harry S Truman on September 19, 1945, to replace Justice Owen J. Roberts, who resigned. Retired October 13, 1958.

After graduation from Harvard, Burton settled in Cleveland and began to practice law. He moved to Utah for a short time to work as an attorney for the local utility company, but then World War I broke out and he served as a captain. After the war, Burton returned to Cleveland, and besides practicing law, became involved in Republican politics. He was elected to a one-year term in the Ohio state legislature, and then was named city counsel for Cleveland. He then won the mayor's job, to which he was twice reelected by a huge margin. He was elected to the U.S. Senate in 1941. There he became a close friend of Harry Truman, and when the Democratic president came under heavy pressure to name a Republican, he chose the moderate Burton.

Burton served for thirteen years, more than half of them as the only Republican on the Court. Early in his tenure he tended to be rigidly conservative and an advocate of judicial restraint, especially in the area of civil liberties. In this period he was often found arguing in

dissent. But in the middle third of his career, he helped form a five-member conservative majority that voted together more than 80 percent of the time. But it should be noted that he helped form a majority on civil rights issues that ruled against all the Southern strategies trying to get around the unanimous *Brown* v. *Board of Education* (1954) school desegregation ruling. In the latter third of his career, once Earl Warren came to the Court, he found himself again in a conservative minority. Burton contracted Parkinson's disease, and this forced his retirement in October of 1958.

## Frederick Moore Vinson, 1946–1953

*Personal Data* Born: January 22, 1890, Louisa, Kentucky. Education: graduated Centre College, A.B. 1909, LL.B. 1911. Married Roberta Dixson, 1923, two children. Died: September 8, 1953, Washington, D.C.

*Career Data* Commonwealth's Attorney (K.), 1921–24. Member, U.S. House, 1924–29, 1931–38. Judge, U.S. Court of Appeals, 1938–43. Director, Office of Economic Stabilization, 1943–45. Secretary of the Treasury, 1945–46.

*Supreme Court Data* Nominated Chief Justice by Harry S Truman on June 6, 1946, to replace Chief Justice Harlan Stone, who died. Served until September 8, 1953.

After law school, Vinson started a law practice in Ashland, Kentucky, which continued until he ran for Congress in 1924. Except for one term in which he lost, Vinson served in the House until

1938. He was critical to the passage of much of the New Deal legislation, and he was rewarded by Roosevelt with a seat on the U.S. Court of Appeals. Then during the war, Vinson ran several war-related agencies, and was named treasury secretary in 1945 by his friend Harry Truman, who had just become president. With the death of Chief Justice Stone, Truman wanted a Chief Justice who would not stand in the way of strong postwar recovery measures, so he named Vinson.

Vinson brought to the Court a view, born of the war, that the federal government needed extraordinary powers to meet the challenges it faced. He presided through the cold war years, sticking closely to this philosophy. He took over a sharply divided Court, and although he did not exactly unify it, relations among justices did improve during his seven years. Vinson was not much of a civil libertarian, adopting a narrow view of the First Amendment and much of the Bill of Rights. The one area in which Vinson did manage to unite his fellow justices was in race relations in a series of decisions starting with *Shelley v. Kraemer* (1948).

Truman then tried to convince Vinson to run for the presidency in 1952, but Vinson declined. Most believe he would have won if he had run, but he took the position that once a person accepts the Chief Justiceship, it should be for life. (For a fuller discussion of the Vinson Court, see pages 104–07.)

Tom Campbell Clark, 1949–1967

*Personal Data* Born: September 23, 1899, Dallas, Texas. Education: graduated University of Texas, A.B. 1921, LL.B. 1922. Married Mary Ramsey, 1924, three children. Died: June 13, 1977, New York City.

*Career Data* Practiced law, 1922–37. Dallas County District attorney, 1927–32. Special Assistant, U.S. Justice Department, 1937–43. Assistant U.S. Attorney General, 1943–45. U.S. Attorney General, 1945–49. Senior judge, U.S. Court of Appeals, 1967–77.

*Supreme Court Data* Nominated by Harry S Truman on August 2, 1949, to replace Justice Frank Murphy, who died. Retired June 12, 1967.

Clark, born into a prominent Texas legal family, started to practice with his father's firm, where he stayed until 1937, with time out for a four-year term as Dallas district attorney. In 1937 he moved to Washington as a special assistant in the Justice Department. In prosecuting fraudulent war claims, he worked closely with then Senator Harry Truman. When Truman became president, he named Clark his attorney general.

In 1949 Truman promoted Clark to the High Court. In his eighteen years on the Court, Clark slowly evolved from a conservative to a champion of civil rights and liberties, in an era dominated by questions over the relationship between state power and individual freedom. But the evolution came slowly. In his first four terms he almost always voted with Chief Justice Vinson. Then in the early years of the Warren Court, he continued to hold conservative views, especially in the areas of loyality-security cases. But as the 1960s dawned and the "red scare" years ended, Clark developed much more tolerance for the liberal activism of the Warren Court and he, himself, authored some of its most controversial opinions. He served until 1967, when he resigned to avoid conflict of interest after his son, Ramsey Clark, was named attorney general. For the next decade he worked for judicial reform and served as a senior judge hearing cases on various courts of appeals.

## Sherman Minton, 1949–1956

*Personal Data* Born: October 20, 1890, Georgetown, Indiana. Education: graduated Indiana University, LL.B. 1915; Yale University, LL.M. 1917. Married Gertrude Gurtz, 1917, three children. Died: April 9, 1965, New Albany, Indiana.

*Career Data* Indiana Public Counselor, 1933–34. Member, U.S. Senate, 1935–41. Assistant to President, 1941. Judge, Court of Appeals, 1941–49.

*Supreme Court Data* Nominated by Harry S Truman on September 15, 1949, to replace Justice Wiley Rutledge, who died. Retired October 15, 1956.

Minton began a law practice in New Albany, Indiana, that continued until 1933. A law school classmate, who had become governor, named him Indiana public counselor in 1933. Two years later, he successfully ran for the U.S. Senate, but was defeated for reelection in 1940. In the Senate, Minton had supported Roosevelt's court-packing plan, so the president brought him to the White House as an assistant. The

next year Roosevelt appointed him to the U.S. Court of Appeals. When Justice Wiley Rutledge died, President Truman knew immediately who he wanted to nominate: his friend and former Senate colleague Sherman Minton.

As often happens, you cannot tell what kind of justice someone will make from his previous politics. Minton as a legislator was an ardent New Dealer, seemingly liberal to the core. But beginning with his service on the lower court, and then on the Supreme Court, he evolved into a conservative who almost always favored government interests over the civil liberties of the individual. He never became a distinguished justice, in some measure because his health slowly deteriorated throughout his seven years on the Court. Health finally forced his retirement in 1956. He spent the last nine years of his life in retirement in New Albany, Indiana, and died in 1965.

## Earl Warren, 1953–1969

*Personal Data* Born: March 19, 1891, Los Angeles, California. Education: graduated University of California 1912, J.D. 1914. Married Nina Meyers, 1925, six children. Died: July 9, 1974, Washington, D.C.

*Career Data* Deputy City Attorney, Oakland, 1919–20. Deputy Assistant District Attorney, Alameda County, 1920–25. District Attorney, 1925–39. Attorney General of California, 1939–43. Governor of California, 1943–53.

*Supreme Court Data* Nominated Chief

Justice by Dwight D. Eisenhower on September 30, 1953, to replace Chief Justice Fred M. Vinson, who died. Retired June 23, 1969.

Warren spent his entire career in public service, much of the time as an assistant and then as district attorney of Alameda County, which includes Oakland and the surrounding areas. Warren, a Republican, decided to run for state attorney general in 1938. He won both the Democratic and Republican nominations. Four years later he ran for governor and won easily. He was then twice reelected.

Warren was high on the list of potential Republican presidential nominees in 1952. But he threw his support to Dwight D. Eisenhower, who probably would not have won the nomination without Warren's support. Eisenhower repaid Warren with the surprise nomination to succeed Chief Justice Fred M. Vinson.

If any man has ever been a surprise on the High Court it was Warren. A moderate conservative governor, he became the focus of one of the most activist liberal Courts ever. In later years, Eisenhower publicly called the appointment "the biggest damn fool mistake I ever made."

Lyndon Johnson gave Warren the additional burden of heading a special commission to investigate the Kennedy assassination; the commission bears his name. In 1968 Warren submitted his resignation, but served an additional year until a successor could be named to replace him. (For a fuller examination of the Warren Court years, see pages 107–13.)

## John Marshall Harlan, 1955–1971

*Personal Data* Born: May 20, 1899, Chicago, Illinois. Education: graduated Princeton University, B.A. 1920; Rhodes Scholar, Oxford University 1923; New York Law School, LL.B. 1925. Married Ethel Andrews, 1928, one child. Died: December 29, 1971, Washington, D.C.

*Career Data* Practiced law, 1926–51. Assistant U.S. Attorney, 1925–27. Assistant Attorney General of New York, 1928–30. Counsel, New York State Crime Commission, 1951–53. Judge, U.S. Court of Appeals, 1954–55.

*Supreme Court Data* Nominated by Dwight D. Eisenhower on November 8, 1954, to replace Justice Robert Jackson. Retired September 23, 1971.

Named after his grandfather, who served on the Supreme Court from 1877 to 1911, Harlan joined a prominent Wall Street law firm, where he remained for twenty-five years except for periods he left to perform such public service as being assistant U.S. attorney, a special prosecutor of municipal graft cases, and, during World War II, a high-level position in the Army Air Corps. In 1951 Governor Thomas E. Dewey appointed Harlan as chief counsel of the New York State Crime Commission. He also served as the chairman of the Ethics Committee of the Bar of New York City. In 1954 President Eisenhower nominated Harlan to the U.S. Court of Appeals and then, only six months later, to the U.S. Supreme Court.

Harlan, in great measure, became the

conservative conscience of the most activist Supreme Court in history. He was always greatly troubled trying to find the line between individual rights and government power. He was a great believer in the federal system, which to him meant a fine balance between states' rights and federal power. He harbored grave doubts of the wisdom of judicial intervention into many political activities, and he was a champion of maintaining the distribution of power among the three branches of government. These views often came into sharp conflict with the majority, and left Harlan to write eloquent dissents.

## William Joseph Brennan, Jr., 1956–1990

*Personal Data* Born: April 25, 1906, Newark, New Jersey. Education: graduated University of Pennsylvania, B.S. 1928; Harvard Law School, LL.B. 1931. Married Marjorie Leonard, 1924, three children; married Mary Fowler, 1983, no children. Still living.
*Career Data* Judge, New Jersey Superior Court, 1949–50; Appellate Division, 1950–52. Judge, New Jersey Supreme Court, 1952–56.
*Supreme Court Data* Nominated by Dwight D. Eisenhower on January 14, 1956, to replace Justice Sherman Minton, who resigned. Resigned July 20, 1990.

After law school, Brennan returned to his home in Newark, New Jersey, joining a prominent local firm specializing in labor law. During World War II, Brennan joined the army, where he served as a special assistant to the undersecretary of war. At war's end he returned to Newark.

In 1949, Brennan accepted a judgeship on the new New Jersey Superior Court, in part because he felt an obligation having served on the commission creating it. A year later he moved to the appellate division and then to the state supreme court. When President Eisenhower was searching for a replacement for Sherman Minton, several members of the New Jersey congressional delegation recommended Brennan. Eisenhower agreed, thinking perhaps that the naming of a Catholic Democrat would help him at the polls.

Brennan ended up serving one of the most distinguished tenures in Court history. His thirty-four years years of service span several eras in the Court's history, from the conservative post–Korean War years through the cold war years, then to activist years of the Warren Court to the progressively more conservative Courts of Warren Burger and William Rehnquist. Through it all Brennan stood as a consistent beacon guarding individual rights. But during his long career he was not quite as absolute in his views as was Douglas or Black. Rather, he always sought to balance conflicting interests and to maintain a prime role for the judiciary in guaranteeing individual rights.

## Charles Evans Whittaker, 1957–1962

*Personal Data* Born: February 22, 1901, Troy, Kansas. Education: graduated University of Kansas City Law School, LL.B. 1924. Married Winifred

Pugh, 1928, three children. Died: November 26, 1973, Kansas City, Missouri.

*Career Data* Practiced law, 1924–54. Judge, U.S. District Court, 1954–56. Judge, Circuit Court of Appeals, 1956–57.

*Supreme Court Data* Nominated by Dwight D. Eisenhower on March 2, 1957, to replace Stanley Reed, who retired. Retired March 31, 1962.

Whittaker never finished high school, let alone college, quitting to help support his family. But he was admitted to Kansas City Law School on the basis of high entrance test results. He worked his way through law school clerking for a local law firm, that he joined after graduation. He remained with that firm for thirty years, becoming a district judge in 1954 and an appeals court judge two years later. When President Eisenhower was considering a replacement for Stanley Reed, Whittaker's reputation as one of the nation's top attorneys, followed by four years on the bench—coupled with strong Republican ties—made him the first choice.

Whittaker's brief five years on the Court were marked by constant health problems. He was basically a conservative, by one count voting with a 5–4 majority forty-one times to limit a claimed civil right or civil liberty. But at other times he voted with the liberal majority in civil rights and civil liberties cases, and in some instances was something of a champion of the rights of criminal defendants. But many of the cases in which he was the critical fifth vote were quickly overturned after he left the Court in 1962. In retirement, Whittaker helped write a new code of senatorial ethics and he continued to be active in bar affairs.

Potter Stewart, 1958–1981

*Personal Data* Born: January 23, 1915, Jackson, Michigan. Education: graduated Yale University, B.A. 1937; Yale Law School, LL.B. 1941. Married Mary Bertles, 1943, three children. Died: December 7, 1985, Hanover, New Hampshire.

*Career Data* Practiced law, 1941–42, 1945–52. Member, Cincinnati Council, 1950–53. Vice Mayor of Cincinnati, 1952–53. Judge, Circuit Court of Appeals, 1954–58.

*Supreme Court Data* Nominated by Dwight D. Eisenhower on January 17, 1959, to replace Harold H. Burton, who retired. Retired July 3, 1981.

Stewart's father was mayor of Cincinnati and served on the Ohio Supreme Court. After graduating from law school, Stewart moved to New York, joining a major Wall Street law firm. But the war began and Stewart joined the navy, where he served as a shipboard officer. After the war he returned to Cincinnati, where he joined the city's top law firm and became involved in Republican politics. Twice he was elected to the City Council, and then elected as vice mayor. His political loyalty was rewarded in 1954 with a seat on the U.S. Court of Appeals. Five years later Eisenhower elevated him to the Supreme Court.

Stewart had a long career, serving twenty-three years before he retired in 1981. In that time he was a centerist swing vote on the Warren Court; then on the Burger Court he emerged as the ideological center. Stewart made important contributions to a number of areas of criminal law, criminal procedure, and the criminal justice system, especially search and seizure. He also made important contributions in the area of civil rights, especially in extending civil rights protections to private, as opposed to public, actions. Also, Stewart played a leading role in the Pentagon Papers cases—*New York Times Company* v. *United States* (1971)—and was a major proponent of freedom of the press.

Byron Raymond White, 1962–

*Personal Data* Born: June 8, 1917, Fort Collins, Colorado. Education: graduated University of Colorado, B.A. 1938; Rhodes Scholar, Oxford University, 1939; Yale Law School, LL.B. 1946. Married Marion Stearns, 1946, two children. Still living.
*Career Data* Clerk to Chief Justice Fred M. Vinson, 1946–47. Practiced law, 1948–62. Deputy U.S. Attorney General, 1961–62.
*Supreme Court Data* Nominated by John F. Kennedy on March 30, 1962, to replace Justice Charles Whittaker, who retired. Still serving.

White enjoyed an extraordinary college career. He was a football all-American, four-year letter man in basketball and baseball, and a Phi Beta Kappa who graduated first in his class and who won a Rhodes Scholarship to Oxford (where he went after playing a year of professional football). He then returned to the United States to attend Yale Law School while continuing his professional football career with the Detroit Lions. He left law school to fight in World War II, and then returned to Yale and graduated at the top of his class. He spent a year clerking for the Chief Justice before returning to his home in Denver and a fourteen-year legal career.

White had become a good friend of John F. Kennedy, and in 1960 ran his primary campaign in Colorado and then was one of his top campaign aides. When Kennedy won, he brought White to Washington to work with his brother as deputy attorney general, and then two years later he named White to the Supreme Court.

In the years that White has served on the Court, he started out as a conservative on a highly liberal Court, and has ended up among the more moderate justices on a highly conservative Court, while not changing his centerist views almost at all. White has suffered the fate of many centerist justices in not being noticed simply because he does not stand out. But in fact, White has played a major role during his long Court tenure, especially during the 1970s, when his was often the swing vote in adopting many of the liberal advances. It was his willingness to go along with the liberal majority that often provided the critical fifth vote. At the same time, in later years he has taken a leading role in limiting criminal defendants' rights. But what comes out most in examining White's long record is his independence.

Arthur Joseph Goldberg, 1962–1965

*Personal Data* Born: August 8, 1908, Chicago, Illinois. Education: graduated Northwestern University, B.S. 1929; J.D. 1930. Married Dorothy Kurgans, 1931, two children. Died 1990.

*Career Data* Practiced law, 1930–61, 1969–90. Secretary of Labor, 1961–62. U.S. Ambassador to the United Nations, 1965–68.

*Supreme Court Data* Nominated by John F. Kennedy on August 29, 1962, to replace Felix Frankfurter, who retired. Resigned July 25, 1965.

After law school graduation, Goldberg established a labor law practice in Chicago and soon came to national attention with his representation of labor unions in strike situations. In World War II, he served in the predecessor to the CIA, the Office of Strategic Services, and then returned to Chicago. He was the primary architect of the 1955 merger of the American Federation of Labor (AFL) and the Congress of Industrial Organizations (CIO).

President Kennedy appointed him secretary of labor. A year later, he nominated Goldberg to the Supreme Court. In his three years on the Court, Goldberg was among the most liberal of justices, a fierce protector of individual liberties. He wrote a surprising number of opinions, including many dealing with civil rights and immigration matters. More than that, he wrote a number of concurring opinions that advanced constitutional law beyond the majority opinion and which since have been adopted as the majority opinion. In 1965, President Lyndon Johnson asked Goldberg to become U.S. ambassador

to the United Nations. Goldberg resigned his seat to comply. He held the post for three years, and then remained in New York to try to run for governor. Defeated, he returned to Washington and the practice of law.

Abe Fortas, 1965–1969

*Personal Data* Born: June 19, 1910, Memphis, Tennessee. Education: graduated Southwestern College, A.B. 1930; Yale Law School, LL.B. 1933. Married Carolyn Agger, 1935, no children. Died: April 5, 1982, Washington, D.C.

*Career Data* Professor, Yale Law School, 1933. Assistant Director, Securities and Exchange Commission, 1934–39. Counsel, Public Works Administration, 1939–40. Counsel, Department of the Interior, 1939–42, Undersecretary, 1942–46. Private practice, 1947–65, 1969–82.

*Supreme Court Data* Nominated by Lyndon B. Johnson on July 28, 1965, to replace Justice Arthur J. Goldberg, who resigned. Resigned May 14, 1969.

After law school, Fortas remained in New Haven to teach for a year and then left for Washington, where he held a series of governmental appointments over the next decade. Fortas left government for private practice and founded what would become one of Washington's most powerful law firms, Arnold, Fortas, and Porter. One of his clients was Lyndon B. Johnson, who became a close friend, and Fortas became one of Johnson's closest advisers. Johnson tried to name Fortas attorney general, but he declined. When Johnson asked Justice

Arthur Goldberg to resign to become U.N. ambassador, it was in part to open a seat for Fortas. Over Fortas's opposition, Johnson nominated him.

Fortas brought to the Court a reputation as a fierce fighter for civil rights and individual liberty. This showed in his opinions during his short stay on the Court. He was especially interested in the rights of juvenile criminal defendants. But at the same time Fortas wanted to keep his foot in the political ring and was probably the most political of modern justices. He acted as both an adviser and a political agent for President Johnson, and his activities angered many conservatives on Capitol Hill. Eventually it led to Fortas's undoing.

In 1968, Chief Justice Earl Warren announced he would retire. Johnson wanted to elevate Fortas. But conservative opponents trying to prevent this dug up dirt on the justice, including that, in violation of federal law, he was paid $15,000 to teach a course at a law school. Then it was revealed that he had accepted a $20,000 check from a charitable foundation controlled by the family of an indicted stock manipulator. His opponents started calling for Fortas's impeachment. Fortas instead quickly resigned and returned to private practice in Washington until his death in 1982.

## Thurgood Marshall, 1967–1991

*Personal Data* Born: July 2, 1908, Baltimore, Maryland. Education: graduated Lincoln University, A.B. 1930; Howard University Law School, LL.B. 1933. Married Vivian Burey, 1929, two children; married Cecelia Suryat, 1955, no children. Still living.
*Career Data* Practiced law, 1934–40. Counsel, NAACP Legal Defense and Education Fund. Judge, Circuit Court of Appeals, 1961–65. U.S. Solicitor General, 1965–67.
*Supreme Court Data* Nominated by Lyndon B. Johnson on June 13, 1967, to replace Justice Tom C. Clark, who retired. Retired, June 23, 1991.

For more than two decades after law school, Marshall was probably the foremost civil rights lawyer in the United States. As head of the NAACP Legal Defense and Education Fund, he argued such historic cases before the Supreme Court as *Brown* v. *Board of Education*. In 1961, Marshall was appointed by President Kennedy to the Second Circuit Court of Appeals, but southern Democratic senators held his confirmation hostage for almost a full year. After four years on the appeals court, Marshall was named solicitor general by Lyndon Johnson and two years later, Johnson selected Marshall as the first black justice.

In case after case, Marshall sought to advance individual liberties. But a hallmark of his many opinions is that almost all are narrow, not broad and dramatic. They feature a balancing of issues, a search for the narrow line between competing interests. At times Marshall has sided with government and law enforcement, surprising his colleagues. But as the Court became more conservative under Chief Justices Burger and Rehnquist, Marshall saw himself part of a shrinking minority. His dissents became bitter and more personal. Finally, with the retirement of William Brennan, the fire seemed to leave Marshall and he retired after the next term.

## Warren Earl Burger, 1969–1986

*Personal Data* Born: September 17, 1907, St. Paul, Minnesota. Education: attended the University of Minnesota, 1925–27; graduated St. Paul College of Law, LL.B. 1931. Married Elvera Stromberg, 1933, two children. Still living.
*Career Data* Practiced law, 1931–53. Assistant U.S. Attorney General, 1953–56. Judge, U.S. Court of Appeals, 1956–69.
*Supreme Court Data* Nominated Chief Justice by Richard Nixon on May 21, 1969, to replace Chief Justice Earl Warren, who retired. Retired September 26, 1986.

Burger worked his way through a night law school as a salesman. After graduation, with honors, he joined a local law firm, where he practiced until 1953. He also became involved in Republican politics, and through his political contacts came to Washington in 1953 to serve as assistant attorney general in charge of the Justice Department's civil division. Three years later he was named to the U.S. Court of Appeals for the District of Columbia. There he earned a reputation as a conservative and as an activist for reform of the federal courts. Burger was not well known outside legal circles, and his nomination as Chief Justice shocked Washington. But he was quickly confirmed.

Burger ended up serving seventeen years as Chief Justice. His tenure will likely go down in history as one of the most important eras in Court history. He himself is a moderate conservative, and as such he began to lead a retreat from the expansive positions taken by the Warren Court. While a staunch defender of First Amendment rights, especially freedom of speech and the press, Burger had markedly less sympathy for those claiming expanded individual rights, and he especially tried to restrict the expansions of rights said to be constitutionally protected. He also led a movement to sharply curtail the rights of criminal defendants, which had been greatly expanded under the Warren Court. But his most important ruling might have been the one that caused the downfall of the man who appointed him. In *United States* v. *Nixon*, Burger required the president to turn over the White House tape recordings to the Watergate special prosecutor.

Since his resignation, Burger chaired the commission that planned the Constitution's bicentennial celebration in 1987, and the Bill of Rights celebration in 1991. (For an expanded view of the Burger Court, see pages 114–119.)

## Harry Andrew Blackmun, 1970–

*Personal Data* Born: November 12, 1908, Nashville, Illinois. Education: graduated Harvard University, B.A. 1929; Harvard Law School, LL.B. 1932. Married Dorothy Clark, 1941, three children. Still living.
*Career Data* Clerk, Circuit Court of Appeals, 1932–33. Practiced law,

1934–50. Counsel, Mayo Clinic, 1950–59. Judge, Eighth Circuit Court of Appeals, 1959–70.

*Supreme Court Data* Nominated by Richard Nixon on April 14, 1970, to replace Justice Abe Fortas, who resigned. Still serving.

Blackmun grew up in Minnesota, where his closest friend in grade school was Warren Burger. He went on an academic scholarship to Harvard, where he graduated with the highest average possible in mathematics. He chose law school over medical school, and after graduation he returned to St. Paul where he clerked on the court of appeals before entering private practice with a Minneapolis law firm. He remained there for sixteen years before becoming counsel at the Mayo Clinic. In 1959 he was named to the Eighth Circuit Court of Appeals, where he gained an instant reputation for his scholarly opinions.

In 1970, President Richard Nixon was having major problems filling the seat of Justice Abe Fortas. Nixon wanted a southerner, but the Senate had rejected his first two nominees, Judge Clement Haynsworth of South Carolina and Judge G. Harrold Carswell of Florida. So Nixon took Chief Justice Burger's advice and nominated his old friend, who was quickly confirmed.

He and Burger quickly became known as the Court's "Minnesota Twins," because they always voted alike. But the two split in the Court's landmark 1973 *Roe* v. *Wade* abortion ruling, which Blackmun authored and on which Burger dissented. From this point on Blackmun became more liberal, to the disappointment of the Chief Justice.

## Lewis Franklin Powell, Jr., 1971–1987

*Personal Data* Born: September 19, 1907, Suffolk, Virginia. Education: graduated Washington and Lee University, B.S. 1929; Washington and Lee University Law School, LL.B. 1931; Harvard Law School, LL.M. 1932. Married Josephine Rucker, 1936, four children. Still living.

*Career Data* Practiced law, 1932–71. President, American Bar Association, 1964–65.

*Supreme Court Data* Nominated by Richard Nixon on October 21, 1971, to replace Hugo L. Black, who retired. Retired June 26, 1987. Still living.

After getting a master's degree in law from Harvard, Powell returned to Richmond, where he joined one of the city's oldest law firms. In almost forty years of practice, Powell rose to managing partner and served a term as president of the American Bar Association and a decade as head of the local school board and the Virginia State Board of Education. He had acquired a reputation as a moderate, which appealed to Richard Nixon who nominated him to the Supreme Court in 1971.

Powell is the only modern justice to come to the Court from a career as a practicing lawyer. As a lawyer often does, he sought to find compromise and middle ground. Soon after taking his seat, Powell developed into the intellectual center of the Court, a position he never relinquished. Not surprising from a lawyer who represented big business for three decades, his decisions expanded the rights of business and state control. He was hard on criminal defendants, but a moderate in the area of civil rights and individual rights. Above all he was pragmatic—one example of which was his opinion in *California Board of Regents* v. *Bakke* (1978), in which he ruled against rigid race-based quotas in admission to professional schools, but allowed race as one of a number of factors for admission. For many of his years on the Court his was the swing vote, including the controversial abortion decision, *Roe* v. *Wade* (1973).

William Hubbs Rehnquist, 1971–

*Personal Data* Born: October 1, 1924, Milwaukee, Wisconsin. Education: graduated Stanford University, B.A. 1948, M.A. 1948; Harvard University, M.A. 1950; Stanford University Law School, LL.B. 1952. Married Natalie Cornell, 1953, three children. Still living.
*Career Data* Clerk to Justice Robert H. Jackson, 1952–53. Practiced law, 1954–69. Assistant U.S. Attorney General, Office of Legal Counsel, 1969–71. *Supreme Court Data* Nominated by Richard Nixon on October 21, 1971, to replace Justice John Marshall Harlan, who retired. Elevated to Chief Justice by Ronald Reagan on June 20, 1986. Still serving.

After World War II service in the Air Force, Rehnquist entered Stanford University, earning both a B.A. and an M.A., and then a second master's from Harvard before returning to Stanford, where he graduated at the top of his law school class. After clerking, he moved to Phoenix, Arizona, to begin law practice and to work in Republican state politics. In 1964, Rehnquist worked on Barry Goldwater's presidential campaign and became close to a number of top Republican political operatives. One was Richard G. Kleindienst, who five years later as Richard Nixon's deputy attorney general, brought Rehnquist to Washington to head the Office of Legal Counsel. In that position, Rehnquist became the point man for the administration on Capitol Hill in all legal matters. In 1971, Nixon surprised most of Washington by nominating Rehnquist to the Supreme Court, despite his lack of judicial experience.

Over the next fifteen years, Rehnquist developed a reputation as the Burger Court's most conservative member. As an associate justice he almost always decided conflicts between an individual and the government in favor of the government, and conflicts between the states and the federal government in favor of the states. He was especially vigorous in expanding the rights of law enforcement and limiting the rights of defendants and the accused.

When Rehnquist was elevated by Ronald Reagan in 1986, a major battle in the Senate ensued, questioning his views on civil rights and his role in Republican harassing of black voters in Phoenix during the early 1960s. The result was that while he was confirmed, it was with more negative votes than any other successful Supreme Court nominee had received in over a hundred years.

As Chief Justice, Rehnquist started presiding over a sharply divided Court. This remained true, through the 1991–92 term, even as more liberal justices have been replaced by justices as conservative as he. (For a fuller examination of the Rehnquist Court, see pages 120–22.)

## John Paul Stevens, 1975–

*Personal Data* Born: April 20, 1920, Chicago, Illinois. Education: graduated University of Chicago, B.A. 1941; Northwestern University School of Law, J.D. 1947. Married Elizabeth Sheeren, 1942, four children; married Maryan Simon, 1980, no children. Still living.

*Career Data* Clerk to Justice Wiley B. Rutledge, 1947–48. Practiced law, 1949–70. Judge, Circuit Court of Appeals, 1970–75.

*Supreme Court Data* Nominated by Gerald R. Ford on November 28, 1975, to replace Justice William O. Douglas, who retired. Still serving.

After clerking for Supreme Court Justice Wiley B. Rutledge, Stevens returned to Chicago and a position at a prominent Chicago law firm. Quickly, he developed a reputation as an innovative antitrust expert, and within three years had started his own law firm, Rothschild, Stevens, Barry, and Myers. He remained there until his appointment by President Nixon in 1970 to the Seventh Circuit Court of Appeals. There he developed a scholarly reputation and was a popular choice to replace the retiring William O. Douglas.

Stevens is another of the justices who has adopted a centerist position, and as such has not had the visibility of some of his colleagues. His entire tenure has been marked by his independence, and his willingness to go it alone in a dissent or a concurring opinion if he does not agree with the majority. His moderate position has changed little, but he has found himself shifted from the philosophical right to the left as the Court has become more conservative. He has developed a reputation as a hard-working justice, one who produces a large number of finely crafted opinions.

## Sandra Day O'Connor, 1981–

*Personal Data* Born: March 26, 1930, El Paso, Texas. Education: graduated Stanford University, B.A. 1950, LL.B. 1952. Married John O'Connor, 1952, three children. Still living.

*Career Data* Deputy County Attorney, San Mateo, California, 1952–53. Lawyer, U.S. Army, 1954–57. Private practice, 1957–65. Assistant Attorney General, Arizona, 1965–69. Member, State Senate, 1969–75. Judge, County Superior Court, 1975–79. Judge, Arizona Court of Appeals, 1979–81.

*Supreme Court Data* Nominated by Ronald Reagan on August 19, 1981, to replace Justice Potter Stewart, who retired. Still serving.

At Stanford Law School, Sandra Day met her future husband, John J. O'Connor, and William Rehnquist. After law school, despite an outstanding academic record, she had difficulty finding a job. So she became a deputy county attorney in San Mateo, California, supporting her husband who still had to finish school. When he did, he had a military service obligation, so he joined the army and the O'Connors left for Germany, where Sandra Day worked as a civilian attorney. Upon returning from the army, the O'Connors settled in Phoenix, and for the next eight years, Sandra Day O'Connor raised her children and practiced law on both a full- and part-time basis.

In 1965 O'Connor became assistant attorney general of Arizona. Four years later she was elected to the State Senate as a Republican. During her six years in the Senate, she became the first woman in America ever to hold the leadership position in a state legislative body. In 1974 she decided she wanted to be a judge, and won election to the superior court of Maricopa County. She served for five years and was becoming a favorite to run for governor. The Democratic incumbent, Bruce Babbitt—possibly looking at his own re-election chances—named her to the Arizona Court of Appeals. She was sitting on that court when Ronald Reagan named her the first woman justice on the Supreme Court.

O'Connor brought to the Court a conservative political philosophy and a deep-seated belief that courts should interpret, not make, law. In her early years on the Burger Court, she stayed in the background, a reliable vote for the emerging conservative majority. On the Rehnquist Court, she has generally moved in lockstep with the activist conservative majority formed by her Arizona colleague. She is especially passionate about states' rights, perhaps because she is the only justice in many

years to have been a state legislator. But while remaining a rock-solid law-and-order proponent in criminal cases, and very willing to limit First Amendment rights, O'Connor remains independent on some issues like women's rights, including reproductive rights. She became something of a swing vote on the Court, and in several major decisions her vote pushed the Chief Justice and his more conservative colleagues into the minority. As new arrivals have pushed the Court further to the right, O'Connor has emerged as something of a centerist on the Court.

## Antonin Scalia, 1986–

*Personal Data* Born: March 11, 1936, Trenton, New Jersey. Education: graduated Georgetown University, A.B. 1957; Harvard Law School, LL.B. 1960. Married Maureen McCarthy, 1960, nine children. Still living.

*Career Data* Practiced law, 1960–68, 1978–82. Professor, University of Virginia Law School, 1968–71; University of Chicago, 1978–82. Counsel, White House Office of Telecommunications Policy, 1971–72. Chairman, Administrative Conference of the United States, 1972–74. Assistant U.S. Attorney General, 1974–77. Judge, U.S. Court of Appeals, 1982–86.

*Supreme Court Data* Nominated by President Ronald Reagan on June 24, 1986, to replace Justice William Rehnquist, who was elevated to Chief Justice. Still serving.

After Scalia graduated from Harvard Law School, he spent seven years in private practice in Cleveland. He then went to teach at the University of Virginia Law School. When Richard Nixon was elected, Scalia came to Washington and served in a series of administration jobs including assistant attorney general, Office of Legal Counsel, a post previously held by William H. Rehnquist. When Jimmy Carter came in, Scalia returned to teaching law at the University of Chicago Law School. From there he was named to the Court of Appeals by Ronald Reagan in 1982, and four years later to the Supreme Court.

Scalia has become the most quirky justice on the Rehnquist Court. On the one hand he is unquestionably its most conservative legal thinker, clearly the intellectual heart of the conservative Court's right wing. But at the same time he can also be its most independent member. More than any justice in recent times, he is prone to writing long, complicated, concurring opinions when he believes in the conclusion reached by the majority, but not its reasoning. At the same time, his complex legal reasoning often becomes almost libertarian, and he reaches what seems on the surface to be surprising "liberal" results.

Anthony McLeod Kennedy, 1988–

*Personal Data* Born: July 23, 1936, Sacramento, California. Education: graduated Stanford University, A.B. 1958; London School of Economics, 1959; Harvard Law School, J.D. 1963. Married Mary Davis, 1963, three children. Still living.
*Career Data* Practiced law, 1961–75.

Judge, U.S. Court of Appeals, 1976–88.
*Supreme Court Data* Nominated by Ronald Reagan on November 30, 1987, to replace Justice Lewis F. Powell, who retired. Still serving.

After graduating from law school, Kennedy began to practice in San Francisco. But he returned home to Sacramento the next year to take over his father's practice upon his death. Practicing in the state capital, and being involved in Republican politics, brought Kennedy to the attention of California's governor, Ronald Reagan. Reagan recommended Kennedy to fill a seat on the Ninth Circuit Court of Appeals in 1976. He served on that Court for a dozen years before Ronald Reagan reached the White House and nominated Kennedy to the Supreme Court.

In his first years on the Court, Kennedy has adopted the lowest of profiles. Moderately conservative, on the Rehnquist Court he has staked out a position at the center and has rarely taken controversial positions.

David Hackett Souter, 1990–

*Personal Data* Born Melrose, Massachusetts, September 17, 1939. Education: graduated Harvard University, A.B. 1961; Rhodes Scholar, Oxford University, 1962–63, Harvard University Law School, LL.B. 1966; Oxford University, M.A. 1989. Never married. Still living.
*Career Data* Practiced law, 1966–68. Assistant Attorney General of New Hampshire, 1968–71; Deputy Attorney

General, 1971–76; Attorney General, 1976–78. Judge, Superior Court of New Hampshire, 1978–83. Judge, New Hampshire Supreme Court, 1983–90. Judge, U.S. Court of Appeals, 1990.

*Supreme Court Data* Nominated by George Bush on October 9, 1990, to replace Justice William Brennan, who resigned. Still serving.

After graduating from law school, Souter returned to his home in Concord, New Hampshire, and practiced law with a local firm for two years. From there he went to the state attorney general's office, where he stayed for the next fifteen years, first as an assistant attorney general, then deputy attorney general, and finally attorney general. From there he accepted a seat on the state bench. After five years he was elevated to the state Supreme Court, where he served for six years. In 1990, George Bush, on the recommendation of his chief-of-staff, former New Hampshire Governor John Sununu, appointed Souter to the Court of Appeals. Only months later, Bush shocked the legal community by elevating Souter to the Supreme Court.

At the time of his appointment, Souter was called the "stealth justice" because he was so little known—perhaps the most obscure choice ever for the Supreme Court. But despite this lack of a public record on where he stood on most issues, he was quickly confirmed. In his first year on the Court, Souter remained in the background, authoring few significant opinions, and giving the appearance of a low-keyed justice who could be counted on to rarely stray from the conservative fold. But to the surprise of many, in his second term, Souter gradually emerged as a genuine intellectual force in the center of the Court— a balance to Scalia on the right. To many observers, Souter seems to be staking out a role for himself as the centrist conscience of the Court; a role much like that played for many years by Justice Lewis Powell until his retirement in 1987.

## Clarence Thomas, 1991–

*Personal Data* Born: June 23, 1948 Savannah, Georgia. Education: graduated Holy Cross College, A.B. 1971; Yale Law School, J.D. 1974. Married Virginia Lamp, 1987, one child. Still living.

*Career Data* Assistant Attorney General of Missouri, 1974–77. Staff Attorney, Monsanto Company, 1977–79. Assistant to Senator John Danforth, R–MO, 1979–81. Counsel, Civil Rights Office of Department of Education, 1981–82. Chairman, U.S. Equal Employment Opportunity Commission, 1982–90. Judge, U.S. Court of Appeals, 1990–91.

*Supreme Court Data* Nominated by George Bush on October 23, 1991, to replace Justice Thurgood Marshall, who retired. Still serving.

After graduating from Yale, Thomas was hired by then Missouri Attorney General John Danforth as an assistant. After two years in corporate law, Thomas followed Danforth to Washington after he had been elected to the Senate. Two years later he joined the Civil Rights Office in the Education Department, and then in 1982 was selected to head the Equal Employment Opportunity Commission (EEOC). His tenure there was controversial amid charges that he did not support affirmative action programs. In 1990 he was appointed to the appeals court by George Bush, and then almost immediately to the Supreme Court.

Because of his ultraconservative views and his stormy tenure at the EEOC, Thomas's confirmation was not easy. Just before the nomination was to go to a vote, the public hearings had to be reopened to air charges that the nominee was guilty of sexual harassment of a former aide. In the end, in what became the bitterest confirmation battle of this century, Thomas was confirmed by a two-vote majority. In his first term on the Court, Thomas's votes have all reflected his ultraconservative views.

# 6.

# Justices Denied

*[The President] shall nominate, and by and with the Advice and Consent of the Senate, shall appoint . . . Judges of the supreme court."*

*Article II, Section 2*

On three occasions since 1968, the Senate has rejected a president's choice for Supreme Court justice; on two other occasions the president has had to withdraw his choice; and one nominee faced a bitter and prolonged confirmation that resulted in his approval by the narrowest of margins. In all cases except the withdrawal of the nomination of Justice Abe Fortas to be Chief Justice in 1968—the defeats of Judges Clement F. Haynesworth in 1969, G. Harrold Carswell in 1970, and Robert Bork in 1987; the withdrawal of the nomination of Judge Douglas Ginsburg in 1987, and the fight over the nomination of Clarence Thomas in 1991—the nominees were conservatives and their opposition a liberal amalgam. Conservatives have reacted to these contentious confirmations by charging that their liberal opponents have somehow perverted and made a mockery of the system. They charge that the only legitimate inquiry into a Supreme Court nominee should be as to his or her competence, intellect, judicial temperament, and moral character. But in point of fact, these confirmation proceedings were not aberrations; rather, they were more like throwbacks to an earlier congressional age. Factors outside the mere competence and ability of the individual have always played a major role in the selection and confirmation of Supreme Court justices, and there is every indication that that is precisely what the Founding Fathers intended.

Before this series of rejections, starting when Justice Fortas was filibustered out of his elevation to the center chair in 1968, the previous Supreme Court nominee to be rejected had been Judge John Parker in 1930. Previous to Parker, the most recent rejections had been almost forty years earlier—the two nominees of President Cleveland in 1893, William Hornblower and Wheeler Peckham. Given the fact that prior to 1968 there had been only one rejection in the previous eighty years, it is easy to understand how people had forgotten how the confirmation process had always worked, when examples could be found only in history texts.

Going back to the debates of the Constitutional Convention, it appears that the idea of having the executive nominate judges, and the legislative then confirm or reject them, was Alexander Hamilton's. As the delegates debated the new High Court, there ended up on the table four competing proposals on judicial selection: by the president alone, by both houses of Congress, by the Senate alone, and Hamilton's compromise that eventually carried the day.

In his Federalist Papers Nos. 76 and 77, Hamilton wrote extensively on this power to advise and consent that was being given to the Senate. He indicated that the Framers realized completely that nomination would be rejected by the Senate, and that they found this concept appealing. "If by influencing the President be meant restraining him," Hamilton wrote in Federalist No. 77, "this is precisely what must have been intended."

When the drafters of the new Constitution went back to their home states to argue its adoption, many brought up the Senate's advise and consent function as a major reason why the document should be accepted. James Iredell of North Carolina, a signer and eventual Supreme Court justice himself, made such a presentation to his home state's ratification convention. "As to offices," Iredell told his home state gathering, "the Senate has no other influences but a restraint on improper appointments. The President proposes such a man for such an office. The Senate has to consider upon it. If they think him improper, the President must nominate another, whose appointment ultimately again depends upon the Senate."

Actually, totaling Supreme Court rejections is a bit difficult. If you look at the number of straight up and down no votes on the Senate floor, only eleven nominees have been rejected after full votes. But more often, especially in the early and the mid-nineteenth century, the Senate would reject a nominee simply by ignoring the nomination, not acting upon it until either the president got the message and submitted another name, or the president's term expired and his successor submitted a new nominee. In one case—Edward King—the Senate twice rejected the same man. In two cases, persons were rejected to later be renominated and eventually confirmed. What follows is probably the most generally accepted tabulation of rejections. It shows that between 1789 and 1894, the Senate rejected about a quarter of all nominees—twenty-one of the first eighty-one. Overall, through 1991, the Senate has rejected, or forced a president to withdraw, a total of twenty-eight nominees.

The list of twenty-eight nominees does not take into consideration some of the epic confirmation battles of the past in which nominees ended up being confirmed. In this category you have to include the classic confirmation hearing of Brandeis in 1916, as well as Trimble in 1826 and Matthews in 1882, and more recently Stone in 1925 and Frankfurter in 1939.

One thing that should be understood is that the confirmation process today is vastly different from the way it was in the past. The holding of elaborate confirmation hearings is a very recent innovation. For much of this country's history, Supreme Court nominations were either taken directly to the Senate floor and voted up or down, often on the same day as they were received, or were quickly reviewed in caucus. In later years, with the start of the formal committee structure, when Judiciary Committee hearings were ordered, the nominees never appeared in person. At most, a nominee would send a letter or a telegram to the committee stating his background and views. To interrogate a potential justice was considered out of the question.

The first recorded instance of a nominee personally appearing before a confirmation hearing occurred in 1925, with the nomination of Harlan Fiske Stone by President Coolidge. Stone was initially approved by the Judiciary Committee without appearing, and his nomination was sent to the Senate floor. There it was blocked on a point of personal privilege by Senator Burton Wheeler of Montana. The matter was recommitted to the Judiciary Committee, and Stone was granted the right to appear in person to answer charges that had been raised by Wheeler. In the end he was easily confirmed.

After Stone's appearance the Senate reverted to its traditional practice of not having personal appearances by nominees. In 1930, during the hotly contested confirmation of Judge John J. Parker, the nominee demanded that he be allowed to testify in person so he could protect his reputation.

## Supreme Court Nominations Rejected or Withdrawn

| Nominee | Year | Nominated By | Action |
|---------|------|--------------|--------|
| John Rutledge | 1795 | Washington | Withdrawn |
| Alexander Wolcott | 1811 | Madison | Rejected |
| John Crittenden | 1828 | Adams | None |
| Roger B. Taney* | 1835 | Jackson | None |
| John Spenser | 1844 | Tyler | Rejected |
| Reuben Walworth | 1844 | Tyler | Withdrawn |
| Edward King | 1844 | Tyler | None |
| Edward King* | 1845 | Tyler | Withdrawn |
| John Read | 1845 | Tyler | None |
| George Woodward | 1845 | Polk | Rejected |
| Edward Bradford | 1852 | Fillmore | None |
| George Badger | 1853 | Fillmore | None |
| William Micou | 1853 | Fillmore | None |
| Jeremiah Black | 1861 | Buchanan | Rejected |
| Henry Stanbery | 1866 | Johnson | None |
| Ebenezer Hoar | 1869 | Grant | Rejected |
| George Williams | 1873 | Grant | Withdrawn |
| Caleb Cushing | 1874 | Grant | Withdrawn |
| Stanley Matthews* | 1881 | Hayes | None |
| William Hornblower | 1893 | Cleveland | Rejected |
| Wheeler Peckham | 1894 | Cleveland | Rejected |
| John Parker | 1930 | Hoover | Rejected |
| Abe Fortas* | 1968 | Johnson | Withdrawn |
| Homer Thornberry | 1968 | Johnson | None |
| Clement Haynsworth | 1969 | Nixon | Rejected |
| G. Harrold Carswell | 1970 | Nixon | Rejected |
| Robert Bork | 1987 | Reagan | Withdrawn |
| Douglas Ginsburg | 1987 | Reagan | Withdrawn |

*Taney and Matthews were later renominated and confirmed. King was nominated for a second time and President Tyler was forced to withdraw him a second time. Fortas, a sitting justice, was rejected when nominated for chief justice.

The committee refused, saying that he could make his arguments in writing.

The modern tradition of personal appearances started with Felix

Frankfurter in 1939. Frankfurter's nomination was controversial. He was attacked before the Judiciary Committee as being too radical, and on the basis of his Jewish faith. The committee asked the nominee to appear and to subject himself to questions. He refused at first. But eventually he did appear, accompanied by his own lawyer, Dean Acheson. He read a short prepared statement, refused to answer any questions about his views on the issues of the day, and would only confirm his belief in America and its institutions. But the appearance began a tradition, and most nominees since then have appeared for personal questioning.

But these appearances have usually been quite perfunctory, and the committee members considered it impropritious to ask nominees about their specific views, let alone how they might be expected to vote in a hypothetical situation. That kind of questioning started in 1959, with the confirmation of Potter Stewart. In his hearing Stewart was questioned—gently—about his views on past Supreme Court decisions, his own judicial philosophy, and issues that the Court would likely be facing in the future. Since 1959, this kind of questioning has become a fixture of confirmation hearings, and various nominees have responded differently. Some have given detailed answers. Other have resorted to generalities and have avoided specifics. A few have flatly refused to answer such questions.

There is still disagreement over what confirmation hearings have become, and even whether nominees should appear. Constitutional Scholar and Harvard Law Professor Paul Freud, writing in the *Harvard Law Review* in 1959 after the confirmation of Justice Stewart, questioned not only the propriety of detailed questioning of nominees but the propriety of their appearing in person before the Judiciary Committee at all. In the wake of the controversy surrounding the Bork confirmation in 1987, the Twentieth Century Fund put together a blue ribbon panel—including some of the leaders of the opposition to Bork—to consider what confirmation hearings have become. They concluded that the process has gotten out of hand. The panel said that hearings have become "too visible and attract too much publicity," and that they are now being used "for other purposes ranging from self-promotion to mobilizing special-interest groups in order to influence public opinion." The panel questioned the appearance and detailed questioning of nominees.

But in fact, if anything, the confirmation hearings that followed the release of this report—David Souter's in 1990 and Clarence Thomas's in 1991—have drawn even more attention to the process. And a new watershed might have been reached in the aftermath of the Thomas hearings.

For the first time, certainly in modern times, political careers of senators have fallen depending on how they voted for the nominee. Illinois Democratic Senator Alan Dixon was defeated in his party's primary by a black woman who used Dixon's vote for Thomas as a major campaign issue. In Pennsylvania, Senator Arlen Specter found his defense of Thomas, and his rough handling of witness Anita Hill, as the leading issues in his campaign for reelection.

The Bork rejection began a debate that still rages among constitutional scholars and Court historians. Bork's supporters charged during the hearings, and after, that his opponents had changed the dynamic of the confirmation process by—for the first time—rejecting a nominee because of his ideology. As their argument goes, the only time in the past that ideology was a major issue in a confirmation was in the Brandeis struggle in 1916. And, say the Bork supporters, when Brandeis's opponents realized what was happening, they backed off, resulting in his eventual confirmation.

In a highly regarded 1985 book on the history of the Court, *God Save This Honorable Court*, Harvard Professor Lawrence Tribe wrote: "The simple truth is that the upper house of Congress has been scrutinizing Supreme Court nominees and rejecting them on the basis of their political, judicial, and economic philosophies ever since George Washington was president."

Examining the history of the confirmation process, Tribe selected six widely spaced rejections to prove his thesis: John Rutledge in 1795, John Crittenden in 1829, George Woodward in 1846, Jeremiah Black in 1861, Caleb Cushing in 1874, and John Parker in 1930. In a detailed examination of each case, Tribe came to the conclusion that ideology played a dominant role in the defeat of each nominee, and this proves conclusively that what happened in the Bork confirmation was not new or novel.

This debate turns on some very fine distinctions: the difference between politics and ideology, and between partisan and philosophical grounds. Those making the argument that the Bork hearings changed the basic equation readily admit that politics has always played a role in the rejection of Court nominees. But they charge that the Senate crossed an impermissible boundary by rejecting Bork, not because he was a Republican and the Senate majority were Democrats, or because they wanted to put a president of the other party in his place, but because of his beliefs and his philosophy.

Stanford University Professor David J. Danelski is an advocate of the position that the Bork confirmation marked a seminal change. He took on

Professor Tribe directly, attempting to show that the real cause of Senate rejection in at least five of the six instances that Tribe selected for his book were for reasons other than ideology. In a nutshell, here are the arguments advanced by Tribe and Danelski in the six specific cases:

• *Rutledge*. The long accepted theory for Rutledge's rejection—recounted by Tribe—was his vociferous objection to the Jay Treaty combined with his petulant previous refusal to serve as an associate justice because he thought that he, and not Jay, should have been Chief Justice. If he was rejected on the basis of his opposition to the treaty, on his ideology, then this alone would seem to be proof that the Framers intended that ideology play a central role in the confirmation process, since many of those who drafted the Constitution were sitting in the Senate that rejected Rutledge. Danelski, however, recounts evidence that what really led to Rutledge's rejection was a concern that he was mentally unstable, and that he was not worthy of the high office because he had led a number of "intemperate" and "wild" antigovernment demonstrations. The fact that he was unstable, says Danelski, was shown in the fact that he attempted suicide the day after the Senate rejected him.

• *Crittenden*. Tribe ascribes the defeat of Crittenden's nomination in 1829 (the Senate's refusal to vote on it before Adams's term expired) to the fact that his Whig views of federal supremacy were at odds with the new Jacksonian democracy. Not so, argues Danelski. He believes that simple party politics were at work. He cites a letter to the nominee from Henry Clay, in which Clay tells Crittenden that if he is rejected he should not take it personally, that it will be "entirely on party ground[s] and ought, therefore, to occasion you no mortification."

• *Woodward*. Tribe and other historians have long believed Woodward's rejection was based on his support of what was then called the American Nativist agenda, which centered on limits to immigration and discrimination against certain ethnic groups. But Danelski says the reasons for Woodward's rejection were purely political. He quotes Polk's diary as showing the president thought his nominee had been defeated by Senate Whigs and six Democrats who were trying to put him in his place, and because of the negative intervention of his secretary of state, James Buchanan, who was mad because he had not been consulted in Woodward's choice.

• *Black*. Tribe acknowledges that some of the opposition to Black in 1861 came from Republicans who thought the seat should remain vacant for Lincoln to fill once he had been inaugurated. But Tribe supports the theory that the main reason that Black was defeated was philosophical: he opposed the outright abolition of slavery. Danelski again believes the basic reason for the rejection was completely political. He quotes Black's biographer, William Brigance, as saying that the Senate was controlled by radical Republicans who would not have confirmed any Democrat under any circumstances.

• *Cushing.* Tribe argues that Cushing's nomination was defeated because of Senate concern about his views on slavery and because "he was too quick to change his political stripes to suit the times." Danelski quotes historians as agreeing that Cushing had spent years making deep personal enemies, and that they joined together to defeat his nomination. The rejection, argues Danelski, was personal and not philosophical.

• *Parker.* Danelski acknowledges that Parker was rejected basically on ideological grounds—some senators opposed the conservative economic decisions of the Court and thought that Parker would add to the majority that was deciding them; racial organizations were against him because they thought his views racist; labor organizations thought him antilabor. But Danelski argues that if Parker is an example of ideological rejection, he is a poor precedent because it was later acknowledged that he was neither racist nor antilabor, and that he went on to have a distinguished career on the appeals court bench.

While Tribe argues that ideological rejection of nominees has been continual and goes all the way back to Rutledge, and Danelski counters that Parker may be the only pre-Bork example of an ideological rejection, other scholars take a middle ground. Some see ideology coming into the process in the fight over Justice Stanley Matthews's confirmation in 1881, or the rejection of the two Cleveland nominees—Hornblower and Peckham—in 1893–94. But most agree that ideology has played a role in many confirmation hearings in this century.

Two changes have also contributed to the altered character of confirmation proceedings. The roles of Congress and the president within our governmental system have largely been reversed. For the first hundred years of the Republic, it was Congress that held the bulk of power. In the twentieth century, that power has shifted to the executive branch. In most of the early and middle history of this nation, presidents were forced to take seriously the "advice" portion of the confirmation function. Presidents would actively work with the Senate to arrive at an agreement on a nominee before the president ever sent the nomination to Capitol Hill. In those instances when a president didn't—Tyler is an example—their nominations were instantly in trouble. In this century, and certainly over the past fifty years, that advice function has largely been ignored. Presidents now choose nominees with little advanced regard for what members of the Senate might think, and then try to ram those nominations down the Senate's throat.

But perhaps more important, over the past forty years, and especially since 1970, Supreme Court nominees have been selected specifically, and in many cases solely, because of their philosophies. If that is the case, many observers ask, isn't it valid for the Senate to inquire about that which is the principal reason a president has made the choice?

In a major 1970 examination of the role of the Senate in the confirmation process published in the *Yale Law Review*,[1] Professor Charles L. Black, Jr., concluded:

> To me, there is just no reason at all for a Senator's not voting . . . on the basis of a full and unrestricted review . . . of a nominee's fitness for the office. . . . A Senator properly may, or even at some times in duty must, vote against a nominee to the Court, on the ground that the nominee holds views which, when transposed into judicial decisions, are likely, in the Senator's judgment, to be very bad for the country. . . . I have seen nothing textual, nothing structural, nothing prudential, nothing historical, that tells against this view.

1. Black, "A Note on the Senatorial Consideration of Supreme Court Nominees, 79," *Yale Journal* 657 (1970). The article played an important role in the Senate's rejection of C. Harrold Carswell in 1970 after a copy of it was given to all senators. It also played a role in the Bork hearings, as an answer to critics who charged that what was happening was improper.

# 7.

# The Court and Its People

## The Court's Early Homes

It was well into the twentieth century before the Supreme Court acquired the magnificent marble home we are familiar with today. Before that, it had had many homes, from crowded courtrooms in various buildings, to several makeshift quarters in the Capitol, to the back rooms of more than one tavern or boardinghouse.

Its first brief home, in 1790, was the Royal Exchange Building at Broad and Water streets, in what is now the heart of New York City's financial district. New York was the nation's capital for only one year because members of Congress from the south were unhappy about the long trip. So it was decided to build a new capital at about the midpoint of the country—at the Maryland-Virginia border on the Potomac River—in what was then a combination of swampland and farms. It would take quite a few years before this new capital could be constructed, so it was decided to temporarily move south to Philadelphia.

The next year when the Court reconvened, it did so in Philadelphia, in the State House—which we now know as Independence Hall. This one building housed most of the government, so it was too crowded. The city of Philadelphia was building a new City Hall, and it was decided that, starting with the August 1791 term, the Court would move there, as would much of the rest of the federal government. The Court reassembled in the east wing of the new Philadelphia City Hall, but still under very crowded conditions. Part of the building housed the Congress. The Pennsylvania legislature and Philadelphia city offices were in another; in the same wing as the Supreme Court were also the state and municipal courts. The Supreme Court actually shared a courtroom with the local Mayor's Court; the plan was for that local court to go out of session when the Supreme Court was in session. But that didn't always work. On more than one occasion, the Supreme Court found that its courtroom was busy trying some local lawbreaker. It then was forced to wander around the building until it could find some available space. One Court term in 1795 was held in the Philadelphia Common Council's chamber. These all were less than prestigious locations for a Court struggling to establish its identity.

By 1800, enough of the new capital was ready in what was now called the city of Washington, in the District of Columbia. But things did not improve at all for the Court when it relocated. Actually, Congress had completely overlooked the Court when it planned the Capitol. As history has it, the Court's clerk arrived in Washington several weeks before the start of the new term and went to the Capitol and asked where the courtroom was. It was then that Congress realized its oversight, so on January 23, 1801, it passed an emergency resolution allowing the Court to meet in the Capitol. It was one of those "better said than done" kind of resolutions. Most of the Capitol was still unfinished, and only the north wing was ready. So a small 25 by 30-foot room in the basement was turned over to the Court. It would be the first of a number of homes for the Court in the Capitol.

The north wing of the Capitol was never really finished, and by 1807 the architect of the Capitol, Benjamin Latrobe, decided he had to finish the lower level of the wing. That meant moving the Court, and Latrobe suggested the House of Representatives library. That, however, was a major step backward for the Court. The room was even smaller than the one it had vacated, and the heating system left much to be desired. By February 1809 the justices had learned all they needed to know about their new quarters, and moved the Court's sessions to a room provided by Long's Tavern, located across the street from the Capitol at about the spot now occupied by the Library of Congress.

Apparently, meeting in a tavern did not greatly offend the justices, but it did Latrobe, the Capitol's architect. He went to President Madison and received permission to build a permanent Court chamber within the Capitol. He found space in the unfinished basement, directly under the Senate's new chambers. By the February 1810 term he had finished what was called the Hall of Justice. In comparison to what the justices had grown accustomed to, their new quarters were both stately and magnificent. They sat on a raised mahogany bench. In front of them there were tables for the lawyers arguing cases to sit and put their law books. There even was seating for spectators in a semicircle around the Court. Attending Court sessions became the thing to do for the ladies of Washington, and on more than one occasion, if a group of ladies arrived after a lawyer had started his argument, the always accommodating Chief Justice Marshall would ask the lawyer to start over.

These new quarters lasted but two years. Then came the War of 1812, the British capture of Washington, and the burning of the Capitol. Various accounts have British troops actually starting the fire in the Hall of Justice, using law books from the Court's small library. When the British fled leaving the White House and Capitol in ruins, Congress moved first to Blodgett's Hotel, the only building in town large enough to hold it. Construction was immediately started on a large structure to act as Congress's temporary home until the Capitol could be rebuilt. Called the Brick Capitol, it was completed by the time the Court met in 1813. This was the Court's home for two years; to relieve crowding in the building, the Court moved its sessions for the next two years to a private home that it leased.

By February 1817, the Capitol had been sufficiently restored to move back in. The only room that could be used by the Court was a tiny space in the north wing basement; it was the Court's official home for the next two years. But the area was so unappealing that most of the justices' work and conferences took place in the boardinghouse in which most of the justices rented quarters, and many of the arguments were heard in one local tavern or another. Finally in 1819, the Hall of Justice in the basement of the Capitol, under the Senate chamber, was rebuilt. Today the room, which still exists, is known as the Old Supreme Court Chamber. This was the courtroom that the justices occupied for the next forty-one years.

The Hall of Justice was certainly the best facility the Court had so far occupied, but it still left much to be desired. The courtroom was somewhere between difficult and impossible to find, for instance. On days when oral arguments were scheduled, guides had to be stationed at the entrances to the building to lead people through what was described as a "twisting labyrinth" of corridors and stairs that led to the courtroom. It was not unusual for lawyers to be late for their arguments because they had got lost between the entrance and the courtroom.

But the biggest problem continued to be space. While the justices had the courtroom with its raised bench, lawyers tables, and seating for a few dozen spectators, that's about all they had. There was one small room for the clerk, which was filled to overflowing. Thus much of the work of the Court—the justices' research, conferences, and so on—still had to take place outside of the Capitol, usually in the boardinghouses where the justices lived and then later, as some of the justices became more permanent residents, in the homes they maintained nearby or in Georgetown.

All during the 1850s, as their docket and work load began to increase rapidly, the justices were constantly complaining—quite rightfully—about the lack of work space in and around their courtroom. The Senate was in the process of building a new chamber for itself, so it was decided that, once it was ready, the Supreme Court would be given its old quarters on the first floor of the Capitol. After a year of renovations and construction, the Court occupied its new home for the first time in 1860.

Except for one two-month period in 1901, when the courtroom was being refurbished and the Court met in the Senate Judiciary Committee's hearing room, this was the Court's home for the next seventy-five years— or well into this century. It gave the Court the major thing it had lacked so far—work space—while at the same time added a sense of grandeur and dignity to the Court's proceedings that had been sorely lacking in its previous homes.

In the elaborately decorated courtroom, the justices sat behind an imposing mahogany bench, which sat atop a raised platform in front of an arched doorway with ten marble columns and topped by a gilded American eagle. The elevation allowed the justices to look down on the lawyers presenting arguments from the half-dozen lawyers tables spread out below. On one side were the desks of the clerk, the marshal, and other court officials. Behind the lawyers were spectator benches for about 100 visitors. Both the carpeting and the drapes were heavy and red, and the rear wall was decorated in busts of former justices.

Almost more important to the ever more complex operation of the Court were the dozen adjoining anterooms given over to the Court for its use. One room was used for the clerk's office, another as a combination robing room and dining room where the justices took their lunch. Still another room was used for the justices' conferences, and this room doubled as a small law library. But what was still missing were chambers for the individual justices. There was a small chamber for the Chief Justice, but the other justices—until the present Supreme Court building opened in 1935—continued to have to work out of their homes or apartments. That is where their clerks worked, and that is where each maintained his own law library. The justices would come into the Court to hear arguments, usually five days a week, and they would usually spend all day Saturday in conference. The rest of the time was spent at home working, with the justices often visiting one another in the evenings or on Sundays to discuss and argue cases.

Despite the relative splendor of their new quarters, at least as compared to the old Hall of Justice in the north wing basement, this lack of space still prevented the Court from fulfilling its ever growing twentieth-century role. William Howard Taft, with his life-long dream of becoming Chief Justice, was always a great champion of the Court. As early as 1912, when he became president, he began to prod Congress to build the Court its own building, to finally give it the room it really needed. The First World War interfered, and then Taft was gone. But when he became Chief Justice in 1921, Taft embarked on a one-man crusade to acquire a new home for the Court. His dream was finally realized in 1929, when Congress appropriated $9.7 million to acquire land and to design and build a new Court.

Having convinced Congress to build the Supreme Court its own home, Chief Justice Taft became almost obsessed with what it should look like. He named himself chairman of the committee overseeing its design, and the committee gave the commission for the building's design to famed architect Cass Gilbert, who was assisted by his son Cass Gilbert, Jr., and by architect John R. Rockart.

The site chosen was a plot of land just across First Street from the Capitol—actually the site of the old Brick Capitol that had served as the home of Congress after the British burned the Capitol in 1812. Today the building is bordered by Maryland Avenue to the north, Second Street to the east, and East Capitol to the south. It took two years to acquire the land and to finish the plans for the building.

Construction began with the laying of the cornerstone on October 13, 1932. Considering how hard he had worked to accomplish this, it is a shame that Taft never lived to see that day. He died in 1931. The cornerstone was laid by President Herbert Hoover and by Taft's successor, Charles Evans Hughes, who remembered Taft's dream and his years of work. "The Republic endures and this is the symbol of its faith," Hughes said that day. "This building is the result of his persistence."

Construction took another three years and, in the interim, the Court continued to meet in the Capitol. That courtroom, called today the Old Senate Chamber, has been lovingly restored, and can be seen by visitors to the Capitol. The last time it was used was the final day of the 1934 term. On October 7, 1935, the Court held session for the first time in its new building. In its 146th year of existence, the Supreme Court finally had a permanent home.

# The New Building

When architect Cass Gilbert delivered his original design for the new Supreme Court Building, he said the plan was for "a building of dignity and importance suitable for its use as a permanent home of the Supreme Court of the United States." He chose to build a stately edifice of classical Corinthian architecture that would blend with the Capitol and the nearby congressional buildings. He determined that the principal building material would be marble—all kinds of marble, from all over the world. When the final bills were paid, more than a third of the entire building cost, almost $3 million, went to buy marble.

From its west front to its east back, the building measures 385 feet. Its north-to-south dimension is 304 feet. At its tallest point, the building is 92 feet—four stories—above ground. Its exterior is done in the finest Vermont marble available. It took over 1,000 freight cars to haul this marble south from the quarries, and the shipments included one 250-ton solid piece that was used by sculptor James Fraser to carve the allegorical figures that tower over the building's front plaza.

The almost-square building is topped with a roof of cream-colored Roman tile, interspersed with bronze strips, all laid over lead-coated copper sitting on a slab of watertight concrete. The inside of the building is broken up by four interior open-air courtyards with small fountains, which are used in good weather by the Court's employees to eat lunch or just to get some sun. The exterior walls of these spaces are made of Georgian marble. A striking feature of the building's interior are two massive, self-supporting elliptical spiral stairways constructed of marble and bronze that connect the building's four floors. They are little used today, but are almost unique in the world. Only a few others like them exist: an original in the Vatican and copies in the Paris Opera and the Minnesota state legislature. Throughout most of the building, the floors, walls, and doors are done in American white, with accents of Honduras mahogany, Alabama marble, and brass. Public areas are separated from the private corridors and offices by gleaming bronze floor-to-ceiling latticework gates.

To enter the building through its formal main entrance, visitors ascend from the street level up a short flight of stairs, flanked by a pair of huge Vermont marble candelabra, to a 100-foot-wide oval plaza. One of the candelabra contains carved panels depicting Justice holding her scales and sword; the other contains panels of the three fates weaving the thread of life.

Thirty-six steep marble stairs ascend from the plaza to the massive bronze doors of the main entrance above. At the base of the stairs are sculptor Fraser's two seated allegorical figures: on the left (looking at the Court), a female who is contemplating justice; on the right, a male who is the guardian of the law.

At the top of the steps, sixteen marble columns at the main west entrance support the pediment, and the architrave above has these aspiring words incised: "Equal Justice Under Law." Although often overlooked by visitors, the building's "east front" (most people would think of it as the back of the building) can be just as inspiring. Its corresponding pediment and columns support an architrave that bears the inscription "Justice the Guardian of Liberty."

Guarding the formal main entrance are two massive bronze doors, each weighing six and one-half tons. On both are four relief panels sculpted by John Donnelly, depicting the growth of the law from ancient Greece and Rome to America. When opened, each of the doors slides into a hidden wall recess.

Through the massive bronze doors, a visitor enters into the building's focal point, the wide corridor known as the Great Hall. At each side, double rows of monolithic marble columns rise to a coffered ceiling. Busts of the fifteen former Chief Justices are displayed on pedestals along the side walls. Gilbert did the massive walls of both the Great Hall and the adjoining Court chamber in ivory vein marble from Alicante, Spain.

The Court chamber itself measures 82 by 91 feet, with a 44-foot-high coffered ceiling. The room is dominated by twenty-four massive pillars. Gilbert knew exactly where he needed to go for the marble for these columns—the Old Convent quarry in Liguria, Italy. There they mine a stone of unique color called light siena—and for Gilbert none other would do. The stone was cut in Italy and then shipped to a marble finishing company in Knoxville, Tennessee, where it was shaped into column form. Then it was reshipped to Washington in 30-foot sections to be reassembled in the courtroom.

The floors of the Great Hall and floor borders of the courtroom were done in a combination of darker marbles from Africa and Italy.

Overhead in the courtroom are large marble panels sculpted by Adolph Weinman. Above the bench are two figures representing the power of government and the majesty of the law. In between the two is a representation of the Ten Commandments. To the left is a depiction of the Rights of the People, to the right a depiction of the Defense of Human Rights. Along the walls are figures instrumental to the growth of law; along the left, the ancients like Moses, Confucius, and Solomon; along the right, more modern figures like Blackstone, Napoleon, and Charlemagne.

Despite its grandeur, the building cost a relatively modest amount. Congress appropriated $10 million for construction, but the building was completed and fully furnished for less. The architect of the Capitol, David Lynn, who supervised construction, returned $94,000 of the $10 million to the treasury. But estimates are that if the same building were constructed today, it would cost between $150 and $200 million—if the materials were still available, which they are not.

As with Taft's dying before he could see his dream realized, the building's designer, Cass Gilbert, also never saw his creation occupied. He died during the first year of construction, and the building was completed by his son.

## Inside the Building Today

Of the Court's four above-ground floors, visitors are allowed to see only the ground floor and a portion of the first floor.

At the building's east rear are two guarded entrances into the Court's subterranean garage. From there justices and staff can take special elevators directly to the justices' chambers, so for security reasons they never have to encounter the public. Also in the lower level are carpentry and furniture refinishing shops, a laundry, and offices for Capitol employees (electricians, plumbers, and groundskeepers) permanently assigned to the Court.

The building's ground floor houses several suites of offices for support officers of the Court and their staffs; those of the court clerk, curator, public information officer, personnel and budget officer, the Chief Justice's administrative assistant; the computer room; a one-chair barber shop; the seamstress's room; and offices and facilities for the Court police force.

The ground floor also features a cafeteria and snack bar that are open to the public, with an adjoining Law Clerk's Dining Room and a small private room known as the Ladies Dining Room, a tradition from the days when the justices' wives would often gather together for lunch or tea.

In the public areas of the ground floor is a gift shop run by the Supreme Court Historical Society and a theater in which films and videotapes are shown detailing the Court's history and its role in American life. Below the Great Hall is a space of similar size, called the Lower Great Hall. It is used for historical exhibitions and as an area where visitors can relax. It is dominated at one end by a massive sculpture of Chief Justice John Marshall, behind which is a large block of marble containing quotes from some of his more famous opinions. The statue, which was carved in 1884, had stood on the West Terrace of the Capitol. It was placed in the Supreme Court Building in 1982.

One level above is the Great Hall and the Court chamber. The courtroom is located at the center of the first floor, surrounded by the nine justices' chambers, which actually are suites of offices containing an outer reception area, the justice's actual office with its working fireplace, and an office for the justice's clerks. Behind the heavy red drapes of the Courtroom is an alcove that contains a small working law library containing a set of the *U.S. Reports* for use by the justices while hearing oral arguments. Adjacent to this alcove is the justices' robing room with its nine oak closets and, in keeping with modern times, a copy machine. The Justices' Conference Room is located adjacent to the Chief Justice's chambers and is used for the twice-weekly conferences where cases are decided. Also on the first floor are two larger oak-paneled ceremonial conference rooms, called simply the East and West Conference Rooms, which are used for meetings, small lunches and dinners, and social occasions. On the first floor too is the office of the Court marshal and his staff.

One floor above the Court chamber are the Court's legal offices housing the Court counsel and his staff, and the office of the reporter of decisions and his staff. Also on the second floor is the small John Marshall dining room, and the justices' private dinning room with its anteroom (along with its spacious kitchen); and a private library and reading room for the justices. In recent years, the second floor also has been home to some of the justices' law clerks and chambers for retired justices.

The Court once had no library of its own, and the justices were forced to maintain their own collections of legal texts. Today, the Court's law library is considered one of the best in America and takes up the building's entire third floor. It contains more than 300,000 volumes. The library houses all of history's Supreme Court decisions, along with all the recorded decisions of lower federal courts and the highest court of each state. In its stacks are volumes of the nation's leading law reviews, federal and state statutory codes, and other law-related texts. The third-floor library features a main reading room that many believe to be one of the most beautiful and impressive rooms in all of Washington, a large expanse of tables and shelves below crystal chandeliers, paneled throughout in hand-carved oak. Again, in keeping with modern times, adjacent to the main reading room is a room of modern computer equipment for database access. The library's use is limited to court staffers, lawyers licensed to practice before the Court (Supreme Court Bar members), government attorneys, and members of Congress and their legal staffs. Members of the public and press generally are allowed access for research projects.

The fourth floor, sometimes referred to by employees as the attic, features a gymnasium. Court employees participate in a volleyball league and pickup basketball games on "the highest court in the land." The gym contains an exercise room and shower stalls.

Even though most of the building is closed to the public, there is much to see in the building for visitors. The Supreme Court Building is open from 9 A.M. to 4:30 P.M. weekdays.

# The People of the Court

As an institution, the Court has grown significantly from its first days in New York, and for years thereafter, when it had a staff of one—its clerk. It has grown quite a bit, but by Washington standards it remains a small institution. It employs only 320 people, 77 of them police officers. The court's budget for fiscal year 1991 was a paltry (again by Washington standards) $20.7 million.

The Court has four officers established by statute: its clerk, marshal, reporter of decisions, and librarian. For fiscal year 1991, the salary for each statutory officer and for the Chief Justice's administrative assistant was $108,000. The Chief Justice of the United States and the Supreme Court's eight associate justices select their own law clerks and staff members. The Chief Justice alone has ultimate hiring and firing control over all other Court employees.

Since 1972, the Chief Justice has relied on an administrative assistant for help with nonjudicial work. The administrative assistant, who has three support staffers, primarily aids the Chief Justice in coordinating personnel policies, preparing the Court budget, and meeting the Chief Justice's growing duties as head of the federal judiciary. By statute, the administrative assistant is to (1) provide research and analysis supportive of the Chief

Justice's public addresses and statements; (2) monitor literature of developments in the fields of judicial administration and court improvement; (3) liaison with the many legal and judicial groups and individuals dealing with problems in those fields, including assistance in organizing legal conferences; (4) assist in the task of explaining to the public the role of the Supreme Court and the federal judicial system; (5) assist the Chief Justice in his overall supervisory responsibilities with respect to the institutional operations of the Supreme Court, such as the supervision and coordination of the various offices of the court.

The Court's nerve center is the office of the Court clerk. All official business must go through it, from litigants to the justices and from the justices to litigants and the American public. All motions, appeals (formally called jurisdictional statements and petitions for writs of certiorari) and briefs are first lodged with the clerk's office, where they are assigned docket numbers and filed, or otherwise officially noted. It is the clerk's office that distributes those documents to the justices. More than 5,000 cases reach the court during a typical term. It is the clerk's office that prepares and releases the Court's Orders List and Journal, where all formal judgments and mandates are noted.

The clerk's office, with a staff of twenty-eight that includes three deputy clerks, also is responsible for preparing those formal judgments and mandates, and for notifying lawyers involved in the case and the appropriate lower courts of all formal actions taken by the Supreme Court. The office also collects filing fees and other Court costs, supervises the printing of briefs and appendices in *in forma pauperis* cases, and obtains lower court records as needed by the justices. These materials are kept for five years and then are sent to the National Archives.

Counsels of record who file documents with the Court or argue before it must be members of the Supreme Court Bar. The clerk's office supervises the admission of lawyers to the Supreme Court Bar, and also their disbarments. During public sessions, the Court clerk often swears in new members of the Supreme Court Bar. And the clerk and his staff continually advise litigants and their lawyers on Court rules and procedures.

No one has direct supervision over more Supreme Court employees than its marshal. He has been described as the Court's operations manager, paymaster, and chief security officer. When not in Court, the marshal is ultimately responsible for paying the Court's bills, paying the justices and the Court's other employees, and ordering supplies. The marshal has an office staff of thirteen, but he also supervises the Court's seventy-seven-member police force, its thirty-three member labor force, and its twenty-five-member housekeeping force. The marshal is responsible for receiving visiting dignitaries at the Court building and for providing for the justices' security when they attend formal functions outside the Court building.

The marshal is most visible in the courtroom, where his job is to announce the beginning and end of each public session. Located to the right of the bench as seen from the courtroom's public seats, the marshal stands and announces: "The honorable, the Chief Justice and the Associate Justices of the Supreme Court of the United States." As the justices enter the courtroom from behind a burgundy drape, the marshal three times announces "Oyez" (Hear ye) and continues: "All persons having business before the Honorable, the Supreme Court of the United States, are admonished to draw near and give their attention, for the Court is now sitting. God save the United States and this Honorable Court."

The post of a Supreme Court librarian was first established in 1887. The librarian supervises a research and support staff of twenty-four, who specialize in acquiring, cataloging, or circulating the resource materials.

The Court's most visible link to the public is its public information office (PIO), with a staff of four. It fields questions from the public and news media, and disseminates information about the justices and the Court. The public information officer is the Court's spokesperson, but does not comment on decisions, orders, or other official business conducted by the justices. The staff believe that written words must speak for themselves.

The PIO plays a key role in getting out early word of Supreme Court rulings. As a decision is being announced from the bench by the Court member who wrote for the majority, a member of the Court clerk's staff calls by telephone the public information officer to relay the information that the particular decision has been announced. Within seconds, the public information officer distributes printed copies (bench opinions) of those rulings to members of the news media who gather each decision day in the PIO's ground-floor suite. The public information officer also provides work space for news reporters in the court's press room, and supervises the assignment of credentials reporters need to cover the Court.

Aside from those of the justices, the most private suite of offices within the Court building houses the reporter of decisions, and his staff of nine. The reporter is one of the very few Court employees not assigned to the justices' chambers who sees a decision before it is announced and released publicly. The reporter of decisions and his staff also edit the Court's opinions, checking all citations of previous decisions and lower court rulings, correcting typographical and other errors that may appear. The reporter supervises getting the Court's initial copies of its decisions, called bench opinions, to the Government Printing Office. The GPO publishes the official Supreme Court compilation, *U.S. Reports*, as thick, bound volumes. A single Court term typically fills five such volumes.

The reporter supervises the printing of a syllabus (headnote) for each signed decision of the Court. It summarizes the background of the case being decided and the legal points decided by the High Court, tells whether a lower court's ruling has been affirmed or reversed, and gives the voting lineup of the Supreme Court's members. Each headnote contains this disclaimer: "The syllabus constitutes no part of the opinion of the court but has been prepared by the Reporter of Decisions for the convenience of the reader."

The first reporter, Alexander J. Dallas, was self-appointed. A journalist, court watcher, and secretary of the treasury, he began writing up Supreme Court decisions as a public service in 1790. The Court's current reporter of decisions is the fifteenth man to hold the job.

By law, each Supreme Court member today is entitled to four law clerks. These men and women are, most often, young lawyers a year or two out of law school. They generally finished at the top of their class and clerked one year for a state or federal judge before signing on for a one-year stint at the highest court. Law clerks make up the bulk of any one justice's personal staff. Justices also are entitled to two secretaries and a messenger.

In fiscal year 1991, law clerks were paid an annual salary of $38,861. But a Supreme Court clerkship is a much sought-after credential among the nation's largest and most prestigious law firms, and former clerks have left the court for law firm jobs that pay beginning salaries of $80,000 or more. In recent years, some firms have imitated sports franchises and paid "signing bonuses" to Supreme Court law clerks who agree to work for them. Some bonuses reportedly go as high as $20,000.

Just what kind of work a law clerk does for his or her justice depends on the work habits of that justice. Some members of the Court have their clerks author initial drafts of opinions and then edit them in their own writing style. In other chambers, it is the clerks who edit and suggest changes to the initial drafts composed by the respective justices.

But in recent years, each Supreme Court member has relied on the clerks to sort through all new appeals and motions and to write a memorandum on each. Some justices have allowed their clerks to unite in a "cert pool" and divide the memorandum-writing work to avoid duplication.

Law clerks often are treated as a member of a justice's family, with all the accompanying perks and chores. Chief Justice William H. Rehnquist's clerks play tennis with him weekly. Justice Harry A. Blackmun's clerks eat breakfast with him daily. On the other end of the spectrum, such bright young lawyers have been expected, on occasion by one justice or another, to retrieve laundry from the dry cleaners or groom the family pet.

Chief Justice Rehnquist and two other Court members—Justices Byron R. White and John Paul Stevens—served as Supreme Court law clerks in their younger years. How much influence law clerks, either individually or collectively, exert over a member of the Court who enjoys life tenure has been a subject of enormous speculation over the years. Even former clerks have differed in their views on that subject.

Retired Justice Thurgood Marshall told the story of an in-chambers conference in which two of his law clerks argued over how "we" should cast a vote in a particular case. Eventually, Marshall said he had to remind the young lawyers that only one person in the room had received a presidential commission.

The practice of hiring law clerks dates back to 1882. For the Court's 1991–92 term, thirty-nine law clerks were hired. Chief Justice Rehnquist had three; the eight associate justices had four each. Four retired Court members—Chief Justice Warren E. Burger and Justices Marshall, William B. Brennan, and Lewis F. Powell—had one each. The four retired members are provided with offices in the Court building, in keeping with Court tradition.

The Court also has its own lawyers. The office of legal counsel was established in 1973 to provide help with questions of law concerning the Court, its employees, and its property. For example, litigants involved in some High Court case on occasion have sued members of the Court clerk's staff in their official capacity. The Court's legal office has represented those employees.

The legal office, comprising two attorneys and a secretary, occasionally deals with personnel grievances and interpretations of the Court's institutional rules. The legal office also can be involved in advising the Court on some substantive matter, especially when one side in a dispute seeks expedited consideration.

More than 700,000 visitors take in the Supreme Court building each year, and the person most responsible for what they see is the Court's curator. The curator is responsible for the exhibits, often featuring historic memorabilia, displayed on the building's ground floor, and for developing educational programs aimed at telling the public about the Court's work and history. One such program yielded the film now on display in the building's ground-floor theater.

The curator's office, with a staff of six, also provides daily courtroom lectures when no oral arguments are being conducted. The office also works with the Court's historical society in adding to the Court collections of antique furniture, documents, and photographs. The Court has had an official curator since 1973.

The Court in recent years has taken on a data systems unit, which now has twenty employees. It is responsible for printing all Court orders and bench opinions and, on an experimental basis, for making the Court's work immediately available far from Washington via the computer-to-computer network dubbed Project Hermes.

Among the Court's other support personnel are four telephone operators, eighteen general messengers, six woodworkers, two first-aid staffers, a food-preparation specialist, a barber, and a seamstress who repairs the justices' robes, the Court police's uniforms, and from time to time the flag that flies over the building.

## Other Court-Related Offices

Tens of thousands of lawyers are members of the Supreme Court Bar, but only a tiny fraction of them ever get to argue a case before the Court. A lawyer is eligible for Supreme Court Bar membership if he or she has been admitted to practice in one of the fifty states, the District of Columbia, or a U.S. territory for three years prior to applying and "shall have been free from any adverse disciplinary action whatsoever during that three-year period and . . . appears to the court to be of good moral and professional character." The admission fee is $100.

The Chief Justice, by virtue of his office, presides over the Judicial Conference of the United States, a kind of board of directors for the federal courts. The conference, created by Congress in 1922, comprises twenty-seven federal trial and appellate judges. The conference is a policymaker that meets twice each year at the Supreme Court Building. Its various committees can meet more often in many locations.

The conference does not have a budget, but its expenses are met by the Administrative Office (AO) of the U.S. Courts, the federal judiciary's administrative arm. The AO's main responsibility is preparing and submitting to Congress the budgetary requests and legislative initiatives of the federal courts. The AO's director and deputy director are appointed by the Supreme Court.

Another support organization for the High Court and the federal judiciary is the Federal Judicial Center, which seeks to improve the administration of justice. It serves as the judiciary's research and training arm.

Founded in 1974, the Supreme Court Historical Society collects and preserves memorabilia and documents relating to the High Court or its members. The society raises money by operating a gift shop in the Supreme Court Building and by assessing most of its 2,600 members dues of $50 annually.

# Glossary of Legal Terms

The following are terms often used by the Supreme Court in its decisions, or are commonly used in describing the Court and its workings.

*Abstention Doctrine* A Supreme Court doctrine whereby it will withhold ruling on a case involving issues of state law until the lower state court has ruled on those issues.

*Accessory* In criminal law, a person who, although not present at the scene of the crime, orders and advises (accessory before the fact) or who aids and assists in concealing the crime (accessory after the fact).

*Accomplice* One who participates with another in a crime, either as a principal or as an accessory.

*Acquittal* The dismissal of charges. May be by a jury with a verdict of innocence, or by a judge who finds insufficient evidence to convict.

*Action* Legal conduct or behavior. Usually refers to a lawsuit.

*Actus Reus* The conduct element of a crime that must be proven for conviction.

*Adjudicate* To judicially determine a case.

*Ad Valorem* Taxes assessed by a state on property within the state as of a particular "tax" day each year.

*Affidavit* A written statement of facts, given under oath.

*A Fortiori* Literally "with more force." Usually refers to a stronger fact or argument.

*Alibi* The legal defense of having been somewhere other than the scene of the crime at the time the crime was committed.

*Amicus Curiae* Literally "friend of the court." Refers to someone—not a direct party to the litigation—who desires to join it in order to call the court's attention to a matter, or issue, involved in the lawsuit that the nonparty has a strong interest in.

*Amicus Curiae Brief* A legal document containing arguments submitted by the nonparty in order to assist the Court in acquiring additional information or to request a particular outcome.

*Answer* A written, filed response to the filed allegations of the aggrieved party.

*Appeal* The taking of a court's decision to a higher court for review.

*Blackmail* A form of extortion by threat of exposure of some conduct by the victim which would operate to his disadvantage if revealed.

*Booking* The formal, administrative step following arrest that normally occurs at the police station and consists of entering the arrestee's name, the alleged crime, and facts in an official log book, and then making a permanent identity record of the accused through fingerprinting and photos.

*Breach* The failure of one party to a contract to perform on a promise that constitutes a basis of the contract.

*Brief* A written document filed with the court outlining a party's view of the facts, legal argument, and position.

*Burden of Proof* The need to provide sufficient evidence in support of a particular issue.

*Case in Chief* That part of the trial in which the party with the initial burden of proof presents his evidence.

*Case Law* Law as determined by previous trial or appellate court decisions.

*Causation* An action that starts a string of events that result in the occurrence of an event.

*Caveat* A warning or notice to beware. Generally refers to an entry in a register serving as notice that no act can occur without notice to the person making the entry.

*Caveat Emptor* Literally, "buyer beware." A rule of common law that the buyer purchases at his own risk.

*Certiorari, Writ of* A judicial document issued from a superior court to a lower court, directing that the case be heard in the superior court. In the U.S. Supreme Court the writ is discretionary and will be issued if at least four of the nine justices agree to hear the case.

*Challenge* The objection, by a lawyer for either side, of a potential juror's service during the *voir dire* process.

*Challenge for Cause* An objection to a potential juror's service for a specific reason that disqualifies. See also *peremptory challenge*.

*Chattel* Personal property, as opposed to land, that is real property.

*Circumstantial Evidence* Indirect evidence, not based on personal knowledge or observation, but evidence from which one might assume an event occurred.

*Civil Law* Generally used to refer to the area of law covering crimes committed against an individual, as opposed to criminal law, which is considered to be against society as a whole.

*Class Action* A legal case brought by several parties who have similar disputes against the same defendant.

*Code* Collection of laws and statutes.

*Codicil* An amendment to a will.

*Collateral Estoppel* A legal doctrine that prohibits the relitigation of an issue already litigated and which was a material part of an earlier judgment.

*Comity* Refers to the relationship of respect that exists between state and federal courts.

*Commerce Clause* The provision of the U.S. Constitution (Article I, Section 8, Cl. 3) that gives Congress the power to regulate interstate commerce.

*Common Carrier* Commercial transportation whose function is to transport passengers and/or goods for hire; i.e., airlines, bus lines, railroads, trucking companies.

*Common Law* Judge-made law, based on law originally developed in England.

*Comparative Negligence* An interpretation of negligence law that distributes the recovery of damages based on the degree of fault of each of the respective parties. It usually compares the negligence of the defendant with that of the plaintiff.

*Competency* The capability to be held responsible, legally and/or physically, for one's actions.

*Complaint* Document filed with the court that commences a law suit. Contains statements claiming damages, the cause of those damages, why the plaintiff should be awarded those damages and a request that the court find in favor of the plaintiff and award his requested damages.

*Condition (precedent, subsequent, concurrent)* A future, uncertain event that, upon its occurrence, an obligation will be owed or will ensure. 1. *precedent*—the event must occur or be performed before the agreement becomes effective; 2. *subsequent*—once the event occurs, the obligation is no longer binding on the other party; 3. *concurrent*—the event must occur at the same time as the effectiveness of the agreement.

*Consent* The voluntary agreement to an act, after a full disclosure of all material facts.

*Consent Decree* An agreement by the parties to a dispute, made under the auspices of the court, but not the result of a judicial decision, in which the parties agree to be bound by stated facts.

*Conspiracy* An agreement between two or more parties to act together in the commission or the furtherance of a crime.

*Contempt* Disobeying an order or the integrity of a court (or judge). Punishable by fine or detention.

*Contribution* Seeking a portion of damages due to a plaintiff from another source, typically a co-defendant.

*Contributory Negligence* An interpretation of law that bars recovery of damages by a plaintiff against a defendant if the plaintiff's negligence contributed at all to his injuries.

*Conversion* The act of wrongfully taking the personal property of another for one's own use.

*Conviction* Being found guilty of a charge.

*Covenant* A formal agreement usually involving conditions on the transfer of land or real property.

*Criminal Law* The body of law that governs crimes against society, as contrasted with civil law, which governs crimes against individuals.


*Declaratory Judgment* When a plaintiff is in doubt as to his legal rights, he may request clarification from the court. The decision of the court is referred to as a declaratory judgment.

*De Facto* Literally "as a matter of fact." Refers to an action or state of affairs that must be accepted for practical purposes, although not legally formed or lawfully recognized. It is distinguished from *de jure*.

*Defamation* An attack, written or oral, on the reputation of an individual.

*Defendant* The party against whom a complaint (lawsuit) is filed.

*De Jure* Literally, "as a matter of law." Complying with the law in all respects; valid under the law.

*Demonstrative Evidence* Nonverbal evidence (i.e., charts, films, maps).

*De Novo* The decision by an appeals court to itself rehear the evidence of a case, rather than rule based on the evidence as presented in a lower court.

*Deposition* The questioning of a witness under oath prior to the commencement of the trial, with counsel for all interested parties present.

*Derivative Action* In corporate law, refers to a lawsuit brought by a shareholder to assert a right of the corporation because of the corporation's failure to otherwise act upon that right.

*Directed Verdict* The ruling by a judge in favor of a particular party if, after all evidence is presented, the judge determines that by law there is no question of fact remaining to be decided by the trier of fact (usually a jury).

*Discovery* The pretrial period to be used by counsel to collect evidence for trial. May consist of depositions, interrogatories, admission of fact.

*Discretion* A judge's prerogative to make decisions.

*Dismissal* The dropping of all charges in a criminal prosecution or the discontinuance of a lawsuit in a civil matter.

*Diversity (of Citizenship)* A rule of federal court subject matter jurisdiction which requires that all parties to a federal court suit be from different states, unless the issue in question is a federal question.

*Docket* A court's calendar.

*Doctrine* A legal rule or principle.

*Double Jeopardy* The Fifth Amendment guarantee against reprosecution for the same offense after acquittal.

*Double Process* Guarantees an individual against arbitrary government interference. Derived from the Fifth Amendment to the Constitution, which states that no person "shall be deprived of life, liberty or property, without due process of law." This provision has been made applicable to the state actions through the Fourteenth Amendment.

*Duty of Care* The standard to which an individual is held, otherwise negligence is said to be present.

*Eminent Domain* The power of the state to seize land for a public use through a judicial proceeding and after just compensation has been paid.

*Equal Protection* The right for certain classes of individuals not to be treated differently from others.

*Equity* 1. An interest in property that a court will protect. 2. A system of established law and jurisprudence. 3. A system of law, or a principle of justice that institutes remedies other than money damages—i.e., injunctions, specific performance.

*Estate* The sum total of an individual's real and personal property.

*Executive Agreement* A treatylike agreement between the president of the United States and a foreign country, which does not need to be ratified by the Senate.

*Executive Privilege* That privilege which exempts the president of the United States from the legal disclosure requirements that apply to ordinary citizens.

*Exigent Circumstances* Those circumstances that require unusual or immediate action. Generally refers to circumstances surrounding the pursuit, arrest, and search of a criminal suspect.

*Ex Parte* Literally, "from one side only." 1. An application made to the court by one party without notifying the adverse parties. 2. A judicial action taken for the benefit of only one side.

*Ex Post Facto* Literally, "after the fact." Refers to laws that are enacted in order to punish for an act already committed.

*Express* Generally used in contract law to refer to a contract that is oral or written, or to terms of the contract that are clear and definite, as opposed to contracts and terms that are implied, to be deduced by actions or prior activity.

*Ex Rel.* Literally, "upon relation or information." Used in case names to mean "in relation to."

*Extortion* The crime of blackmail. The unlawful obtaining of property by means of threat to do harm or reveal information.


*Federal Question* A genuine controversy arising under the Constitution, a federal law, or a treaty presented in such a form that a court is capable of acting upon it.

*Felony* A more serious crime punishable by death or imprisonment for more than one year.

*First Impression* Usually an issue facing a court for the first time with no preceding precedent.

*Forbear* To refrain from an action.

*Foreseeability* The ability to reasonably predict that one's actions will result in a particular reaction.

*Forum* The court.

*Forum Non Conveniens* Literally, "an inconvenient forum." Doctrine whereby a judge can transfer a case to another court, where the suit could have originally been brought, for the convenience of the parties and witnesses.

*"Fruit of the Poisonous Tree" Doctrine* A criminal law concept that refers to the inadmissibility of evidence that was obtained as a result of an illegal search.

*Fundamental Rights* Those basic rights accorded to all individuals under the Constitution. Includes rights such as free speech, to practice religion free from state control, to vote, and to travel.

*Grand Jury* A panel of individuals numbering from six to twelve or more depending upon the state, whose purpose is to hear prosecutorial evidence of an accused individual's alleged involvement in a crime in order to determine if sufficient evidence exists to hold that individual for trial.

*Habeas Corpus* Literally "you may have the body." Originally an English common law writ to secure the release of an improperly confined person. Now a generic term applicable to several kinds of writs and actions designed to allow convicted individuals to request release from unlawful imprisonment.

*Hearsay* Testimony by a witness relating to matters that the witness did not actually see or hear firsthand, but rather was told by others.

*Hung Jury* A jury that is unable to come to a decision on whether to convict or acquit.

*Immunity* Freedom from fear of prosecution, usually under an agreement made with the prosecution in return for giving evidence.

*Impeach* To discredit a witness's testimony.

*In Camera* Literally "in the chamber." Refers to a private meeting with a judge in his chambers.

*Inchoate* Those crimes which generally are committed owing to state of mind of a defendant and which lead to the commission of another crime. For instance, solicitation, attempt, or conspiracy.

*Indemnity* 1. Receiving money or other valuable property in compensation for a loss. 2. A contract to save a party from the legal consequences of the conduct of one of the parties or of a third party. 3. Security by way of payment of a deposit or a bond.

*Indictment* A criminal charge issued by a grand jury.

*In Forma Pauperis* Literally "in the form of a poor person." Refers to an indigent's ability to be excused from paying court fees.

*Information* An indictment presented by a prosecutor, rather than a grand jury.

*Injunction* A formal command by a court prohibiting an action or commanding a certain act be done.

*In Pari Delicto* Literally "equally at fault." Refers to the occasion when a plaintiff and defendant are deemed equally at fault in a matter.

*In Personam* "Over the person." Refers to a court's jurisdiction over an individual; i.e., the court's ability to force a person to appear in court.

*In Re* Regarding. . . .

*Interlocutory Action* A temporary action taken by a judge that remains in effect during the life of the trial.

*Interrogatory* A set of written questions prepared by one side in a litigation that must be answered, as if under oath, by the opposing side.

*Intervention (Intervene, Intervenor)* The act of someone other than the original parties to a lawsuit, who requests to become a party to the action in order to protect an affected right.

*Intestate* Dying without a will.

*Invitee* A guest on your property who is there primarily for business purposes.

*Irresistible Impulse Test* A legal test for insanity which states that because of a mental defect or disease, a defendant does not have the ability to control his own actions.

*Issue* Relating to matters or questions in the dispute.


*Joint and Several* A liability concept, whereby if you have multiple defendants, each can be held fully responsible for the total amount of damages due to a plaintiff.

*Judgment* A decision of a court.

*Jurisdiction* See *In personam jurisdiction* and *Subject matter jurisdiction*.

*Jury* A panel of individuals selected to hear the evidence and decide a case.

*Jury Instructions* Guidelines to assist a jury in coming to a verdict, given by the judge at the close of the lawyers' final arguments and before the jury begins deliberations.


*Larceny* The taking and transporting away of the personal property of another with the intent of permanently depriving the owner of his property.

*Last Clear Chance Doctrine* In a jurisdiction that allows the defense of contributory negligence, a doctrine that holds that a plaintiff can still recover, even if shown partly at fault, if he can show that the defendant had the "last clear chance" to avoid the accident.

*Lay Witness* A nonexpert witness.

*Lex Fori* Literally "law of the forum." A method used by the court to determine whose law should apply in deciding the issues in a case; usually that the law of the court where the case is being tried is the law that will apply to the case.

*Lex Loci* Literally "law of the location." Another choice of law method, where the law of the location where the accident occurred is the law that will apply to the case.

*Liability* The legal responsibility for an action and the damages caused by that action.

*Libel* Written defamation.

*Licensee* A guest on the property of another, whose purpose is primarily social, and who while not invited, is tolerated.

*Liquidated Damages* A contract clause that expressly states the amount of damages to be paid in the event of a material breach.

*Litigant* A participant in a legal case.


*Magistrate* A judicial officer, in either the federal or state court system, with limited jurisdiction and authority, primarily at the local level.

*Malice* A state of mind involving the reckless disregard of the law and legal rights of another. The state of mind that prompts the intentional commission of a wrong against another.

*Malicious Prosecution* The filing of a legal action solely for the purposes of harassment.

*Malum In Se* A wrong that is prohibited because it is evil in itself—i.e., murder—as opposed to an act simply prohibited by a legislative act—such as speeding.

*Malum Prohibitum* A wrong that is prohibited by statute—i.e., running a traffic light.

*Mandamus* A legal document issued by a higher court ordering the performance of a particular act.

*Manslaughter* The causing of the death of another without the necessary intent and premeditation requirements of murder.

*Material* Important and vital to the issue.

*Mayhem* A crime that results in permanent disfigurement or bodily dismemberment.

*Mediation* A dispute settlement system, similar to arbitration, except that the decision by the neutral third party is advisory and not binding.

*Mens Rea* Literally "a guilty mind." A necessary element in a criminal case. The prosecutor must prove that a guilty state of mind accompanied the commission of the criminal act—that the defendant intended to commit a crime.

*Misdemeanor* A crime deemed lesser than a felony and punished accordingly.

*Mitigation of Damages* Generally, every fact tending to decrease damages. For instance, the showing that a plaintiff could reasonably have avoided all or part of an injury. Also refers to the duty not to aggravate one's injury and to refrain from increasing one's damages.

*M'Naughten Rule* An insanity test which states that insanity exists when a mental disease causes a defect of reason whereby the defendant did not know the quality or nature of his actions.

*Moot* A question is moot when it presents no actual controversy, usually because the issues involved no longer exist; i.e., questions regarding pregnancy when the pregnancy has passed, or issues involving academic institutions when the complainant has already graduated.

*Motion (Move)* A request for judicial action in favor of the requesting party.

*Natural Law* A body of law that derives its validity inherently from society. Basically, it deems certain laws valid because society has determined them to be so.

*Negligence* The theory that the failure to exercise a proper standard of case has resulted in injury or loss to another.

*Nexus* Connection.

*Nolo Contendere* Literally "no contest." A plea in a criminal action that has the same result as a guilty plea, but which is not an actual admission of guilt which could be used against pleader in a subsequent action.

*Nuisance* Activity that arises from a person's unreasonable or unlawful use of his own property which interferes with the enjoyment of another's property; i.e., noise, odors.

*Obiter Dictum ("Dicta")* Parts of a judicial opinion not necessary to the decision itself, often in the form of footnotes. Cannot be used as precedent, but often used for persuasion.

*Objection* In a trial, a protest by counsel.

*Ordinance* A municipal law.

*Overbreadth Doctrine* A principle of constitutional law whereby a statute will be found unconstitutional if it is so broadly written that it forbids constitutionally protected activity as well as unprotected action.

*Parole* A conditional release from prison. Normally requires the parolee to periodically check in with authorities (parole officer) and may limit travel or other activities.

*Per Curiam* Most judicial opinions, issued by courts of more than one judge, are issued by one judge and concurred in by the others. A *per curiam* opinion is issued by the entire panel of judges.

*Peremptory Challenge* The dismissal of a perspective juror by lawyers for either side with no reason given or necessary. Each side is allowed a limited number of such challenges.

*Petit Jury* Literally "small jury." Refers to a trial jury, usually twelve individuals, but can be as small as six, as opposed to a grand jury.

*Petitioner* The party who files the initial statement with the court.

*Plain View Doctrine* Allows police to gather evidence that is in plain sight in a situation where the police are lawfully present. For example, when the police are in hot pursuit of a subject and follow him into his home without a prior search warrant, they are entitled to gather any evidence that is openly visible.

*Plaintiff* The party who files a complaint.

*Plea Bargain* The process in which the defendant makes a deal with the prosecutor usually to plead guilty to a lesser charge, or for a guarantee of a lesser sentence, in exchange for information or testimony or to forgo the time and cost of a trial.

*Pleading* Refers to a complaint or answer in a civil case.

*Political Question* Questions that the federal courts will not hear, since to decide such issues would be considered an encroachment on the legislative and/or executive branches.

*Precedent* The law as determined by previous judicial decisions.

*Preemption Doctrine* Refers to the doctrine whereby federal law supplants state law regarding the same situation.

*Preliminary Hearing* A judicial hearing held postarrest to determine if enough evidence exists that a crime has been committed and that the person charged should be held for trial.

*Presumption* A judicially applied prediction of factual legal probability, such as a presumption of innocence.

*Prima Facie Case* Literally "at first sight." Refers to the plaintiff's burden to present sufficient evidence to permit the jury to infer that a genuine question of fact exists.

*Procedural Due Process* The guarantee of fairness stemming from the Fifth and Fourth Amendment to a notice and hearing before a government agency deprives him of life, liberty, or property.

*Prior Restraint* Censorship before publication. Except in very rare circumstances, the First Amendment guarantee of freedom of speech and press has been held to preclude preventing publication before the fact.

*Privilege* An exemption from having to disclose certain conversations and situations. Some privileges include attorney-client, doctor-patient, husband-wife.

*Probable Cause* Reasonable belief in certain alleged facts. Refers to the belief necessary for law enforcement officers to detain an individual.

*Probation* A form of punishment consisting of a set time by which a convicted individual must submit to close monitoring in lieu of incarceration. Monitoring usually consists of periodic visits to a probation officer and possible limitations on travel and activity.

*Proximate Cause* An action that, in a normal and continuous sequence, produces an injury.


*Quash* To suppress or subdue.

*Question* The point in controversy or to be decided.


*Reasonable Cause* Basis upon which a law enforcement officer may stop or arrest without a warrant if a situation exists where an ordinary person would believe that the person to be stopped or arrested committed a crime.

*Reasonable Person ("Reasonable Man")* The basic objective standard of negligence whereby one's conduct is measured against the conduct of a mythical average person.

*Recognizance* A promise made before the court to perform some act; i.e., appear in court at a later date.

*Relevance* Evidence submitted and questions asked in court and at pretrial must relate to the issue at hand.

*Remand* When an appeals court sends a case back to the lower court to have certain issues relitigated.

*Res Ipsa Loquitur* Literally "the act speaks for itself." When no evidence exists regarding negligence, the plaintiff may establish a breach of duty by showing that the accident is of the type that would not have occurred absent negligence and that the instrumentality causing the injury was in the defendant's control at the time of the accident. This doctrine allows plaintiff to avoid a directed verdict against him.

*Res Judicata* When a matter has been finally adjudicated, it may not be challenged by any of the involved parties.

*Ripeness* Federal courts will not hear a case where the controversy at issue is theoretical or speculative.


*Search and Seizure* The looking for and taking of property by law enforcement officers. Unlawful search and seizure is forbidden by the Constitution.

*Settlement* An agreement to damages and fault entered into by the parties in dispute in order to avoid trial.

*Sine Qua Non* "But for." A causation test . . . "but for" the particular action, the injury would not have occurred.

*Situs* Location.

*Slander* Spoken defamation.

*Solicitation* The crime of requesting another to commit a crime for your benefit.

*Sovereign* The "state"—i.e., the government.

*Sovereign Immunity* Doctrine that prevents the state from being sued or made the defendant in a prosecution, except in certain limited and clearly defined circumstances.

*Standing* The right to bring suit. Federal law requires that a person bringing suit must be directly affected by the issues involved in the suit.

*Stare Decisis* The doctrine of precedent, whereby it is necessary to abide by prior case decisions.

*State Action* Refers to claims under the due process clause and Civil Rights Act, where an individual seeking damages must show a significant enough connection between the government and the challenged action that the action can be treated as an action of the state itself.

*Statement of Admissions* A written document stating facts that both sides agree are not in dispute.

*Substantive Due Process* The right of an individual not to be arbitrarily deprived of life, liberty, or property. Depending on the status of the individual affected, the courts will apply one of the three "scrutiny" tests to determine if the individual's rights have been unconstitutionally denied.

*Status Conference* An interim judicial conference held in order to ascertain how a case is proceeding.

*Statute* Legislatively enacted law.

*Stay* To postpone or halt.

*Stop and Frisk* Police officers who are suspicious of individuals may lightly pat down the exterior of their clothing in order to determine if the individual is carrying a weapon.

*Strict Liability* Liability without fault. Applies in product liability cases to find a seller or manufacturer of a product liable for any and all defective products.

*Subject Matter Jurisdiction* Refers to the type of cases that can be heard by a federal court. These are 1. cases that involve parties from different states and that involve damages in excess of $50,000.00; and 2. cases that involve a question regarding a federal law.

*Subpoena* An order from a court to appear at trial.

*Subpoena Duces Tecum* An order from the court to produce documents at trial.

*Superseding Cause* An intervening act of a third party that is significant enough to insulate the individual who was originally negligent from liability.

*Supremacy Clause* The clause of the Constitution (Article VI, Section 2) that states that federal law preempts state law.

*Testimony* Statements made under oath in regard to a legal proceeding.

*Tort* A civil wrong against an individual's rights, as opposed to a criminal wrong, which is against the state. Includes assault, battery, false imprisonment, intentional infliction of emotional distress, and trespass.

*Tortfeasor* One who commits a tort.

*Treaty* A binding pact between two sovereigns, normally foreign countries.

*Trespass* The intentional entering onto another's property.

*Trier of Fact* He who decides a case. In a jury trial, it is the jury; in a bench trial, it is the judge.

*True Bill* An endorsement by a grand jury of an indictment when it has determined that sufficient evidence exists to bring the individual to trial.

*Trust* A legal entity involving a third party (trustee) who holds property (trust corpus) of one person (settlor) for the benefit of another (beneficiary).

*Unconstitutional* A law or an action of the state that is held to be in violation of some part of the Constitution, and therefore is null and void and of no force, and is treated legally as if it had never existed.

*Uniform Commercial Code* A legislatively enacted body of statutes governing commercial transactions. Enacted in all states, except Louisiana.

*Vacate* To overrule and set aside a verdict.

*Vagueness Doctrine* A Constitutional principle that finds a statute unconstitutional if a person reading it would not know what specific actions are prohibited.

*Verdict* The opinion of the jury or of the judge on a particular issue of fact.

*Vest* The point of time at which a beneficiary can claim his or her rights.

*Voir Dire* The process whereby a judge and lawyers for the litigants (or for the state and the defendant in a criminal matter) can question potential jurors to determine their fitness to serve.


*Waiver* An agreement among the parties to a contract or an agreement that a particular clause or obligation will not apply.

*Warranty* A guarantee, usually granted by a manufacturer, regarding the fitness of his product.

*Writ* A legal document issued from or submitted to a court.

# Bibliography

The following represents a sample of the significant books written about the U.S. Supreme Court and its justices over the past twenty years.

## Books on the Supreme Court

Abraham, Henry Julian. *The Judiciary: The Supreme Court in the Governmental Process*, 6th ed. Boston: Allyn and Bacon, 1983.

———. *Justices and Presidents: A Political History of Appointments to the Supreme Court*, 3rd ed. New York: Oxford University Press, 1992.

———. *Freedom and the Court: Civil Rights and Liberties in the United States*, 5th ed. New York: Oxford University Press, 1990.

Asch, Sidney H. *The Supreme Court and its Great Justices*. New York: Arco Press, 1971.

Baker, Leonard. *Back to Back: The Duel Between FDR and the Supreme Court*. New York, Macmillan, 1967.

Baum, Lawrence. *The Supreme Court*, 4th ed. Washington, D.C.: CQ Press, 1991.

Beard, Charles Austin. *The Supreme Court and the Constitution*. Englewood Cliffs, N.J.: Prentice-Hall, 1962.

Berger, Raoul. *Congress vs. The Supreme Court*. Cambridge: Harvard University Press, 1969.

Bickel, Alexander M. *The Supreme Court and the Idea of Progress*. New York: Harper & Row, 1970.

———. *Politics and the Warren Court*. New York: Da Capo Press, 1973 (1965).

Blandford, Linda A. *Supreme Court of the United States, 1789–1980: An Index to Opinions Arranged by Justice*, 2 vols. Millwood, N.Y.: Kraus International Publications, 1983.

Carr, Robert K. *The Supreme Court and Judicial Review*. Westport, Conn.: Greenwood Press, 1970 (1942).

Cox, Archibald. *The Role of the Supreme Court in American Government*. New York: Oxford University Press, 1976.

———. *The Court and the Constitution*. Boston: Houghton Mifflin, 1987.

———. *The Warren Court: Constitutional Decision as an Instrument of Reform*. Cambridge, Mass.: Harvard University Press, 1968.

Currie, David P. *The Constitution in the Supreme Court: The First Hundred Years, 1789–1888*. Chicago: University of Chicago Press, 1985.

———. *The Constitution in the Supreme Court: The Second Century, 1888–1986*. Chicago: University of Chicago Press, 1990.

Danelski, David. *A Supreme Court Justice Is Appointed*. New York: Random House, 1965.

Ernst, Morris Leopold. *The Great Reversals: Tales of the Supreme Court*. New York: Weybright and Talley, 1973.

Ervin, Sam J. *The Role of the Supreme Court: Policymaker or Adjudicator?* Washington, D.C.: American Enterprise Institute, 1970.

Frank, John P. *Marble Palace: The Supreme Court in American Life*. New York: Alfred A. Knopf, 1961.

Freund, Paul A. *On Law and Justice*. Cambridge, Mass.: Harvard University Press, 1968.

———. *The Supreme Court of the United States*. New York: Meridian Books, 1961.

Friedman, Leon, comp. *The Justices of the United States Supreme Court: Their Lives and Major Opinions*, 5 vols. New York: Chelsea House in association with Bowker Press, 1969–1978.

Galloway, Russell. *Justice for All? Rich and Poor in Supreme Court History, 1790–1990*. Durham, N.C.: Carolina Academic Press, 1991.

Garraty, John. *Quarrels that Have Shaped the Constitution.* New York: Harper & Row, 1975.

Goodman, Elaine. *The Rights of the People: The Major Decisions of the Warren Court.* New York: Farrar, Straus and Giroux, 1971.

Harell, Mary Ann. *Equal Justice Under Law: The Supreme Court in American Life,* 5th ed. Washington, D.C.: Supreme Court Historical Society, 1988.

Irons, Peter H. *The Courage of Their Convictions: Sixteen Americans Who Fought Their Way to the Supreme Court.* New York: Penguin, 1990.

Ivers, Gregg. *Redefining the First Freedom: The Supreme Court and the Consolidation of State Power, 1980–1990.* New Brunswick, N.J.: Transaction Press, 1992.

Keynes, Edward. *The Court vs. Congress: Prayer, Busing, and Abortion.* Durham, N.C.: Duke University Press, 1989.

Krislov, Samuel. *The Supreme Court in the Political Process.* New York: Macmillan, 1965.

Kurland, Philip B. *Politics, the Constitution, and the Warren Court.* Chicago: University of Chicago Press, 1970.

Lasser, William. *The Limits of Judicial Power: The Supreme Court in American Politics.* Chapel Hill: University of North Carolina Press, 1988.

Levy, Leonard W. *Original Intent and the Framers' Constitution.* New York: Macmillan, 1988.

———. *The Supreme Court Under Earl Warren.* New York: Quadrangle Books, 1972.

Lyons, Thomas T. *The Supreme Court and Individual Rights in Contemporary Society.* Menlo Park, Calif.: Addison-Wesley, 1975.

Martin, Fenton S. *The U.S. Supreme Court: A Bibliography.* Washington, D.C.: CQ Press, 1990.

McCloskey, Robert G. *The Modern Supreme Court.* Cambridge, Mass.: Harvard University Press, 1972.

———. *The American Supreme Court.* Chicago: University of Chicago Press, 1960.

Menez, Joseph Francis. *Decision Making in the Supreme Court of the United States: A Political and Behavioral View.* Lanham, Md.: University Press of America, 1984.

Miller, Arthur Selwyn. *The Supreme Court and the Living Constitution.* Washington: Lerner Law Book, 1969 (1968).

————. *The Supreme Court: Myth and Reality*. Westport, Conn.: Greenwood Press, 1978.

Murphy, Walter F. *Congress and the Court: A Case Study in the American Political Process*. Chicago: University of Chicago Press, 1988.

Newmyer, R. Kent. *The Supreme Court Under Marshall and Taney*. Arlington Heights, Ill.: Harlan Davidson, 1986 (1968).

O'Brien, David M. *Storm Center: The Supreme Court in American Politics*, 2nd ed. New York: Norton, 1990.

Pacelle, Richard L. *The Transformation of the Supreme Court's Agenda: From the New Deal to the Reagan Administration*. Boulder, Colo.: Westview Press, 1991.

Perry, H. W. *Deciding to Decide: Agenda Setting in the United States Supreme Court*. Cambridge, Mass.: Harvard University Press, 1991.

Pfeffer, Leo. *This Honorable Court: A History of the United States Supreme Court*. New York: Octagon Books, 1978 (1965).

Pollak, Louis H., ed. *The Constitution and the Supreme Court*, 2 vols. Cleveland: World Publishing, 1966.

Rehnquist, William H. *The Supreme Court: How It Was, How It Is*. New York: Quill, 1989.

Rodell, Fred. *Nine Men: A Political History of the Supreme Court from 1790 to 1955*. Littleton, Colo.: F. B. Rothman, 1988.

Rostow, Eugene V. *The Sovereign Perogative: The Supreme Court and the Quest for Law*. Westport, Conn.: Greenwood Press, 1974 (1962).

Shnayerson, Robert. *The Illustrated History of the Supreme Court of the United States*. New York: Abrams in association with the Supreme Court Historical Society, 1986.

Spaeth, Harold J. *Studies in U.S. Supreme Court Behavior*. New York: Garland, 1990.

Steamer, Robert J. *Chief Justice: Leadership and the Supreme Court*, 1st ed. Columbia, S.C.: University of South Carolina Press, 1986.

Stephenson, D. Grier. *The Supreme Court and the American Republic: An Annotated Bibliography*. New York: Garland, 1981.

Strum, Philippa. *The Supreme Court and 'Political Questions': A Study in Judicial Evasion*. Alabama: University of Alabama Press, 1973.

Tribe, Laurence H. *God Save This Honorable Court: How the Choice of Supreme Court Justices Shapes Our History*. New York: Random House, 1985.

Ulmer, S. Sidney. *Supreme Court Policymaking and Constitutional Law*. New York: McGraw-Hill, 1986.

Van Geel, Tyll. *Understanding Supreme Court Opinions*. New York: Longman, 1991.

Warren, Charles. *Congress, the Constitution and the Supreme Court*. New York: Johnson Reprint Corp., 1968 (1932).

———. *The Supreme Court in United States History*. Littleton, Colo.: F. B. Rothman, 1987 (1926).

Wasby, Stephen L. *The Supreme Court in the Federal Judicial System*, 3rd ed. Chicago: Nelson-Hall, 1988.

Westin, Alan F. *The Supreme Court: Views from the Inside*. New York: W.W. Norton, 1961.

Wiecek, William M. *Liberty Under Law: The Supreme Court in American Life*. Baltimore: Johns Hopkins University Press, 1988.

Wilkinson, J. Harvie. *Serving Justice: A Supreme Court Clerk's View*. New York: Charterhouse, 1974.

Witt, Elder. *Congressional Quarterly's Guide to the U.S. Supreme Court*, 2nd ed. Washington, D.C.: Congressional Quarterly, Inc., 1990.

Woodward, Bob. *The Brethren: Inside the Supreme Court*. New York: Simon and Schuster, 1979.

# Books on the Justices

Hugo L. Black

Ball, Howard. *Of Power and Right: Hugo Black, William O. Douglas, and America's Constitutional Revolution*. New York: Oxford University Press, 1992.

Dunne, Gerald T. *Hugo Black and the Judicial Revolution*. New York: Simon and Schuster, 1977.

Frank, John P. *Mr. Justice Black*. Westport, Conn.: Greenwood Press, 1977 (1948).

Freyer, Tony A. *Hugo L. Black and the Dilemma of American Liberalism*. Glenview, Ill.: Scott, Foresman/Little, Brown, 1990.

Louis D. Brandeis

Baker, Leonard. *Brandeis and Frankfurter: A Dual Biography*. New York: Harper & Row, 1984.

Burt, Robert. *Two Jewish Justices: Outcasts in the Promised Land*. Berkeley: University of California Press, 1988.

Gross, David C. *A Justice for All the People: Louis D. Brandeis*. New York: Lodestar Books, 1987.

Mason, Alpheus Thomas. *Brandeis: A Free Man's Life*. New York: Viking Press, 1946.

Mersky, Roy M. *Louis Dembitz Brandeis, 1856–1941: A Bibliography*. Littleton, Colo.: F.B. Rothman Co., 1987.

Paper, Lewis J. *Brandeis*. Englewood Cliffs, N.J.: Prentice Hall, 1983.

Strum, Philippa. *Louis D. Brandeis: Justice for the People*. New York: Schocken Books, 1989.

William J. Brennan, Jr.

Friedman, ed. *An Affair with Freedom: Justice William J. Brennan, Jr*. New York, Atheneum, 1967.

Warren Burger

Blasi, Vincent, ed. *The Burger Court: The Counter-Revolution that Wasn't*. New Haven, Conn.: Yale University Press, 1983.

Galub, Arthur L. *The Burger Court, 1968–1984*. Millwood, N.Y.: Associated Faculty Press, 1986.

May, Daniel L. *A Bibliography on the Supreme Court Under Chief Justice Warren E. Burger*. Hempstead, N.Y.: Hofstra University School of Law, 1985.

Schwartz, Bernard. *The Ascent of Pragmatism: The Burger Court in Action*. Reading, Mass.: Addison-Wesley, 1990.

Schwartz, Herman, ed. *The Burger Years: Rights and Wrongs in the Supreme Court. 1969–1986*, New York: Penguin Books, 1988.

Harold Burton

Berry, Mary Frances. *Stability, Security, and Continuity: Mr. Justice Burton and the Supreme Court, 1945–1958*. Westport, Conn.: Greenwood Press, 1978.

John A. Campbell

Connor, Henry G. *John Archibald Campbell.* New York: Houghton Mifflin, 1920.


Benjamin Cardozo

Posner, Richard A. *Cardozo: A Study in Reputation.* Chicago: University of Chicago Press, 1990.

Hellman, George S. *Benjamin N. Cardozo, American Judge.* New York: Russell & Russell, 1969 (1940).


Salmon P. Chase

Blue, Frederick J. *Salmon P. Chase: A Life in Politics.* Kent, Ohio: Kent State University Press, 1987.


John H. Clarke

Warner, Hoyt L. *Life of Mr. Justice Clarke.* Cleveland: Western Reserve University Press, 1959.


Benjamin R. Curtis

Leach, Richard H. *Benjamin R. Curtis: Case Study of a Supreme Court Justice.* Princeton University, 1951 (unpublished doctoral dissertation).


Peter V. Daniel

Frank, John P. *Justice Daniel Dissenting: A Biography of Peter V. Daniel, 1784–1860.* Cambridge, Mass.: Harvard University Press, 1964.


David Davis

King, Willard L. *Lincoln's Manager: David Davis.* Cambridge, Mass.: Harvard University Press, 1960.


William R. Day

McLean, Joseph E. *William Rufus Day: Supreme Court Justice from Ohio.* New York: New York University Press, 1946.

William O. Douglas

Countryman, Vern. *The Judicial Record of Justice William O. Douglas*. Cambridge, Mass.: Harvard University Press, 1974.

Douglas, William O. *The Court Years, 1939–1975: The Autobiography of William O. Douglas*. New York: Vintage Books, 1981.

Simon, James F. *Independent Journey*: The Life of William O. Douglas. New York: Penguin Books, 1981.


Oliver Ellsworth

Brown, William G. *The Life of Oliver Ellsworth*. New York: Da Capo Press, 1970 (1905).


Abe Fortas

Lewis, Anthony. *Gideon's Trumpet*. New York: Vintage Books, 1989 (1964).


Felix Frankfurter

Baker, Leonard. *Brandeis and Frankfurter*. A Dual Biography. New York: Harper & Row, 1984.

Baker, Liva. *Felix Frankfurter*. New York: Coward-McCann, 1969.

Burt, Robert. *Two Jewish Justices: Outcasts in the Promised Land*. Berkeley: University of California Press, 1988.

Hirsch, H. N. *The Enigma of Felix Frankfurter*. New York: Basic Books, 1981.

Kurland, Philip B. *Mr. Justice Frankfurter and the Constitution*. Chicago: University of Chicago Press, 1971.

Parrish, Michael E. *Felix Frankfurter and His Times*. New York: Free Press, 1982.


Melville W. Fuller

Furer, Howard B. *The Fuller Court, 1888–1910*. Millwood, N.Y.: Associated Faculty Press, 1986.

King, Willard L. *Melville Weston Fuller*. Chicago: University of Chicago Press, 1967.

Arthur J. Goldberg

Moynihan, ed. *Defenses of Freedom: The Public Papers of Arthur Goldberg*. New York: Harper & Row, 1966.


Oliver Wendell Holmes

Biddle, Francis. *Justice Holmes, Natural Law and the Supreme Court*. New York: Macmillan, 1961.

Cohen, Jeremy. *Congress Shall Make No Law: Oliver Wendell Holmes and Judicial Decision Making*. Ames, Iowa: Iowa State University Press, 1989.

Holmes, Oliver Wendell. *Collected Legal Papers*. New York: Harcourt Brace, 1920.

Hurst, James Willard. *Justice Holmes on Legal History*. New York: Macmillan, 1964.

Lerner, Max. *The Mind and Faith of Justice Holmes*. Boston: Little Brown & Co., 1943.

Pohlman, H. L. *Justice Oliver Wendell Holmes: Free Speech and the Living Constitution*. New York: New York University Press, 1991.


Charles Evans Hughes

Hendel, Samuel. *Charles Evans Hughes and the Supreme Court*. New York: Russell & Russell, 1968 (1951).

Hughes, Charles Evans. *The Autobiographical Notes of Charles Evans Hughes*. Cambridge, Mass.: Harvard University Press, 1973.

Pusey, Merlo. *Charles Evans Hughes, 2 vols*. New York: Macmillan, 1951.


Robert H. Jackson

Gerhart, Eugene. *America's Advocate: Robert H. Jackson*. Indianapolis: Bobbs-Merrill, 1958.

Jackson, Robert H. *Dispassionate Justice: a Synthesis of the Judicial Opinions of Robert H. Jackson*. Indianapolis: Bobbs-Merrill Co., 1969.


John Jay

Pellew, George. *John Jay*. Boston: Houghton Mifflin & Co., 1890.

Morris, Richard B. *John Jay and the Court*. Boston: Boston University Press, 1967.

Thomas Johnson

Delaplaine, Edward S. *The Life of Thomas Johnson*. New York: F.H. Hitchcock & Co., 1927.

William Johnson

Morgan, Donald G. *Justice William Johnson, the First Dissenter: the Career and Constitutional Philosophy of a Jeffersonian Judge*. Columbia, S.C.: University of South Carolina Press, 1954.

John Marshall

Baker, Leonard. *John Marshall: A Life in Law*. New York: Collier Books, 1981 (1974).

Beveridge, Albert J. *The Life of John Marshall, 4 vols*. Boston: Houghton Mifflin, 1916–1919.

Cuneo, John R. *John Marshall, Judicial Statesman*. New York: McGraw-Hill, 1975.

Loth, David Goldsmith. *Chief Justice John Marshall and the Growth of the Republic*. New York: Greenwood Press, 1970.

Rudko, Frances H. *John Marshall, Statesman and Chief Justice*. New York: Greenwood Press, 1991.

Swindler, William Finley. *The Constitution and Chief Justice Marshall*. New York: Dodd, Mead, & Co., 1978.

White, G. Edward. *The Marshall Court and Cultural Change, 1815–1835, abridged ed*. New York: Oxford University Press, 1991.

Thurgood Marshall

Aldred, Lisa. *Thurgood Marshall*. New York: Chelsea House, 1990.

Haskins, James. *Thurgood Marshall: A Life for Justice*. New York: Henry Holt, 1992.

Hess, Debra. *Thurgood Marshall: The Fight for Equal Justice*. Englewood Cliffs, N.J.: Silver Burdett Press, 1990.

Joseph McKenna

McDevitt, Brother Matthew. *Joseph McKenna, Associate Justice of the United States*. New York: Da Capo Press, 1974 (1946).

John McLean

Weisenburger, Francis P. *Life of John McLean: A Politician on the United States Supreme Court.* Columbus, S.C.: University of South Carolina Press, 1937.

Samuel Miller

Fairman, Charles. *Mr. Justice Miller and the Supreme Court, 1862–1890.* Cambridge, Mass. Harvard University Press, 1939.

Sandra Day O'Connor

Bentley, Judith. *Justice Sandra Day O'Connor.* New York: J. Messner, 1983.

Fox, Mary V. *Justice Sandra Day O'Connor.* Hillside, N.J.: Enslow Publishers, 1983.

Gherman, Beverly. *Sandra Day O'Connor: Justice for All.* New York: Viking, 1991.

Stanley Reed

O'Brien, F. William. *Justice Reed and the First Amendment.* Washington, D.C.: Georgetown University Press, 1958.

William Rehnquist

Davis, Sue. *Justice Rehnquist and the Constitution.* Princeton, N.J.: Princeton University Press, 1989.

Savage, David G. *Turning Right: The Making of the Rehnquist Supreme Court.* New York: Wiley, 1992.

Wiley Rutledge

Harper, Fowler. *Justice Rutledge and the Bright Constellation.* Indianapolis: Bobbs-Merill, 1965.

Harlan Fiske Stone

Konefsky, Samuel J. *Chief Justice Stone and the Supreme Court.* New York: Hafner, 1971.

Mason, Alpheus T. *Harlan Fiske Stone: Pillar of the Law.* Hamden, Conn.: Archon Books, 1968 (1956).

Joseph Story

McClellan, James. *Joseph Story and the American Constitution.* Norman, Okla.: University of Oklahoma Press, 1990 (1971).

Newmyer, R. Kent. *Supreme Court Justice Joseph Story: Statesman of the Old Republic.* Chapel Hill, N.C.: University of North Carolina Press, 1985.

George Sutherland

Paschal, Joel. *Mr. Justice Sutherland.* Princeton: Princeton University Press, 1951.

William Howard Taft

Anderson, Judith Icke. *William Howard Taft: An Intimate History.* New York: Norton, 1981.

Mason, Alpheus T. *William Howard Taft, Chief Justice.* New York: Simon and Schuster, 1965; Lanham, Md.: University Press of America, 1983.

Pringle, Henry F. *The Life and Times of William Howard Taft.* Norwalk, Conn.: Easton Press, 1986.

Roger B. Taney

Newmyer, R. Kent. *The Supreme Court Under Marshall and Taney.* Arlington Heights, Ill.: Harlan Davidson, 1986 (1968).

Siegel, Martin. *The Taney Court, 1836–1864.* Millwood, N.Y.: Associated Faculty Press, 1987.

Smith, Charles W. *Roger B. Taney: Jacksonian Jurist.* New York: Da Capo Press, 1973 (1936).

Steiner, Bernard C. *Life of Roger Brooke Taney: Chief Justice of the United States Supreme Court.* Westport, Conn.: Greenwood Press 1970 (1922).

Swisher, Carl Brent. *The Taney Period, 1836–64.* New York: Macmillan, 1974.

Tyler, Samuel. *Memoir of Roger Brooke Taney.* New York: Da Capo Press, 1970 (1872).

Smith Thompson

Roper, Donald M. *Mr. Justice Thompson and the Constitution*. New York: Garland Press, 1987.


Fred M. Vinson

Palmer, Jan S. *The Vinson Court Era*. New York, N.Y.: AMS Press, 1990.

Pritchett, C. Herman. *Civil Liberties and the Vinson Court*. Chicago: University of Chicago Press, 1954.


Morrison R. Waite

Magrath, C. Peter. *Morrison R. Waite: The Triumph of Character*. New York, Macmillan, 1963.


Earl Warren

Christman, Henry H., ed. *The Public Papers of Chief Justice Earl Warren*. Westport, Conn., Greenwood Press, 1974.

Pollack, Jack H. *Earl Warren, the Judge Who Changed America*. Englewood Cliffs, N.J.: Prentice Hall, 1979.

Rice, Arnold S. *The Warren Court, 1953–1969*. Millwood, N.Y.: Associated Faculty Press, 1987.

Schwartz, Bernard. *Super Chief: Earl Warren and His Supreme Court*. New York: New York University Press, 1983.

White, G. Edward. *Earl Warren, A Public Life*. New York: Oxford University Press, 1982.


Edward Douglass White

Highsaw, Robert B. *Edward Douglass White: Defender of the Conservative Faith*. Baton Rouge: Louisiana State University Press, 1981.


James Wilson

Smith, C. P. *James Wilson, Founding Father: 1742–1798*. Chapel Hill: University of North Carolina Press, 1956.

# Appendix

## CHIEF JUSTICES
### In Chronological Order

| Justice | Tenure | Appointed By | Political Party |
|---|---|---|---|
| John Jay | 1789–1795 | George Washington | F |
| John Rutledge | 1795 | George Washington | F |
| Oliver Ellsworth | 1796–1800 | George Washington | F |
| John Marshall | 1801–1835 | John Adams | F |
| Roger B. Taney | 1836–1864 | Andrew Jackson | D |
| Salmon P. Chase | 1864–1873 | Abraham Lincoln | R |
| Morrison R. Waite | 1874–1888 | Ulysses S. Grant | R |
| Melville W. Fuller | 1888–1910 | Grover Cleveland | D |
| Edward D. White | 1910–1921 | William H. Taft | D |
| William H. Taft | 1921–1930 | Warren G. Harding | R |
| Charles E. Hughes | 1930–1940 | Herbert Hoover | R |
| Harlan F. Stone | 1941–1946 | Franklin D. Roosevelt | D |
| Frederick M. Vinson | 1946–1952 | Harry S. Truman | D |
| Earl Warren | 1953–1969 | Dwight D. Eisenhower | R |
| Warren E. Burger | 1969–1986 | Richard M. Nixon | R |
| William E. Rehnquist | 1986– | Ronald Reagan | R |

## ASSOCIATE JUSTICES
### In Alphabetical Order

| Justice | Tenure | Appointed By | Political Party |
|---|---|---|---|
| Baldwin, Henry | 1830–1844 | Andrew Jackson | D |
| Barbour, Philip P. | 1836–1841 | Andrew Jackson | D |
| Black, Hugo L. | 1937–1971 | Franklin D. Roosevelt | D |
| Blackmun, Harry A. | 1970– | Richard M. Nixon | R |
| Blair, John | 1789–1796 | George Washington | F |
| Blatchford, Samuel | 1882–1893 | Chester A. Arthur | R |
| Bradley, Joseph P. | 1870–1892 | Ulysses S. Grant | R |
| Brandeis, Louis D. | 1916–1939 | Woodrow Wilson | D |
| Brennen, William J. | 1956–1990 | Dwight D. Eisenhower | R |
| Brewer, David J. | 1889–1910 | Benjamin Harrison | R |
| Brown, Henry B. | 1890–1906 | Benjamin Harrison | R |
| Burton, Harold H. | 1945–1958 | Harry S. Truman | D |

[Party Abbreviations: **D**: Democrat; **R**: Republican; **DR**: Democrat-Republican; **F**: Federalist; **W**: Whig]

| Justice | Tenure | Appointed By | Political Party |
|---|---|---|---|
| Butler, Pierce | 1922–1939 | Warren G. Harding | D |
| Byrnes, James F. | 1941–1942 | Franklin D. Roosevelt | D |
| Campbell, John A. | 1853–1861 | Franklin Pierce | D |
| Cardozo, Benjamin N. | 1932–1938 | Herbert Hoover | D |
| Catron, John | 1837–1865 | Martin Van Buren | D |
| Chase, Samuel | 1796–1811 | George Washington | F |
| Clark, Tom C. | 1949–1967 | Harry S. Truman | D |
| Clarke, John H. | 1916–1922 | Woodrow Wilson | D |
| Clifford, Nathan | 1858–1881 | James Buchanan | D |
| Curtis, Benjamin R. | 1851–1857 | Millard Fillmore | W |
| Cushing, William | 1789–1810 | George Washington | F |
| Daniel, Peter V. | 1841–1860 | Martin Van Buren | D |
| Davis, David | 1862–1877 | Abraham Lincoln | R |
| Day, William R. | 1903–1922 | Theodore Roosevelt | R |
| Douglas, William O. | 1939–1975 | Franklin D. Roosevelt | D |
| Duvall, Gabriel | 1811–1835 | James Madison | DR |
| Field, Stephen J. | 1863–1897 | Martin Van Buren | D |
| Fortas, Abe | 1965–1969 | Lyndon B. Johnson | D |
| Frankfurter, Felix | 1939–1962 | Franklin D. Roosevelt | D |
| Goldberg, Arthur J. | 1962–1965 | John F. Kennedy | D |
| Gray, Horace | 1881–1902 | Chester A. Arthur | R |
| Grier, Robert O. | 1846–1870 | James M. Polk | D |
| Harlan, John Marshall (1) | 1877–1911 | Rutherford B. Hayes | R |
| Harlan, John Marshall (2) | 1955–1971 | Dwight D. Eisenhower | R |
| Holmes, Oliver W. Jr. | 1902–1932 | Theodore Roosevelt | R |
| Hughes, Charles E. | 1910–1915 | William H. Taft | R |
| | 1930–1941, Chief Justice | Herbert Hoover | R |
| Hunt, Ward | 1872–1882 | Ulysses S. Grant | R |
| Iredell, James | 1790–1799 | George Washington | F |
| Jackson, Howell E. | 1893–1895 | Benjamin Harrison | D |
| Jackson, Robert H. | 1941–1954 | Franklin D. Roosevelt | D |
| Johnson, Thomas | 1791–1793 | George Washington | F |
| Johnson, William | 1804–1834 | Thomas Jefferson | DR |
| Kennedy, Anthony M. | 1988– | Ronald Reagan | R |
| Lamar, Joseph R. | 1910–1916 | William H. Taft | D |
| Lamar, Lucius Q. C. | 1888–1893 | Grover Cleveland | DR |
| Livingston, Henry B. | 1806–1823 | Thomas Jefferson | DR |
| Lurton, Horace H. | 1909–1914 | William H. Taft | D |
| Marshall, Thurgood | 1967–1991 | Lyndon B. Johnson | D |
| Matthews, Stanley | 1881–1889 | James A. Garfield | R |
| McKenna, Joseph | 1898–1925 | William McKinley | R |
| McKinley, John | 1837–1852 | Martin Van Buren | D |
| McLean, John | 1829–1861 | Andrew Jackson | W |
| McReynolds, James C. | 1914–1941 | Woodrow Wilson | D |
| Miller, Samuel F. | 1862–1890 | Abraham Lincoln | R |
| Minton, Sherman | 1949–1956 | Harry S. Truman | D |

| Justice | Tenure | Appointed By | Political Party |
|---------|--------|--------------|-----------------|
| Moody, William H. | 1906–1910 | Theodore Roosevelt | R |
| Moore, Alfred | 1799–1804 | John Adams | F |
| Murphy, Frank | 1940–1949 | Franklin D. Roosevelt | D |
| Nelson, Samuel | 1845–1872 | John Tyler | D |
| O'Connor, Sandra D. | 1981– | Ronald Reagan | R |
| Paterson, William | 1793–1806 | George Washington | F |
| Peckham, Rufus W. | 1895–1909 | Grover Cleveland | D |
| Pitney, Mahlon | 1912–1922 | William H. Taft | R |
| Powell, Lewis F. | 1972–1987 | Richard M. Nixon | R |
| Reed, Stanley F. | 1938–1957 | Franklin D. Roosevelt | D |
| Rehnquist, William H. | 1972–1986 | Richard M. Nixon | R |
|  | 1986–, Chief Justice | Ronald Reagan | R |
| Roberts, Owen J. | 1930–1945 | Herbert Hoover | R |
| Rutledge, John | 1789–1791 | George Washington | F |
|  | 1795, Chief Justice | George Washington |  |
| Rutledge, Wiley B. | 1943–1949 | Franklin D. Roosevelt | D |
| Sanford, Edward T. | 1923–1930 | Warren G. Harding | R |
| Scalia, Antonin | 1986– | Ronald Reagan | R |
| Shiras, George | 1892–1903 | Benjamin Harrison | R |
| Souter, David H. | 1990– | George H. W. Bush | R |
| Stevens, John P. | 1975– | Gerald R. Ford | R |
| Stewart, Potter | 1958–1981 | Dwight D. Eisenhower | R |
| Stone, Harlan F. | 1925–1941 | Calvin Coolidge | R |
|  | 1941–1946, Chief Justice | Franklin D. Roosevelt | D |
| Story, Joseph | 1811–1845 | James Madison | DR |
| Strong, William | 1870–1880 | Ulysses S. Grant | R |
| Sutherland, George | 1922–1938 | Warren G. Harding | R |
| Swayne, Noah H. | 1862–1881 | Abraham Lincoln | R |
| Thomas, Clarence | 1991– | George H. W. Bush | R |
| Thompson, Smith | 1823–1843 | James Monroe | DR |
| Todd, Thomas | 1807–1826 | Thomas Jefferson | DR |
| Trimble, Robert | 1826–1828 | John Adams | DR |
| Van Devanter, Willis | 1910–1937 | William H. Taft | R |
| Washington, Bushrod | 1789–1829 | John Adams | F |
| Wayne, James M. | 1835–1867 | Andrew Jackson | D |
| White, Byron R. | 1962– | John F. Kennedy | D |
| White, Edward D. | 1894–1910 | William H. Taft | D |
|  | 1910–1921, Chief Justice | Grover Cleveland | D |
| Whittaker, Charles E. | 1957–1962 | Dwight D. Eisenhower | R |
| Wilson, James | 1789–1798 | George Washington | F |
| Woodbury, Levi | 1845–1851 | James M. Polk | D |
| Woods, William B. | 1880–1887 | Rutherford B. Hayes | R |

## PRESIDENTS AND THEIR SUPREME COURT APPOINTMENTS

| Name of President | Presidential Term | Name of Justice | Appointed |
|---|---|---|---|
| George Washington | 1789–1797 | John Jay (Chief Justice) | 1789 |
| | | John Rutledge | 1789 |
| | | William Cushing | 1789 |
| | | James Wilson | 1789 |
| | | John Blair | 1789 |
| | | James Iredell | 1790 |
| | | Thomas Johnson | 1791 |
| | | William Paterson | 1793 |
| | | John Rutledge (Chief Justice) | 1795 |
| | | Samuel Chase | 1796 |
| | | Oliver Ellsworth (Chief Justice) | 1796 |
| John Adams | 1797–1801 | Bushrod Washington | 1798 |
| | | Alfred Moore | 1799 |
| | | John Marshall (Chief Justice) | 1801 |
| Thomas Jefferson | 1801–1809 | William Johnson | 1804 |
| | | Henry B. Livingston | 1806 |
| | | Thomas Todd | 1807 |
| James Madison | 1809–1817 | Gabriel Duvall | 1811 |
| | | Joseph Story | 1811 |
| James Monroe | 1817–1825 | Smith Thompson | 1823 |
| John Quincy Adams | 1825–1829 | Robert Trimble | 1826 |
| Andrew Jackson | 1829–1837 | John McLean | 1829 |
| | | Henry Baldwin | 1830 |
| | | James M. Wayne | 1835 |
| | | Roger B. Taney (Chief Justice) | 1836 |
| | | Philip P. Barbour | 1836 |
| Martin Van Buren | 1837–1841 | John Catron | 1837 |
| | | John McKinley | 1837 |
| | | Peter V. Daniel | 1841 |
| John Tyler | 1841–1845 | Samuel Nelson | 1845 |
| James M. Polk | 1845–1849 | Levi Woodbury | 1845 |
| | | Robert C. Grier | 1846 |

| Name of President | Presidential Term | Name of Justice | Appointed |
|---|---|---|---|
| Millard Fillmore | 1850–1853 | Benjamin R. Curtis | 1851 |
| Franklin Pierce | 1853–1857 | John A. Campbell | 1853 |
| James Buchanan | 1857–1861 | Nathan Clifford | 1858 |
| Abraham Lincoln | 1861–1865 | Noah H. Swayne | 1862 |
| | | Samuel F. Miller | 1862 |
| | | David Davis | 1862 |
| | | Stephen J. Field | 1863 |
| | | Salmon P. Chase (Chief Justice) | 1864 |
| Ulysses S. Grant | 1869–1877 | William Strong | 1870 |
| | | Joseph P. Bradley | 1870 |
| | | Ward Hunt | 1872 |
| | | Morrison Waite (Chief Justice) | 1874 |
| Rutherford B. Hayes | 1877–1881 | John Marshall Harlan | 1877 |
| | | William B. Woods | 1880 |
| James A. Garfield | Mar.–Sept. 1881 | Stanley Matthews | 1881 |
| Chester A. Arthur | 1881–1885 | Horace Gray | 1881 |
| | | Samuel Blatchford | 1882 |
| Grover Cleveland | 1885–1889 | Lucius Q. C. Lamar | 1888 |
| | | Melville W. Fuller (Chief Justice) | 1888 |
| Benjamin Harrison | 1889–1893 | David J. Brewer | 1889 |
| | | Henry B. Brown | 1890 |
| | | George Shiras Jr. | 1892 |
| | | Howell E. Jackson | 1893 |
| Grover Cleveland | 1893–1897 | Edward D. White | 1894 |
| | | Rufus W. Peckham | 1895 |
| William McKinley | 1897–1901 | Joseph McKenna | 1898 |
| Theodore Roosevelt | 1901–1909 | Oliver W. Holmes Jr. | 1902 |
| | | William R. Day | 1903 |
| | | William H. Moody | 1906 |
| William H. Taft | 1909–1913 | Horace H. Lurton | 1909 |
| | | Charles E. Hughes | 1910 |
| | | Edward D. White (Chief Justice) | 1910 |
| | | Willis Van Devanter | 1910 |
| | | Joseph R. Lamar | 1910 |
| | | Mahlon Pitney | 1912 |

| Name of President | Presidential Term | Name of Justice | Appointed |
|---|---|---|---|
| Woodrow Wilson | 1913–1921 | James C. McReynolds | 1914 |
| | | Louis D. Brandeis | 1916 |
| | | John H. Clarke | 1916 |
| Warren G. Harding | 1921–1923 | William H. Taft (Chief Justice) | 1921 |
| | | George Sutherland | 1922 |
| | | Pierce Butler | 1922 |
| | | Edward T. Sanford | 1923 |
| Calvin Coolidge | 1923–1929 | Harlan F. Stone | 1925 |
| Herbert Hoover | 1929–1933 | Charles E. Hughes (Chief Justice) | 1930 |
| | | Owen J. Roberts | 1930 |
| | | Benjamin N. Cardozo | 1932 |
| Franklin D. Roosevelt | 1933–1945 | Hugo L. Black | 1937 |
| | | Stanley F. Reed | 1938 |
| | | Felix Frankfurter | 1939 |
| | | William O. Douglas | 1939 |
| | | Frank Murphy | 1940 |
| | | James F. Byrnes | 1941 |
| | | Harlan F. Stone (Chief Justice) | 1941 |
| | | Robert H. Jackson | 1941 |
| | | Wiley B. Rutledge | 1943 |
| Harry S. Truman | 1945–1953 | Harold H. Burton | 1945 |
| | | Fred M. Vinson (Chief Justice) | 1946 |
| | | Tom C. Clark | 1949 |
| | | Sherman Minton | 1949 |
| Dwight D. Eisenhower | 1953–1961 | Earl Warren (Chief Justice) | 1953 |
| | | John Marshall Harlan | 1955 |
| | | William J. Brennen Jr. | 1956 |
| | | Charles E. Whittaker | 1957 |
| | | Potter Stewart | 1958 |
| John F. Kennedy | 1961–1963 | Byron R. White | 1962 |
| | | Arthur J. Goldberg III | 1962 |
| Lyndon B. Johnson | 1963–1969 | Abe Fortas | 1965 |
| | | Thurgood Marshall | 1967 |

| Name of President | Presidential Term | Name of Justice | Appointed |
|---|---|---|---|
| Richard M. Nixon | 1969–1974 | Warren E. Burger (Chief Justice) | 1969 |
| | | Harry A.Blackmun | 1970 |
| | | Lewis F. Powell Jr. | 1972 |
| | | William H. Rehnquist | 1972 |
| Gerald R. Ford | 1974–1977 | John P. Stevens | 1975 |
| Ronald Reagan | 1981–1988 | Sandra D. O'Connor | 1981 |
| | | Antonin Scalia | 1986 |
| | | Anthony M. Kennedy | 1988 |
| George H. W. Bush | 1988–1993 | David H. Souter | 1990 |
| | | Clarence Thomas | 1991 |

APPOINTMENTS TO THE SUPREME COURT
By Seat

| CHIEF JUSTICE | SEAT 2 | SEAT 3 | SEAT 4 | SEAT 5 | SEAT 6 | SEAT 7 | SEAT 8 | SEAT 9 | SEAT 10 |
|---|---|---|---|---|---|---|---|---|---|
| John Jay 1789–1795 | John Rutledge 1789–1791 | William Cushing 1789–1810 | James Wilson 1789–1798 | John Blair 1789–1796 | James Iredell 1790–1799 | Thomas Todd 1807–1826 | John Catron 1837–1865 | John McKinley 1837–1852 | Stephen J. Field 1863–1897 |
| John Rutledge 1795 | Thomas Johnson 1791–1793 | Joseph Story 1811–1845 | Bushrod Washington 1798–1829 | Samuel Chase 1796–1811 | Alfred Moore 1799–1804 | Robert Trimble 1826–1828 | | John A. Campbell 1853–1861 | Joseph McKenna 1898–1925 |
| Oliver Ellsworth 1796–1799 | William Paterson 1793–1806 | Levi Woodbury 1845–1851 | Henry Baldwin 1830–1844 | Gabriel Duvall 1812–1835 | William Johnson 1804–1834 | John McLean 1829–1861 | | David Davis 1862–1877 | Harlan F. Stone 1925–1941 |
| John Marshall 1801–1835 | Brockholst Livingston 1806–1823 | Benjamin R. Curtis 1851–1857 | Robert C. Grier 1846–1870 | Phillip Barbour 1836–1841 | James M. Wayne 1835–1867 | Noah H. Swayne 1862–1881 | | John Marshall Harlan 1877–1911 | Robert H. Jackson 1941–1954 |

| | | | |
|---|---|---|---|
| Roger B. Taney 1836–1864 | Salmon P. Chase 1864–1873 | Morrison R. Waite 1874–1888 | Melville W. Fuller 1888–1910 |
| Smith Thompson 1823–1843 | Samuel Nelson 1845–1872 | Ward Hunt 1873–1882 | Samuel Blatchford 1882–1893 |
| Nathan Clifford 1858–1881 | Horace Gray 1882–1902 | Oliver W. Holmes 1902–1932 | Benjamin Cardozo 1932–1938 |
| William Strong 1870–1880 | William B. Woods 1881–1887 | Lucius Q. C. Lamar 1888–1893 | Howell E. Jackson 1893–1895 |
| Peter V. Daniel 1841–1860 | Samuel F. Miller 1862–1890 | Henry B. Brown 1891–1906 | William H. Moody 1906–1910 |
| Stanley Matthews 1881–1889 | George Shiras 1892–1903 | William R. Day 1903–1922 | Pierce Butler 1922–1939 |
| Joseph P. Bradley 1870–1892 | David J. Brewer 1890–1910 | Charles E. Hughes 1910–1916 | John H. Clarke 1916–1922 |

| | |
|---|---|
| John Marshall Harlan 1955–1971 | Mahon Pitney 1912–1922 |
| William Rehnquist 1972–1986 | Edward T. Sanford 1923–1930 |
| Antonin Scalia 1986– | Owen J. Roberts 1930–1945 |
| | Harold H. Burton 1945–1958 |

## APPOINTMENTS TO THE SUPREME COURT
### By Seat

| CHIEF JUSTICE | SEAT 2 | SEAT 3 | SEAT 4 | SEAT 5 | SEAT 6 | SEAT 7 | SEAT 8 | SEAT 9 | SEAT 10 |
|---|---|---|---|---|---|---|---|---|---|
| Edward D. White 1910–1921 | Edward D. White 1894–1910 | Felix Frankfurter 1939–1962 | Rufus W. Peckham 1896–1909 | Joseph R. Lamar 1911–1916 | Tom C. Clark 1949–1967 | George Sutherland 1922–1938 | | Potter Stewart 1958–1981 | |
| William H. Taft 1921–1930 | Willis Van Devanter 1911–1937 | Arthur J. Goldberg 1962–1965 | Horace H. Lurton 1910–1914 | Louis D. Brandeis 1916–1939 | Thurgood Marshall 1967–1991 | Stanley F. Reed 1938–1957 | | Sandra Day O'Connor 1981– | |
| Charles E. Hughes 1930–1941 | Hugo L. Black 1937–1971 | Abe Fortas 1965–1969 | James C. McReynolds 1914–1941 | William O. Douglas 1939–1975 | Clarence Thomas 1991– | Charles Whittaker 1957–1962 | | | |
| Harlan F. Stone 1941–1946 | Lewis Powell 1972–1987 | Harry A. Blackmun 1970– | James F. Byrnes 1941–1942 | John Paul Stevens 1975– | | Byron R. White 1962– | | | |

| | | |
|---|---|---|
| | | Wiley B. Rutledge 1943–1949 |
| | | Sherman Minton 1949–1956 |
| | | William J. Brennan, Jr. 1956–1990 |
| | | David Souter 1990– |
| | Anthony Kennedy 1988– | |
| Fred M. Vinson 1946–1953 | | |
| Earl Warren 1953–1969 | | |
| Warren E. Burger 1969–1986 | | |
| William Rehnquist 1986– | | |

# Index

3 1978 02760 0014

347.9973
Wagman,R.J.
The Supreme Court
[26218646]

JUN 0 2 1993

WITHDRAWAL

20-8/96
35-2/99
56c.2/11

INDIANAPOLIS-MARION COUNTY
PUBLIC LIBRARY

offers you:         MAGAZINES        PAMPHLETS
BOOKS              MAPS             PICTURES
RECORDS            FRAMED ART       PROGRAMS
FILMS              VIDEOTAPES       FOR ADULTS
MUSIC              AUDIOCASSETTES   AND CHILDREN

Other borrowers will appreciate the prompt return of this book.
A CHARGE IS MADE FOR OVERDUE MATERIALS

GAYLORD